HOW CAME OUR FAITH

HOW CAME OUR FAITH

A STUDY OF THE RELIGION OF ISRAEL
AND ITS SIGNIFICANCE FOR
THE MODERN WORLD

BY

W. A. L. ELMSLIE

D.D. Cambridge; Hon. D.D. Aberdeen and Edinburgh;
Formerly Fellow of Christ's College; Sometime Principal and
Professor of Old Testament Theology at
Westminster College, Cambridge

CAMBRIDGE
AT THE UNIVERSITY PRESS
1958

PUBLISHED BY
THE SYNDICS OF THE CAMBRIDGE UNIVERSITY PRESS

Bentley House, 200 Euston Road, London, N.W. 1
American Branch: 32 East 57th Street, New York 22, N.Y.

First Edition 1948
Reprinted 1950
1958

First printed in Great Britain at the University Press, Cambridge
Reprinted by offset-litho by Bradford & Dickens, London W.C. 1

TO
THE DEAR MEMORY OF MY FATHER
WILLIAM GRAY ELMSLIE
(*obiit* 1889)
WHO HOPED TO HAVE WRITTEN
UPON THIS THEME

CONTENTS

Preface   *p.* ix

Part I   THE OLD TESTAMENT TO-DAY

   I   Ancient Israel and Modern Life   3
  II   Modern Study of the Old Testament   25
 III   The Old Testament as Literature   43
 IV   The Bible as Sacred Scripture   56

Part II   THE RELIGION OF THE HEBREWS

   V   The Land of Israel and its Peoples   91
 VI   The God of the Hebrews   112
 VII   The Gods of Canaan   141
VIII   Jehovah: God of Israel   158

Part III   THE FAITH OF THE PROPHETS

 IX   Hebrew Puritans   179
  X   'God with us' (Moses)   198
 XI   Conscience and Reason (Samuel and Elijah)   224
 XII   Mercy (Amos)   245
XIII   Love (Hosea)   264
XIV   The Eternal in the Temporal (Isaiah)   286
 XV   God and the Individual (Jeremiah)   306

CONTENTS

XVI   God and the Nations (The Poet-Prophet)   *p.* 335

XVII   Wisdom   363

XVIII   Power   382

Scripture References Index   403

General Index   405

MAPS

The World of the Old Testament   24

Palestine   91

Jerusalem   169

Route of "The Exodus"   206

A table of dates is given on p. 178.

PREFACE

This work is addressed to any one who takes a responsible interest in his own life, his neighbours' lives, affairs of State in his own and other lands, and the trend of thought and morals at this momentous period. Its claim is that in the course of Hebrew history beliefs were attained—attained in an extraordinary way—that are in essence eternally valid, that speak to the heart of our manifold anxieties and fundamentally concern right understanding of the Christian Faith and its presentation in the modern world. Therefore, it is also designed to be of service to professional students of religion and morals, especially to those whose difficult privilege it is to teach the contents of the Bible and its values. In outward form this work is a study of Hebrew religion; but its primary purpose is seen in the underlying argument that its subject is profoundly relevant to present issues, social and personal.

The author has set himself a difficult task in seeking to serve both general readers and students. As regards the former, the Books of the Old Testament present an impenetrable jungle to such as have not from their youth up been shown the way through. The method here pursued has regard to that fact. Therefore, basic information on the leading facts of Hebrew history, and on the structure of the literature, is provided more often and more simply than students would require. The first Chapter states the general argument about the present relevance of the subject. The survey of modern Biblical study (Chapters II–IV), and the subjects treated in Chapters IX–XVIII, have obvious application to present-day interests. But the book includes (Chapters V–VIII) consideration of early religious ideas and the shaping of the Hebrew nation. Those topics might seem to be the concern of students only. They are, however, very much in place, if one is to understand clearly the achievement of the men of genius in Hebrew history; and they shed useful, lurid, light on popular misconceptions of religion and morality, prevalent then and prevalent now. Occasionally outlines of specialist discussion regarding puzzling problems in the literature or history of Israel have been sketched in the text or footnotes. Where non-specialists feel their patience overtaxed by such matters, it is hoped they will exercise the art of skipping, but come to earth again on less debatable and more delectable territory. A risk has been taken, in trust that readers will recognize that a great subject yields its values to those who will yield to it time and thought. There used to be an American Guidebook, designed for rapid travellers, under the title *Britain at a Bite*. Comparatively small this island may be, but there is enough in its length and breadth to reward a more extended visit. The 'country' of the Bible likewise responds to those who give it more than a passing glance.

Students will find that the work is concentrated on Hebrew religion. It provides them neither with a political History of Israel, nor a handbook to Hebrew archaeology. It touches upon politics and ancient customs only in so far as those matters contribute to better understanding of the progress of Israel's ideas of God and duty. Moreover, although this volume is designed to form a complete study having its own unity of discourse, it carries the valuation of Israel's religion only to the stage at which the last of the truly great Hebrew Prophets had rendered his service to God and testimony to men, and a 'Faith for Mankind' had come into existence. To develop the underlying argument upon the bearing of Israel's religious genius on the nature and advocacy of Christianity in the modern world a further volume is required— covering the leading interests of the five centuries that elapsed between the last of the great Prophets and the Christian Era. This later period is apt to be regarded as a somewhat dull pedestrian interlude in religious history, a period during which (so to say) Faith had to descend from the heights to walk the plains. One reflection alone should have warned against that impression. The course of Jewish religion subsequent to the great Prophets is no more of secondary importance for perceiving what is, and what is not, 'religion pure and undefiled' than is Christian history as sequel to the Gospel. Those four or five centuries afford the first, large-scale, illustration of what may happen when men, having recognized in their Faith an absolute moral demand, attempt to apply it to inherited customs and urgent, practical problems.

To provide sufficiently the ampler and more technical information which students are bound to desiderate, and yet not exhaust the patience of other readers, presents a dilemma. Footnotes are an irritant interruption of the text, but they seem to the writer to afford the only solution. Liberal use has therefore been made of them in order to mention, or develop, points of scholarly interest. References to books have been selected, as far as possible, from works likely to be accessible to students. Biblical quotations follow the text of the Authorised or Revised Versions or the American Standard Version as the writer felt preferable, and occasionally he has altered word or phrase, if the Hebrew seemed to warrant it and the sense might thus be clearer.

Anyone who has the temerity to write about the Old Testament is confronted by great difficulties. So many fields of study are involved. The output of expert literature is daunting. In 1925 Dr S. A. Cook filled twenty-five of the spacious pages of *The Cambridge Ancient History* with a list which he described as 'only the most general guide to the most recent works'. Minor technical problems are innumerable. But it can be said with confidence that the large issues, which are of essential importance for knowledge of the development of Hebrew religion, have been determined; and it is with those conclusions that this study is concerned. Scholars will feel that, as regards certain notable problems still in debate, the writer has left the view which he has taken inadequately argued and documented. His defence is desire to 'temper the wind' for non-specialist readers.

In 1914 Dr J. P. Peters in the Preface to his book, *The Religion of the Hebrews*, wrote these words: 'This volume is the result of the special labour of over twenty years. I began the work light-heartedly, thinking that I knew my theme. It was years before I succeeded in writing the first chapter; and many a time I have been tempted to lay down my pen and abandon the task as too hard for me.' The present writer confesses to a like experience and a fellow-feeling. But the Old Testament steels men against 'turning back in the day of battle', and the words of the noblest and most sorely-tried of all the great Hebrews refuse to be put out of mind: 'If I say I will not make mention of God, nor speak any more in his name, then there is in mine heart as it were a burning fire shut up in my bones, and I cannot desist.'

I welcome this opportunity to thank my students. Lecturing is a privilege and a discipline. For students, even without voicing their feelings, have swift power to apprise the speaker when his material is dull or his thoughts confused, but also heartening ways of teaching him what aspects of the subject quicken interest. I am deeply indebted to the University Press;

to Miss Wolstencroft, who was indefatigably patient in typing
my manuscript; to my colleagues, Professor H. H. Farmer and
Professor R. D. Whitehorn, who gave me helpful comments on
certain chapters; to the Reverend W. S. Robertson, who did me
the great kindness of reading the proofs and preparing the Index.
There was a time when I resolved to abandon the work. I now
record with gratitude the encouragement given me by friends,
whose interest and insistence have enabled me to continue and
to bring this volume to completion.

W. A. L. ELMSLIE

WESTMINSTER COLLEGE
    CAMBRIDGE
September 1948

NOTE

Some errata in the first printing have been corrected, and an
explanatory footnote has been added to p. 42.

W. A. L. ELMSLIE

January 1950

The third printing of this book has enabled a number of minor
alterations to be made in its text and footnotes. Attention is
specially called to the following changes:
(1) On p. 42 comment is offered regarding interpretation of the
'Patriarchal' traditions. (2) On p. 88 the problem of treating the
general theological significance of the Old Testament is considered, and reference made to some important recent publica-
tions. (3) On pp. 101 and 111 it will be found that a different,
earlier, dating of the Exodus from Egypt and the 'Conquest' of
Canaan has been adopted. (4) On pp. 175, 176 an Additional Note
supplements certain drastic and unduly brief remarks in the text
regarding *popular* Hebrew religion at the time of the fall of
Jersualem.

W. A. L. ELMSLIE

June 1958

PART I
THE OLD TESTAMENT TO-DAY

CHAPTER I

ANCIENT ISRAEL AND MODERN LIFE

An author should not choose a misleading title. The one here chosen, *How came our Faith*, clearly indicates that the work claims to be relevant for *our* times, and will be concerned with the most important of all questions—What is the nature of Ultimate Reality in relation to human life. For, although basic conviction about any subject might be styled *Faith*, the normal usage is in connexion with religion and signifies confidence that the belief, when tested by reason and tried out in life, will approve itself as valid—is such that one may reasonably put trust therein.[1] But the words *How came* are obscure; for they do not (as might be expected) refer directly to Christian history, but to the development of religion in ancient 'Israel' (the Hebrew-Jewish People), which led up to Christ. If, however, this book had been called *The Religion of Israel*, that would have been gravely misleading. For it would have afforded no hint of the argument, stated in the Preface, that the religious significance of certain Hebrew beliefs, and of the way in which they were reached, was not properly understood, and was disastrously undervalued in Christian history; and that the facts are of the utmost importance if the truth in Christianity is to be reasserted powerfully in modern life. Incidentally, *The Religion of Israel* might have risked losing the battle without even a chance of firing a shot! For persons who take a lively interest in affairs must needs pick and choose what they will read. Hope and anxiety beset us as we watch the careers of certain fateful abstractions ('ideologies' is the fashionable word)—Democracy and Communism, The Four Freedoms, Power Politics. Current events so rapidly make contemporary history that there seems no time to spare for history in the past. But there is *one* past history invaluable to know—so searchingly does it lay bare the motives that determine what ideological attitude men adopt, or (in simpler phrase) their aims and conduct.

[1] It is tragic that there has been so great reason for the popular notion that in Theology *Faith*, unlike the hypotheses used in the Sciences, implies that religious beliefs (doctrines) ought to be accepted credulously—'taken on faith'

That 'history' is the unique religious development in the centuries of ancient Hebrew life, culminating in Jesus Christ. Its nature and its present relevance form the subject of this work.

Yet it is safe to say that most people think of Hebrew religion as out-of-date since the beginning of the Christian Era, and are positive the history of a small nation that flourished two and three thousand years ago does not concern the modern world. How can it be true that present and future interests are vitally related to what happened to the Hebrews and what they felt about things in general and religion in particular? To that initial, and very reasonable question, answer is given in this Chapter.

Hebrew religion did not perish of old age. In a superlatively wonderful way it showed capacity not only to reach certain permanent truths, but progressively to respond to changing circumstance and see deeper into complex problems. There was in it *vitality*, enabling obsolete ideas to be transcended, and giving rise to a continuity of religious conviction down to the present time. History shows two principal sequels. One has been the powerful monotheism which religious Jews have maintained throughout the Christian Era. Judaism in all generations has never ceased to produce countless good men and women, and its full share of men of learning and genius (scientists, scholars, artists, musicians, philosophers, theologians), *and* its saints and martyrs. That is fact which neither the unsaintliness of many Jews, nor present political problems, should be allowed to obscure. The other sequel to Hebrew religion was the supreme fact in spiritual history—Jesus of Nazareth, 'after the flesh' a son of David, born in Bethlehem of Judaea when Herod was king. But, since we know the Faith which came by Jesus Christ, why turn back to consider what preceded it? How can facts about pre-Christian Hebrew religion be of radical importance for the understanding and advocacy of Christianity in these days?

A Christian, instructed in the history of the Church, is keenly aware that at two periods outstanding effort was made to give formulated expression to the doctrines of the Christian Faith—first, during the Greek and Roman Age through the Creeds of the ancient Church; and, secondly, in the sixteenth century through the Confessions of Faith drawn up by the Reformed Churches. If he happens to be a member of the Roman Catholic communion, he values the former; if a Protestant he values both, believing that the principles emphasized in Protestant theology rightly interpret the Catholic Apostolic Faith. Supposing, however, that he is desired by someone, for whom religion is a blur, to explain: (1) Why he is Roman Catholic or Protestant and (2) What in plain terms modern Christians believe—two initial difficulties have to be surmounted. First, facts that seem elementary to him will almost certainly be as good as unknown to his questioner. Even outline knowledge of the landmarks in Church History is rare among the non-churchgoing. (Ask the next hundred passers-by their views as to the orthodoxy of the Council of Nicaea, or as to the justification for the Diet of Worms, and answers are likely to be few.) Secondly (and here is the testing task), in order to help his hearer to understand precisely what are the cardinal beliefs of Christianity, he will find himself *translating* into the vocabulary of present thought *either* Christian doctrine as it was set forth in the ancient Creeds formulated in the Greek and Roman Age, *or* the interpretative principles of the Faith declared in the Protestant Confessions of the sixteenth century. Moreover, discussion cannot possibly go deep or proceed far, unless, first of all, this much common ground exists—that the questioner knows, or is willing to learn, the primary records about Jesus—the way He lived, why He was crucified, and what happened immediately thereafter. All Christian belief has derived from the creative fact: Christ Himself. Prior to, and source of, the historic Creeds and Confessions there is what one may venture to call *God's Creed*—what God eternally believes. What did Jesus feel that He had come to fulfil? What are the truths which God made manifest through Israel and fulfilled in Jesus? Therein is the fullness of the Christian Faith, to which the changing Ages endeavour to give expression. With a fervency and sincerity and wisdom that only the untaught can fail to reverence, the makers of the historic Creeds and Confessions sought to do so.

There has been no need to be restlessly Creed-making genera-tion after generation; for Christian belief is not tossed to and fro by every wind of developing knowledge. It has to do with the unalterable experiences of Man's spirit, with 'temptations, motives and desires, loves, hates, struggles, defeats and victories'; with 'heartbreak, grief, and tragedy, joy, hope, and the need of God'.[1] But the advance in knowledge during the last two or three centuries has vastly altered our outlook from that of the Greeks and

[1] Cp. Fosdick, *Modern Use of the Bible*, Lecture II.

Romans or our sixteenth-century forefathers. He is blind who does not see that we belong, veritably, to a new epoch in world history. We may well ask ourselves whether correspondingly fuller understanding and fresh interpretation of the Christian Faith is not required of us? Sixty years ago the following, far-sighted, comment was made by Professor A. B. Davidson: '*The effort of this age is to get behind the Greek influences and to present Christianity as the Semitic mind presented and left it.*'[1] By 'the Semitic mind' Davidson referred essentially to the genius of the Hebrews for religion and morals. He was not suggesting that the truth and worth of Christianity would be illumined by considering Babylonian religion, and his remark would not have been made if the Hebrews had not existed; especially those supremely spiritual Hebrews whom we style 'the Great Prophets'. Davidson was too learned, and fully Christian, a theologian not to be thoroughly aware of the permanent wisdom of the historic Creeds. He was not calling their validity into question. But he was pointing to the fact that weaknesses in the Greek methods of dealing with religious belief and its propagation have become apparent; and that the deep contrasts between Greek and Hebrew mentality increasingly show themselves to be of radical importance. He meant that, whereas the Greek contribution to understanding the Faith has not been undervalued, *the Hebrew has*; and that the progress of modern thought is emphasizing the fact. To this matter reference must be made later in the chapter. Suffice it for the moment to say that the Greeks were very clever, but for perceiving the things of the Spirit, and knowing how to com-municate religious and moral ideas from mind to mind and translate assent into action, the Hebrews had *genius*. That was their gift from God.

Genius discerns essentials and patiently insists on their impor-tance. Then the scientific problem is solved, the artistic master-piece created. The vitality in Hebrew religion was due to the impact made on the nation's intelligence and conscience by men whose genius it was to believe that morality is not the title of a haphazard game without rules, in which one opinion is as good as

[1] *Theology of the O.T.* p. 250 (cp. Snaith, *Distinctive Ideas of the O.T.* pp. 14, 184f.). *Semitic* denotes the ancient Asiatic nations of the Near East, of whom the Hebrews were a very minor part politically and numerically, but otherwise incomparably the most important race.

another. They held that certain qualities are *really* right, and others *really* perversion of what men should be. Effort to discriminate Right from Wrong is not pursuing a will-o'-the-wisp illusion, because Ultimate Reality (God) is Absolute Goodness. In the strength of that fundamental principle—testing finite virtue by a transcendent standard—the great Hebrews sought to distinguish the better from the worse in the tangled ways of life. They were wise; for when men aim at less than the best, visualize the target vaguely, they are likely to miss the mark completely. Unless individuals, classes, nations and social systems resolutely seek to test their aims and attainments over against an unattained, absolute, ideal, they lack humility and with appalling swiftness lose capacity for drastic self-criticism, making *expediency* their only ruler and guide. It has been truly said that 'the logic of expediency leads to the atomic dissolution of morality; a kind of radioactive decay of all virtues'. The Hebrews of genius did not confuse expediency with honesty, truth and right. Great consequences result from men's attitude in this basic matter. 'What is a promise,' scoffed Hitler, 'save a tool wherewith to dupe trusting fools?' 'What is truth?' said jesting Pilate; and would not stay for an answer. 'It is expedient', said a High Priest, 'that one man die for the people'; and thereby he divided history into *before* and *after* Christ. But he was flouting the religious and moral genius of his Race, which had learnt to ask: 'What is right *in God's sight?*' The great Hebrews gave a clear and marvellous answer to that question. And the modern world has need to understand that answer clearly, if civilization is to steer safely between Scylla and Charybdis, and not be wrecked on the jagged rocks of Isolationism or engulfed by the Totalitarian whirlpool.

Our world is in a tragic state: the newspapers, the 'wireless' and our own observation allow no respite from the daunting facts. If only there were not so many evil persons, if only we ourselves were better, if only nations could be relied on to act in accordance with the noble ideals they profess; if scientific discoveries could be used only for the benefit of mankind; if high finance and big business could be trusted to work together for the greatest good of the greatest number; if the realistic view in politics were not so frequently the pernicious; if only the Churches gave sound and united answer in defining the essence of the Faith; if all professing Christians embodied the very spirit of Christ—this world would be in a much less tragic state. Having regard to the distressing facts—the appalling misuse of power in past time; the appalling atomic power which Science is now placing in our unreliable hands—Hebrew religion (if we know what we are looking for in it) is a very 'live' issue.

Even earlier than 1939 interest in the problems of Ethics and Religion was considered to be on the up-grade. Science, it appeared, had not 'knocked the bottom out of religion'. Very many scientists remained philosophically agnostic, feeling like men in so thick a mist as to be dubious whether there be such a thing as the sun. But some leading physicists prescribed bounds to their inquiry, saying: 'Hitherto shalt thou come, but no further; and here shall thy proud waves be stayed.' The door leading to religion had not been scientifically bricked-up, but stood open or ajar. Beyond it was country which the human mind should endeavour to explore. Moreover, concern was deepening about the extent to which formerly accepted standards of personal behaviour were challenged and experimentally flouted. And in public affairs progress did not seem to be advancing as had been expected. Things were being said in Germany, and were happening in Europe, too disconcerting to be fully credible, yet giving rise to puzzled anxiety. Nevertheless, both in Britain and in America interest in religion and morality was scarcely more than languid— literary and discussional—rather than systematic and urgent.[1] Amiability was easier than ardour. Public opinion shut its eyes to hard choices and remained incredulous, whilst the furnace was being heated seven times hotter than before for both great Democracies and for many other nations.

In 1939 the Nazis dealt an awakening blow to the dream that a mildly moral, tepidly Christian, disposition would suffice to be getting on with. Blitzing across the frontiers its ardent Faith that might is right, bludgeoning into our consciousness its horrible delight in cruelty, exhibiting its terrible power to enlist the support of the masses and to hypnotize the mind of its youth, the Nazi philosophy taught what can happen when the Christian reading of life's values has been flung to the dogs—rejected lock, stock and barrel. The Nazis' beliefs, we realized, were not ours. But to oppose the Nazis' certainty about the 'hell' they wanted to create we had no similar clarity about 'heaven'. A well-known phrase

[1] See Agar, *A Time for Greatness*.

from a soldier's letter hits the mark: 'All of us out here know what we are fighting against. *We wish it were just as clear what we are fighting for.*'

Rosenberg, the Nazi sociologist, had no dubiety about the nature of the struggle and that it was more than political. Said he: 'The war of to-day is a struggle between two opposing philosophies, the outcome of which will decide the structure of the world for the next few centuries.' To which a British historian retorted: 'Rosenberg completely understates the gravity of the issue. The outcome will decide the issue for all time as surely as did the conflicts enshrined in the history behind and in the Bible. To-day it is a fight for the soul of the world, the eternal world of which we are by the grace of God members and participators.'

It is one thing, however, to resolve that one will read 'something' about religion; quite another to venture on a book that proposes to tackle the subject *via* the Bible; whilst one that means to draw its material from the *Old* Testament clearly seems to make a quite unreasonable demand on limited patience and much-occupied time. As a plain man plainly put it at an open-air meeting: 'What have we men of to-day got to do with Jehovah, the bloodthirsty war-God of the ancient 'Ebrews?' Perhaps the attitude of very many people to the Old Testament may be summed up as follows: No doubt it contains many beautiful sayings, lovely words from a far-away world. Some of these passages, incorporated in a National Service or the daily Epilogue, seem remarkably appropriate and moving. Christianity might sensibly have approved an Anthology of Old Testament verses, but ought never to have got tangled up with the multifarious Hebrew Books. A vast number of people, therefore, feel it sense to keep the Old Testament at a respectful distance; regarding it as a sort of gloomy labyrinth into whose intricacies it would be waste of time to enter, since they are sure they would never reach its centre and, anyway, would be bored in making the attempt. They have no right to be so pessimistically sure. It is true that without guidance they are likely to get lost in its maze. Given the guiding thread which modern study of the Bible and ancient history have provided, one can follow the path to the centre, and discover treasure that is worth a lifetime's search. Concerning his own experience the writer can affirm that thirty years' study of the Old Testament has not outworn its value for him. On the contrary, ever increasingly he finds in it resources of strength. The Old Testament is unsparingly honest about human nature, it is also indomitably enheartening. It exposes our besetting weaknesses, and shows how swiftly ruin can come upon the unteachable. But it is eloquent of what high courage can effect, what great things even one wise and steadfast soul may achieve for the many, and how despair can change to hope. But why not state quite briefly anything of importance the Old Testament may have to tell us? Why not tabulate that such and such ideas were held by early Hebrews; and that, later on, the following more advanced ideas were held by less early Hebrews? That is the anatomical method of dealing with the religion of Israel, and its result is that one looks at a corpse or a skeleton instead of a living man: the marvel of vitality has gone a-missing. The rewarding task is not simply to tabulate the beliefs, profound though they became. Under modern methods of study the Old Testament has yielded documented evidence of a religious history which shows to a quite unparalleled degree vital power—'the history of a perpetual renaissance'. The impressive truth is that the thoughts became what they were *through the fortitude and fineness of persons*, who faced the stress of life in the strength of the one principle—God and His righteousness. So regarded, the facts shape themselves in a way that is enthralling—not just worth knowing, but enthralling. They speak to one's own personal problems. But one also becomes conscious how acutely Israel's life and thought bear upon anxieties about which we are all talking to-day. Very plainly Israel's history illuminates the clash of States, the structure of Society, the rights of the Individual, the rights of the State; and, above all, the *limits* of the rights of Individual and State respectively. We begin to perceive how great wisdom in these matters the Hebrew mind attained, taught by grim failures. A time came when the Hebrews were politically broken and dispersed; but by then they had found in their religion means of communal cohesion which they put into practice and by its strength were enabled to survive disasters that would have been fatal to any other nation. To know these facts vividly is to find oneself asking old questions with a new intensity: Why have the Peoples of Gentile Christendom (and they have known 'Christ', as well as 'The Law and the Prophets') so poorly learnt, or so feebly practised, the wisdom and goodness that saved the Jews? Why has powerful industrialized Europe so heartlessly and disastrously allowed 'the tenth' to remain 'submerged' in misery? Why have the nations destroyed one another in wars, thinking of glory in terms of conquest? Why could those who love darkness so prevail that in 1939 'the lamps went out'? The war ended. Why do persons and parties remain influential, who have no ideas save to direct present effort towards what may be grabbed out of the wreckage instead of what can be given to rebuild?

This work accordingly does not profess to be a dispassionate survey of the beliefs, customs, social organization, and political vicissitudes of ancient Israel. It is written under passionate conviction that the Old Testament writings, passed through the furnace of modern investigation, have yielded pure gold— true belief concerning Ultimate Reality and immediate human duty; and cogent factual evidence, psychological and historical, for the validity of the essential convictions. It is of the religion of Israel so perceived, and as culminating in Christ, that a Christian scholar—alive to philosophic, historical and scientific knowledge —could write these burning words: 'The history of Israel is not closed. It is continued in the history of mankind. The religion of Israel is not superseded. It remains man's only religion. The theology of Israel is not an anachronism. It is the abiding truth of God.'[1] It is with the religion of Israel thus understood that this work is concerned. The literature of the Old Testament is intricate and extensive. The story of Israel unfolds for more than 1000 years. There is a long journey to make. But the scenery is wonderful all the way; for it follows the royal road of history, ascending into the hill of the Lord, to the heavenly city not built with hands.

If the reader feels this claim to be extravagant, he may be pardoned. The evidence on which it rests should be known to many, but is known to relatively few. By far the most important result of modern Old Testament study is its recognition of the religious and moral significance of certain men (less than ten in number) whose quality determined the course of Hebrew history. Concerning these men it is no exaggeration to say that 'they stand in the highest category of spiritual genius', or to say of their particular spiritual experience that 'if we could penetrate its mystery, we should know the last secret of personal religion....In their work we see clearly the crucial issue between nature and

[1] Kilpatrick, *The Encyclopaedia of Religion and Ethics*, vol. XI, p. 112.

spirit, which perhaps every generation—and none more obviously than our own—has to face.'[1] They were not individually founders of *a* philosophy or *a* religion, as were Plato or Mohammed. But cumulatively, and in a very impressive way, their convictions cohere so as to present at last a comprehensive interpretation of the meaning of life—a Religion for the World—an Ethic for Humanity. No less impressive is it that there should have been the sequence of them within the confines of a single small nation. But there is far more to it than that: as Old Testament scholars and certain philosophical theologians, especially during the last twenty years, have been insisting—to say no more than that about these men is to be blind to the wonder of the facts. The Faith that we owe to them confronts us as something incomparably more vital and practical than a 'Theory of Existence'; and, closely regarded, the men through whom it was declared present by what they were in themselves singular and moving evidence for the validity of their thought of God. And it is plain enough that the core of their religious experience might be ours also—provided we choose to meet the challenge of life as they did. Further, the evidence for the essential truth of their Faith, which we perceive in the men themselves, is writ large in the extraordinary history of their race—as they insisted it was and would be. From that flows the wider suggestion that all history and every personal life, if intently considered, sustains the truth of their interpretation of the mystery of existence. Finally, it has grown more and more evident that to understand these men (and the way they made their Faith convincing) opens the direct road to the deepest apprehension of what Christ taught, of how He taught it, and of what He Himself uniquely was.

Can we find some satisfying designation for these vital Hebrews? They lashed religious and social abuses with a passion disconcerting to all who would rather leave things to right themselves, and turn a short-sighted eye and a deaf ear to wrongs. Shall we entitle them Social Reformers? The notion is comically anaemic. Should we call them Intellectuals? Their discernment was great, but they would have said that the question whether they were clever or ultra-clever men was neither here nor there, because they were what they were, and believed what they believed, for a reason they could describe only by saying that *God* had 'laid

[1] H. W. Robinson, *Redemption and Revelation*, pp. 130, 138.

His hand upon them' and 'put His Word in their mouth', giving them knowledge of truth. How then shall we term them? Their contemporaries often called them *Men of God*; and perhaps it had been well if that had been their only title. Usually, however, the Hebrews referred to them by a word (*Nābhi*) which meant *One who declares* ('tells forth') *a divine message*. This term the Greek translations of the Hebrew text rendered by the Greek word (προφήτης) which our translations did not attempt to translate but simply transliterated as *Prophet*. That was a misfortune; because in the Greek period the idea of a Prophet uppermost in men's minds had come to be *One who predicts future events by divine inspiration*, and for many subsequent centuries that notion was dominant. (Even now, those to whom the Old Testament is a closely sealed book are apt to suppose that Hebrew Prophets served their day and generation, and should serve our own, as a sort of 'Old Moore's Almanack'.)

The supremely great Hebrew Prophets were primarily men who sought to face facts, instead of cherishing easy hopes by evading actualities. They 'saw life steadily and saw it whole'. Their hearts delighted in peaceful harvests and the beauty of fruitful vines and olives. But they also witnessed at first hand the devastation wrought by plague and famine, and the atrocities of pitiless warfare. They watched the happiness of homes and children; but what open eyes they had for corruption and cruelty and the Palestinian equivalent of the slums! The end to which those bitter things would lead they foresaw. But they had more than the gift of foresight. They were forthright men; and they were given a forthright Word to declare.

It was the great Prophets who saw the supreme principle—that men must measure what is right and wrong by the test of Absolute Goodness. Great insight followed. The Prophets were in no dubiety about the rights of the community over the individual or the limits of its rights. They declared it was the duty, and should be the joy, of each to serve his fellows to the utmost in his power. But the Prophets were assuredly not the tame slaves of kings! The individual must not surrender his conscience to the State, nor must the State seek to silence him. On no account whatsoever must a man agree to be its conscienceless, passive, agent. They were right—that way lies Nazified Germany, and the outcome is individuals like Goering, Himmler, Streicher and Irma Grese, claiming irresponsibility for their diabolical actions because they were merely carrying out the Führer's orders. The Prophets lived what they thought and taught; and gave such definiteness to 'God and His righteousness' that their nation had to take heed to its ways asking whether they were good or evil. In these men, above all others, the genius of the 'Hebrew mind' is disclosed. In their lives we touch the pulse of Israel's spiritual vitality. They stood for belief in the 'law' of God—the significance of the operation of cause and effect in the moral sphere. Therefore they were rigorous: they would not suffer the voice of Conscience to be drowned in a cackle of irrelevance. And they were piercingly clear-sighted to distinguish the better from the worse course, because they judged by the standard of Right and not by the counsel of Expediency: they did not confuse grey with white, or black with blue. As G. A. Smith has said of the shepherd-Prophet, Amos, 'he carried with him his clear desert atmosphere and his desert eyes. He saw the raw facts....He had no illusions: he knew a mirage when he saw one.'[1] (This capacity for keen moral discernment they eventually imparted to the deep consciousness of their People. Hence amidst the glittering confusion of Greek and Roman civilization great Jews knew the difference between the compromise which is reasonable and the compromise with evil which leads straight to perdition. They knew when to stand and, if need be, die for principles. And, broadly speaking, their nation as a whole acquired the same capacity; if it had not, it would ignominiously have ceased to exist.) But the Prophets held that this inexorable moral law is written in the heart of things by God, not for condemnation but in order that Humanity can learn what is right and be saved from self-destruction. Therefore, they could confront individuals and nation with the standard of moral perfection, face dire actualities honestly, and yet remain constant in hope. The surpassing moral demand made sense in relation to its *religious* foundation—belief that God is good and His purpose for men their welfare. For the Prophets morality and religion were indivisible. 'Only a vital Christian faith, renewing its youth in its prophetic origin,' writes a modern philosopher, 'is capable of dealing adequately with the moral and social problems of our age.'[2] For very great reasons

---

[1] *The Twelve Prophets*, vol. I, p. 84.
[2] Niebuhr, *An Interpretation of Christian Ethics*, p. 44. Cp. also p. 392.

this study will revert again and again to the significance of the supremely great Prophets.

Modern thought tends to settled conviction that, if Ultimate Reality is rightly conceived to be an infinite 'Intelligence' in *Whom* exist in absolute degree the qualities we finitely know as Truth, Goodness and Beauty, it is not to the universe in general but to human personality at its noblest that we should turn for clearest evidence. Trust that God in relation to Man is 'Truth, Goodness and Beauty in perfection' centres therefore in the supreme marvel of the Person of Jesus. But the great Hebrew Prophets had earlier brought into existence a faith in God vital and vitalizing. We may well ask whether these men, who prepared 'a highway in the desert' for the feet of Christ to walk, have not timeless spiritual value for right comprehension of the Christian Faith. These were men who gave of their best that others might possess. They sought truth, and loved goodness; and, in so doing, created that subtle fragrant excellence we call beauty—'an added benediction which may be awarded when you have done the right thing rightly'. We may well ask ourselves exactly what qualities enabled them in the circumstances of their lives to be discerners of righteousness, veritably servants of God, and mediators of an increasing wisdom? How exactly did they, and how did Jesus, make belief so apparent to the minds of others, and so effective in their wills? How do they stand related to Him, who 'after the flesh' was a son of David, born in Bethlehem of Judaea when Herod was king?

In the ever-imperfect expression of historic Christianity nineteen centuries have shown the same resurgent vitality. Immense intellectual and social changes have occurred during the Christian Era. Again and again, it has looked as if the Faith would prove unable to answer the challenge and respond to the new environment. Things that had grown old looked to be irremediably ready to pass away. The fires died down; as if the last embers would soon become cold grey ash. '*Then the Lord awaked as one out of sleep*', said a boldly poetic Psalmist of Israel. '*He that sitteth upon the throne said, Behold I make all things new*', declared the writer of the Book of Revelation. The renewals of spiritual energy during the Christian Era are heartening facts. But there is a sombre way in which these nineteen centuries ought to be regarded. How came it to pass that the Church so often, and to so lamentable an extent, has been shockingly unlike its Master? Why did the Gospel, which went forth conquering and to conquer, in time come to have so pitiably feeble a hold, or none at all, over the intelligence of masses of men, or not in a way that caused the profession of the lips to be translated effectively into the desires of their hearts and the acts of their lives? Did our Christian forefathers make some tragic mistake concerning the statement or presentation of the Faith?

Whenever ideas and ideals answer a deep-felt need, confront men with a challenge, and are stated with crystal clarity, the effect is tremendous. We have no excuse to-day for ignoring that fact. The Nazis contrived to state their devilish creed (*Blood and Soil*) with quintessential clarity, and Russian Communism made its social philosophy intelligible to millions of men and women— with prodigious consequences. So also it was seen, when the great Hebrew Prophets made their belief concerning God and His righteousness intelligible and unforgettable, changed the 'mind' of their nation, and gave it new vitality. So also, when Christ taught the multitudes the things that belong to our peace. So also, when the first Apostles went forth to preach the Gospel in His name. How stands it now? Men say that they know not what we say. 'Those of us who believe that the religion of which Jesus Christ is the centre holds the key to all the problems of life and thought must not blind ourselves to the fact that under its name are preached the most diverse beliefs: an infallible Church; an infallible Book; a moral ideal for human conduct; an other-worldly pietism; a social and international programme; a pure pacificism; the consecration of force; the corporate State; the communist State. I might multiply endlessly the opposites which are to-day preached by reputable Christians as things necessary to or proceeding from the understanding of the Christian religion.'[1] Why does the trumpet give forth an uncertain sound? Where does the fault lie that essential Christian belief is so widely unknown, so bewilderingly presented, or so feebly held?

To toss the question aside with a shrug of the shoulders and lay the blame on 'obdurate sinners who ought to know better' is a wicked answer; for it is the answer of the self-satisfied. To answer that there is no need to reconsider anything about Christianity because in the Conciliar Creeds the early Church was led by the

---

[1] W. Paton, *Christianity in the Eastern Conflicts*, p. 130.

Spirit to give exact and full definition of the Faith—is a very lazy answer; first, because it is perspicuous to theologians but to extremely few others; but secondly, for the following deep reason —the expression which any period, with its distinctive problems and cultural temperament, gives to eternal spiritual truth does not exhaust the full meaning. To suppose that it does is not listed among the heresies, but it comes not far short of proposing to limit the work of God and the boundlessness of His wisdom. It is possible to honour the validity of the Creeds of the early Church in a numb way, as if (so to say) God had been so fully satisfied with the achievement of the Greeks and Romans that He considered translation into other tongues would completely suffice for the remainder of history. The Creeds safeguarded the metaphysical and historical character of the Faith by giving correct (i.e. *orthodox*) replies to certain subtle and dangerous misconceptions propounded in the Greek and Roman Age, and they have a timeless relevance inasmuch as ancient heresies have a way of reappearing in modern disguises. But it is matter of fact that in the first few centuries of the Christian Era Greek dialectical ability changed the mode of presenting the claims of Faith and Duty. It ceased to be the method used by the great Prophets, the method used by Christ Himself, the method used by the Apostles. What had been simple but profound became profoundly intellectual. In 1888 an expert student of early Christianity, Dr Edwin Hatch, penned these words: 'the Greeks changed the rushing torrent of the river of God into a broad and feeble stream. Christianity was profoundly modified by the habit of mind of those who received it. Around it thronged the race of eloquent talkers, who persuaded it to change its dress and to assimilate its language to their own.'[1] What

---

[1] See *The Influence of Greek Ideas upon the Christian Church* (Hibbert Lectures, 1888), pp. 49, 114. The inevitable linguistic transition from the Semitic Hebrew-Aramaic to the Indo-European Greek and Latin idiom, to which Hatch refers, is of the utmost importance. Languages as means of thought and expression reflect specific casts of mind. No finer precision-instrument than Greek has ever been used by the lips of men. But the Semitic languages (Hebrew, in especial) were characterized by a vividness and directness that made them singularly suited for effective presentation of religious and moral feeling: they go straight to the heart of the matter and speak lucidly. For instance, the qualities of Semitic speech led the Hebrews to invaluable insight into that hard problem—the relation of things temporal to things eternal—in ways far more practically important than the

of to-day? It is true that the extension of authentic Christian belief, religious and moral, in Africa and the Eastern hemisphere is a giant phenomenon in modern history. The effects, if less spectacular, are as profound and revolutionizing as the spread of Communism. (The facts concerning it are absurdly little known.) But in the West the position for Christianity is different indeed. Only a small percentage of the population profess definitely Christian belief. The tragedy is that so very many do not so much as know what the Faith is; that so many entertain a distorted notion of what it affirms and confidently conclude that 'Christianity is superstition'. And—no less tragic—many Christians have but a vague conception of their Faith, or how it stands in relation to modern thought. Beliefs vaguely held have no cutting edge.

Recall the observation stressed earlier in this chapter: 'The effort of this age is to get behind the Greek influences and to present Christianity as the Semitic mind presented and left it.' That summons to consider again the essential nature of our Faith, and the mode of its presentation, is not a proposal to unthink what the Greeks rightly thought, or to undo what they rightly did. But it may save us from the tempting assumption that the Greeks did

Greek philosophers could compass. As regards contrast of mental temperament—the intellectual perspicacity of the Greeks stands above criticism. Nevertheless, Hebrew intelligence (despite its ancient Eastern garments)— as regards that high mystery, Man's personal consciousness—is more in accord with recent opinion (philosophical and psychological) than is that of the Greeks. The Greek approach to the basic problem was too restrictedly intellectual and argumentative; whereas the Hebrews reached their convictions by following a wider route. Their conclusions were the outcome of a more unified effort of personality, in which the will was co-operating with the intelligence closely. As for morals, the *non-Christian* Greeks eventually talked themselves into a tangle of impotence, paralleled only by the same phenomenon in the modern world. Greek ethical opinions and systems were eager, manifold, and shaky. The trouble was that (Platonism excepted) they doubted or denied that *Right* is based on a secure, metaphysical foundation. As for religion, the non-Christian Greeks yielded almost totalitarian authority to reasoning about Ultimate Reality, and their speculations never became a fully religious philosophy; whereas the view of life's final meaning held by the Hebrews of genius began, continued and ended a religion: a *religion*, however, which can be classified philosophically as 'Ethical Theism'. The *Christian* Greeks enriched the Faith by giving it the definition and defence required by the mentality of the Greek and Roman Age. But they enfeebled the amazing power with which Semitic genius had endowed it.

all Christian thinking for all men for all time; or that, being very wise, they were wise in all ways. It may lead us to perceive what, notwithstanding their piety and intelligence, they did amiss or failed to do.[1] It may aid us to hear what God wants us to learn in this our Age, and how to say it with lucidity in a world which has put questions about the validity of religion unknown to the Greeks; a world which, even when it asks old questions which the Greek and Roman Christians answered correctly, insists on formulating them differently. If the present situation does not sound and resound in the conscience of sincere Christians as the Voice of God demanding that we should be thinking what has been done amiss, or left undone, about our Faith, it ought to do so! As men who are aware of what the Greeks achieved doctrinally, but who are also aware of modern knowledge, *and* of what God has wrought in Christ for the seekers of truth in every age and in continents other than our own, we of to-day should be able to present the greatness of the Faith more deeply and more effectively than has been possible at any previous time. That is our task, and our unequalled opportunity.

Will the argument underlying this study of the development of Hebrew religion prove to be that the needs of our Age would be met by proclaiming what was customarily called 'the simple Gospel'—its so-called 'simplicity' being an attenuated version of the Christian Faith ascribing no value to the wisdom and experience of the Church? The writer regards the continuity of the Christian Church as seen in the triumphs and tragedies of its history as a revealing fact, instructive in the highest degree. But not least instructive in its warnings—how inadequately each and all of the passing generations realized that the fullness of Christ's significance exceeded their immediate comprehension; how reluctant they were to believe that God is the living God to whom men must for ever listen in order that they may learn yet more. This work does not consider the task of religious thought in our times to be rightly summed in the formula 'Back to Christ', as if we should forget Christian history. Neither does the writer envisage the object of

---

[1] It has been said that 'the Greeks took Christianity into the University, and set it forth in a form suitable for examination purposes—as if entrance into the Kingdom of Heaven would be the reward of those able to matriculate'. That is a forceful remark; too forceful, and ungenerous—for urgent intellectual problems of the time had to be faced.

this study as 'Back to the beliefs of the great Prophets, *forgetting Christ*'—as though, forsooth, our Faith were not in Christ Himself, and our interest not in the broad river of Christianity as it flows down the centuries; as though our aim were merely to trace the river's mighty current back to a tiny streamlet in the hinterland of early Hebrew history, and the ultimate hope of our journeying to descry at last (with the aid of binoculars and the archaeologists) its original spring in primitive Semitic customs. 'The river and its source' is here the wrong similitude. If metaphor be desired to suggest the thought that guides this work, let it be drawn from the Gospel of St John, from its narrative concerning Jesus and the Woman of Samaria when He spake with her at the well of Jacob. Christ and the beliefs of the great Prophets, which flowed through Him, are like a well of living water—an inexhaustible source, to which men can resort at all seasons and, even in the heat of summer, will not depart unsatisfied. The ancient well from which Jacob drank ('he and his sons and his cattle'), where Jesus talked with the Samaritan woman, is in the Vale of Shechem beneath the Mountain of Blessing in the very centre of the Holy Land. Thither the Peoples of our world from East and West have need to journey; for from the fullness of its depths we should all receive. If, enriched by the wealth of modern knowledge and by the experience which the long centuries have yielded, we come to that well thankfully and humbly, He who will talk with us there can give us to drink of 'the water of life' freely. Then He could take us up with Him to the Mount of Blessing; and Christ with the Prophets would stand transfigured before our modern eyes. But a wiser thought should rise in our minds as we think of Jesus at the well of Jacob. The well and the mountain are still near Shechem. But the spirit of Christ went forth from the Holy Land, passing through time and space, that He might be ever present with men, ever in our midst. If, with that truth in mind, we ask expectantly 'How came our Faith?', God may show us in yet more splendid Vision 'What is our Faith'.

There is yet another reason why the story of Israel ought not to be forgotten—its aesthetic quality. All lovely things ought to be cherished, even when they can make no other claim than that of their intrinsic beauty. It is good for a man to look up to the stars in the night skies, although the discipline of trying to tell their number will not aid him to balance his budget next morning.

Because the critics have dug out of Homer every scrap of historical information his poems can yield concerning the break-up of Mycenaean civilization in the thirteenth century B.C., we do not think the *Iliad* and the *Odyssey* may suitably now be consigned to the salvage dump. At Athens the ruins of the Parthenon should be preserved, although they will not serve as a convenient civic centre. When the Athenian writer, Thucydides, set himself to relate the history of the war that ended in the capture of the fair city by its uninspired Spartan foes, he knew that if he could but describe Athens in its Golden Age—the complex of ambition, valour and achievement; the mistakes, misfortunes and dawn of fear; the wisdom of great leaders and the perils of demagogic oratory; the disaster of the plague; how the expedition to Sicily on which all was staked came within an ace of success but ended in irretrievable ruin; how Athens received the news and faced its fall—Thucydides knew that, if he could livingly relate these things, he would leave a thing of beauty, 'a possession for ever'.

'Israel' also is epic history in immortal words. It has the rich diversity of Nature—line and colour, grandeur and detail. It is music: the whole symphony of human life. As Heine said of the Psalms: 'Sunrise and sunset, birth and death, promise and fulfilment.' It possesses the rare and lovely characteristic of a great complexity which, seen in its totality, is found to be a unity. The origins of Israel are veiled in the mists of antiquity; the sequel extends for over 1000 years in the light of history. As the great drama develops many trivial persons play small parts in its unfolding. Then fragments, now from one quarter now from another, are seen to come together. For long, however, it is not evident that a majestic unity is in the making. In the end the complexity reveals itself as a marvellous pattern. As the centuries passed, the threads were woven together and the Christ seen. But the aesthetic quality in the history of Israel cannot be rightly valued apart from the inherent religious and moral significance. For this 'drama' is not a masterpiece of the imagination. It had for its 'stage' the real world; the 'characters' were living persons; its theme is the actualities of our common experience; and its strength is that at last it found in human life no enigma of darkness but a mystery of light. The treasure in the Old Testament is ever-relevant to human affairs. It is not right to hand it over, disinterestedly, to students of antiquity, as if it were something other men could with little loss leave buried in the dust of ages. It is not right to think of it as notable ancient literature, which, if anyone should want to examine its pages, can be found safely stowed away in reverent custody of theologians and duly entered in their library catalogue. The treasure in the Bible offers itself as present wisdom and power which any man can grasp, and of which all stand in need. For the marvellous fact about what Christ and the Prophets said and did was that they cut through tangled perplexities to make profound things simple, by revealing that certain simple things are profound. Moreover, Christ and the Prophets bring the issues in life before us in such a way that, when our mind assents, saying 'Yes, that was right', conscience speaks within us, saying 'It is right for me to-day'.

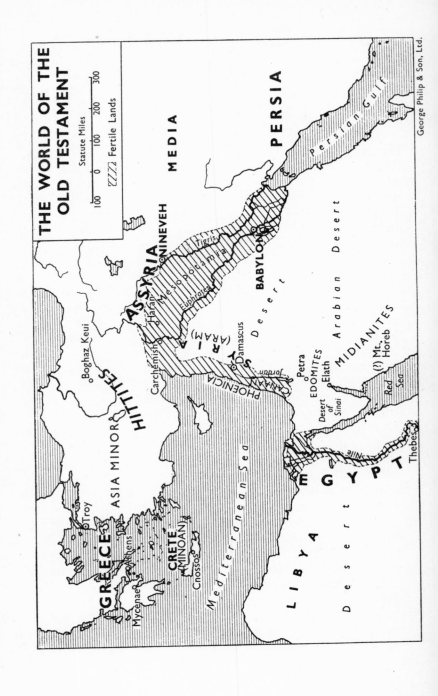

THE WORLD OF THE
OLD TESTAMENT

Statute Miles

100   0   100   200   300

▨ Fertile Lands

George Philip & Son, Ltd.

GREECE
Troy
ASIA MINOR
Athens
Mycenae
HITTITES
Boghaz Keui
CRETE
(MINOAN)
Cnossos
Mediterranean Sea

ASSYRIA
NINEVEH
Carchemish
Haran
Tigris
Meso potamia
Euphrates
MEDIA
BABYLON
PERSIA
Persian Gulf

SYRIA
(ARAM)
Damascus
PHOENICIA
CANAAN
Jordan
Desert
Arabian Desert

Petra
EDOMITES
Elath
Desert
of
Sinai
MIDIANITES
(?) Mt.
Horeb
Red Sea

EGYPT
Nile
Thebes
LIBYA
Desert
Desert

CHAPTER II

MODERN STUDY OF THE OLD TESTAMENT

The net of Introduction has been cast widely in the foregoing Chapter. Ought not Page 1, line 1, of the history of Hebrew religion immediately to follow? But there are three general matters of prime importance for appreciating that history. First (in this Chapter)—what precisely is meant by saying that recent study has opened up the treasures discoverable in the Old Testament? Second (in Chapter III)—the Hebrews did not talk our language, and certain surprising facts about theirs illuminate their mental attitude and all their literature. Third (in Chapter IV, on The use and misuse of the Scriptures)—the great truth has to be made clear that the events in Hebrew history, and the various Books of the Old Testament, are not isolated *items*, but (so to speak) leaves and branches of an organic growth, 'The Tree of the Knowledge of Good and Evil', 'The planting of the Lord'. The Parts are parts of a Whole: namely, for Jewish belief, eventual Jewish theology; for Christians, Christ and Christianity—whereby the Old and New Testaments together constitute a profound unity of written record. Therefore these three Chapters are NOT failure to begin to build, but foundations of the building. (If general readers find more detail than is welcome, it is hoped they will extract the gist of the matter from Chapters II and III, and will not fail to read IV on 'The Bible as sacred scripture'.)

Nothing of importance to the modern world would be known about the People of Israel earlier than the third century B.C., if the literature of the Old Testament Books had perished. Rich and intimate, however, is the information provided by that marvellous literature. Moreover, in the course of the past century archaeological investigation of the ancient civilizations of the Near East, comparative study of religious beliefs and customs, and the application of literary science to the Old Testament writings themselves, have together shown the Old Testament to be an incomparably richer source of knowledge concerning Israel's history and thought than had previously been realized. The religious quality of the Old Testament, and the relation of its contents to the New Testament writings, will be considered in Chapter IV. The purpose of the present Chapter is to outline the ways in which the three branches of modern research, referred to above, have corrected misconceptions and increased historical information. No more, of course, can here be done than to mention a few salient and memorable facts.

§ 1. *Archaeological Science*

The work of the archaeologists who, little more than a century ago, set themselves to explore the traces of ancient civilization in the lands of the Near East may justly be termed a *Science*. A highly skilled technique of excavation, and mastery of several languages written in alphabets or pictorial signs that for long baffled accurate translation, had to be developed before assured information could be derived from the material remains of the ancient civilizations —from excavated temples and tombs and city sites, from inscriptions and manuscripts, from implements, ornaments, and fragments of pottery. But the labours of the investigators might with equal justice be styled a *Romance*, so startling have been the results, and so comparatively short the time in which they have been won. The pioneers began with only the slightest idea of the really ancient history of the lands in question—Egypt, Babylonia, Assyria, Asia Minor, Syria, Palestine. Not in their wildest dreams could they have anticipated the magnitude and difficulty of the task they had commenced. During the course of a century fragments of astonishing interest came to light, now from one quarter, now from another. Right inferences were gradually drawn; growing knowledge checked and interrelated. The pioneers in the gigantic task may have hoped to reach back even to the age of Abraham, *c.* 1700 years before Christ. Their successors have been able to present us with so comprehensive a survey of the ancient history of the Near East that detailed knowledge of its civilization has been carried back generally to 3000 B.C., and in Egypt and Mesopotamia to over 4000 B.C.

(*a*) *Egypt*. Throughout the centuries the Sphinx and the Pyramids of Egypt have been visible to men. But the Sphinx guarded its secret inscrutably, and the Pyramids stirred the curiosity of very few. It seemed there was really nothing one could do save gaze upon them! In 1798 a French scholar, attached to Napoleon's army in Egypt, recognized the possible importance of an inscribed slab of black stone at Rosetta. When Alexandria was captured by the British in 1801, this stone was removed to the British Museum. It bears in three languages inscriptions that proved to be identical—one is in Greek, one in 'popular' Egyptian, and one (on the topmost portion) is written in the then-mysterious picture-writing which we now know was used in ancient Egypt for royal and sacred purposes, and which we call the hieroglyphic script. Fortunately the name of King Ptolemy occurred in the Greek version, and the corresponding hieroglyph was deciphered. By 1830 a French scholar (Champollion) and a British (Young) between them had succeeded in understanding the whole of the hieroglyphic inscription on the Rosetta Stone. The road lay open to mastery of the ancient Egyptian language, and accurate translation of the multitude of inscriptions and papyrus documents subsequently found has become easy. Ever since then Egypt has yielded up marvel on marvel in profusion—temples and statues of its Gods, tombs and mummies of its great men and its monarchs, records of dynasty on dynasty stretching back to 4000 years before Christ.

The most fascinating, though by no means the best known, discovery commenced when a peasant woman in 1887, searching rubbish heaps at a place called Tell-el-Amarna, found in a small store chamber a number of inscribed tablets which she sold to a neighbour for the equivalent of two shillings. Now the site of Tell-el-Amarna covered the ruins of a city which the youthful King Amenhotep IV, who reigned from 1375–1358 B.C., built to replace Thebes as the capital of Egypt and to be the royal centre from which he sought to promulgate his own brilliant conception of true religion. And the store chamber proved to have been no less important a building than 'the place of the records of the palace of the King'! And the tablets no less a treasure than Foreign Office correspondence exchanged between the Egyptian Government, the rulers of the towns of Syria and Palestine, and the king of the great Hittite Power in Asia Minor. These and other Tell-el-Amarna tablets threw a flood of light not only on the events and general ideas of this period, which though brief was momentous, but also on the wonderful personality of Amenhotep IV, or (as he styled himself in relation to his religious effort) Ikhnaton. The political aspect of his reign will be referred to in Chapter V. Here the far more important subject of Ikhnaton's personality may be mentioned.[1] He is the one permanently interesting individual known to us in the whole 4000 years of Egyptian history; beyond doubt a genius, whose brilliance and originality showed itself alike in matters aesthetic, moral, intellectual and religious. Ikhnaton sought to replace the immemorial polytheism of Egypt by belief in a sole, *beneficent*, Deity. He is justly called 'the world's first monotheist', but his real greatness is that he conceived the character of the *One* God to be wholly good—enlightening, healing, helpful to mankind. The symbol which Ikhnaton adopted to promote comprehension of the new conception of God, and to put an end to the gross polytheism of Egypt, was the golden disk of the sun with rays streaming from it, each terminating in a human hand. The relentless antagonism of the immensely powerful organization of the priests of the ancient Sun-God, Amon, of Thebes is one indication that Ikhnaton's attempted reform was no mere inculcation of sun-worship. It is certain he was proclaiming a new conception of religion, profound and spiritual. He died about the age of 30, and immediately on his death those who had hated and opposed him swept away his work. They even sought to obliterate his very memory, and it was enacted that in the records of Egypt he should be referred to, not by his name, but as 'the criminal of Akhetaton'— Akhetaton being the name of his royal city at El-Amarna. The epitaph he truly deserved waited to be written by a modern scholar 3000 years later: 'There died with him such a spirit as the world had never seen before—a brave soul, undauntedly facing the momentum of immemorial tradition... that he might disseminate ideas far beyond and above the capacity of his age to understand.... The modern world has yet adequately to value or even acquaint itself with this man, who, in an age so remote and under conditions so adverse, became not only the world's first idealist and the world's first *individual*, but also the earliest monotheist, and the first prophet of internationalism—the most remarkable figure of the Ancient World before the Hebrews.'[2]

Far more widely known than the story of Tell-el-Amarna is the

---

[1] Many, to whom the name of Ikhnaton may be unknown, are familiar with the replicas of the lovely statuette of the head of his beautiful and beloved Queen, Nefertiti.

[2] Breasted, in *The Cambridge Ancient History*, vol. II, p. 127.

discovery in 1922 of the unplundered tomb of Ikhnaton's son-in-law, Tutankhamen. Tutankhamen was no more than a boy-king who reigned for six years. But the glories of his sepulchre with its golden coffins and mummies, its jewels and thrones and beds and sculptured figures, were a revelation of the wealth and craftsmanship of ancient Egypt. Accordingly 'all the world and his wife' hastened to acquaint themselves with the details of *that* discovery: for here was no strange tale of a reformed theology, but material treasure beyond the dreams of avarice.

(*b*) *Babylonia and Assyria.* As late as A.D. 1840 'a case hardly three feet square in the British Museum contained almost all that was known to remain both of Babylon and Nineveh'.[1] In 1835, however, Sir Henry Rawlinson had succeeded in making a copy of an inscription graven on a nearly inaccessible rock some 300 ft. above the Plain of Behistun in western Persia. Like the Rosetta Stone it bore a royal decree in three languages, and, since one of the scripts was a wedge-shaped form of writing (*cuneiform*) used by the Assyrians and Babylonians (and the still earlier Sumerian-Accadian inhabitants of the Mesopotamian river-plains), its decipherment was the key to translation of the mass of cuneiform tablets subsequently discovered. Huge earthen mounds cover the remains of the cities, palaces and temples, of ancient civilization in Mesopotamia. The first really rewarding excavations were carried out in 1840. In 1846 an obelisk, sent to London, furnished the first reference found outside the Old Testament to an episode in early Hebrew history; for among the various triumphs of Shalmaneser III of Assyria recorded on the obelisk there was mention of tribute paid to him by Jehu, King of Israel. About the same time, by great good fortune, the state libraries of two Assyrian monarchs, Nebo and Asshurbanipal I, were unearthed; and from these were recovered tens of thousands of brick tablets inscribed in cuneiform. When in 1872 a young Assyriologist, George Smith, in a paper read to the Society of Biblical Archaeology quietly announced that he had transcribed in the British Museum tablets giving a Babylonian version of Noah's Flood, a sensation was caused. By the beginning of this century it could be stated that 'Buildings, sculptures, and inscriptions have been disinterred in almost countless numbers, testifying to the industrial activity

[1] The capitals respectively of the southern (Babylonian) and of the northern (Assyrian) Empires of Mesopotamia.

which existed in ancient Babylonia more than 2000 years before Christ. Hymns, epics, poems, letters, chronicles, annals of kings, paradigms and vocabularies, inscriptions relating to ritual, astrology and magic; besides a very important Code of Laws,[1] have also been discovered.'[2]

Since then knowledge of the Sumerian-Accadian civilization preceding the Babylonian Age has been won. Sir Leonard Woolley's excavations[3] at Ur (the Biblical 'Ur of the Chaldees') have been particularly notable. Its temple-mound ('Tower of Babel', *Ziggurat*) was of immense size. The royal tombs at Ur, opened up in 1926, revealed quantities of gold and silver implements, fine mosaics, jewelled ornaments most artistically wrought, together with a gruesome array of skeletons of men, women and animals, slain to serve as retinue for the dead king and queen. At Ur also, in 1929, beneath the *strata* of civilized centuries, Woolley dug down to a layer of clay 8 ft. thick which had certainly been deposited by a tremendous inundation about 3000 B.C.; and beneath the clay he further found relics of habitation from 4000 B.C. In the excavation of another Sumerian city, Kish, a similar 'Flood' *stratum* was found, but its catastrophe antedates that at Ur by 1000 years.[4] Traces of civilized occupation at Kish reach back to 5000 B.C.

(c) *Asia Minor*. The chief result of excavation in this region has been the discovery that from about 2000 B.C. a people (partly of Indo-European ancestry) known as Hittites formed a mighty nation, closely connected with a number of lesser States. For long the Hittite language proved very difficult to master. Now we have intimate knowledge of their affairs—religious, social, military, political and commercial. One of their kings had a Hitleresque talent for duplicity! At his capital (Boghaz-Keui) there was found the Hittite counterpart of the Tell-el-Amarna correspondence

---

[1] That of Hammurabi, King of Babylon, now dated about 1700 B.C. Their resemblance to many Hebrew laws is of deep interest.

[2] Driver, *Modern Research as illustrating the Bible*, p. 5.

[3] See Woolley, *The Sumerians* (1928). The book contains most interesting illustrations.

[4] These two 'Flood' discoveries, in relation to the story of a Universal Deluge in Gen. vi–ix and the comparable but *polytheistic* version found in the Babylonian literature, afforded an illuminating example of the way in which an ancient tradition may combine memory of fact with features of myth and legend.

mentioned above in connexion with the Egyptian King, Ikhnaton; and it reveals Hittite diplomacy shamelessly lying and scheming to subvert Egyptian control in Syria and Palestine.

(*d*) *Syria and Phoenicia.* In this great area the most striking 'find' is of more recent date. In 1929 some hundreds of tablets were unearthed at Ras Shamra, a site on the Syrian coast. They date from about 1470–1366 B.C., but many may be reproductions of still older writings. These tablets are inscribed in a previously unknown alphabetic form of cuneiform, and the language is *not Babylonian* but similar to Phoenician and Hebrew, though less developed. Many of the tablets record public and commercial matters, but many are of religious interest—mentioning ritual customs and mythological traditions. The Ras Shamra evidence illuminates Phoenician-Syrian culture and bears upon Canaanite and later Hebrew religious ideas and rites.[1]

(*e*) *Arabia.* Even the sands of Arabia, vast remote and secretive, have yielded up some valuable information about the location and wanderings, the worship and customs, of its great tribes in antiquity; and the importance of the caravan traffic on the routes from the rich incense-bearing lands of southern Arabia through the deserts to Egypt and the northern Semitic countries.[2]

(*f*) *The Mediterranean Sea Empire.* The history of the Classical Age in Greece was 'solid ground', documented and dated. But what inferences could be drawn from Homer's immortal poems, the *Iliad* and the *Odyssey*? Was it possible, as Homer's songs seemed to imply, that a beautiful civilization had preceded the 'Classical Age'? Surely the *Iliad's* tale of the siege of Troy, in which Olympian Gods and Goddesses took so active a part, was only myth and legend. Surely its contending heroes—Priam, Agamemnon, Achilles and the rest—were never mortal men, but only the creation of the poet's golden imagination. Surely the Mediterranean wanderings of resourceful Odysseus, striving to return from Troy to his island home in Ithaca, were no more than 'magic casements opening on the foam of perilous seas in faery lands forlorn'. We know now that the *Iliad* and the *Odyssey* are poetry turning to enchantment the prose of Mediterranean history

---

[1] Cp. Albright, *Archaeology and the Religion of Israel*, ch. 3. (H. W. Robinson's discriminating reviews of this book, and of the same author's *From the Stone Age to Christianity*, in the *Journal of Theological Studies*, 1941, 1943, should be noted.) [2] Cp. Freya Stark, *Southern Gates of Arabia*.

about 1200 B.C.—the very time (in the writer's opinion) when Hebrew tribes were struggling to fight their way across Jordan and into the highlands of central Canaan.[1] Nothing could well be more romantic than the effort, begun by Schliemann in 1870, to find the remains of an actual city of Troy in the mound of Hissarlik on the north-western coast of Asia Minor: for the eventual result was knowledge of a 'lost' civilization—a Sea Empire which during 2000 years had controlled the waters of the eastern Mediterranean! Schliemann was right as to the site of Troy, but the 'Homeric' city lay buried three layers deeper than the foundations he unearthed and supposed to be the relics of Homer's Troy. In 1876, however, at Mycenae on the Greek mainland Schliemann successfully laid bare the foundations of the palace of Agamemnon; and its artistic treasures proved conclusively that here had been a splendid civilization, not only earlier than, but distinct in culture from that of the Classical Greeks. It was evident that a fresh labyrinthine problem invited solution. There was a clue to it in Greek mythology; for the tale of Theseus and the Minotaur in Crete is legendary, but the legend covers history. The secret was penetrated by Sir Arthur Evans' excavations at Cnossos in Crete. It then became certain that this great island had been the centre of a very ancient, seafaring civilization; that the rulers of Cnossos had been lords of the eastern Mediterranean Sea, and that, as time went on, they had established their distinctive culture at different strongholds (such as Agamemnon's Mycenae) on the coasts of Greece and of Asia Minor. *Minoan-Mycenaean* is therefore the name used to denote this civilization. In its eventual breakdown the siege of Troy was one incident. Another (and this touches the history of Israel) was the settlement of the Philistines on the shore of Palestine.

(g) *Palestine.* The first triumph of excavation in Palestine itself was achieved by Flinders Petrie in 1890. In the mound of Tell-el-Hesy (probably the site of the ancient Eglon) he laid bare the foundations of no less than eleven cities which in the course of 1300 years (1700–400 B.C.) had been superimposed each on the ruins of its predecessor. In 1902–8 R. A. S. Macalister excavated a great mound at Gezer, situated in the Judaean foothills overlooking the coastal plain.[2] There he was able to dig down through

[1] Cp. Chapter v, pp. 102 ff.
[2] Cp. his volume *Bible Sidelights from the Mound of Gezer*, and *The Palestinian Exploration Fund Quarterly* for 1902–8.

the strata of many cities to the earliest Amorite settlement about 3000 B.C., and found caverns in the rock which had been used by aboriginal men of the Stone Age, men short of stature and certainly not of Semitic race, since (for one thing) they cremated their dead. The excavations at Gezer yielded the first splendid example of a typical Canaanite Sanctuary (the Biblical term is 'High-Place'), with a rock-altar and a row of huge standing stones. Another remarkable find at Gezer was a tunnel 23 ft. high and 12 ft. wide, which about 2000 B.C. had been hewn down into the rock to a length of 219 ft. until a water-spring to supply the city had been found at a depth of 94 ft.: an amazing achievement. At Jerusalem excavation outside its present wall has laid bare the lower courses of the wall of the Jebusite town which David conquered and made his capital.[1] In the past fifty years site after site in Palestine has surrendered to us 'treasures of darkness, and hidden riches of secret places'. We know now how men lived and died and worshipped in Palestine for 2000 years before David was king in Zion; for 3000 years before Christ was born in Bethlehem.

§2. Comparative Study of Religions

This title denotes a very wide range of investigation. The subject deals with vastly more than comparing the religious systems of *civilized* nations. When the ideas and customs of uncivilized races, ancient and modern, are collated, it is apparent not only that they throw light upon beliefs and usages cherished in advanced religions, but also that they are in their own right of very deep interest. We are apt condescendingly to refer to uncivilized communities as *savage* or *primitive*. 'The so-called savage is a gentleman', said an eminent anthropologist (Dr A. C. Haddon), 'and the only real savages are to be found in the governments and cities of the West.' Sir J. G. Frazer also cautions us regarding the term *primitive*, observing that the outlook of races whose culture in relation to our own may properly be styled *rudimentary* or *backward* was, or is, far above the level of neolithic and palaeolithic men.[2] Moreover, it should be borne in mind that the uncivilized peoples of the present time have behind them as long a history as the civilized, although they are not conscious of it to anything like the same extent, and cannot profit by written records of the past. In the first place, anthropologists have shown that

[1] See *The P.E.F. Quarterly* for 1924.   [2] *Psyche*, p. 163.

E F

3

savage customs, which seem to the inexpert to be simple and superstitious, in reality are by no means so simple as they seem. The expression which early men, and unsophisticated tribes of the present time, give to their thoughts may be crude; but the principles underlying their ideas and actions may be profound.

Secondly, comparative study of Religion involves consideration of matters that might seem to us at first sight not relevant to religion. But among uncivilized peoples, and generally in antiquity, social organization, the arts of peace, and warfare, are closely linked with their religious beliefs.[1] In a multiplicity of ways this field of study has illuminated the thought and customs of the early Hebrews. An immense store of comparable ideas and practices among uncivilized races the world over is to be found in Sir J. G. Frazer's massive volumes entitled *Folklore in the Old Testament*. The similarities he cites are impressive, but the subtle dissimilarities which mark the emerging genius of the Hebrews in religion and morals are much more so.[2]

§3. *Biblical Criticism*

Most important of all for revealing the wealth of historical information in the Old Testament writings has been the examination

---

[1] Religious beliefs and magical practices seem to be ultimately distinct in origin. Savage Magic is an attempt to apply to the problems presented by Nature logical reasoning based on inadequate knowledge: it is, in fact, rudimentary science. (Cp. Malinowski in *Science, Religion and Reality*, ed. Needham.) Most primitive peoples, however, appear to believe in, or mystically 'sense', the existence of a diffused, *impersonal*, 'Power': *Mana* (a Melanesian word) is used in reference to this fact. It is possible that there is a subtle connexion in savage minds between *Mana* and Magic.

[2] A cautionary word is in place. There is danger in drawing sweeping conclusions from similarities of custom obtaining in communities widely sundered by place and time. Frazer's encyclopaedic parallels are sometimes open to criticism on that score. When, however, the matter for comparison derives from nations of Semitic antiquity related to Israel, the relevance is unimpeachable. A point of particular interest is the fact that in 1889, when Robertson Smith wrote his brilliant book on the *Religion of the Semites*, knowledge of the totemic system of the Australian aborigines was a recent and thrilling discovery. Smith held that traces of a somewhat similar system had obtained among the ancestors of the Hebrews. The evidence is impressive, but it is now generally held that he pressed the evidence too hard in his discussion of Hebrew sacrificial ideas. (Cp. S. A. Cook's Notes to the 3rd edition of Smith's volume; also his article 'Israel and Totemism' in the *Jewish Quarterly Review*, 1902.)

of their contents by methods of literary investigation. The pioneers in this essential study gave their labours a most tactless designation —*Criticism*. *Criticism* is a word with two meanings. Technically, it denotes 'the art or science of estimating the qualities of literary work', and was therefore the appropriate term. Unfortunately, it has also a popular sense which the dictionary thus defines: 'The action of passing judgement, especially unfavourable judgement, upon the qualities of anything; fault-finding.' It has been a very grave misfortune that the notion could thus gain currency that 'a Biblical Critic' (especially one styled 'a Higher Critic') was a presumptuous scholar who dared to think himself competent to pass unfavourable judgements on Holy Writ!

(*a*) *Textual Criticism* (or, as it is sometimes styled, *Lower Criticism*) investigates whether the words in the printed Hebrew Bible reproduce faithfully the words of the original Biblical writers. Indubitably they are not a *verbatim* transcript. The printed Hebrew does present with marvellous exactitude the words of a manuscript which the Jewish authorities prepared with meticulous care about A.D. 150 in order that from it all subsequent Hebrew manuscripts should be copied.[1] In making it they selected what they judged to be the most correct readings. But it had to be made, precisely because at that time the existing manuscripts were full of differences, great and small. It is curiously hard to copy without any errors a manuscript in any language; it was virtually

---

[1] The Rabbis entrusted with the task *either* selected what seemed to them the finest extant manuscript, *or* compared the best three they could find, and prepared to the best of their judgement an eclectic text. There were minor variations even in the five Books of the Law. But by A.D. 150 the Law was held to be word-perfect in every 'jot and tittle'; and it was felt intolerable that the manuscripts showed any discrepancies. As for *The Prophets* and the *Other Writings* proof of how many, and often how great, were the differences of text found in manuscripts is furnished by the Greek versions (and to a much less extent other early versions). Translation of the Old Testament into Greek had been accomplished long before the Christian Era from Hebrew manuscripts therefore much earlier than the standard Hebrew of A.D. 150. Modern scholars, seeking to ascertain the most reliable text, accordingly consider the divergencies between the standard Hebrew (Massoretic) text and the early versions. In very many verses neither the Massoretic text nor the readings in the versions give sense, or tolerable grammar and syntax. In all such cases the only resort is to conjecture (with the aid of common sense and philological knowledge) what the original text is likely to have been—a hazardous procedure, which, however, not infrequently affords a convincing or highly probable emendation.

impossible for the early Hebrew scribes to do so. Ancient Hebrew manuscripts recorded only the *consonants* (not the vowels) of words, and seldom marked any division between words; leather rolls presented a poor surface for writing, and the ink used was liable to fade.[1] We do not possess an infallibly accurate reproduction of the original Biblical documents. On the other hand, for many and conclusive reasons, it is equally certain that in view of the great difficulties in transmission the present text preserves the original writings to a wonderful extent. The craftsmanship and devoted zeal of the Jewish scribes is worthy of all admiration.

Lower Criticism has also in its scope this question—Why were certain Jewish writings (we term them the Apocryphal Books) not included among the Sacred writings, for they were highly esteemed? A few of these Books are of great merit— notably Ecclesiasticus (also called The Wisdom of Ben Sirach), The Wisdom of Solomon, and I Maccabees.[2] Many express courageous predictions that God's righteous purpose is about to be fulfilled, and Israel's faith and hope vindicated. Strange that

[1] Add the further difficulty that about 300 B.C. the forms of Hebrew letters changed from rounded (archaic) shapes to the square characters seen in our printed Bibles. Consider also that great numbers of manuscripts were destroyed during the persecution in the Maccabaean period, when it was penalty of death for a Jew to be found in possession of a manuscript of the Law. But greatest of all reasons for divergencies arising in early manuscripts is this— Eventually it was recognized that the sole duty of a scribe was to make an exact copy. Earlier, however, those who possessed manuscripts took a less literary attitude towards preparing a new manuscript: their aim was primarily to preserve the maximum of Holy writings. Hence marginal comments in an old manuscript were apt piously to be copied into the text itself of the new document. Again, if (say) a roll of prophetic oracles was being transcribed and the new roll was of larger size, its additional space could be filled from other prophetic utterances found elsewhere: these also were 'holy words', and the question whether they had been spoken by the same prophet did not greatly trouble the devout scribes. Such processes account for the grouping of passages of different periods and authorship in the larger prophetic Books, especially the great rolls of Isaiah, Jeremiah and Ezekiel.

[2] The general term we use for the excluded writings is 'the Apocryphal Books'. Those of them that predict the coming End determined by God are called Apocalypses—i.e. Revelations. Ecclesiasticus is a collection of 'Wise' Sayings like those in the canonical Book of Proverbs and Ecclesiastes, but more closely wrought; and it contains many lovely and moving passages. I Maccabees is a vivid, contemporary, account of the heroic struggle of the Jews for religious and civil freedom at the time of the terrible persecution by Antiochus Epiphanes IV, Greek King of Syria, in 176–164 B.C.

such earnest religious writings should not be in the Jewish Bible! *Lower Criticism* can give the explanation, but its detail is proper in a footnote.[1] The exclusion of these so-called Apocryphal Books, however, was perhaps for the best; certainly if all had been included harm would have been done. In general, they do not rise to the extraordinary quality that makes the Biblical Books in a deep sense a unity and the Bible a completed work, unique in the world's literature. The Jewish scholars were in effect giving the stamp of their approval to the sound religious judgement of earlier generations. 'For the great mass of the Scriptures', writes Skinner, 'the real sanction lies in the witness borne to their inspiration by the experience of devout minds in Israel, whose spiritual insight had discerned their unique value for the nourishment of the religious life of fellowship with God.'[2]

(*b*) *Higher Criticism* (unfortunate name!) deals with the sources, date, authorship, and detailed structure of the Biblical Books.[3]

[1] When, about A.D. 150, the Jewish scholars resolved that there should be a standard text of the Sacred Books, obviously it was also urgent to decide precisely which were those Books. It was laid down that to be accounted one of the Sacred writings a Book must fulfil three conditions—its teachings must be in accordance with the Books of the Law; it must not be later in date than the time of Ezra, about 400 B.C.; and it must have been written in Hebrew. There is nothing in the Old Testament later in date than about 150 B.C. There is *much* (some Books and many passages and verses) a great deal later than the date of Ezra. The Rabbis in A.D. 150, however, did not recognize the fact, and supposed they were complying with the three principles they had decreed. The rules were the wisest they could devise, but were really arbitrary, and had some unhappy consequences. All the Apocryphal Books were known to have been written later than 250 B.C., and therefore all had to be excluded— among them the fine Ecclesiasticus, Wisdom of Solomon and I Maccabees; whereas the really irreligious Ecclesiastes 'got in', because mistakenly it was supposed to have King Solomon as its author. The Song of Songs was included for the same reason; and its contents interpreted as an allegory of God's love for Israel. In the Book of Ezekiel there were passages which ran counter to the system of the Law. But there could be no doubt about its antiquity or its just reputation as a great prophetical Book. It *had* to be included; and the difficulty was met by a sensible, humorous, assertion that a very learned Rabbi had found out how to account satisfactorily for the apparent divergences from the Law, although it had cost him a huge amount of 'midnight oil' in order to do so!

[2] Skinner, in Peake's *Commentary on the Bible*, p. 40.

[3] The Books in the Hebrew text are arranged in different order from the English translations, in which the sequence follows that found in the early Latin (Vulgate) and Greek (Septuagint) versions. In the Hebrew there are

What it had to say on those subjects was startling in the extreme,
when its findings were first made known and debated. Angry,
hysterical, fears were expressed that the Higher Critics were
'tearing the Bible to tatters'. Actually the outcome of higher
critical study has been to disclose previously unrealized riches in
the Old Testament as a source of historical knowledge, and to
open up the religious wonder of the life and thought of Israel.[1]
Literary analysis swiftly reveals that the structure of most of the
Books of the Old Testament is much more complex than might
be supposed. The appearance of an ancient cathedral provides a
helpful analogy: its existing structure is, in a sense, a unity; but
'it was not built in a day'. It is easy to distinguish the Norman
from the Early English parts of the edifice. Perhaps even Roman
tiles are visible here and there in its walls, much as there are
visible occasionally in Hebrew narratives traces of pre-Israelite,
Canaanitish, ideas and practices. The trained eye of the architect
can perceive how many 'sources' have gone into the making of
the cathedral through the centuries. So likewise with most of the
Books of the Old Testament. When the strands of their component
sources are separated out, the gain—both for religious and
historical purposes—is astonishingly great. This subject is of
prime importance for students, and is therefore amplified below
in the footnote.[2]

three groups: (a) The Books of the Torah, or Law [i.e. Genesis to Deutero-
nomy]; (b) The Books of the Prophets, subdivided into the Former Prophets
[i.e. Joshua to II Kings (Ruth excepted). That these, as we should say,
historical Books were classed as Prophets shows the Jewish realization that
the emphasis in them was on the religious aspect of history]; and the Later
Prophets [i.e. Isaiah to Malachi]; and (c) The Other Writings [i.e. Psalms,
Proverbs, Job; five, minor Books,.among them Daniel; and the historical
Books Ezra, Nehemiah, Chronicles.]

[1] Summary of the particular results will be found in works on *Introduction
to the Bible*, e.g. volumes by S. R. Driver, Sellin, Oesterley and Robinson,
H. W. Robinson, Eissfeldt. For comment on recent discussions, see *The
People and the Book* (ed. Peake), and *Record and Revelation* (ed. H. W.
Robinson).

[2] As regards the 'history' Books (or, as the Jews entitled them, The
Former Prophets), it is essential to appreciate the difference of outlook
between ancient and modern history writers. A modern historian consults
original documents and the works of other historians, passing the material
through his own mind so as to produce an account of the period in his own
words, and when he quotes he gives the references. Fortunately for us the
Hebrew narrators, like the Arabian chroniclers, worked on different lines

(cp. Bevan, in *Cambridge Theological Essays*, pp. 1–19). They were not so much authors as purposeful compilers, who recorded ancient traditions, preserving long-familiar popular wording, yet conscientiously and dexterously touching the phrasing and shaping the tales to make them the vehicle of their own highest standards of faith and conduct; who drew from older records of history or legal codes all that it seemed right to transmit, incorporating the material in their book with only a rare mention of sources from which it was derived (cp. II Sam. i. 18; II Kings xii. 19); and who showed their own standpoint by the excerpts they selected, the way they pieced them together, and (revealingly) sometimes in connective verses of their own composition. Thus it is certain the compilers of the Books of Judges, Samuel, and Kings were men of Jerusalem, moved by the overwhelming disasters which had put an end first to the Kingdom of Israel in 721, and later of Judah in 586 B.C.; and that they aimed so to relate the history of the two kingdoms that the reality of God's control of events (as shown by the consequences of right and wrongdoing) might be made convincing. Further, it is clear that they had been profoundly impressed by the definition of right conduct for Israel laid down in the Code of Deuteronomy, which in its present form is not earlier than the end of the Judaean kingdom. Hence in their own *connective* verses we find that their interpretation of all that had happened to the nation, and their estimates of its kings, are based on 'Deuteronomic' principles and phrased in its characteristic style (e.g. Judges iii. 7, 8 or II Kings xv. 34, 35).

As for major sources in the historical Books—in I Samuel the compilers have woven together at least two documents, one of which viewed the institution of a Hebrew monarchy with approval as consonant with the will of God, the other (and later) regards it as a Divine concession to Israel's sinful mistrust of God's immediate rule of His people: a faithful Israel would have needed no human king, and in its selfish kings it had therefore got what it deserved! In II Samuel (chs. ix–xx) there is preserved a magnificent source, usually called 'The Court History of David'. This document is the oldest, first-rate, historical narrative in existence, written probably by a friend and contemporary of King David. The compilers of Kings drew excerpts from official records of Judah and Samaria, but used chiefly Tales of the Prophets; since their object was not to record the bare bones of history but to show Jehovah's righteous working in history. What are we to make of the strange work, I and II Chronicles—which opens with nine genealogical chapters of names; which ignores the existence of the northern kingdom of Israel; which consists chiefly of *verbatim* quotations from Kings, augmented by passages concerning the zeal of David in preparing for the building of the temple and concerning the piety of certain later monarchs in observance of the Law; which exalts the glories of Solomon's temple and the importance of its Levitical ministrants; and which magnifies amounts and numbers fantastically? The explanation is that the author (or compiler) of Chronicles was a Levite serving the second temple. He could think of David only as his patron saint. For the David of actual history we must confine our attention to Kings. But Chronicles is invaluable for the light it gives on the post-exilic, priestly, standpoint towards the past.

In brief—and to name only salient points—literary analysis shows that the Psalter was not composed by David 'all of a piece', but was made piecemeal at sundry times and places by many earnest and eager men 'as the Spirit moved them', and as the religious sense of the community and its priests took possession of the words and adapted them for continued use generation after generation. The present Psalter is an epitome of the growth of Israel's Faith, especially as it developed from the sixth century B.C. down to the third. The actual personalities of the great Prophets live before us when their authentic words have been disentangled from the mass of later additions in the Books that bear their names. When the bewildering multitudes of statutes and judgements in Exodus to Deuteronomy are realized to be an amalgam of four chief sources (dating in their written form from, say, the ninth to the fourth century B.C.), we find an 'open book' wherein to read the story of Israel's developing religious, and social, conscience.

As regards Genesis three of the four, great, sources found in Exodus to Leviticus are present. One of these is a *Judaean* account first of 'the beginning of all things' (parts of Genesis i–xi), and then of the remotest ancestors of the Hebrew People (the 'Patriarchs—Abraham, Isaac, Jacob and his children'). The second is an *Israelite* document concerning the Patriarchs. Neither can be earlier in composition than the ninth century, both are almost certainly much later. Moreover (not earlier than the fall of Samaria in 721 B.C.) these two were so skilfully blended that sometimes it is hard to say whether certain verses should be assigned to the Judaean or to the Israelite account. The third source in Genesis (known as *The Priests' Code*) is later still in date, and in style as different as a State proclamation or lawyer's deed from a page in a story. It presents the beliefs of the Jerusalem priests, probably about the fifth century B.C. In its solemn splendid diction it seeks to emphasize their paramount concern to uphold the sanctity of the essential Jewish institutions of the Faith— the obligations of keeping the Sabbath, abstinence from eating flesh with the blood in it, circumcision: practices which in the fifth century were necessities for preserving the Jews from melting into Gentile, heathen, civilization. The *priestly* passages consti- tute a frame for the older *Judaean-Israelite* document, and are found interspersed through its narratives. Most skilfully the priest-writers improved, modified, supplemented the older traditions, and drove home their insistence on the customs of the Faith by claiming thus that these obligations for Israel's welfare had been made known by God even in the far-past Patriarchal Age.[1] But, despite the grandeur of the *Priests'* document, the achievement (artistic, moral, and religious) of both the Judaean and the Israelite sources must not be belittled. Concerning the Judaean, Sellin writes: 'Out of all these materials there was created a work with a definite purpose, a work of such historical breadth and such religious insight and depth, a work through which there so breathes the spirit of a living, saving, sin-punishing, but above all a gracious and all-merciful God, that no nation in antiquity has anything to set beside it.'[2] Moreover, it is patent that the Israelite document is religiously more refined than the Judaean and no less powerful. As for the artistic merits of both, it has been said: 'The short stories of Genesis, even those of the most elementary type, are exquisite works of art, almost as unique in their own kind as the parables of our Lord are in theirs. They are certainly not random productions of fireside gossip, but bear the unmistakable mark of individual genius.'[3] In sum—Archaeology, providing its comprehensive picture of civilization far earlier than the Age of 'Abraham, Isaac and Jacob', shows that the tales of the Patriarchs in Genesis yield only fragments of historical knowledge of those remote centuries; and yield it only to expert study. But, as Skinner has truly said, 'it is a suicidal

---

[1] Thus, the Flood narrative culminates in *priestly* verses requiring abstinence from flesh with the blood in it, and proclaiming the absolute sinfulness of murder (ix. 1–17). In the story of Abraham the priests inserted a solemn chapter (xvii) on the duty of circumcision. In Gen. i–ii. 4 we have the priests' theological account of Creation—poetically giving expression to profound beliefs concerning the relations of God, Nature and Man. Note how this account insists on the duty of keeping the *Sabbath*, by declaring (ii. 1–3) that God Himself is not enmeshed in His labours but rested on the Sabbath Day! In the middle of verse 4 the style abruptly changes. That marks the deft blending of the priests' version with the centuries-older Judaean account of Creation. The exact point of union is more apparent in the Hebrew text than in the English Bible; but one does not need to know Hebrew to sense the difference in style and level of thought between the two accounts. The Judaean version is naïve in comparison with the priestly. Yet it also was a medium of deep religious insight.

[2] *Introduction to the Old Testament*, p. 60.

[3] Skinner, *Genesis (I.C.C.)*, p. xxix.

error to suppose that the value of Genesis resides in the residuum of historical fact that underlies the present form of the narratives'.[1] And literary research, enabling us to distinguish and date the component sources in Genesis—has provided invaluable evidence as to the ideals of the men who shaped the ancient traditions to their present form.

Anyone who wishes to estimate for himself the value of the tales of the Patriarchs in Genesis—their relative unimportance for history in the remote period, and the very great importance of the long process of oral transmission from which emerged first the earlier *written* narratives and eventually the solemn religious ('theological') presentation—ought certainly to consult the thorough survey of the subject in Skinner's Introduction to his volume on Genesis in the *International Critical Commentary* series, 1910. The years that have elapsed since its publication have amplified knowledge of the environing civilization in the (so-called) Patriarchal Age. Nothing affects adversely the soundness of the interpretative principles indicated by Skinner, and nothing detracts from the religious discernment and appreciation shown in his work.

[1] Cp. Skinner, *Genesis* (*I.C.C.*), pp. iv, viii.

CHAPTER III

THE OLD TESTAMENT AS LITERATURE

'The Bible is an indivisible whole, and to rest content either with the Old Testament alone, or with the New Testament alone, is to miss the real inwardness of that which makes the Bible the most remarkable book in the world'—so writes a historian and Biblical critic.[1]

'If I am asked why I receive Scripture as the Word of God and as the only perfect rule of faith and life, I answer with all the Fathers of the Protestant Church: because the Bible is the only record of the redeeming love of God, because in the Bible alone I find God drawing near to man in Christ Jesus and declaring in Him His will for our salvation. And this record I know to be true by the witness of His Spirit in my heart, whereby I am assured that none other than God Himself is able to speak such words to my soul'—so answered a scholar of encyclopaedic range of knowledge, orientalist and theologian.[2]

'In this Book there is more that finds me than I have experienced in all other books put together. Here I have met everywhere with copious sources of truth and power and purifying impulses. Here I have found words for my inmost thoughts, songs for my joy, utterances for my hidden grief, pleadings for my shame and feebleness'—so witnessed a poet, voicing what unnumbered men and women through the centuries have found to be true of the Bible.[3]

Critic, theologian, poet—agreed that there is in the Bible value beyond compute, unequalled power to touch every mood and moment in human experience.

The writings that make up the Hebrew Bible exhibit utmost diversity of literary form. They contain myth, legend, and history. They include popular stories of ancestors and national heroes; accounts of wars and policies and kings; composite collections of laws concerning worship and social duties; oratorical speeches; lyrical odes, and in the Psalter an unparalleled collection of religious poetry; in Proverbs an assembly of 'Words of the

[1] S. A. Cook, *The Old Testament*, p. 224.
[2] W. Robertson Smith (cited by Denney in *Studies in Theology*, p. 205).
[3] S. T. Coleridge.

Wise', which are not merely popular maxims, but present a 'philosophy' of conduct; and in the Prophetical Books a unique type of literature (partly in prose but chiefly in rhythmic form) for which *Rhapsody* has been suggested as the best designation. Drama alone is absent from Hebrew composition; but the impassioned poetry of the Book of Job is truly dramatic. Some passages in the Old Testament are tedious or commonplace writing. But a very large amount both of its prose and its poetry maintains a high level of style, whilst much admittedly ranks with the masterpieces of all time: a fact which is the more impressive in that, almost always, Hebrew writings were the product of unsophisticated, though not unpractised, art. In comparison with Hebrew, Greek is a vastly richer and more flexible language. Yet a literary expert can commit himself to the statement that the Bible contains 'lyrics which Pindar cannot surpass, rhetoric as forcible as Demosthenes, contemplative prose not inferior to Plato's'.[1]

Literature is necessarily affected by the fundamental qualities of the language in which it is cast. The basic experiences and instincts of a race create its mode of speech, and then in turn the formed language moulds the thoughts and utterances of its users. Hebrew is one of the dialects of the Semitic group of languages, and they have curious characteristics that sharply differentiate them from the Indo-European group to which Greek, Latin and English belong. It is important, therefore, to grasp the features in which the Hebrew language differs greatly from our own. To an interesting extent Hebrew reflects the restricting, yet tremendously powerful, influences of nomadic life in the desert.[2] As known to us through the Old Testament and a few inscriptions, Hebrew had a remarkably small vocabulary—some 5000 words, of which only about 500 were in frequent use.[3] Moreover, the great majority of its words refer to natural objects or physical actions; and of these many are synonyms. Hebrew uses but the barest minimum of

---

[1] Prof. R. G. Moulton, *Literary Study of the Bible*, p. xiii.

[2] The remark is no more than a generalization. Cp. S. A. Cook's penetrating analysis of Semitic temperament and speech in *C.A.H.* vol. I, ch. v; also Mullo-Weir, *A Companion to the Bible* (ed. Manson), pp. 13–21.

[3] The vocabulary was not nearly so meagre as it seems, thanks to the economy made possible by the most characteristic feature of Semitic languages, known as *tri-literalism*. For example, the general notion of *Greatness* was conveyed by the three consonants G–D–L; by vocalizing them in different ways a range of words all relevant to the basic notion was obtained. Thus *Gadal* means *to become great*; *Gadhol*, *great*; *Godel*, *greatness*, or *magnificence*.

abstract nouns—such as *justice, sin, faithfulness, truth, glory*. Its syntax is of the simplest nature. In consequence of the restricted vocabulary and lack of syntactical subtlety Hebrew was not suited for philosophical reasoning. But the inference must not be drawn that Hebrew thinking was shallow. Leon Roth, writing on the Jewish contribution to European thought, remarks: 'The Hebrew Prophets defined the knowledge of God as judging the cause of the poor and the needy: and the legislators and moralists produced no theoretical treatise on Justice but practical rules such as "Thou shalt not have divers weights". Such thoughts seem banal; yet they contain in sum, and in the simplest language, lessons for society which the analytic mind never managed to evolve.'[1]

The Bible speaks of God and Man with limpid simplicity, which we are too prone to consider naïve, regarding only surface appearance: let down the line, and the sea is deep. When the Scriptures call upon God as Father, there is a religious philosophy involved: it is an excellent way of affirming that Ultimate Reality is 'Divine Personality', not an impersonal First Cause.

Hebrew was a splendid instrument for powerful, terse, and vivid expression. Ten thousand instances in the Old Testament witness to its strength. The language was spoken by keen-sighted men, intently observant of all that happens; watchful and reflective. Everything that the Hebrew saw he saw with wonderful precision, and expressed with almost photographic exactitude. To illustrate the *terseness*, here is Quiller-Couch's comment on the narrative about Michal, Saul's daughter (II Sam. vi. 14–16, 20): 'The whole story goes into about ten lines. Your psychological novelist nowadays, given the wit to invent it, would make it cover 500 pages at least.'[2] As regards the vividness of Hebrew speech, consider the quaint precision that gives rise to the frequent phrase, 'And he opened his mouth, and spake...'.[3]

[1] *The Legacy of Israel*, p. 464.

[2] *The Art of Reading*, p. 150. Quiller-Couch's three Lectures in this volume on 'Reading the Bible' are delightful and illuminating.

[3] Or note the point-to-point detail set out in Gen. xxii. 9, 10: 'And Abraham built the altar there, and laid the wood in order, and bound Isaac his son, and laid him on the altar upon the wood. And Abraham stretched forth his hand, and took the knife to slay his son.' Yet with what economy of words the narrator manages to compress into nineteen verses the whole of the popular story of the averted sacrifice; and, even so, skilfully contrives to reiterate certain phrases and give the impression of the slow pace of the father and son walking side by side.

In comparison with other languages Hebrew conditional sentences are dexterously simple. Conditional particles were sometimes employed, but often the need was met by setting two phrases—two pictures—side by side, leaving it to the intelligence of the hearer to grasp that the one was conditioned by the other. Thus Hebrew can express 'If a man were to lean upon it, it would pierce his hand', by saying 'He leans on it; it pierces his hand'. This extraordinarily graphic attitude of mind dominates the Hebrew *verbal* system. We have to employ a complicated system of tenses and moods. Hebrew got along differently and excellently by making its verb-forms tell us only whether we ought to see the action in question as *completed* (a finished fact) or as *uncompleted* —in process of happening. It is essential to realize that Hebrew verbs do not of themselves indicate the time of the action, whether past, present, or future. This would seem likely to give rise to constant perplexities; actually one finds there is seldom in Hebrew sentences obscurity as to the time implied by the verb. Nor were the remarkable features just mentioned the linguistic hindrances they seem to us to be. What the Hebrews could reckon on was swift apprehension in the mind of the hearer or reader. The *nuances* were there; Hebrews seized them at once, and it is we who are apt to be too slow to grasp them. One example out of many is Ps. xlv. 5: 'Thine arrows are sharp; the peoples fall under thee; in the heart of the king's enemies.' The staccato verse demands instant visualization of a scene of battle. As Robertson Smith puts it: 'In the first line the warrior bends his bow, in the second his chariot sweeps over the fallen, and then, when he has passed by, it is seen that his shafts are truly planted in the heart of the slain.'[1] So comparatively sluggish and unpictorial is our imagination, so habituated our minds to using abstract nouns, that the finer points of language in the Old Testament escape our notice. True, the English-speaking peoples are singularly fortunate in that the Authorised Version of the Bible issued in 1611 is itself a miracle of literary genius.[2] Yet, one way and another, so different is English from Hebrew that even the best translation misses much.

[1] *Lectures and Essays*, p. 438.
[2] Cp. Quiller-Couch, *On the Art of Writing*, p. 121: 'And then, as already had happened to our Verse, to our Prose too there befel a miracle. You will not ask me "What miracle?" I mean, of course, the Authorised Version of the Bible....I grant you that the forty-seven men who produced the

Over against that fact stands a most fortunate circumstance. However well the prose of one language can be rendered into the prose of another, it is next to impossible to translate its poetry satisfactorily. Approximately half of the Old Testament is written in poetic rhythm.[1] Fortunate indeed it is that the prime characteristic of Hebrew poetry can be, and has been, successfully preserved in translation. How comes that to pass, and why is Hebrew literature so full of poetry? In reply, first, let this famous passage be quoted from one of the earliest works concerned with the literary aspect of the Bible: 'Since action and delineation are of the essence of poetry, and since the *verb* is the part of speech that depicts action, or rather sets action directly before us, the language that is rich in expressive pictorial verbs is a poetical language, and is more poetical the more it can turn nouns to verbs. What a noun sets forth is dead, the verb sets everything in motion....Now

Authorised Version worked in the main upon Tyndale's version, taking that for their basis. Nay, if you choose to say that Tyndale was a miracle in himself, I cheerfully grant you that as well. But...when Tyndale has been granted you have yet to face the miracle that forty-seven men—not one of them known, outside of this performance, for any superlative talent—sat in committee and almost consistently, over a vast extent of work, improved upon what Genius had done. I give you the word of an old committee-man that this is not the way of committees—that only by miracle is it the way of any committee.'

[1] The Authorised Version most effectively blanketed that fact by printing everything as prose! The Revised and the American Versions show that the Psalter, Proverbs, Job, and certain passages elsewhere (e.g. Judges v) are not plain prose; but cannot essay the difficult, yet most important, task of discriminating prose from verse in the Prophetical Books. 'The Bible is the worst printed book in the world'—the author of that scathing remark did not intend by it any aspersion on the actual printers. He had in mind various handicaps consequent on the fact that the translators of the A.V. and R.V. had to conserve exactly the form and order of the Hebrew and Greek text. Hence the irritating, 'chapter and verse', subdivision of the contents in our versions; the inadequate differentiation between prose and verse; the dislocation of the flow of historical narrative by such disconcerting matter as genealogical lists and massive legal codes; the fact that the final text as we read it is often built of a mosaic of sources not indicated; and, above all, that the material in the Hebrew Bible is not arranged in anything like chronological order. These features are far greater deterrents to the modern reader than probably he realizes. It is exhilarating to read selected portions of the literature set out in better order and more attractive form—as, for instance, in Bates, *The Bible to be read as Literature*; *The Bible for To-day* (ed. J. Stirling); J. B. T. Davies, *The Heart of the Bible*.

in Hebrew almost everything is verb; that is, everything lives and acts....The language is a very abyss of verbs, a sea of waves where action rolls surging into ever new action.... I conceive the language is as poetic as any upon earth.'[1] Secondly, the desperate difficulty involved in translating rhyme into rhyme does not arise, since Hebrew poetry makes no use of rhymes.[2] The normal unit of Hebrew poetic utterance is a two-line couplet, having two characteristics: (a) a fairly regular balance of stressed accents in the two lines, thus: '*The Lord of Hosts is with us; the God of Jacob is our refuge*'; or, '*He suffered no man to do them wrong; Yea, He reproved Kings for their sake*'; and (b) a balance of *thought* between the two lines, the second expressing reiteration or antithesis or supplement: for instance, 'Weeping may tarry for the night, but joy cometh in the morning'. The first feature (stress-accent structure) was not recognized until comparatively recent times; and, although it can be reproduced in translation, account is not taken of it in our English versions. But the second feature (and it is by far the more impressive) cannot be missed by any accurate translation; for it is inherent in the very words to be translated. We term it *parallelism*, and its wavelike rhythmic movement is the secret of the memorable, lovely mode of speech which pervades so many passages in the Bible: 'Scarce has a sentence fallen on the ear, than straight another comes to echo it.' For example:

> God is our refuge and strength,
> A very present help in trouble.
> Therefore will we not fear, though the earth do change,
> And though the mountains be moved in the heart of the seas.

Whenever the minds of the men of Israel were deeply stirred, they spoke thus rhythmically, and the pendulum correlation of sense and sound sinks into the consciousness of the hearer almost hypnotically.

May we go further? This instinct of the Hebrews for balanced thought and utterance—does it arise from intuition that the universe is an ultimate harmony, an orderly Creation not a Chaos?

[1] Herder (A.D. 1783), *Vom Geist der Ebräischen Poesie* (cited by W. R. Smith, *Lectures*, p. 414).

[2] Occasional assonances are the nearest approach, e.g. (Judg. xvi. 24): 'Nathan elohenu bheyadhenu eth oyebhenu....' This elementary device was characteristic of early rather than of later and cultured style; and was in any case an adornment, not a necessity, for poetic diction.

Perhaps, in their different way, the Greeks witness to the same instinct; for their famous watchword, μηδὲν ἄγαν (*Nothing in excess*), set up as the Ideal, not the middle path of mediocrity, but the equipoise of perfection. The very form of Hebrew poetry voiced the faith that, under the baffling confusion on the surface, there is a deep peace at the heart of things, the peace not of death but of the pulse of life. Laurence Binyon phrased this suggestion in the following memorable words:[1]

[The] one thing which may especially impress the mind in reading Hebrew poetry [is] the seeking for a harmony, a correspondence, between the actions of mankind and the larger movements of the universe in which man's life is set. There is no description of things for their own sake; they are vividly seen, but all things are related to one another; we are made aware of them all—the mountains and the streams, the vineyards, the olives, the desert places, the sheep and cattle, the wild ass and the lion in the wilderness, the tender grass, the rocks, the sea and the ships upon the sea, the fishes under the water, the stars, the rain, the wind, and in all this world men moving and going about their business, acting, suffering, rejoicing; all these are related to one another because united by the presence in the poet's consciousness of the pervading power of the invisible Creator. A modern reader may have quite other ideas about the constitution of the universe, a quite different approach to it; but he will hardly deny that it is a living and mysterious whole; and through this profound conviction of the unity of life and the power of the pervading, eternal spirit, touching all life with a kind of glory, Hebrew poetry has a grandeur of horizon together with a kindling warmth and passion which we find in no other poetry with the same constancy or to the same degree.

A large part of the Old Testament can assuredly be ranked as noble literature. Now great writing very rarely has for its subjects trivial matters. The *Idylls* of Theocritus, the *Georgics* and *Eclogues* of Virgil, were not really concerned with the affairs of individual shepherds in Sicily or Italy; they tell the mystery and beauty of Nature, the sweetness and pathos of human life. The speeches of Demosthenes may for a moment seem to waste their passion on the petty politicians of Athens on the road to decadence, but the orator was in fact the champion of the ideal of Democracy against the menace of corruption and despotism. So also the Hebrew writers possessed the great gift of being able to reveal the

---

[1] In his Preface to Bates, *The Bible to be read as Literature.*

heights and depths in passing events and individual characters. Their skill was partly due to aptitude for exact observance, and to the direct language at their command. There is nothing forced and artificial in their writing. Action and motive were unsparingly and brilliantly delineated, so that the Old Testament is like a flawless mirror in which life is reflected with absolute fidelity. But a far more profound cause than literary skill lies at the root of the achievement: *The subject-matter of the Bible is not 'Man', but 'Man in relation to God'*.

Every Book in the Old Testament is concerned with religion: its demands, and its aid.[1] There is no parallel in national literature elsewhere. Other races produced 'Sacred Books'. The point is that gifted Israel produced no secular writings! Or, rather, in so far as the Hebrews did, they let them perish in that form or, later, shaped the secular to serve religious purposes.[2] The Hebrews relished proverbial maxims, and collections of proverbs were made. But they architected the prudent sayings as the instruction of *Wisdom*, guiding men to act rightly in relation to life's multifarious interests, and conceived *Wisdom* itself as emanating from God, having served Him in the creation of the world.[3] Thus, as it were, they made the many proverbs into a cumulative sermon on the grand theme: 'Reverence for God is the chief part of sound understanding.'[4]

Consider, next, *Songs*. The Hebrews were not unmelodious (Eastern fashion). The shepherd piped to his flock; the nomad sang praise to the life-giving water of the well; and the cultivator to his pleasant vineyard.[5] But nobody made an anthology of 'Popular Hebrew Songs'. Israel's gift for music and singing

---

[1] The one near exception is the Song of Songs, a collection of love-poetry or wedding-songs, worked into a unity. As was said in the last chapter, the Book is in the Bible only because King Solomon was supposed to be its author and its contents could be read allegorically as the love of God for Israel.

[2] One or two, very early, collections of brief triumph-verses, celebrating successes in battle, once existed. But these Victory Songs were entitled The Wars of Jehovah, and Israel's historians drew from them only a few fragments. The 'Collections' were not preserved.

[3] See Prov. viii.

[4] This prosy phrase gives the true sense of the Biblical rendering (e.g. Prov. i. 7): 'The fear of the Lord is the beginning of knowledge.'

[5] See Judges v. 16; Num. xxi. 17; Isa. v. 1, xxvii. 2.

poured itself into the creation of The Psalter: 'the most wonderful collection of religious poetry in the world.'

Israel formulated its Codes of Rules and Regulations, but did not separate its standards of morality from its religion. The ethical aspect of Hebrew Law is definite indeed—This and this and this shalt thou do! Public sense of Right and Wrong was vehemently asserted—'No such thing ought to be done in Israel';[1] and Hebrew society (in its early days) took drastic action against the offender. A state of affairs when every man felt free to do 'that which was right in his own eyes'[2] spelt sheer anarchy. But note that the virtues honoured by the uncivilized Hebrew tribesmen were assumed to be consonant with the will of their God, and closely related to His blessing. As the Hebrews developed in ethical sensitiveness the superior codes of right behaviour never ceased to be regarded as not of Man's devising but of God's ordinance and revelation. Of course, Israel urgently needed to outgrow its early notions of Right and Wrong. And how marvellously in the end it did outgrow them: 'So long as the world lasts', wrote Matthew Arnold, 'all who want to make progress in righteousness will come to Israel for inspiration, as the people who have had the sense of righteousness most glowing and strongest.'[3] That happened because from first to last Israel's standards of conduct were rooted in the sense of religious obligation. Hence Lofthouse rightly says: 'Although we may find Ethics in the Bible, we cannot call the Biblical writers ethical. Their main interest was not with men but with God—His will, His purposes, His commands, His pleasure and displeasure. The Decalogue itself begins with "God spake these words and said". And the rules that follow on the Ten Commandments are not so much rules between man and man (which is what we mean by Ethics) as between man and God.'[4]

Hebrew historians chose out what they recorded in order to inculcate the duty of national fidelity to the Faith. In the royal cities annals concerning national affairs were kept. The compilers of Samuel and Kings drew from those public archives only such

---

[1] II Sam. xiii. 12.   [2] Judges xvii. 6.

[3] Cp. R. G. Moulton, op. cit. p. xiii: 'A people dominated by an utter passion for righteousness, a people in whom ideas of purity, of infinite good, of universal order, of faith in the irresistible downfall of all moral evil, moved to a poetic passion as fervid, and to speech as musical, as when Sappho sang of love or Aeschylus thundered his deep notes of destiny.'

[4] In *A Companion to the Bible* (ed. Manson), p. 349.

excerpts as emphasized their religious purpose. If their aim had been to prepare as full a political narrative as possible, how different—how disastrously different for our interests—would have been the contents of their work. Ample space, for example, would have been devoted to Omri, builder of Samaria, a monarch so influential that for generations after his death the Assyrian historians referred to Palestine as 'The Land of Omri'. As it is, in Kings he gets but seven contemptuous verses, the purport of which is to put on record that 'he did that which was evil in the sight of the Lord'. The compilers gave space to the traditions about the great religious personalities and incidents in history, finding therein the very meaning of history. So also in the Book of Judges the stories of the champions of Israel make not a collection of Heroic Ballads, but enforce the doctrine that the Hebrews' weal or woe turned on fidelity to known duty to Jehovah. The triumphant invasion of Canaan ascribed to Joshua gave rise to no Hebrew *Iliad* of 'The Conquest', nor was the romantic career of patient Moses given immortality in the form of a Hebrew *Odyssey* on 'The Wanderings of the Tribes'. Instead that splendid raw material of literature was immortalized as manifesting in history Jehovah's power and mercy, and the enunciation of how rightly to live. Pursue the point yet further back—to the tales of the Patriarchs in Genesis; and we find the popular traditions were brought together to proclaim a grandly religious conception— belief that the very existence of Israel had been due to an act of God, who had called Abraham to be His servant and had promised that in his children all nations would see a People fully blest.

Turn to another extraordinary feature which is characteristic of Hebrew literature, and which has its justification in the primary religious standpoint. The Hebrews were astonishingly subjective in their attitude towards the physical world. In the Old Testament *Man* is (so to say) spelt with a capital letter; *nature* is written small.[1] The Hebrews were thoroughly sensitive to Nature in its varied aspects, beautiful, majestic, terrifying. But unlike ourselves, or the Greeks, they never took a dispassionate view of it. Their interest was absorbed in the way physical objects affect human life, and this intense and serene subjectivity could on occasion give rise to what we feel to be grotesquely inartistic metaphors. As they saw it,

[1] See, however, for further comment and qualification, p. 379.

Nature's duty was to align its behaviour to human moods, and most certainly to Divine intentions. Thus, the Psalmists call upon the sea to roar and the trees to sing for joy, when God cometh to judge the earth. They declare that, when Israel escaped out of Egypt and crossed the sundering waters of the 'Red Sea' and the Jordan, 'the mountains skipped like rams, the little hills like young sheep'.[1] David, lamenting for Saul and Jonathan slain on Mount Gilboa by the Philistines, declares that nor rain nor dew ought to fall on its heights, since there the bodies of royal Saul and his valiant son lie fallen in defeat and death.[2] It is easy to stigmatize this unrestrained subjectivity as megalomania. But there is another side to the matter. Let justice be done. The Hebrews stoutly maintained that Man is 'the crown of creation' solely in virtue of his moral affinity with God shared by no other created being. Hebrew pride over against Nature was balanced by humility towards the supernatural. As their religious insight developed into rational awe of one sublime Deity, they looked on Man as nothing before God;[3] and yet not *nothing*, since God, who created the immensities of the heavens, is 'mindful of him' and has willed that he should have 'dominion over the works of His hand'.[4] 'The art of the Hebrew', as Robertson Smith said, 'is true art for all who can rise to the level of his passion. For religious conviction is supreme where it exists at all. And the aesthetic necessity that all things in heaven and earth shall bend to the divine purpose of salvation revealed to the prophet's faith is also the ethical necessity on which the whole religious life depends....To assert with unwavering confidence the victory of spiritual certainties over all empirical contradiction, to vanquish earthly fears in the assurance of transcendental fellowship with God, to lay down for all ages the pattern of a faith which endures as seeing Him who is invisible—such is the great work for which the poetic genius of the Hebrews was consecrated by the providence and inspiration of the Most High.'[5]

The influence which the Bible has so long exercised over the minds and consciences of countless persons is due to their finding in it not great literature, but the literature of a great religion. If, however, even the essence of that religion be rejected, or if, being superficially misunderstood, it is assumed to be totally anti-

---

[1] Ps. cxiv. 4.
[2] II Sam. i. 21.
[3] Cp. Isa. xxxi. 3.
[4] Cp. Ps. viii.
[5] *Lectures and Essays*, p. 432.

quated—what will happen to the former influence of the Bible on people's lives? Precisely what is happening at the present time: it will rapidly vanish. The Bible will cease to be read; or, when read, will be read uncomprehendingly. Some, who reject the religion but have a conscience, will occasionally turn to its pages in search of a moral tonic; but, not knowing how to handle the Books, they will find as much that they disapprove as approve. Moreover, the motive that gave driving power to Hebrew and Christian moral demands is missing from their thoughts. The Old Testament lays on our shoulders absolute responsibility for our 'neighbour's' welfare. But it makes the yoke easy and the burden light, because it believes that God is with us in that task, bidding us feel that we are each precious in His sight. A few aesthetically-minded persons might continue to seek occasional artistic pleasure in some of the Bible's pages. But Fine Art is the interest of the few, not of the myriad. When the Bible is not cherished for religious reasons, it is soon placed (less assimilated than Shakespeare) on the bookshelf. That is happening; and in the interests of culture alone the fact is a disaster for our times. As a fugitive article in a newspaper put it: 'It is clear to anyone who goes about with his eyes open that masses of people, educated and uneducated, now grow up with only a vague notion of the New Testament and none at all of the Old.... For centuries the majestic and enthralling Biblical narratives were for many people their sole contact with great literature—and a very adequate one too.' Laurence Binyon phrased it: 'To forego the opportunity, accessible to all, of frequenting this surpassing literature of the Bible, with its grandeur and abundance— a world of mind and spirit and passionate drama, far transcending the horizons of the little private world we each of us inhabit—is as if one should resolve of set choice to be poor in the midst of plenty and to dwell in a mean street.'

Religion is the one subject of paramount practical importance on which multitudes are tamely willing to remain ill-informed and behind the times. Modern study has long ago shown what are the transient features, and what the lasting treasure in the Bible. Yet very many, otherwise competent, citizens of the Western World would be mystified by, or might absurdly misunderstand, the convictions expressed by the two scholars quoted at the start of this chapter. They might be completely unable to understand why the one—a man of the widest range of modern knowledge—

should affirm that he 'received Scripture as the Word of God and as the only perfect rule of faith and life'. When the other writes: 'The Bible is an indivisible whole', some are capable of inferring from the remark that he must be a man who still 'believes the Bible from cover to cover'—a queer fish who credits that Almighty God really commanded a whale to swallow Jonah, and Hebrews to massacre Canaanites. It is not right at any time, least of all in the gravity of our times, that people, otherwise sensible, should be content to hold notions about the Old Testament that are as obsolete as the Dodo. For many the Old Testament calls to mind only some colourful pictures of Noah's Ark, David and Goliath, Moses in the bulrushes and Jonah in the whale. In the middle of the twentieth century that ought not to be. Nor is it right that responsible, conscientious, citizens should float through life with only a hazy idea of what Christian doctrine maintains, and for what reasons.

CHAPTER IV

THE BIBLE AS SACRED SCRIPTURE

Seeing that *sacred* means 'pertaining to religious belief and practice', Jews and Christians had been blind if they had not recognized that quality in the Books of the Old and New Testaments. 'There is impressed upon the writings that make up the Bible a breadth and variety, an intensity and purity of religious life that are without parallel in any other literature.'[1] Nobody, whatever his views upon the validity of religious belief, would deny that the Biblical writings have justly a place, and a preeminent place, among the Books that men of diverse races have classed as sacred. But both Jews and Christians possessed other religious writings which they highly esteemed. How came it to pass that they regarded only the Books included in the Old and New Testaments as their Sacred Scriptures?

(1) *The Jewish Scriptures.* Suppose that a supercilious Gentile had twitted a Jew (*a*) for reverencing Books that told of God Himself writing on stone tablets or actually speaking to men (whereas no educated gentleman, still less a philosopher, would accept such childish notions); and (*b*) for his arrogance in claiming the Jews were God's Chosen People, to whom He had vouchsafed a special revelation of truth. To such a man the Jew might have replied by quoting (with emphasis) a single sentence from Ps. ciii: 'He made known his *ways* unto Moses, his *acts* unto the children of Israel.' If the Gentile contemptuously asked no further explanation, the fool had been well answered according to his folly. For the verse quoted by the Jew states succinctly two religious convictions which caused the Jews to regard their ancient Books as supremely holy writings. The first claim ('His *ways*') was that through Moses God had revealed to His People how rightly to worship and behave, and that in the five Books of the Law (Genesis to Deuteronomy) they possessed exact record of what God had thus made known. The second claim ('His *acts*') was that the history of Israel witnessed to the initiative and power of the living God, bringing this People into existence through the response of

---

[1] Sanday in *The Encyclopaedia of Religion and Ethics*, vol. II, p. 579.

Abraham, delivering their fathers from slavery in Egypt, leading them in the desert, disciplining and preserving them through the ensuing centuries in Canaan: to the end that Israel should learn to know and to obey His will, and thus should serve His final purpose for mankind. (This, the Jew would have argued, was an inspiring, rational, view of history compared with the Gentiles' nightmare notion that human events display a meaningless recurrence of *Ages*—'Golden, Silver, Brass, Iron'—revolving from the best to the worst, and vice versa!) Sole record of Israel's significant history was to be found in the Books of the Law, and also in the historical and prophetic writings. Wherefore all those Books were esteemed as *sacred*; together with certain other venerable writings as well—Psalms, Proverbs, Job, and a few minor Books. The precise number and precise text of the Books ranked as sacred was determined authoritatively by the discussions of Jewish scholars about A.D. 150.[1] All other Jewish writings (which were mostly of later date than those found in the Old Testament) were from that time considered not to have equal regulative value for the Jewish Faith, however praiseworthy they might be. And the text of the great manuscript of the Sacred Books then prepared (from which all subsequent copies were to be made) was regarded as impeccably correct. Thus were the *Jewish Scriptures* completed.

(2) *The Christian Bible*. At the end of the second century A.D. the Books contained in the New Testament were in existence. In addition Christians had produced, and were producing, many other religious writings that were influential.[2] But it was self-evident that the Gospels and the Epistles of St Paul and the other Apostles, together with the Book of Revelation ascribed to St John, were primary documents; and, so far, there was no need of ecclesiastical ruling that these, exclusively, should be the authoritative (in Greek phrase, *canonical*) Scriptures for the Christian Faith. A grim turn was given to the latent question (Whether any other Christian documents had comparable value?) through the ferocious persecution instituted by the Emperor Diocletian in A.D. 303; for one of the imperial edicts enacted that Christian Scriptures were to be burnt. To which of the many valued writings did the decree refer? About A.D. 400 a great scholar, Jerome,

---

[1] See Chapter II, p. 35.
[2] See M. R. James, *The Apocryphal New Testament*.

translated into Latin both the Jewish, and the specifically Christian, Holy Scriptures; including in the New Testament the documents it now contains. His judgement was wholly wise; for the other early Christian Books are all in fact of secondary interest, and many of them have indisputably lower religious quality. Jerome's translation, known as the *Vulgate*, shortly afterwards received formal ecclesiastical sanction: only the Books included in its *Vulgate* were to be deemed *canonical*.

Besides the New Testament writings the early Christians instinctively and properly counted themselves heir to the treasures of the Jewish Scriptures, holding that the revelation of God given to Israel of old had come to its fulfilment in Jesus. About the end of the second century, controversy whether the Jewish Books ought to be revered by Christians became acute owing to the insistent arguments of Marcion, who could see only an impassable gulf between the God of the Hebrew Law and the true God revealed in Jesus Christ. Marcion's theology was perceived to be dualistic. The orthodox decision rejected his polemic against the worth of the Old Testament, and the Church continued to esteem its Books as Sacred Scripture.[1]

Like the Jews, Christians were not swiftly perturbed about divergent readings in manuscripts, despite the fact that the Greek translations they used differed greatly among themselves as well as from the Hebrew text. Occasionally textual differences could set at cross-purposes discussion between Jew and Christian as to the significance of certain verses.[2] In time, however, the divergencies

---

[1] After the first decades of the preaching of Christ the spread of the Faith was among Gentiles and Jews of the Greek-speaking world. Hence it happened that certain Books (notably Ecclesiasticus, the Wisdom of Solomon and the Books of the Maccabees), eventually known as the Apocrypha, were regarded by Christians as properly part of the Old Testament, although they were not found in the Hebrew Bible. The influence of Augustine in their favour was great; and that of Jerome (*c.* 400) still more so, since he had included them in his authoritative translation, the Vulgate. Dubiety about their sanctity, however, continued; and eventually it was felt that they ought not to be regarded as authoritative for 'proof of doctrine'. At the time of the Reformation the tendency among Protestants was to consider only the Books in the Hebrew text as Sacred Scriptures of the Old Testament.

[2] The famous instance is Isa. vii. 14 ('A virgin shall conceive, and bear a son, and shall call his name Immanuel'). The Hebrew word, translated in the English text as 'A virgin', is *almah*, and means vaguely 'A young woman'— one who might, or might not, be married. The early Christian argument was

began to distress the learned, and a very great scholar—Origen of Alexandria (A.D. 185–254)—prepared a massive work in which he collated the variant readings with a view to determining what was most likely to be the correct text.[1] Origen's labours may be said to anticipate modern textual technique. Unhappily his systematic study was too complicated and too extensive for lesser men; and the upshot was that manuscript confusion became the worse confounded. Eventually the Church settled its textual anxieties in a most unscientific way, by ruling that the Latin text in Jerome's translation (c. A.D. 400) was inerrant, and alone authoritative. A modern writer has ungenerously said: 'Jerome stunned Old Testament study for a thousand years.' The caustic comment is broadly true as regards textual study. Even so Jerome rendered great service, for his claim that his choice of readings was in accord with the best Jewish tradition was accurate.[2]

In such wise the Church assembled and approved the contents of *The Holy Bible*, and came to suppose that in the Vulgate Version it possessed an infallibly correct translation of the original documents. But official decisions that only certain Books should be regarded as *sacred* are of secondary consequence compared to the fundamental issue—What use men will make of their Sacred Books; what meaning attach to their contents? With that primary subject the rest of this chapter deals—the use (and alas! also the unwitting misuse) of the Sacred Scriptures throughout the Christian centuries. It is an immense theme.[3] The following pages seek but to sketch successive phases of interpretation, especially as regards the use, misuse, and present disuse, of the Old Testament.

that Isaiah had thus predicted the Virgin Birth of Jesus, and it relied on the fact that *almah* had been translated into Greek by *parthenos* which does regularly mean 'A virgin'. But, disconcertingly, there were other Greek versions which read *neanis*, and that word (like the Hebrew *almah*) denotes 'A young woman'.

[1] The fragments of Origen's work that survive are of value to modern scholars as witness of the texts of the versions in his time.

[2] Cp. W. R. Smith, *The Old Testament in the Jewish Church*, pp. 25, 28–30. In preparing the Vulgate Jerome assailed the propriety of the labours of Origen, the man he should most have honoured for his effort to obtain the most accurate possible text. His own work was in no wise unscholarly in intention, but its acceptance as the sole legitimate text was a disaster from our standpoint, since earlier MSS. with their variant readings were suppressed or forgotten.

[3] See Von Dobschütz's article 'The Bible in the Church' in *E.R.E.* vol. II, pp. 579–615; also Fullerton, *Prophecy and Authority*.

§ 1. *'Morning Glory'* (*The Proclamation of the Gospel*)

In the years immediately following the Crucifixion there was no
need of written documents concerning Jesus. The Apostles went
forth to tell what they themselves had seen and heard in the three
years when they had been with Him. We possess in written form
fragments of what they said. Listening to them, it was as if all the
books in the world could not contain the outpouring of their
memories, or transmit the ardour in their voices. They tried to
make men understand why inexpressible wonder and love had
grown in their minds as they listened to what Jesus said, and
witnessed the way in which unsparingly He gave Himself to heal
and help. Above all, they told that His strength and tenderness
were drawn from God in a way that overawed them. They had
been conscious that He possessed an intimate certainty of God's
Reality—intimacy more wonderful than confidence that God
was *with Him* (as the Prophets used to say). They felt as if somehow Jesus lived *with God*; and when He saw and spoke to men He
seemed aware of what is in each one of us and needed not that any
should tell Him. Therefore, boundless hope had risen in their
hearts that Jesus was going to reveal Himself as the supernatural King, the *Messiah*,[1] whom God would send to deliver
Israel and rule in righteousness over the nations. But, instead, He
had told them He would be put to death at Jerusalem. That would
happen because He must accomplish the work God had sent
Him to do. When He tried to make them understand that only so
could God's power and purpose be for ever revealed to men, they
were dumbfounded. When they besought Him not to go to
Jerusalem, He would not hear: He knew there was no other way.
They told about the Last Supper with their Lord, the Trial and
Crucifixion, and said that at that terrible moment their hopes
had been shattered.

But all this they related in the process of *proclaiming the Gospel*
('the Good News')—how that to them and many others Jesus had
manifested Himself existent beyond death; in form not subject to
the limitations of our earthly body, yet no doubtful apparition:
Jesus Himself, whom they had known and loved, still knowing and
loving them, alive for evermore. God had raised Jesus from the

---

[1] I.e. 'The anointed One'—the Hebrew word is *Messiah*, the Greek
Christos (Christ).

power of death! God's mighty act had made all things new; for thus had been revealed the final victory of Goodness over Evil. Not Caesar, not Pilate, not Herod, not Caiaphas; but Christ in the wisdom and power of God is the Judge of Men; and Christ can be their Saviour. God's words, spoken of old through Moses and the Prophets, had become in Christ Jesus *The Word Incarnate*.

Now when those that were listening heard them say that God had made Jesus victorious over death, many used to laugh and go away. But some said: 'We will hear you again about this matter'; and one there might be who said passionately: 'My wife and children are dead. Why are you certain that Jesus rose from the dead? And how can He free others from sin and the grave? Tell me more.' Him perhaps they would take to a house in Bethany where Jesus had sometimes stayed, and would arrange for him to talk with Peter—the disciple to whom Jesus had said that his name *Simon* would be changed to *Peter* (which is Greek for *the Rock*). Simon Peter used to speak after this manner: 'I and my brother Andrew were fishermen on the Lake of Galilee when Jesus called us to become His disciples. We said we would follow Him. We knew Him to be a wonderful man. So wonderful was Jesus I became positive He would reveal Himself as the promised *Messiah*, and I was very very sure I loved Him more than anyone else could do. Listen! I was then an unstable impetuous man, weak because I thought myself strong. On the night Jesus was betrayed I told the Master I was ready to die for Him. But the moment He allowed the mob to seize Him, I was filled with consternation. However, I followed the crowd to the chief priest's house whither they took Him. There a maid accused me of being one of His disciples. I cried out that I had never known Him, and then fled in terror. That is the man I was.... From a distance I watched Him die upon the Cross. When on the first day of the week certain women ran to tell us that He was risen from death, I did not in the least believe their story. Ah! how I wondered when I heard them; but I did not believe. If ever a man deserved to be unforgiven it was I. Then to me also, even as to the other disciples, Jesus showed Himself alive beyond death—the selfsame Jesus who had been so patient with me, whom I had loved so much and yet had failed so dreadfully....A few weeks after He had been crucified, we, His disciples, defied our rulers, proclaiming openly in Jerusalem the saving power of God made manifest in Jesus Christ. They arrested and flogged us; but the rulers grew afraid of our truth, not we of their threats. In their hearts they knew that they had slain the Innocent....Consider this—Jesus (who knew the hearts of men) chose *me* to be a disciple: He said that Simon the proud, Simon the weakling, would be changed; and it would come to pass that upon me men would build as upon a rock. How that may be fulfilled, I cannot tell. Also He told me the time would come when I should be arrested for His sake and condemned to death. I shall not again try to escape....Do you begin to understand what God has spoken to men in Christ; what Jesus can do for me, for you, for everyone? To-morrow John and I will be at the Beautiful Gate of the Temple where we often go to declare the Faith. Come and hear.'

Sometimes a learned Jew would earnestly inquire. To such a one Peter might add these words: 'You may feel that I was a fisherman, not a man of education. I wish you could meet Paul, a citizen of Tarsus, who has been convinced of the truth of this our Faith in Christ. Paul is a Jew deeply instructed in the Law, who knows also the Wisdom of the Greeks. So zealous a Jew was Paul that at one time he persecuted bitterly the followers of Jesus. But there came to him a vision of our risen Lord. We others feel that Paul understands what has happened more deeply than any of us. It was Paul who first enabled me to comprehend that Jesus came from God to be the Redeemer, not of Israel only, but of all men, and how it could be that God was in Him and He in God.

Thus used the Apostles at first to speak about Jesus, proclaiming the Gospel. Then they began to write down what they had seen and known. Later, others set down what they had learnt from those who had been with Jesus: and in time the narratives were gathered from which the four Gospels were made. Letters that Paul had written to groups of Christians in different cities were cherished, and copied. Eventually the Books which constitute the New Testament were solemnly declared to be *canonical* Scriptures of the Christian Faith—the sacred record of 'the Word of God in Jesus Christ'.

§2. The Clouds gather (Typology)

How sublimely different Jesus had been from the conquering Messiah expected by the Jews. How glorious His triumph over wrong and the power of the grave. How different from the 'Day of the Lord' depicted in certain ancient prophecies, and in recent writings that claimed to foretell how and when God would avenge Him of His adversaries and exalt His chosen People. All that had been good in Israel's heroic hope that God would cause Right to triumph over Wrong, Jesus had fulfilled. All that had been amiss in Jewish expectations, His life and death and resurrection refuted. Ardently therefore Christians turned to search the Sacred Books, expectant to find therein indications that pointed towards God's real purpose as it had come to pass in Jesus Christ—'signs' which the Jews had not seen or had misunderstood. Surely Jesus shed illumination on Israel's past, and surely it would be found that what was true in the ancient Scriptures witnessed to Him. For this mode of studying the Old Testament scholars ought to have used a more pleasing term than *Prefiguration* or *Typology*.[1] Unhappily Christian seekers in antiquity conducted the search with greater eagerness than wisdom.

(i) *Analogies*. In the first place, the Old Testament could be scrutinized to find features that seemed comparable one way or another with the life of Jesus. Such analogies or comparisons might be felt to be intellectually or devotionally stimulating. To say '*This* is like *that*' is often a valuable way of assisting understanding. Christ Himself used such a comparison when He said: 'As Moses lifted up the serpent in the wilderness, so must the Son of Man be lifted up.' His strange words were memorable: when spoken they perplexed the hearers, but after the Crucifixion they became illuminating. St Paul several times (e.g. I Cor. x. 4) makes analogical references to Old Testament passages. One feels he knew exactly what he was doing, and does not in the least imply that the ancient events or institutions to which he refers had no religious significance save to furnish the comparison with Christ. Indeed,

---

[1] 'TYPE: a symbol, emblem; in Theology a person, object, or event of Old Testament history, prefiguring some person or thing revealed in the new dispensation.' (*The Oxford Dictionary*). For a thorough and reliable study of Hebrew Messianic hope in relation to New Testament fulfilment, see *The Evidential Value of Prophecy* (1906) by E. A. Edghill—a scholar whose early death was a grievous loss to Biblical studies.

in almost all the analogies drawn by the New Testament writers one senses their consciousness of historical reality and its value.[1]

When, however, we pass beyond the borders of the New Testament into the works of the ancient and medieval expositors of the Scriptures, it is everywhere evident that disastrous influences were given full scope, producing endless artificialities. The sincerity of their interpretations is obvious, but 'the zeal was not according to knowledge'. Even analogies require restraint in their exercise, if they are to be justifiable and seemly. Their value always depends on the extent to which they are apt or inept. Easily they can become far-fetched and unreal. A single instance will serve. If anyone can bring himself to think it a comparison either sensible or reverent, the story of Joseph in Egypt (suffering humiliation, overcoming temptation, finally vindicated and exalted) might be alleged as 'prefiguring' Christ's human life, His Passion, and Resurrection. Tertullian (c. A.D. 200) does thus refer to the story; indeed goes further, for in the context of his Treatise it is plain his argument is that the Deity ordained those experiences should happen to Joseph and be recorded, in order that centuries later the Jews ought thereby to have been guided to recognize their Saviour in Jesus.[2]

(ii) *Predictions*. So great are the truths concerning God and Man which it was given to the supreme Hebrew Prophets to perceive that their convictions reach out towards the fullness of truth that actually came in Christ. But in this matter the intelligence of the early Christian expositors of Scripture was beclouded by an assumption that caused them to plunge into a morass of fanciful interpretations. They were heirs of the centuries during which the

[1] Even in the Epistle to the Hebrews, which may be influenced by Alexandrian, as well as Rabbinic, modes of exegesis.

[2] *Adversus Judaeos*. Tertullian writes the Treatise to confute and convince the Jews by 'proofs' from Scripture. A modern writer (Hebert, *The Throne of David*, p. 36) also commends the story of Joseph as offering 'an excellent instance' and 'a real analogy of principle'. Does Hebert go further (like Tertullian) and regard it as *more* than a devotionally helpful comparison? He refers to it again (p. 260) under a heading 'Mystical Interpretation'. Not thus should the Gospel be commended to men of the Tank Corps or Dons of the University. The Gospels exist. Let a man take his temptations and prosperity direct to the foot of the Cross and not *via* Genesis thus misused. Let him also learn what are the historical, religious values of Genesis in the long process of the revelation of God to His people. The analogical style of preaching was in vogue as late as the middle of the last century.

idea of the inspiration of a Prophet had lamentably contracted to the notion that his prime function had been to utter (with or without his conscious knowledge) predictions of future events. In consequence of that attitude Christian students ransacked the prophetic writings for 'hidden' meanings in which they found Jesus foretold. They were entitled, of course, to fasten on definitely Messianic verses, but even in these they should have perceived more often matter for contrast than for comparison. And constantly their discoveries were absurdly artificial. Out of countless cases a single illustration (again from Tertullian) will suffice. Tertullian pondered the memorable verse in which Amos (denouncing merciless Hebrews for enslaving brethren unable to discharge paltry debts) declares: 'They have sold the righteous for silver, and the needy for a pair of shoes.' From it he drew the conclusion that God caused the Prophet to use those indignant words in order that it might thus, cryptically, be predicted that Judas would betray Jesus for a price![1]

(iii) *Growth of Ideas and Ideals.* (*Modern Typology.*) S. A. Cook quotes a remark 'the old Typology is dead and buried'; and proceeds to stress that *modern* typological method in Old Testament study effectively and movingly traces the development of ideas, ideals and institutions: 'The idea that is at first implicit', Cook observes, 'becomes explicit; there is a definite similarity of function when the earlier and "lower" examples are compared with the later and "higher".'[2] So regarded, the Old Testament is

[1] Expectation of finding hidden predictions was extended beyond the Books of the Prophets to other Old Testament Writings. An example (cited by J. R. Darbyshire in *E.R.E.* vol. XII, p. 501) may be taken from The Epistle of Barnabas (*c.* A.D. 100)—'the puerilities of which' (as Bishop Westcott remarked) 'degrade the Old Testament to a mere riddle of which Christianity is the answer'. The writer of this Epistle noted that in Gen. xiv it is said that, when Abraham pursued five kings who had invaded the land and captured his brother Lot, Abraham had with him 318 trained men. 'Ah!' thought the godly author of Barnabas, 'in that number God foretold that Jesus would be crucified'. He thought so for this hyper-ingenious reason. The Greek language used letters of the alphabet to denote numerals, and 318 was represented by the Greek capital letters T.I.E.—in the 'T' he perceived a symbol of the cross, whilst 'I' 'E' are in Greek the first two letters of the name of Jesus. Obviously, mistaken principles were at work. Such absurdities have no place in the right use of the Scriptures.

[2] The quotation is from Strahan, *Life of A. B. Davidson*, p. 199. See Cook's memoir on G. A. Smith in *The Proceedings of the British Academy*, vol. XXVIII, p. 33.

inexhaustibly stimulating.[1] Its record of the actualities of the whole course of Hebrew life and thought illuminates the final fullness of truth not only in virtue of all that, dimly or brightly, is comparable with the mind and work of Christ, but also through all that stands in sharp or subtle contrast. If, for example, we trace the usage of the term *holiness*, we find that it expressed an idea at first morally colourless, then moralized; at first externalized in connection with material objects, then deeply spiritualized in thought of personal-moral relationships. It was used anciently (by the Hebrews as by other Peoples) in allusion to the Gods simply as mysterious powerful beings, who must be approached with anxious precaution and deference, lest their anger be kindled by some offence to their dignity (however unintended it might be).[2] Places where they were deemed to be present, and utensils used in their worship, were *holy*, and must be treated with utmost caution. The transforming development from materialistic to moral reverence is visible in Isaiah, because the Prophet conceived God, the Holy One of Israel, to be exalted in *righteousness*. The development points towards the insight of Him who illuminated every personal relationship, and who warned men lest they be content to 'cleanse the outside of the cup and of the platter, but within they are full of extortion and excess'. Again, as regards the custom of worship by means of animal-sacrifice, we trace its antiquity, complexities, and persistence; then the radical denunciations of it uttered by the great Prophets, and the effort made to reform and justify its continuance; finally its abolition by sublimation. The comprehensive instance of growth of Idea is, of course, seen in the developing conception of the nature of God—how it moved upwards from the archaic level—to the Prophetic—to Christ's.

In illustration of modern typological attitude to *Ideals*, we may

[1] Cp. G. A. Smith, *Modern Preaching and the Criticism of the Old Testament*, Lecture V.

[2] See Otto, *The Idea of the Holy*. Cp. Exod. iii. 5; and xix. 12 (concerning Sinai, the holy mountain—'Whosoever toucheth the mount shall be surely put to death; no hand shall touch him, but he shall surely be stoned, or shot through; whether it be beast or man, it shall not live'; so infectious was the sinner's guilt that the death penalty had to be carried out by a method that did not involve physical contact with him); and II Sam. vi. 6, 7 (Uzzah stricken dead because he touched the holy Ark of God. His pious intention was to save it from being overturned!). Gods, and all that pertained to them, were like a 'live wire' charged with perilous electric current.

consider the problem of Justice and of Man's yet greater need of Mercy. When at length the law of civilized Israel decreed the social principle, 'An eye for an eye, a tooth for a tooth', we perceive Conscience emerging from the wilderness of unrestrained barbaric vengeance into the stern yet cultivated territory of Justice. But in the agonized pleadings of the great Prophets that justice reflects not the Mind of God, comes short of the height that even human nature should attain, can in no wise suffice the necessity of our being, we listen beforehand to Him who was to say in His dying agony: 'Father, forgive them, for they know not what they do.' One of the Hebrew proverbs enjoins: 'If thine enemy hunger, give him bread to eat.' That, indeed, foreshadows the mind that was in Christ Jesus. But nothing anticipated the attainment in Jesus of the unity of the perfected ideal wherein Justice and Mercy were one. Seeking Messianic analogies (however strained), peering about in the Prophetic Books for Messianic predictions, the early Christian expositors let riches slip from their hands. They were too little awed and enthralled by the Prophets' invective against cruel deeds and the futility of ritual that did not stir the conscience and quicken genuine adoration of God; nor did they thoroughly lay to heart the Prophets' Christlike tenderness for the poor, the ignorant and the suffering; nor sense the overshadowing divine Presence in the consecration of the Prophets' own lives. One anticipation of a true idea and ideal they could not wholly fail to grasp: for Christ had pointed it out. That was the resemblance to what Jesus had to be to suffer and achieve, visible in certain passages in Isaiah xl–lxvi concerning the suffering 'Servant of the Lord'.[1] Yet even there they did not discern Christ's meaning as profoundly as they should. As for the Jewish Law, the ancient expositors showed keen interest in seeking figurative meanings in its sacrificial system viewed in relation to Christ; but the tremendous demands made by the Law in its application of the great Commandments to the obligations of life were little noted. More and more the Books of the Law were dismissed as obsolete Jewish ordinances—an expanse of thirsty sands with rare oases where a little water might be drawn by aid of typological wells.

Human beings are so tightly held within the thought-limits of their time that a measure of sympathy is due to the early expositors of Scripture. Nevertheless, they ought to have achieved better

[1] See Isa. xlii. 1–4; xlix. 1–6; l. 4–9; liii; lxi. 1–10. Cp. St Luke iv. 16–19.

things; for there were among them men of splendid intelligence, spiritual sensitiveness and saintly devotion. Worse things were in the making; for fanciful Typology was but 'Little Sister' to an unprincipled, domineering, 'Big Brother', called *Allegory*.

§3. 'The Ice-Age' (*Allegory*)

When Jew and Christian commended their Sacred Scriptures to unbelievers, what could they answer when an astute Gentile scornfully pointed out passages of crude theology, barbaric morality or scandalous incident in the Old Testament? How indeed justify to their own minds the presence of such things in Holy Writ? Neither Jew nor Christian had cause to fear (nor did they fear) the pride of Greek and Roman civilization; for they had what that civilization—which welcomed every sort of creed and cult, and stirred them all together into an indigestible pudding of pious confusion—fatally lacked: a truly profound Religion.[1] But in this matter some reply had to be found to rebut the derision of the heathen. (Remember that they had not the explanation that is answer to-day—that revelation of truth came gradually as men's minds grew more able to perceive it.)

Oddly enough, the Greeks had forged the weapon wherewith the attack could be repelled. For the Greeks had had to face a parallel problem in regard to the Homeric poems, which Greek culture used in the education of its youth—used not without good reason; for the *Iliad* and the *Odyssey* faithfully and inspiringly depict the ways of mortal men and women. They show the weaknesses in human nature, but tell of errors retrieved and temptations overcome, and they immortalize heroic enterprise and endurance: 'Homer, thy song men liken to the sea, With every note of music in his tune....' But for men's adoration those poems hold up the Gods of Mount Olympus; and, not infrequently, ascribe to the Deities quarrels, intrigues, treacheries and *amours*. As taste developed, thoughtful Greeks felt it intolerable to believe such shocking statements to be literally true. Way out was found by the contention that any scandalous or ridiculous assertions concerning Gods must conceal some intellectually deep significance. The edifying meanings which accordingly were

[1] Cp. T. R. Glover, *The Conflict of Religions in the Early Roman Empire*; *The Jesus of History*; *Jesus in the Experience of Men*; *The Influence of Christ in the Ancient World*.

superimposed on the literal sense of such passages are termed allegorical, or *mystical*, interpretations.[1] Thus, Greek philosophers maintained *allegorically* that the unsavoury behaviour of the Gods to one another, which Homer naïvely relates, really betokens the interrelations of the forces of Nature. By allegory, Zeus could be claimed to be a symbol for *Intelligence*; and the Goddess Athene (sprung from his head) *Art*. The device was a transparent subterfuge: 'Zeus' was the best idea the early Greeks could form of the creative Deity, and only unintentionally a caricature of truth. Plato would have nothing to do with its evasive nonsense.[2] The Stoic philosophers tried to institute rules to control its use, for Allegory was like a Fairy's wand—there was no guessing into what shapes it would transform the various Gods! The Greek allegorists, however, went gaily ahead; each confidently propounding his own mystical interpretations, and between them unwittingly demonstrating how unreal the whole business was.[3]

But how could the sophisticated Gentile complain if he was hoist with his own petard? Obviously he could not logically deny the use of allegory to Jews or Christians commending their Holy Scriptures. Naturally they used it vigorously both as shield and spear: as shield to ward off the jibes of the scoffer; as spear to pierce the pride of the heathen. For by allegory it could be maintained that all the vaunted wisdom of the Greeks was mystically concealed in the Old and New Testament Scriptures. Moreover, it was useful to be free by this means to interpret texts in a way that seemed to support doctrines. And recourse to allegory was further cherished because it could be so devotionally reassuring: by its aid piety could extract no end of salutary lessons from otherwise unpromising passages in the Bible.

Among the Jews Philo (early in the first century) was the outstanding exponent of allegory, claiming to show that Gentile philosophy and science had been anticipated in the Hebrew writings. By the second and third centuries Christian defenders

---

[1] Long usage of the term in this connexion makes protest too late. But *mystical* ought to have been allowed always to wear the ethereal halo proper to a supernormal, psychic, experience; not the motley of 'hidden' meanings autocratically imposed.

[2] *Republic* ii. 278 ff.

[3] Devastating information, as regards both Greek and Christian usage of the device, is given in Geffcken's article 'Allegory' in *E.R.E.*

of the Faith were in full sail on the uncharted seas of allegory.[1]
The learned Origen of Alexandria tried to lay down 'Laws of
Navigation'; he recognized value in the actual (historical and
moral) sense in the Scriptures, but he ascribed highest value to
mystical interpretations of passages; and held that, wherever the
Scriptures recorded something physically impossible or religiously
absurd or morally reprehensible, there God had intended a
'hidden' spiritual meaning to be discerned.[2] Not until the
thirteenth century was an effective attack delivered against
allegorizing, when St Thomas Aquinas (1227–74) insisted that
only the literal sense of Scripture should be cited as supporting
doctrines. (It should be noted that eventually Roman Catholic
theologians, in general, accepted the view taken by St Thomas.)
Otherwise, for full 1500 years, Christian expositors ranged over
the Scriptures, allegorizing without misgiving as seemed to them
good. To name one of countless examples—St Ambrose (Bishop
of Milan c. 380) interpreted allegorically the words in Gen. iii. 16
said to be spoken by God to Eve—as also the narrative of Isaac
and Rebecca—holding that the relations between Christ and the
Christian soul were therein mystically declared aforehand by
God.[3] The thoughts of Ambrose, and many like him, concerning

---

[1] The scathing attack made c. A.D. 200 by Celsus (a pagan thinker of keen
intelligence and biting tongue) on the fatuities of allegorizing ought to have
been sufficient warning.

[2] Valiant, but unavailing, protest against allegorizing was made in the
fourth century by theologians of the School of Antioch (notably, by Diodorus,
Bishop of Tarsus; Chrysostom; and Theodore of Mopsuestia), who insisted
that sound interpretation must be drawn from the grammatical and historical
sense only. Thus St Chrysostom comments on Isa. vi. 6, 7: 'There are those
who say these things are the symbols of future mysteries; that the altar and
the fire laid upon it symbolize "The Power of Ministering", and the coal
placed on the mouth "The Cleansing of Sins": but we keep hold of the
history.' In regard to certain widely esteemed, Messianic, passages the
Antiochenes compromised considerably.

[3] Instanced by Darwell Stone in Gore's *New Commentary*, p. 693. Stone's
article discusses the use of Psalms and Old Testament Lessons in Christian
worship, tentatively suggesting that worshippers should accustom themselves
by aid of allegory to attach a Christian significance to anything which is, or
seems, sub-Christian in Old Testament passages. In the writer's opinion,
Christian worshippers should instead be made aware of the truth that theirs
is a Faith that developed in history, and should glory in the fact. They should
know that the Old Testament is record of God's mercy and patience in
dealing with wayward uncomprehending men, and rejoice in the marvel of

Christ the Church and the soul of Man were often both intel-lectually and devotionally profound. What we are here concerned with is *the unconscious unreality in their treatment of the Old Testament Scriptures*, and the resultant failure to see clearly its actual values. It is a chilly business to wander through the permu-tations and combinations of so-called mystical meanings which ingenuity in the cause of piety and doctrine arbitrarily extracted, and managed to believe in as profound expositions of the spiritual truth in the Bible. Let allegory in by the door, and it asserts it has right to run riot through the house.

A calamitous misconception (in which allegorizing played its convenient role) beset the use of the Scriptures for doctrinal purposes in the Early Medieval and Reformation centuries. The deadly error was the notion that the Biblical Books, being *inspired writings*, were therefore everywhere equally authoritative, and from that it followed that words found anywhere in the Scriptures might serve as proof that a doctrine was true;[1] no regard need be paid to the meaning of the words in their actual context, and (if so desired) an allegorical significance might be read into them. This was treating the Bible like a huge refrigerator, in which superabundant proofs of doctrine had been laid up in cold storage. Application of the theory quickly led to a disconcerting situation. The unorthodox (it was found) might insist that only the literal meaning of the passage in question was valid (so Marcion), and reject the 'mystical' meaning claimed for it by the orthodox; *or* they might champion a different allegorical interpretation (so the Gnostics)! And how could the 'mystical' expositions of the heretics be demonstrated to be erroneous? For, 'When the his-torical sense of a passage is abandoned there is lacking any sound regulative principle to govern exegesis.'[2]

Israel's gradual ascent towards heavenly wisdom, understanding that they are not, as Christians, assenting to what they may hear in the First Lesson or the Psalms as if it were 'Gospel Truth'.

[1] Cp. many chapter-headings in the A.V. (1611), and 'Scripture proofs' in the Westminster Confession (1643).

[2] Fullerton, *Prophecy and Authority*, p. 75. Cp. W. R. Smith, *The Old Testa-ment in the Jewish Church*, p. 23: 'Of course, the allegorical exegesis yielded to every party exactly those principles which that party desired; and so the controversy between the Gnostics and the Catholic Church could not be decided on the ground of the Bible alone, which both sides interpreted in an equally arbitrary manner.'

From this quandary the orthodox sought deliverance by contending that the proper interpretation and allegory would always be that given by representatives of the Churches which could claim to preserve a tradition of sound doctrine handed down through their bishops from Christ and the Apostles. It was an authoritarian theory; and (operating with proof-texts snatched from anywhere in the Bible) it caused a deal of nonsense to be affirmed regarding the significance of Scriptural passages, and a vast deal of good sense to be ignored. On the other hand, amidst the subtleties of keen minds and the incessant chatter of glib tongues in the Greek and Roman Age, it assisted the orthodox authorities in their defence of certain positions vital for the Faith. This expedient solution of the quandary was, however, a device which could, and in the long run did, work out calamitously for deep appreciation of the real value of the Scriptures. Adequate regard was not being paid to the final principle that the Church is the servant of Truth, not Truth the slave of the Church. Students of the Bible—whether laymen, archbishops or oecumenical councils—must seek first the facts; then all good things exegetically will be added unto them, and to those they teach. It is tragic that throughout this immensely long stretch of history Christian piety made so distorted, and so needlessly jejune, use of the spiritual resources of the Bible. Devoutly desiring to find the maximum anticipation of Christ in the Old Testament, the ancient interpreters found the minimum—for lack of the right perspective. They ought to have been wiser, or grown wiser.

Three general comments on this 'Ice-Age of Allegory' may now be made:

(i) It should have been realized that allegory exalts individual opinion in a way that makes rational discussion impossible, because allegorizing entails that anything can be asserted to mean whatsoever the allegorist chooses to declare is its mystical meaning. A skilled practitioner of the art would not be at a loss to discover Messianic predictions in the legends of the early Latin kings, or when Kai-Lung unrolls his mat of Chinese tales. A worthy gentleman once published a volume to demonstrate that Horace's *Odes* mystically anticipate the findings of modern geology. (If the writer's memory serves, the author seriously propounded that Lydia, the Lady of the *Odes*, signified the Old Red Devonian Sandstone.) A medically-minded enthusiast for allegorizing might insist that Ps. xxvi. 2 ('Examine me, O Lord, and prove me; try my reins and my heart') mystically prefigured discoveries of modern curative science—insulin, penicillin and the rest.[1]

(ii) It should have been realized that, when whole tracts of the Old Testament were being treated as spiritually negligible—attention being concentrated on search for proof-texts of doctrine, and on verses that were (or might be constrained to seem) Messianic—something was gravely amiss. The general attitude of the ancients pitched on to the scrap-heap a vast part of the evidence for revelation in the Holy Scriptures—like a bundle of outworn rags, *junk*! 'The medieval Church', said W. R. Smith severely but not unjustly, 'understanding by God's Word an intellectual revelation looked in Scripture for that *alone*, and where no intellectual mysteries appeared, saw only, as Luther complains, "bare dead histories that concern men no more".'[2]

(iii) It should have been perceived that a repellent idea of the Deity underlay the device of allegorizing. Recognition of enlightening analogies as between Old and New Testament passages is valuable. So also (and very rewarding) is perception that further depth of meaning may be latent in the early forms of beliefs, institutions and ideals. But the theory that crudities in the Old Testament can be happily explained because God, forsooth, had buried in them secret salutary edification which only the spade of allegory could unearth—that was mistaken and bad. The notion implies a shockingly unworthy conception of God. As if the Divine Self-revelation in the ages before Christ had been given through a series of enigmas, useless to those who received them (since the solutions could not be reached until Christ lived), and needless to all who have actual knowledge of Jesus Himself! Profound indications of the consummation towards which Hebrew religion was travelling are indeed perceptible in the Old Testament;

[1] Here is an earnest allegorist at work on a modern secular scene: 'I thought I saw a lawyer's clerk alighting from a bus; I looked again and saw it was a hippopotamus.' Of course others are free to disagree and insist that he is wrong about the hidden meaning he thinks he sees; but the exponent can stand to it he is mystically right.

[2] W. R. Smith, *Lectures and Essays*, p. 228. Also (pp. 212, 214): 'A true historical sense of the organic connection between the Old and New Testaments was altogether lacking....The real reason why men failed rightly to understand the *record* of redemption was because they had no true comprehension of the *work* of redemption.'

but they are visible in the process of a unique history and the development of sound beliefs. God's concern with the Hebrews was real, not fictitious. God did not treat Israel as a sort of picture-gallery, in which to hang up from time to time futurist sketches of the life of Jesus, so mistily painted that their subject would remain hopelessly obscure until Christ had come. In the Old Testament God is not playing a parlour game with devout Jews or devout Christians: 'First, find the conundrums in the Old Testament, and then try and find the answers.' Plato, awed by the regularities of the universe, spoke of God as the supreme Geometrician. That is a noble thought—but not the allegorist's nightmare presentation of God as the Master-maker of crosswords.

Throughout 1500 years something in the nature of an Ice-Age descended on the proper use of the Scriptures, and to a deplorable extent 'the good seed of the Word' lay buried in iron-bound soil. For over a thousand years of this period effort to ascertain the original text, and actual authors and sources of the sacred documents, was left in abeyance, benumbed. It is fair to say that the keen tools requisite for scholarly investigation did not yet exist. But the point is, nobody wanted to make the tools. Acceptance of the Vulgate Version as inerrantly accurate froze textual interest stiff. The learned valued the Old Testament principally as a storehouse for proof-texts in relation to Christian doctrines. The full spiritual significance in Israel's history and in the lives of the great Prophets was buried under glaciers of allegory and neglect. A cold bewildering fog lay heavy upon the waters, and the good ship *Interpretation* could not speed on its way. Or, better, one might say that the gold of the Bible had been safely stored in the vaults of the Church, but the treasure remained for the most part a frozen asset.

It does not follow, however, that the spiritual temperature of the Age was at freezing-point or below. The reader (it is hoped) may have judged that these strictures on the methods of ancient interpretation are merited; but he ought also to feel strongly that a noble aspect of the long period has been ignored. We humans are so swift to fasten on what calls for blame, so slow to appreciate things well done. Consider the following statement concerning these centuries: 'The believer had need of Christ as well as of a Creed, but Christ was held forth to him in the Mass, not in the Bible.'[1] There is a measure of truth in that saying, but *faithfully*

[1] W. R. Smith, *The Old Testament in the Jewish Church*, p. 7.

Christ was thus held forth to the people—if one looks to the broad scene. How else could the sacred duty have been fulfilled in that age, save by maintenance of the Sacraments and solemn liturgy of the Church, and by the clergy teaching the Creed and the cardinal moral obligations of the Faith? How in those years could knowledge of the general contents of the Scriptures be mediated to the multitude? There were no printed Bibles to circulate. Where were the records of the Sacred writings? A few complete and splendid manuscripts (joy of the learned) were guarded in great ecclesiastical establishments; and a few—beautifully wrought on finest parchment, and elaborately decorated—existed as treasure in Kings' palaces.[1] The great fact is that tireless effort was being made by thousands of faithful men working to preserve and multiply the sacred records—copying by hand the most precious portions of the Bible. All through these centuries, in the heat of the summer days, in the cold of the wintry skies, monks were toiling, toiling, toiling to reproduce the Holy Books. No one can examine the products of their industry and not confess that devotion, as well as skill and patience, went to the making of their manuscripts.

And always among their number there were good and thoughtful souls who pondered the meaning of the words their hands were copying. Many recorded the meditation of their hearts in massive commentaries. These men heard the thunder of the Law from Sinai; listened to the teaching of Jesus by the Lake of Galilee; bowed their spirits at the story of the Cross; sought by their character and teaching, by their care for the sick and poor, to reveal the living Presence of the Lord. Had it not been so, the Faith could not have been preserved.[2] It would have been swept

---

[1] Cp. Cranage, *The Home of the Monk*, p. 7: 'To the early monks we owe without doubt, not only the preservation by copying of many important books, sacred and profane, but some of the most beautiful illuminations the world has ever seen. In Ireland the Book of Kells, now at Trinity College, Dublin, is the most famous.... The Lindisfarne Gospel Book, now in the British Museum, is a little later, and was written on Holy Island "for God and St Cuthbert"....It is difficult to imagine anything more magnificent, in colour or design, than this Gospel Book. One page must often have taken months to complete, but time was of little account to a monk who could look forward to years of such regular work....An artist who need not think of time and money has an enormous advantage over his fellows.' Cp. also Oakeshott, *The Artists of the Winchester Bible*. (This Bible, produced in England, is probably the finest 'illuminated' manuscript of the twelfth century.)

[2] See Miss Smalley's admirable study, *The Bible in the Middle Ages*.

away when the avalanche of barbarians from Asia destroyed the civilization of Rome. This was an Ice-Age as regards the full and proper use of the treasure in the Old Testament. But noble and famous Christians, and a host of less famous men also great in faith, lived during it. One thinks of golden-voiced Chrysostom preaching; of Augustine, Anselm, Aquinas, deep in thought; of Bede, kindly scholar, at Jarrow in Northumberland in A.D. 735 using the last hours of his last days to complete the first translation of St John's Gospel into Anglo-Saxon. One thinks of Bernard of Clairvaux, writer of hymns that move our hearts. And may one remember also Chaucer's portrait of a gentle Clerk in Holy Orders, seeking no higher station and emolument, right diligent to help the people of his Charge, teaching the truth of Christ and His Apostles, but 'first he followed it himself'?

To each Age its own task. What are we making of ours, for whom Bibles are available by the million, and aid of learning to interpret them? It is an icy finger of rebuke that points to us from the Age of Allegory.

§4. 'The Sun returns' (Renaissance and Reformation)

The fourteenth and fifteenth centuries saw a new epoch in Western civilization. By A.D. 1500 the invention of printing had begun to provide the many with the means for learning. Gutenberg's Press had issued texts of the most important Greek and Roman ('Classical') literature, and thereby awakened interest in a magnificent civilization—artistic, philosophic, and scientific—that had owed nothing to the doctrines of the Church. Contact was established with Jewish scholars, and the Hebrew text of the Old Testament began to be studied efficiently.[1] By 1500 Erasmus and others were at work on the Greek of the New Testament. It became indisputable that the Latin Vulgate was not an impeccable translation of original documents. Moreover, startling discoveries in the heavens and on the earth assailed belief that the Biblical writers had

[1] *Occasional* contacts with Jewish scholarship had been made much earlier. Miss Smalley (op. cit.) stresses the nearly forgotten and important influence of Andrew of St Victor in Paris, c. 1200. The labours of the German scholar, Reuchlin, who learnt Hebrew from the Jews in 1494 and was the first Professor to introduce its study into the curriculum of a University, should be mentioned, *honoris causa*. 'But for the Jewish contribution to the Reformation Europe would have missed one-half of the harvest of Humanism.' (L. Magnus in *The Legacy of Israel*, p. 504.)

been so inspired as to be inerrant on all matters. As for the heavens, fixed ideas were now confronted by the astronomical-mathematical conclusions of Copernicus, sustained and amplified by Tycho Brahe, Galileo (inventor of the telescope), and later by Kepler and Newton.[1] Our globe is not, as the ancient Ptolemaic astronomy and the men of Biblical times had believed, a fixed point round which sun, moon and planets revolve. As for the earth, sailors were doing things impossible, if Biblical notions of geography were correct. But there was no gainsaying the voyages of Columbus to America, of Vasco da Gama to India round Southern Africa, and finally Magellan's circumnavigation of the world in 1519–21. These were dumbfoundering events.

It was in that situation that a new epoch also dawned in Biblical interpretation, through the conception of the Word of God in Scripture that shone forth in the spiritual experience of Luther and Calvin. We are apt to think of Luther and Calvin only as challenging theologians; and to be keenly observant of their theological defects as well as their virtues. But they were also fresh and bold expositors of the Bible. One thing they, and others of the great early Reformers, knew beyond dispute. In the Gospels their soul was confronted with Jesus Christ crucified and risen; there they saw the glory of God, as had those who walked this earth beside Him; knew with the impact of direct personal apprehension why the Creeds had had to say of Him 'very God of very God'; and were moved to the inmost core of their being. In the Epistles they met Paul, preaching to the Gentiles the unsearchable riches of Christ; Paul for whom to live was Christ and to die was gain. In the Old Testament, in Narratives, Prophets, Psalmists, they found again and again examples of faith and heroism, and heard words of rebuke and comfort, that spoke compelling truths direct to their minds and consciences. For them light had arisen in the Bible, shining more and more unto the perfect day. What mattered the presence of aught else in the Bible beside this incomparable, irrefutable, fact? Therein the living God had spoken to men of old. Therein, with patient redeeming righteousness and grace, God now spake to them—which thing they knew to be true by the witness of His Spirit in their souls. What need had they of allegorical meanings, when the vision of the glory and wisdom of God pervaded the *literal* meaning of the Scriptures? In the actualities

[1] See Alfred Noyes' poem, *The Torch-bearers*.

of Israel's preservation, in the record of the New Testament concerning Christ, was testimony of the Work and Word of God among men; and they asked but to trace the marvel of His ways. Their spiritual insight initiated the emancipation of Biblical study from the thraldom of the medieval outlook. In an age of momentous cultural transition it was rediscovery of that wisdom which in the early years of the second century had enabled martyred Ignatius to brush aside controversy as to this and that, and declare: 'For me the documents are Jesus Christ; my unassailable documents are His Cross and His death and resurrection and the faith which is through Him: in which things I hope, with your prayers, to be saved.'[1]

The shock of the Reformers' convictions had a salutary effect: it caused men to 'see to the ploughs and break up fallow ground'. But Rome set its face against the urgency of the Reformers. Centuries earlier the Western Church of Rome and the Orthodox Churches of the East had divided in counsel and organization. Now Western Christendom was sundered into Catholics and Protestants. Catholics denounced the Reformed Churches as guilty of the sin of schism. Protestants knew Whom they had believed; and felt that Rome ought to have taken the Reformers to its heart and itself reformed. Of both sides it is true that sincere men can do no other than obey what they are convinced is right. The tragedy is that the 'envy, malice and all uncharitableness' of unrighteous men played a wicked part in the Roman-Protestant controversy. If the Hebrew mind were asked for comment on the situation, might it not answer that, mercifully, the wisdom of God and the patience of His working is greater than the unwisdom of impatient men, and that God is forever reminding us—'When the vessel...was marred in the hand of the potter, he made it again another vessel as seemed good to Him'?[2] But the proper subject of this chapter is not the history of the Church, or questions of disunion and reunion; but the history of the use of the Bible.

As to that, the certitude of the great Reformers was that spiritual truth is spiritually discerned; and that vital religious truth inevitably and authoritatively discloses itself in the sacred Books to the pure in mind, the eager and sincere in heart. This claim ought not to have been misunderstood, either by the Catholic Church or by the Protestants of subsequent generations. Authentic

[1] *Letter to the Philadelphians*, § 8.   [2] Jer. xviii. 4.

Reformation theology did not mean by it, 'One man's judgement is as good as another's', but that the teaching of Scripture must be ascertained by careful and competent consideration, not by declarations raised above scrutiny as to facts.[1] Theory, however, is one thing; practice another. Not until the present century has Biblical scholarship (both Protestant and Catholic) become master of the situation. Until then opinionated Protestants, often very ill qualified to judge, were apt to take the bit between their teeth like a runaway horse: Rome was given much reason to think: 'I foresaw how it would be—Your doctrine of Scriptural authority will end by breaking your schismatic Church into little pieces!' (Rome, however, continued to have its own grievous reasons to repent, and not to be overproud.)

In another matter, however, Catholic and Protestant in the sixteenth and seventeenth centuries found themselves more or less of one mind. The Ice-Age was ending; but when Christian thought (emerging from long hibernation) looked around—either from the portals of St Peter's, or from Protestantism with the open Bible in its hand—the light of Renaissance learning and achievement showed to the puzzled eyes of the faithful skies in which, although the sun was shining, there were also portentous clouds.

§5. 'A Depression from Iceland' (The Infallible Bible)

The responsible leaders of the Roman and the Reformed Churches were aghast at the new astronomy and the new geography that seemed plainly to run counter to the teaching of the inspired Scriptures. Rome decided astronomers must not affirm that the earth revolves round the sun. It is easy for us, so long after the crisis, to smile amusedly; but the Christian staunchness was not without rational justification *for the time being*. Galileo's telescope was propounding a theory of the heavens and the earth which appeared to falsify the system of religion and morality that had been the acknowledged standard of human duty for 1600 years. Might there not be a flaw in the instrument, or in the astronomer's arithmetic? The Church was going to make very very sure before deciding that Faith and the Bible had to be aligned to what the scientists alleged to be fact; and very clear how that could be done. (When Einstein announces his theory of Relativity, mathematicians do not accept the theory confidently, until they are very

[1] Cp. W. R. Smith, *O.T.J.C.* p. 27.

very sure there has been no slip-up in the calculations.) Where theologians, and official Church pronouncements, have been grievously at fault is not in being hesitant about accepting new ideas the instant they appear, but in being reluctant to investigate their truth and value, and far too slow in trying to relate well-established facts to the Faith; lacking courage to believe that deepened knowledge will lead to deepened understanding of the Faith.

In the sixteenth century Rome took its stand on the ancient view of the Bible—namely that inspiration made it unerring on all matters, that its text was perfectly presented by the Latin (Vulgate) translation, and correct interpretation given only through the infallible guidance of the Roman Church. It is no wonder that Protestants, bewildered by the findings of the new learning, brow-beaten by the authority of the Church Infallible, sought refuge in the fortress of the Infallible Bible, justly confident that at any rate their translations rested on the original Greek and the original Hebrew—'Hebraica Veritas'.[1] *The Bible, verbally inspired, in-errant in all matters and authoritative in all its parts*[2]—it was wholeheartedly believed that upon that granite rock the waves of unbelief would beat in vain. In reality, that theory of the Bible was a house built on sand, and it could not sustain itself against the surging tide of incoming knowledge.[3] Changing the metaphor— from the time of the Reformation down to the middle of the nineteenth century Christian defenders of the worth of the Bible shut themselves up, as it were, in a medieval castle assailed by the

[1] A quaint instance of over-confidence is found in the Helvetic Confession of Faith, which laid down as regards the Hebrew text of the Old Testament that 'both the consonants and the vowels, yes! and the points themselves, and the very meaning of the points, are inspired; and this in respect not only of the words, but also of the matter'. The authors of this statement betrayed their ignorance that the *points* are but signs to denote vowels in a Hebrew text, and were invented by Jewish scholars centuries after the Christian era as a means of indicating the proper pronunciation of the consonants which alone ancient manuscripts had recorded.

[2] I.e —in the Roman view, the Vulgate text interpreted by the Apostolic Church as sole custodian and expositor; for Protestants, the new translations made from the *original* Hebrew and Greek—the spiritual meaning of which would be made clear by the promised Spirit of God to the Christ-dedicated soul.

[3] See A. E. Garvie's article on 'Inspiration' in *The Encyclopaedia Britannica* (11th ed.). Also H. W. Robinson, *Redemption and Revelation*, 1942.

artillery of the several sciences—including scientific investigation of the literature of the Bible. They did not realize that it was wholly in the interest of their rightly cherished ideals that scientists were battering down obsolete walls, and Biblical scholars toiling to rescue them from an exegetical morass in order that they might be rearmed to contend efficiently on firm ground. In the battle against evil they ought to have been out in the open, in close alliance with sincere and responsible scientists, outflanking and out-fighting the foes of human welfare.

Conscientiousness, if indiscriminate, is apt to produce a tangled crop of 'tares and wheat'. Both good and bad results followed from the supreme reverence with which the Bible was regarded during this period. There was the excellent consequence that the Bible was read, read diligently, by many devout people read from cover to cover. Its pages were 'marked and learnt', and effort made 'inwardly to digest' its teaching. Youth was educated into familiarity with its contents, and great numbers of adults continued throughout life to seek its counsel and wisdom, its rebuke and encouragement. There is something solid to build on when people know their Bibles. Because honest hearts are more common than astute brains, the vast majority of the Bible's readers drew not perplexities but authentic spiritual sustenance from its words. So far, so good. But there was a reverse, and dreadful, side to the picture, due to the continuing assumption that the Bible every-where spake authoritative divine truth. That notion suited the wooden-headed and the hard-hearted, grandly. 'Thou shalt not suffer a witch to live', says Ex. xxii. 18—'On with the witch-hunt! The Bible enjoins it!' Hebrews had slaves—therefore 'Slavery is justified. Wilberforce's notion that they are souls for whom Christ died is captious nonsense; his campaign to liberate them not merely infuriating, but contrary to the plain teaching of Holy Writ!' The last-ditch defence of the Bible as verbally inspired, and infallible on all matters, had in the long run catastrophically harmful results. It buttressed hopelessly muddle-headed ideas of God. Nowadays it is hard to credit that certain things early Hebrews supposed to be true about God, or set down God as saying, were obstinately or unreflectingly held to be as truly inspired and authoritative as what Christ declared. Yet so it was—at least, in theory.

It proved disastrous that the validity of Christian belief was so long linked with the dogma of the infallibility of the Bible. In consequence, during the eighteenth and nineteenth centuries, as it became increasingly impossible for educated people to take that view of the Bible, they felt intellectually estranged from professing Christian Faith. Altogether it was a misguided stage in interpretation. There were Deans still doggedly defending the wooden walls of Noah's Ark, whilst fulminating against those theologians who were talking sense. The scientists were busy men intent on their own difficult, fascinating jobs. All too few of them perceived that all too many theological pundits were fumbling *their* job, and as regards the Bible propounding rank bad theology. By the twentieth century news of the war had floated down from the altitudes of Learning to the Plain Man and his Wife in the form of a sharp alternative—'Believe the Bible from cover to cover', or else 'Believe the Scientists'. How could the Plain Man readily discern this was a false dilemma? His wife thought the children had better go to Sunday School. As for himself, if he had to make choice, scientists (he was pretty sure) knew more about geology, geography and astronomy than Genesis did. Retribution upon the sincere but mistaken theory of Biblical Infallibility was roundly declared by the Plain Man's verdict: 'The Bible is out-of-date. Not that there isn't a lot of good in the Bible. Well, that's the parson's business, not ours.' But public morality suffered as a consequence. Formerly men and women had done evil in defiance of unchallenged standards of Right and Wrong. Now the old constraints were down: God and Heaven, Hell and the Devil, had been scientifically vapourized. The West felt morally free to travel according to inclination. In Europe, the British Isles and America, many chose to go east of Suez, 'where there ain't no Ten Commandments' and the garbage of the East meets the sewage of the West. Very popular became the foolish question—'If you can't believe everything in the Bible, how can you tell what to believe?'; and the questioners did not stop for an answer. Diligent readers of Society Journals found an easy excuse: 'Really, one hasn't time to find out what the Bible's all about?' The old idea of the authority of Scripture was tossed aside; and the Public in general has made disgracefully little effort to substitute sensible use of the Bible, discover that its value is enhanced by modern knowledge, and so obtain, at least, the basic education in wise treatment of life which the Bible affords. Its contents were viewed

as unreal and remote—stained-glass windows in a church, deserving an occasional glance. Then, as the Bible became a book
unknown save to a few, speedily there arose a youthful generation
(now men and women) that 'knew not Joseph', and for whom
Moses was useful only as a joke: 'Holy Moses!' The situation
to-day would be very desperate, were it not for two facts; one that
the character of Jesus remains unscathed in the deeps of men's
hearts and conscience—like St Paul's Cathedral rising marvellously preserved amid surrounding ruins; and the other that
there is so much good in human nature—generous, eager youth;
fathers and mothers caring for their children; brave old age.

§6. *'The Clouds disperse'* (*Opportunity*)

Modern understanding of the Bible reaffirms, as quintessential
wisdom, what the intuition of the great Reformers had seen concerning it.[1] Approach the Bible in the right way and truth is to be
found therein—truth which 'finds' men; truth which should come
home as the voice of Ultimate Reality, summoning the mind to
honest thinking, awakening and enlightening the conscience,
opening the eyes of the soul to ineffable beauty: timeless wisdom,
which bespeaks the continual influence of the living God on
human life, and leads to perception of the measureless spiritual
glory manifested in Jesus Christ.

Ours is a far greater opportunity to discern the fullness of truth
and wisdom in the Faith than was given to men in earlier centuries.
To realize the magnitude of Christ in relation to the never-
changing needs of the *individual* is a task equally incumbent on all
generations. As regards the forms of *Society*, the first Christians
unreservedly declared that God in Christ judges the nations, not

---

[1] The phrase 'the Religion of the Bible'—used to signify the essential unity
of the Old and New Testaments—is avoided in this work. It is in vogue
among theologians, for whom it is convenient shorthand. But others may
readily suppose it to mean that everything said about God and morality in
the pages of the Bible somehow constitutes 'the Religion of the Bible', and
that they are expected to regard the amalgam as Infallible Truth. That notion
creates utter confusion of mind, and the reaction: 'If some parsons manage
to believe it, we don't.' Therefore for theologians to give currency to the
phrase seems to the writer unwise in the last degree. It repeats (in another
way) the inconsiderateness which at an earlier period allowed the technical
term 'Criticism' to come into general use in reference to modern methods
in Biblical study.

the nations Christ; but they could make that affirmation only from knowledge of the ancient world—which was for them essentially Jewish, Greek and Roman civilization. We are aware of other great forms of culture—Mohammedan (strong but hard); Indian (pantheistic in thought, polytheistic in practice); Chinese (whose genius the West has barbarously ignored, and must now take into account); Western nationalism and industrialism (destroying its material success for lack of moral commonsense); and the Russian experiment (whither bound?). Which of them all has been wiser than Jesus concerning the things that belong to our peace? What is truth or illusion, beauty or horror, wisdom or folly for men? From how much greater a range of evidence it is open to us to answer that the first Christians rightly saw in Christ 'the Light that lighteneth every man coming into the world'. The social consequences which follow increasing knowledge of Jesus demonstrably prove momentous; but not less so are the religious. It is fact that throughout the whole of the present world there are men and women of all its diverse races who do not feel Jesus a Palestinian of long ago, and who find in the Bible, not an ancient alien book, but religious illumination as well as challenge to noble living. This Faith speaks a universal language which the human soul understands right well.

The Sciences have provided, and will provide, fresh insight (of immense importance) concerning human nature. We are learning how intimately and intricately human behaviour is influenced by physical condition and social environment—factors very largely beyond the power of the individual to control. There is place for a wiser and kinder, although a no less firm, insistence on personal responsibility. Now the Christian claim has always been that true knowledge of Ultimate Reality (and therefore of the meaning of human life) came through Israel and became in Jesus full and final revelation of the truth. Seeing that knowledge is progressive, in what sense can a single life lived at a point in time present final truth? The answer is that the spirit of Christ will lead into truth those who seek to live as He lived. This Faith presents, not a static attitude to life and knowledge, but dynamic, vitalizing belief. And therein Christianity stands in full accord with the Hebrew mind— or, rather, with the faith of the great Prophets, from Moses onwards.

And ours is also unequalled opportunity to find God's Word for ourselves in the record of God's teaching of Israel. To-day we can appreciate (as the supercilious Gentile, imagined at the start of this chapter, failed to do) that the reasons why the Jew felt so sure Israel's history was religiously unique, and the preservation of his race 'the doing of the Lord', were mighty reasons. We can realize how strong was the Jewish claim that *What righteousness truly is* had been shown to Israel.[1] Moreover, the crudities of belief and conduct recorded in the Old Testament—which so perplexed the ancient Church that it had to have recourse to allegory—are 'difficulties' no longer, but indeed are gain. For it is helpful that the Old Testament reveals the baseness as well as the nobility in human nature; is like a clear mirror reflecting the education of a race. The 'education of the race' is repeated in each individual— that should be remembered. Let a modern take note even of 'the abominations of the Canaanites', and he should become more quick to see how many to-day still 'do according to their ways'— ferocious, greedy, unconsciously polytheistic. Let a modern observe how 'stiff-necked' was early Israel, and he should find himself wondering—'Am I less custom-ridden?' So much negatively. Look at the gentler scenes in Israel's story. Is not the Spirit of God there to be seen moving upon the face of chaotic waters, and the voice of God audible, saying to the darkness 'Let there be light'? The road which Israel travelled led to Christ, although the travellers did not know the end from the beginning.[2] But we, who know—as we mark each faltering onward step—

[1] Jewish monotheism and ethical ideals have been upheld by good Jews throughout the Christian era despite persecutions and temptations that would have broken the staunchness of any other race. Gentiles are acutely conscious of Jewish faults. Those faults are largely of Gentile making. Jewish virtues have been silently and persistently nurtured within their own homes. That is too little known. Those who are surprised by the remark, and inclined to question its accuracy, should read Israel Abrahams' volume, *Jewish Life in the Middle Ages*.

[2] Because of its technical meaning in biological science, it is desirable to avoid the word 'Evolution' in reference to the course taken by Hebrew Religion. Development of belief is manifest as the centuries passed, but its stages had not the inevitability with which station succeeds station on a railway line. It does not follow that pure monotheism was the natural, or necessary, sequel to monolatry. The great changes were due to men of faith and courage interpreting events and discerning a Moral Order as witness to One Divine Reality, and the supreme achievement was due to the Prophets. As Söderblom puts it: 'The religion of the Prophets is not a stage in the development of religion, but a phenomenon by itself.' (*The Nature of Revelation*, p. 30.)

should everywhere perceive the guardian, guiding, hand of God: 'When Israel was a child, then I loved him, and called my son out of Egypt.' In the New Testament there is an exquisite phrase concerning Jesus, which truly sums up the story of Israel: *Out of darkness into His marvellous light*. To us is given opportunity to watch the passing of that darkness, the coming of the dawn—aware that even the earliest rays of light streamed from Him who is forever the Way, the Truth, and the Life.

Can it justly be said that we are making diligent use of our opportunity, or should Conscience call us to account? It is true that a century ago, in face of advancing scientific discoveries, misconceived defence of the Bible's inerrancy precipitated a landslide of incredulity across the trunk road to Christian belief.[1] But alert and wise people ought to have bull-dozed that debris off the road long ago. It is not the fault of modern Biblical scholars that the enlightening facts about the value of the Bible remain so little known. Book after book, intended to help every type of reader, has appeared. But for the most part even the educated and the religiously disposed leave them to the clergy to purchase. Sipping spoonfuls occasionally from sermons in Church may be a good tonic, but is no way for responsible people to set about gaining adequate knowledge of a vital subject. The kindliness, decency and devotion to daily duty, shown by multitudes, is basically the Christlike spirit. But to a calamitous extent the West is living on religious capital instead of interest, so much so that cheques it would like to draw on the children's behalf are ceasing to be cashed. There is widespread a degree of ignorance concerning the essential convictions of the Faith, their sources in the Bible, and their effect in history, which is a menace to good intentions. The Fighting Forces were a cross-section of the public. Ask the padres what they found regarding knowledge of the Bible? If intelligent people gave to study of the Faith one ten-thousandth part of the hours expended on daily politics, finance, the latest catastrophe, sport and fashions —the will for good in the world would be immensely strengthened and enlightened.

[1] Clerical obscurantism in the past did much harm. So also did the rashness with which some scientists dismissed as untenable any spiritual view of life. The lesson should have been learnt, and ought not to have to be repeated. Debatable issues should be treated with a finer mutual respect between scientists and theologians than in the regrettable nineteenth century.

§7. 'The Open Vision' (Responsibility)

Opportunity spells responsibility: 'Walk while ye have the light, that the darkness overtake you not.' Our great opportunity to regain and reassert the first clarity and ardour of the essential Faith is also urgent responsibility. For two frightful wars have made it plain enough that the use to which men will put the resources modern knowledge places at their disposal depends on their view of the right ends of life. Voice after voice of great leaders, on this side of the Atlantic and on that, during the war and after it, declare that what civilization everywhere needs is a great faith in righteousness. Differences as to method (for all their importance) are secondary questions, provided there can be trust among the nations that their final aims are good. Then there is hope of defeating the ruthless selfishness of those who remain unchanged in mind by the sacrifice of brave men's lives, untouched in heart by the continuing miseries of millions of men women and children.

Ours has become appalling responsibility. 'To-day the fundamental power of the universe, the power manifested in the sunshine that has been recognized from the remotest ages as the sustaining force of earthly life, has been entrusted to human hands. In a most terrible sense it is a choice of life and death.'[1] We are hopefully bidden to expect that the skill of scientists will ere long make atomic energy available for peaceful purposes—unless meantime there should be war waged with atomic bombs. Nineteen hundred years ago the basic energy of the *spiritual* universe was made available in our Faith. Mankind has been neither skilful nor swift in relating that energy to basic needs. It is time that we should release its power. It is time that we understood very clearly just what is this Faith concerning God and duty; time that we knew exactly why the Apostles gave thanks to God for Jesus Christ. If we do not so much as understand what is meant by saying that in Christ was fulfilled 'the Hope of Israel', we shall not be keen-sighted about Him now as 'Lord of our life and Hope of every nation'.

---

[1] *The Times* (London)—the words were written in the week after the first atomic bomb fell on Hiroshima.

For 20 years after the start of this century volumes bearing some such title as *The Theology of the Old Testament* virtually ceased to appear. They had rested on insufficiently sifted data. Time was needed to clarify the results of literary, archaeological and comparative-religious studies. The Old Testament does not exhibit Systematic Theology. Its Writings witness to beliefs by which the Hebrews lived, developing in the vicissitudes of history. Ought not the religion of Israel, therefore, to be described rather than appraised, and be treated as an entity in itself: it led both to Judaism and Christianity? Meantime Biblical research was eleucidating the actualities in Israel's history. And the Old Testament cannot sensibly be isolated from the New, or the New from the Old. The Bible began again to be considered as a unity:[1] in the sense that its contents sufficiently furnish evidence to support the claim (relevant for all men) that here in history God imparted, and Israel gradually apprehended, valid knowledge of Ultimate Truth and Ultimate Right. From the 1920's books about the Old Testament other than strictly analytic and descriptive reappeared.[2] 'Then', says Hahn, 'slowly, but gathering momentum as the implications of the new approach awakened interest, the discussion of theological problems took on an increasing importance, until in the last decade it predominated over the discussion of all other problems.'[3] Due recognition is being given to the profound significance of the Prophets' religious consciousness and conscience. Differences, hitherto inadequately perceived, between Hebrew and Greek psychology and terminology are seen to have affected Christian Dogma radically.[4] Eichrodt treated covenant-relationship as the unifying concept in the Bible.[5] Some writers prefer to indicate theological inferences in close relation to the historical stages[6]—in which category the present volume aims to be. It stresses the superlative quality of the great Prophets and points to the Christian sequel, but it also urges that in the early stages God's purpose should be discerned: 'When Israel was a child then I led him, and called my son out of Egypt.'

[1] E.g. Rowley, *The Unity of the Bible*; Dodd, *The Bible Today*.

[2] The shift of emphasis is illustrated by S. A. Cook's later books (*The Old Testament: A Reinterpretation*, 1936; and *The 'Truth' of the Bible*, 1938) in comparison with his survey in *The Cambridge Ancient History*, Vol. III, 1925.

[3] Hahn, *The Old Testament in Modern Research* (Philadelphia, 1954).

[4] Cf. Snaith, *Distinctive Ideas of the Old Testament*.

[5] *Theologie des Alten Testaments* (1933–9).

[6] Dodd, *The Authority of the Bible*; H. W. Robinson, *Inspiration and Revelation in the Old Testament*. Also (in his latest work, 1957) Von Rad, *Theologie des Alten Testaments*, I.

PART II

THE RELIGION OF THE HEBREWS

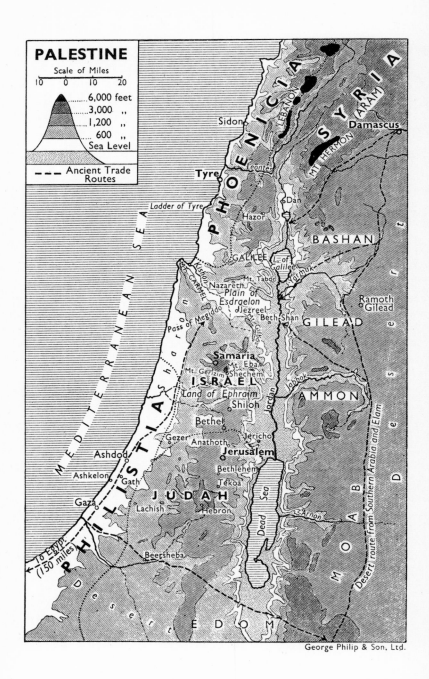

PALESTINE

Scale of Miles
10   0   10   20

6,000 feet
3,000 ,,
1,200 ,,
600 ,,
Sea Level

Ancient Trade Routes

MEDITERRANEAN SEA

PHOENICIA

Sidon

LEBANON

SYRIA (ARAM)

Damascus

MT HERMON

Tyre

Orontes

Ladder of Tyre

Dan

Hazor

BASHAN

GALILEE

L. of Galilee

Kishon

CARMEL

Nazareth

Mt. Tabor

Yarmuk

Plain of Esdraelon

Ramoth Gilead

Jezreel

Beth-Shan

Pass of Megiddo

Kelana

GILEAD

Sharon

Samaria

Mt. Ebal

Mt. Gerizim   Shechem

ISRAEL

Jabbok

AMMON

Land of Ephraim

Shiloh

Jordan

Bethel

Gezer

Anathoth

Jericho

Ashdod

Jerusalem

Ashkelon

Gath

Bethlehem

Tekoa

Gaza

JUDAH

Lachish

Hebron

Dead Sea

Arnon

PHILISTIA

To Egypt (150 miles)

Beersheba

M O A B

Desert route from Southern Arabia and Elam

Desert

E D O M

George Philip & Son, Ltd.

CHAPTER V

THE LAND OF ISRAEL AND ITS PEOPLES

Palestine (or, to give it its ancient name, Canaan) has been the most influential of all countries in religious history.[1] But it did not owe that distinction to the genius of its inhabitants in general. 'The Semitic natives, Amorite, Hebrew, or Arab', writes R. A. S. Macalister, 'never invented anything: they assimilated all the elements of their civilization from without. This principle is the key to the interpretation of all remains of antiquity found in the land.... From first to last there was not a native potter in Palestine who could so much as invent a new design to paint on his waterpots. There was not an armourer who could invent a new pattern of sword or arrowhead. The modern peasants live in houses practically identical in style and construction with those which sheltered the peasants of 2000 B.C.—a community of white ants could not be more unprogressive. It is the last country in the world, perhaps, where it would be natural for us to expect the development of an original conception of divinity so totally at variance with "the gods of the nations" as that which we find in the writings of the Hebrew prophets.'[2]

§1. *The Land of Israel*

Not all of Palestine was possessed by Israel, and Palestine itself is minute in size—from north to south about 130 miles; from west to east about 70, i.e. some 40 miles from the Mediterranean to the Valley of the Jordan, and a further 25 miles from Jordan to the desert border on the east.[3] Its western boundary is the sea, and the

---

[1] *Palestine* (i.e. The land of the *Philistines*) is a Greek designation, which came into general use about the period of the Greek historian, Herodotus, 450 B.C.

[2] *History of Civilization in Palestine*, pp. 31, 32.

[3] Cf. Schofield, *Historical Background of the Bible* (1937). G. A. Smith's detailed survey (*Historical Geography of the Holy Land*, 1894, many subsequent editions) is unsurpassed in the beauty of its descriptions.

coast is almost devoid of harbours. On the east it is bounded by
the north Arabian desert; and on the south again by the desert
(Edomitic), which begins a few miles south of the town of Gaza
and extends to the Delta of the Nile about 150 miles distant.
North of Palestine was the Land of the Syrians or Aramaeans,[1] its
boundary in mountainous country not precisely defined.[2] But so
diversified in character is this tiny country that it has been called
'a world in miniature'.

The physical features of Canaan are easily memorized: (i) Along
the Mediterranean border runs a plain about 15 miles wide. This
was the 'Land of the Philistines' up to the point where the pro-
montory of Mount Carmel juts out to within a mile of the sea;
farther north (west of Galilee and Syria) it was possessed by the
Phoenicians. (ii) East of this sea-plain rises a belt of low hills
through which, especially in the northern and southern ends of the
plain, valleys lead up to the most conspicuous feature of the
country—the central range of mountains, approximately 2000 ft.
above sea-level, which (with one break, the Plain of Esdraelon)
stretches directly south from the Syrian Lebanons to the southern
border of Canaan. (iii) The southern part of this central hill-
country is plateau-land and became the kingdom of Judah; its one
important town and capital, Jerusalem. The central part (more
rugged and broken than Judah) was the heart of the kingdom of
Israel, having in it Samaria which Omri built in 887 B.C. to be its

[1] More anciently called 'the Land of Amor'.
[2] The east-to-west valley of the Leontes and the range of hills from the
Ladder of Tyre on the coast across to the snow-clad mountain of Hermon
(9000 ft. high) constituted an effective physical demarcation. The natural outlet
of the Syrian hill-country ran northwards by the great valley of the Orontes,
and its communications with Canaan were not directly north to south but
circuitous—either by sea or from the north-east by the great route which
traversed the desert from Damascus to reach the Jordan north of the Sea of
Galilee, where the great Canaanite fortress camp of Hazor was a dominating
position as early as 1600 B.C. (cp. Joshua xi. 10). Thence tracks led westwards
across Galilee to the Phoenician ports, but the main thoroughfare continued
south-east, past the Horns of Hattin, to the Plain of Esdraelon and across the
foothills of Samaria by the famous Pass of Megiddo to descend into the
coastal plain of Canaan. Phythian-Adams, op. cit. p. 138, notes that when
the Egyptian king, Thutmose III, in 1479 crushed the Amorites in battle at
Megiddo, instead of attempting to invade Syria by driving direct north
through the hills, he embarked his army at Acre and landed it on the Syrian
coast 100 miles farther north.

capital. (iv) Twenty miles north of Samaria the mountain 'back-bone' of Palestine is broken across by the wide Plain of Esdraelon which traverses the land (west-to-east) from the coast north of Mount Carmel to the Valley of the Jordan south of the Sea of Galilee. (v) North of the Plain of Esdraelon the mountains resume —some of the highest points reaching an elevation of 4000 ft. In later history this region was known as Galilee; its northern border being the Syrian country. (vi) The cultivated or pastoral tract (some 25 miles wide) between the Jordan and the desert boundary of Canaan on the east was, in Biblical times, divided into three principal regions—the northern area known as Bashan (opposite Galilee), the central as Gilead (opposite Samaria), and the southern as Moab (opposite Judah). Of these, only Gilead was firmly held by the Israelites. Bashan is lofty plateau—part of it stony and barren, but the rest magnificent soil for grain. The mountainous territory of Gilead and Moab rises to heights of over 2000 ft. above Jordan; Gilead being country so rugged that it is almost entirely pastoral in character, whilst Moab afforded greater agricultural opportunity but was also famous as land for sheep-rearing. All this territory east of Jordan declines gradually in height to the level of its eastern fringe, the north Arabian desert. (vii) The most remarkable topographical feature of Palestine is the Valley of the Jordan.[1] The river takes its start 1700 ft. high in the Lebanons, and flows southwards through the Lake of Galilee. Even at that comparatively short distance from its source it has dropped to 700 ft. below the level of the Mediterranean. Thence its course runs due south for 65 miles to terminate in the Dead Sea, which it enters at no less than 1300 ft. below sea-level: and the Dead Sea itself is 1200 ft. deep! Thus the Valley of Jordan is an astonishing rift in the earth's surface. South-west of the Dead Sea the rift (here known as the Wadi Arabah) continues on to the Red Sea. No river issues from the Dead Sea to fertilize the Wadi. The torrid heat evaporates the Jordan's incoming stream, and the waters of the Sea are so salt that nothing can live in them, save the tetanus bacillus. Overhung by the bare and precipitous heights of Judah on the west, and by the rose-red mountain-wall of Moab on the east, the Dead Sea is a place of mingled beauty and terror: 'this awful hollow, this bit of the infernal regions come up to the surface, this hell with the sun shining into it.'[2]

[1] See Nelson Glueck, *The River Jordan*.   [2] G. A. Smith, op. cit. p. 504.

It is important to realize how impressive are the mountainous regions of Palestine—Galilee, Gilead, Samaria and Judah; for it was there that the Israelites had their homes; and it is to the People of Israel alone that Palestine owes its pre-eminence in religious history. One has only to read the Old Testament to perceive how poetically sensitive were the Israelites to the loftiness of their land. In the vivid words of Sir G. A. Smith:

The Hebrews were men who for the most part looked down upon their prospects, and painted their scenes from above....The narrow platform of their life fell eastward to an invisible depth....Their stage slopes away from them, every apparition upon it is described as *coming up*. And there is that singular sense which I do not think appears in any other literature, but which pervades the Old Testament, of seeing mountain-tops from above. Israel *treadeth upon his high-places*, as if mountain-tops were a common road; and *Jehovah marcheth upon his high-places*, as if it were a usual thing to see clouds below, and yet on the top of hills....We owe to the high station of Israel those long approaches and very distant prospects both of war and peace; the trails of armies across the plains in fire and smoke, the land spreading very far forth, and, though Israel was no maritime people, the wonderful visions of the coast and the sea.[1]

Its differences in elevation give Palestine great diversity in climate, and corresponding variety in its products. The coastal plain and the foothills are sub-tropical; the highlands (both east and west of Jordan) bracing, with wide changes of temperature between day and night, winter and summer; the Valley of Jordan and the Dead Sea Plain fully tropical. Moreover it should be noted that in antiquity the fertility was greater than it is now; for the ranges of Lebanon were clothed in forests of cedar and pine which induced a heavier rainfall. Moreover, Canaan itself was richer in trees and shrubs,[2] and its soil better protected against erosion by the labour of its inhabitants terracing the hillsides to make vineyards. The land afforded pasturage for flocks of sheep and goats; and also for cattle, especially east of the Jordan. Grain flourished in many parts, and fruit-trees were abundant, particularly olive and fig and vine. An Egyptian traveller in 2000 B.C.

[1] Op. cit. pp. 103 f.
[2] Grievous damage to the vegetation of Palestine was caused in the last century by a Turkish law which imposed a tax on the number of trees a man possessed—a regulation, says Schofield, 'as foolish as the British window-tax of earlier times'. (*Historical Background of the Bible*, p. 9.)

records that he found there 'wine more plentiful than water, copious honey and oil, all kinds of fruit and cereals, and countless cattle'. No perennial rivers, however, meander through the hills of Canaan down to the plains. There are numerous gushing springs, but the brooks to which these give rise dry up in the heat of summer just when they are necessary.[1] This is a most important point. If the land is to yield its increase, rain must fall from heaven to counteract the scorching heat of the summer and promote growth in the spring. Rain usually does fall, but *not with unfailing regularity*; and that fact had a deep effect on the religious outlook of the inhabitants.[2] They were conscious of the contrast with Egypt's reliable crops, where the Nile can be counted on almost invariably to irrigate the fields: 'The land, whither thou goest in to possess it, is not as the land of Egypt, from whence ye came out, where thou sowedst thy seed, and wateredst it with thy foot, as a garden of herbs: but the land, whither ye go over to possess it, is a land of hills and valleys, and drinketh water of the rain of heaven: a land which the Lord thy God careth for; the eyes of the Lord thy God are always upon it, from the beginning of the year even unto the end of the year.'[3] But far more vividly (and how thankfully) the Hebrews could compare its richness with the austerity of the desert. As R. A. S. Macalister forcibly puts it, 'the promise of "a land flowing with milk and honey" was not made to . . . beef-fed excursionists, coming from cultivated and developed lands of the modern West, but to tribes of half-starved wanderers, fighting their way from oasis to oasis over sterile sands'.[4] But even the modern traveller may well be conscious of the quality of this country: 'Let Canaan be seen with the year at the flood, with the rush of colour across the field, the flush of green on the desert, and in imagination clothe again the stony terraces with the vines which in ancient times trailed from foot to summit of many of the hills—then, even though your eye be western, you will feel the charm and intoxication of the land.'[5] To its ancient inhabitants it could not fail to seem an exceeding goodly land. And yet, despite the comparative luxuriance and great diversity of their land, extreme lack of originality was the outstanding characteristic of the Palestinians. How can that curious fact be explained?

[1] Cp. Jer. xv. 18.
[3] Deut. xi. 10–12.
[5] G. A. Smith, op. cit. p. 84.
[2] Cp. pp. 144, 149.
[4] Macalister, op. cit. p. 29.

The situation of Palestine in relation to other lands affords a weighty answer. It was too much a 'bone of contention' for other Peoples to keep out of it and let its inhabitants become a homogeneous race, developing specific charateristics. Palestine was traversed by two great routes of communication. One, following the coast plain of Canaan, was of vital importance; for the sea on the west and the desert on the east made Palestine a *bridge*—the only line of communication between Egypt to the south and the Great Powers to the north.[1] From the dawn of history their armies and merchants moved through its narrow land, like a tide canalized into a single channel. The other great route traversed the Plain of Esdraelon from the Jordan to the Mediterranean; and it carried the riches of the Arabian caravans across to the Phoenician seaports (Tyre and Sidon).[2] Thus Canaan, besides its exposure to the ambitions of mighty neighbours north and south, also lay open to the envious eyes of the men of the deserts on the south and on the east.[3]

[1] Cp. Isa. xix. 23. Starting from Egypt the route (sometimes termed 'the Way of the East') crossed the desert to Canaan and, following its coast to south of Mount Carmel, climbed the foothills by the famous Pass of Megiddo, to descend into the Plain of Esdraelon. There its traffic could branch westwards to the Mediterranean at Acre to be sent overseas or north along the coast by the difficult ascent known as the 'Ladder of Tyre' to the great Phoenician ports. The main route, however, passed across the Plain of Esdraelon to the northern end of the Sea of Galilee at Kinnereth, on to the focal town and fortress-camp at Hazor, whence it crossed the Jordan and traversed the desert to reach Damascus and eventually the great centres of population in Mesopotamia and Asia Minor.

[2] Cp. Isa. lx. 6, 7. The incense trade from southern Arabia was alone of astonishing value. (See Freya Stark, *Southern Gates of Arabia*.) The main route from southern Arabia to Damascus and beyond followed the eastern (Transjordanian) border of Palestine. But the caravans might turn westwards from the Edomite city of Petra across the southern border of Judah to arrive at Gaza and the Philistine cities on the coast or might ascend through Hebron to Jerusalem and the Canaanite hill-towns; or (farther north along the great desert route) they could enter Palestine by way of the Plain of Esdraelon and the roads through Galilee.

[3] From time to time violent irruptions of the desert-dwellers (the Israelite invasions are a case in point) took place; for although a single nomad-clan can scarcely ever overcome the defences of a civilized district or fortified town, if the nomads—rendered desperate by famine or drought or impelled by some fanatical enthusiast—attack in large numbers, 'they are as difficult to keep out as a sandstorm'. Peaceful infiltration of nomad families into the fringes of the settled land has ever been, and continues to be, a small but cumulatively important factor in the peopling of Canaan. (An illuminating

Palestine had no choice but to become a settling-ground of races. In the course of many centuries commerce, conquering armies and tidal-waves of folk-migrations, deposited within its narrow borders layer on layer of inhabitants of diverse racial origin. What chance had its settlers to become a distinctive nation? Even into its mountains the successive invaders penetrated. Moreover, the configuration of these highlands is such that their inhabitants tend to isolate themselves in small groups, concerned only with petty local interests. In comparison with the plains, the heights presented a bare possibility of creating a national unity. The stimulating mountain climate bred men of fine physique, 'at once tough and adaptable'. The highlanders were not wholly cut off from culture, yet were not trampled under foot by the march of civilization; they were, so to speak, 'in the world, but not of the world'. Nevertheless, men dwelt in those hills for 2000 years before the rise of Israel, and proved themselves incorrigibly divisive and uninspired. Even on the heights of Canaan national coherence, and original qualities, were no more than a possibility. Israel, and Israel alone, translated the possible into the actual; and this feat Israel accomplished only in virtue of the element of genius in its religious beliefs.

§2. The Peoples of Canaan

(i) *The Aborigines*. There are impressive remains of Canaan's inhabitants during the Neolithic period—notably the menhirs, dolmens and stone-circles, that are abundant east of the Jordan; aboriginal habitations on the hill of Gezer overlooking the Philistine plain, and extensive limestone caverns near Hebron in Judah which afforded Stone-Age men strongholds from which the Canaanites were unable to expel them down to the coming of Israel. The cave-men of Gezer were short of stature; but those of the Hebron caverns exceptionally tall—Hebrew tradition said that their envoys, sent to spy out the land, were scared by their size: 'we were in our own sight as grasshoppers!'[1] That these Stone-Age men were not *Semites* is certain from their custom of burning

description, alike of the process of steady penetration, and of large-scale movements by the Arab tribes towards Palestine in recent years, may be found in Garstang, *The Heritage of Solomon*, pp. 42–8.)

[1] Num. xiii. 33.

E F

their dead and of offering swine as sacrifices, and they can have had little or no influence on the subsequent inhabitants.

(ii) *The First (Amorite) Civilization.* It was formerly supposed that the first civilized race in Canaan (using bronze, able to build walled towns) were—not Amorites—but northerners, their original home probably in the Caucasus mountains, and their name *Hurrians*: the Egyptians called them *Haru*, and the later Palestinians knew them as the *Horites* or *Hivites*.[1] Four fortified towns in Judah were associated with them. But about 3000 B.C. Semitic tribes erupted from the north Arabian desert, to become known in history as the *Amurru* or *Amorites*. They occupied Syria. They pressed into Mesopotamia, and with its earlier Sumerian inhabitants created a great Sumerian-Semitic kingdom there, having Babylon as its chief city. They spread also into the hill-country of Palestine. About 2750 B.C. it appears that another incursion of desert men into Palestine took place, coming this time from the south—the movement perhaps due to disturbances starting in distant southern Arabia. They penetrated Galilee,[2] occupied the coastal plain, and eventually had much to do with the rise of the great Phoenician ports. It is convenient to term these invaders *the Canaanites*. Amorites-Canaanites became a real civilization.[3]

---

[1] Since *Hor* in Hebrew means *cave*, it had long been supposed that the Biblical references to Horites or Hivites denoted descendants of the aborigines in Canaan. G. A. Speiser (*Ethnic Movements in the Near East*, and *Mesopotamian Origins*) has shown that, almost always, the name denotes Hurrians. Remarkable correspondence between Hurrian law and custom and the patriarchal tales in Genesis has been pointed out by Speiser, Albright and others. The parallels include certain details of which it can be said that writers of a much later period could not have invented them. The word *Hivites*, so prominent in the Hebrew traditions of the pre-Israelite population of Canaan, is a late, scribal, error for *Horites*, due to confusion of a single letter. The names *Perizzites* and *Jebusites* would also appear to have no racial significance; the first word probably means *villagers* (see *Record and Revelation*, pp. 360–6), although Garstang (*Heritage of Solomon*, p. 26) is inclined to think that the Perizzites were a non-Semitic element in the population who lived in the wooded hills between Shechem and Bethlehem.

[2] Cp. Garstang, op. cit. pp. 19, 23, 31, 32; especially in reference to the strategic Amorite centre at Hazor.

[3] They were in contact with Egypt and the great countries in Asia Minor and Mesopotamia at a very early date, sometimes to their discomfiture. Thus the Mesopotamian kings, Sargon of Agade (*c.* 2870 B.C.), and Hammurabi of Babylon, *c.* 1700 (whose fame, however, rests less on military conquest than on his promulgation of a remarkable Code of Law), claimed that their rule

Their towns were powerfully fortified, and it is likely they first invented that invaluable device—a *consonantal* alphabet, as distinct from the cumbersome Babylonian cuneiform and the Egyptian hieroglyphic writing. For 1000 years (3000–2000 B.C.) Canaan was in their hands, and they remained the solid *substratum* of the later population. Fifteen hundred years later the Prophet Ezekiel (xvi. 3) reproached the lax citizens of Hebrew Jerusalem by saying of the city, 'Thy birth and thy nativity is of the land of the Canaanite; the Amorite was thy father, and thy mother was an Hittite'.

(iii) *The Hittites.* By 2000 B.C. a horse-riding race of European and Central Asian origin, known as *the Hittites*, had established a very powerful kingdom in Asia Minor on the Anatolian plateau; its capital at Boghaz-Keui (Hattushah). About 1750 B.C., under Hittite leadership, a huge invasion came south into Palestine, carrying in with it numbers of Aramaean (Syrian) desert tribes. Marvellously the host managed to cross the desert south of Palestine, and burst through the defences of the Nile. For 200 years Hittite kings controlled nearly all Egypt, to the disgust of its cultured ancient people, who called their conquerors *the Hyksos* ('Princes of the desert'?). The triumph was due to the Hittites' horses and chariots. The slow-moving Egyptian infantry could not cope with the 'blitzkrieg' methods of their adversaries. Hittite settlements were consolidated at various places in Canaan, notable among them Hebron (Gen. xxiii. 2, 10) and Jerusalem.

(iv) *Egyptian ascendancy.* In 1580 the Egyptians drove the Hyksos out of Egypt, and ended their control of Palestine and Syria. Conscious now of the need to sustain those countries as a buffer-state against the Hittite kingdom, the Egyptians garrisoned strategic towns in Palestine, and (less effectively) those in Syria. Certainly for the ensuing 350 years (with one short interval) Egypt ruled Palestine. But Egyptian suzerainty was prompted by motives of pride and military security, not by the need to find *lebensraum* for a swarming population anxious to migrate from the

included the land of the Amorites. Pepy I, King of Egypt in 2800, sent an army into Palestine, and records the event in terms suggesting that thus the natives would learn their insignificance in the scheme of things! An exiled Egyptian grandee, Sinuhe (*c.* 2100), left an account of his sojourn among them, indicating his agreeable surprise at finding that the uncultured Amorite was quite an estimable person.

Nile Valley. Hence their domination did not result in a strong admixture of Egyptian blood among the Palestinians. Although worship of Egyptian gods was fostered, even in matters of religion and culture Egyptian influence in Canaan was that of a ruling class, and more superficial than might be expected.

(v) *Habiru-Hebrews.* The few years 1375–1359 B.C. were stormy times—because on the throne of the Hittites reigned a conquering king and thorough-paced liar (Shubbiluliumma, his glorious name), and on the throne of Egypt a religious idealist, philosopher, artist—*Ikhnaton* (to whose effort to reform the ways of Egypt earlier reference has been made). The Hittite king, ostensibly friendly, worked craftily. He corrupted the bribable among the governors of Egypt's garrison towns in Syria and Palestine, until the loyalists of them knew not whom to trust; and stirred up the desert tribes to essay invasion.[1] By great good fortune we have recovered correspondence of the time from the Hittite archives as well as from Ikhnaton's capital at Tell-el-Amarna; and thus understand the situation vividly. The Egyptian Foreign Office was slow in answering the contradictory, mutually accusing, agitated letters from its provincial governors and, when it answered, answered in platitudes. So Egypt fumbled the crisis, was tricked, battered and swamped out of Syria and Palestine; and Ikhnaton gets all the blame.[2] The Habiru poured into the land, the towns revolted, and Egyptian rule collapsed.

Now *Habiru* is philologically equivalent to *Hebrews*, and the theory was naturally urged that here was non-Biblical record of the Biblical tradition of the conquest led by Joshua. But *Hebrews* was a term of wide application meaning Nomads, Wanderers.[3]

---

[1] Of special interest are the letters sent by Abdi-Khiba, the genuinely loyal governor of Jerusalem. His name means 'Servant of Khiba', a Hittite goddess.

[2] Perhaps he deserves it: we have to recognize that he was no Cromwell. Perhaps the fury of the Theban priesthood and other high aristocrats in Egypt against Ikhnaton's reformed Faith paralysed the executive, and the armies could not be set in motion. A hyper-ingenious 'guess in the dark' is that the tradition of the Hebrew Joseph is memory that Ikhnaton installed this Palestinian foreigner in power, and that Joseph—pro-Semitic Premier!— kept the facts from the King. Breasted (*C.A.H.* vol. II, pp. 126, 131) points out that Ikhnaton had in his service an 'able organizer and skilful man of affairs', in the person of the Egyptian Harmhab, who also held the confidence of the Theban priesthood, and who gained the throne of Egypt in 1350 B.C.

[3] Hooke (*Record and Revelation*, p. 359) comments: 'The range of the term Habiru, both in time and geographical distribution, is far too wide to

There are weighty, even conclusive, reasons for holding that the Aramean Habiru who plagued Canaan in the 14th century cannot simply be equated with the Aramean Hebrews whom Joshua led across the River Jordan. That historically momentous incursion happened probably a century later: the Exodus from Egypt about 1270, the penetration into Canaan about 1240.

But it does not follow that these Aramaean Habiru-Hebrews have no connexion at all with the Hebrews of Biblical fame. The Biblical echo of the Habiru incursion is heard in certain of the traditions concerning Jacob, Joseph, and their 'children'. The view here taken is that some of the Habiru families migrated into the borders of Egypt (perhaps in a time of drought).[1] *Their* descendants would be the Hebrews in Egypt—whom Moses brought out of Egypt, and Joshua brought into Canaan. But others of the Habiru invaders settled permanently in Canaan, and *their* descendants became constituent tribes in the brotherhood of the historic People of Israel which eventually formed in Canaan: these were the tribes of Asher, Zebulun, Dan, and perhaps also Issachar and Naphtali.[2] This means that we have to envisage an older

allow of any simple identification with the Hebrews', i.e. of Joshua's invasion. And S. A. Cook (in *C.A.H.* vol. II, pp. 356 f.) sums up his opinion thus: 'The events in the Amarna letters cannot be identified with Joshua's invasion from the south without entirely stultifying the biblical narrative....There is no agreement between the letters and the Old Testament as regards the names of the kings of Jerusalem,...Lachish,...Hazor....The divergence between the conditions as described in the Old Testament and the contemporary evidence is crucial.' Garstang, whose excavations at Jericho showed that a powerful city there had been destroyed in 1400, was entirely confident that the Habiru invasion and Joshua's were one and the same movement, and he put forward an ingenious view to meet the very grave objection that some 300 years must in that case have elapsed before the time of Saul and David. Vincent (whose opinion in such matters is weighty) does not accept Garstang's conclusion that Jericho was destroyed in 1400. Even if a powerful Jericho was ruined at that time, there now seems to be evidence that a weaker city arose on its site. Joshua's triumph may record *its* downfall. Finally, Canaanite memory of the 1400 disaster may have been mistakenly worked into the Hebrew story of their success (*c.* 1340) in entering Canaan across Jordan.

[1] An Egyptian record shows that, at the time that Habiru tribesmen were harassing their garrisons in Palestine, starving nomads were begging at the frontier of Egypt for permission to enter and obtain food. (Cp. Gen. xlii ff.)

[2] Two (Habiru?) tribes known as Simeon and Levi experienced a disaster in conflict with Canaanites at Shechem so serious that they were broken as coherent tribes, their surviving families making their way into southern Canaan and some (almost certainly some families of Levi) going on into

'Israel' in Canaan before the Biblical People of Israel; and a very important inference follows, on which S. A. Cook rightly lays stress in these words: 'Not all the Hebrews or Israelites went down into Egypt; those who remained in the land would have traditions of settlement very different from those who took part in the Exodus; and of these traditions Genesis preserves fragments.'[1]

(vi) *Egyptian control renewed.* In 1314 Egypt, under Sety I, recovered Palestine, and held it for a century. But the Hittites were able to strengthen their hold on Syria. In 1288 at Kadesh in Syria one of history's famous battles took place between the Hittites and the Egyptians (under Rameses II) in which only the courage of Rameses averted catastrophic disaster. Then, dramatically, in 1272 the rivalry of the two Powers ended in a Treaty of Peace. Behind that fact lies a story: both Powers had realized they had to face a life-and-death struggle against a mass migration of peoples coming from the north and across the Mediterranean.

(vii) *The Philistines.* The ancient Minoan-Mycenaean civilization (its chief centre at Cnossos in Crete) had been disrupted by European races pressing south. Conditions in the eastern Mediterranean now became chaotic—what with the newcomers seeking plunder and land, and dispossessed peoples in search of another place to settle. The mass migration overwhelmed the Hittites. Between 1225–1215 B.C. the Egyptians were struggling to beat off attacks of 'sea-peoples' who had crossed into North Africa and were thrusting along the coast of Libya towards the Nile—exactly like Rommel's army to the battle of El-Alamein! Then, like an irresistible stream of lava, in 1192 an enormous host —transported by ships following the coast, and on land with great

Egypt. Tribes called Asher, Zebulun, and Dan seem at first to have found locations in Judaean country, but at a later date these—as also the tribes Issachar and Naphtali—are mentioned as settled on the coast north of Carmel and inland in Galilee. An Egyptian notice in the reign of Sety I, *c.* 1300, seems clearly to refer to Asher as settled on the Galilaean coast, where the tribe was located at the time of the Hebrews' battle against Sisera celebrated in Judges v. 17. The same verse refers to Dan as a coastal tribe. On the other hand, Judges xviii relates a migration at some time of Danites from Judah to Laish in Galilee, near the springs of Jordan.

[1] In *C.A.H.* vol. II, p. 360. Cook observes that certain genealogies in I Chron., and certain traditions regarding the patriarchs and their deeds, 'allow no room for any account of a sojourn in Egypt and an exodus; and they presuppose some considerable body of tradition which has disappeared in favour of the now prevailing outline'.

wheeled carts that carried the women and children—poured along the shores of Syria into Phoenicia and on into the coast-plain of Palestine. An important part of the warriors went by the name of *Pelesati* (*Philistines*). The army and navy of Rameses III met and dispersed the multitude in a battle near the border of Egypt. But the Egyptians were exhausted, and had to be content to keep possession of their Nile Valley and allow the Philistines to settle in the fortified towns of Canaan's coastal plain. The Philistines were neither Europeans nor Semites, but men of the Cretan-Mycenaean culture.[1] Therefore they added to the already complex population of Canaan a new element and a highly advanced culture. 'Uncircumcised Philistines', said the Hebrews, scornfully; but they learnt to their cost that Philistines were first-class fighting men.[2]

(viii) *The Hebrew 'Conquest'*. This was the stage in Palestinian history (so the writer believes) when the Aramaean tribes who were the invaders ('Hebrews') led by Joshua crossed the Jordan, and occupied the Plain of Jericho.[3] After a time they got up to the central highlands (probably by the Valley of Achor), where they surprised themselves by defeating a Canaanite force gathered against them. They managed to get possession of the little towns of Gibeon, Bethel and Ai (the last by a ruse, after suffering a defeat which rather shocked them, for they lost 36 men). They were few in numbers, but great in spirit (for they had been under the influence of Moses), and their entry into Canaan was the most influential racial movement in history—although it was so numerically small a happening. Probably the invaders amounted to some six or seven thousand persons.[4]

The Hebrews had gained no more than a foothold beyond Jordan—but they clung to it: existing as tent-dwelling shepherd-warriors in the hills. From an ancient record in Judges (i. 25–36) we know that they had to leave the Canaanites in possession of the fortified towns—such as Megiddo and others controlling the

---

[1] Prior to the migration, their homeland seems to have been in Lycia and Cappadocia. Cp. Amos ix. 7.

[2] Cp. Macalister, *The Philistines* (Schweich Lectures, 1911).

[3] An Additional Note on the subject follows this chapter.

[4] As to small numbers, Garstang usefully notes that Canaanite towns with 3000 inhabitants would be larger than the average, and their fighting strength might number at most 500 men; also that the army of the earlier kings of Egypt could barely have exceeded 5000. (See his *Heritage of Solomon*, pp. 107, 139.)

Plain of Esdraelon and the coast south of Carmel; Bethshan in the Valley of Jezreel, guarding the all-important ford across the Jordan; Jerusalem and various strongholds in Judah;[1] the great towns of the Philistine plain. How could they (armed with clubs, stone axes, short spears and slings) overcome Canaanites, using chariots and horses, bows and arrows, long spears and swords of bronze? The sense of affinity with these incomers felt by the resident Habiru tribes of earlier 'Israel' (settled north of Esdraelon) was, however, latent strength. But very, very nearly such unity as there was among the invading 'Mosaic' tribes (Ephraim and Manasseh the most important) disintegrated, and very nearly they became subject to the Canaanites, and assimilated to the ancient population.

This will seem a surprising account to those who picture the conquest in terms of the Book of Joshua—Walls of Jericho falling flat miraculously, victory on victory won, Canaanites subdued or exterminated, and the final triumphal scene when Joshua apportions the Land to the twelve valiant tribes. The results of archaeology suffice by themselves to show that picture to be unreal: no completely catastrophic overthrow of Canaan's ancient civilization took place. In general, the Book of Joshua presents what pious Jews of (say) the sixth century felt ought to have happened, and perhaps believed did so happen: it teaches an *Idea*, but is not History. The Hebrew historians were in a quandary how to think about the relations between their ancestors under Joshua and the Amorite-Canaanite population. *Theory* by that time held to it that it had been the bounden duty of good, Mosaic, Hebrews to repudiate utterly the gods of the ancient Canaanites and the horrid ways of the Canaanites: therefore it was to be inferred that conquering Israel had not come to terms with them. But historical memory *knew* it had not really happened that way; and here and there in the records quaint, lame, explanations of why it did not so happen peep out—e.g. Judges iii. 2 (some Canaanites had been

[1] It appears that the 'Mosaic' tribes essayed first to enter southern Judah from their rallying point at Kadesh Barnea (Petra), and failed, having suffered defeat at Hormah (Karnub). They had then to circumvent the hostile territory of the Moabites, but succeeded in capturing the region of Gilead and Bashan from the Amorite kings called Sihon and Og. It was from Gilead that the Jordan was at last crossed. Hebrew control of Judah became effective only in the time of David; and perhaps Judah *as a tribe* is but a name for his consolidation of the southern highlands.

spared to exercise Israel in warfare); Joshua xxiii. 13 (God needed them to be an occasional rod of correction for His peccant people); Exodus xxiii. 29 (to prevent the increase of wild beasts from ruining the country, since at first the Hebrews were not numerous enough to cultivate the whole territory). But the real reason is, perplexedly, admitted in Judges i. 27 ('the Canaanites would dwell in that land'). Some towns were captured;[1] and the persisting Canaanite strongholds did not unite to destroy the Hebrews. The invasion became no trivial event: '*Mosaic*' Hebrews entered the land, stayed in it and eventually shaped its history—and World History.

§3.   *The Consolidation of Israel*

Basically friendly relations between the old Aramaean (Habiru) tribesmen and the 'Mosaic' newcomers were natural. Both were sturdily, wisely, conscious that they were *not* Amorites, *not* Canaanites, *not* Hittites; but men of the desert, with its ideas and ideals in their blood and the welcome fertility of Canaan beneath their feet: they were *Hebrews* of desert Aramaean stock. Their traditions emphasized it: Isaac must not marry a Canaanitish woman; his duty is to seek a wife among his Aramaean kindred.[2] Their ritual-practice taught it: a Hebrew, presenting his offering of first-fruits to the priest, was enjoined to make solemn declaration saying, 'A wandering [i.e. nomadic] Aramaean was my father'.[3] The Canaanites could not (or would not trouble to) drive out the Hebrews, and the Hebrews could not conquer the Canaanites. But as time went on, it is certain that the Hebrews lost cohesion, felt their weakness insurmountable, and were increasingly cowed by the townsmen. And then, at last—probably some 30 or 40 years after the entry—they won a resounding, astonishing victory over a force of Canaanite chariots and horses, led by Sisera. The wonderful, contemporary, poem (Judges v) which tells of the triumph also reveals how dispirited and disunited the tribes had become— the Hebrews had been driven from their villages, and were even unable to use the roads. A Hebrew woman, Deborah, roused them to gather and fight, under a leader named Barak. Only six tribes

---

[1] The Book of Joshua in places drew upon ancient records and traditions.
[2] Gen. xxiv. 2, 3.   [3] Deut. xxvi. 5 (R.V. mg.).

responded to the call.[1] The Canaanite force was in the northern part of the Plain of Esdraelon, and its utter defeat was due, not simply to Hebrew valour, but to a sudden storm which flooded the river Kishon so that the chariots and horses were helplessly bogged in the soft ground. To the exultant Hebrews it seems that their God had come to their aid on the wings of the storm from the distant desert. The victory was a turning-point in the fortunes of the Hebrews.

But consider more widely the uneasy situation that still obtained between them and the townsmen. Canaanites wanted to sleep peacefully in bed and to enjoy their harvests without anxiety or having to pay blackmail for security to the wild men of the hills. Hebrews were tempted to think that houses might be preferable to tents, and that it must be pleasant to sit every man under his vine and fig tree, with grain in the storehouse, cattle in the stalls, and wine in the vessels. If blackmail was refused, firing Canaanite corn and ravaging vineyards did not result in eating and drinking the fruits thereof! Surely the sensible policy was to come to terms and intermarry. History shows that when a fighting race of inferior civilization enters a land more advanced in culture and blends with the older population, it is itself taken captive intellectually by the conquered. That did not happen to the Hebrews among the Canaanites. In another chapter we shall note why their vigour of thought and of action in the long run made Canaan *the Land of Israel*. But eventual Hebrew dominance was not due to wholesale massacre of the Canaanites. Indeed, the generous Hebrew laws concerning the rights of 'sojourners' probably arise from the will to deal fairly by families of Canaanite descent in the period of the Hebrew monarchies. 'If in David's time', writes Pedersen, 'we hear of no antagonism between Israelites and Canaanites, it can only mean that the Canaanites were merged in the Israelite unity, and thus disappeared, naturally infusing Canaanite life and culture into Israel.'[2]

These facts lead to a fundamentally important inference. Among

---

[1] Ephraim, Manasseh, Benjamin, and (the northern tribes) Zebulun, Issachar, Naphtali. Asher would not leave its coast in Galilee; Gad (Gilead) remained aloof east of the Jordan; Reuben after debate decided to do nothing about it, and continued piping to its flocks. Judah (in the south; but did it yet exist?) is not mentioned.

[2] *Israel*, p. 22.

the subjects of the Hebrew kings only a small minority of the families would be of pure descent from the Hebrew tribesmen who had experienced the influence of Moses: some would be of Habiru ('Old Israel') lineage (whose ancestors did not go down to Egypt), and probably the great majority were of Amorite-Canaanite-Hittite descent. Nevertheless it was the 'Mosaic' minority that imposed its traditions, and trust in the God of Moses, upon the entire Nation; so that 'Israel' became One—a People whose bounden duty it was *to understand the gift and the obligations of Liberty*. That is a wonderful fact.

But (to conclude) is it a fact really worth our interest to-day? What have these men of old—their thoughts or their deeds—to do with us? Thomas Carlyle penned this thought-provoking sentence: 'The Present has in it both the whole Past and the whole Future.' *The Present has in it the whole Past*—Carlyle meant that the delusions as well as the truths, the follies as well as the wisdom of our ancestors, persist in us in subtle ways and importantly.

Sometimes the ideas of early men are latent in our minds to our great advantage.[1] Abrahams expresses the point thus: 'To me the permanent value of primitive ideas lies rather in this: they not only prepared the way for higher ideas, but they left their impress on those higher ideas; rise as we will, there is always residue of the primitive left; the higher ideas would be different but for that residue; and *not only different but worse*. It is the primitive in the advanced that gives the advanced its flavour. It is the abiding, indelible, eternal survival of the past in the present that binds the generations in a true tradition, that makes the present livingly adaptable to conditions of life.'[2] In illustration Abrahams says: 'If Judaism had not gone through stages in which God was conceived anthropomorphically, we could not commune with Him as now we can....It is primitive to think of God as close at hand, speaking to Moses face to face as a man to his fellow; it is primitive to place God in a local heaven, above the earth, for science has left us no room for any divine seat in the skies. Yet these two primitive ideas in interaction gave us in Judaism, on the one hand the immanent God, and on the other the transcendent'; and he adds:

[1] That is the argument of J. G. Frazer's volume, *Psyche's Task*, in regard to 'those great institutions which still form the framework of modern society'—Government, Private Property, Marriage, etc.

[2] *Some Permanent Values in Judaism*, Lecture I, p. 7.

'Religions which seek to accept either alternative exclusively must end in pantheism or mysticism.'

Sometimes a primitive way of thinking persists to our undoing; and that is especially true in regard to our deference to Custom—unreasoned mistrust of innovations—indifference or opposition to sorely needed reforms. The closed-mind attitude is in no small degree harmful heritage from the Past. For the ancients above all things feared and hated change: in religion what mattered was to carry out traditional rites with unaltering exactitude; and Justice was what the ancestors had deemed just. 'Theirs not to reason why', or ask whether the statutes reflected Right, or only Man's inhumanity to Man. Even the Athenians put Socrates to death for persisting in questioning customary ideas, and the Hebrews tried to silence Prophets who rebuked them. Indeed, it is surprising that in antiquity CUSTOM was not given the status of a God. His Lordship has not departed from our midst, but sits on a throne behind the scenes, cynically observant of our subconscious worship. At times he takes a seat in Church; for there are some godly people who vote against any change before they consider its suitability. The grin on the face of ancient CUSTOM escapes their notice. But, when others, progressively minded, scornfully sneer at their old-fashioned attitude, CUSTOM still grins —at *them*: for is it not a custom of men to see things only as black or white, and to be uncharitable one to another?

'The tares and the wheat', said Jesus, 'must grow together until the harvest.' The truth is that in our heritage from the Past good things and bad things are subtly intermixed. An illustration is the blend of beauty and dread associated with the word *holy*. Primitively the term was applied to the Gods and all that pertains to them: humans must treat the holy Beings and holy things with anxious care lest somehow offence is given.[1] Only in so far as moral qualities came to be ascribed confidently to the Deity did *holiness* acquire truly ethical significance. Our need is to refine the gold from the dross in the ancient concept—to outgrow unreasoning dread of the 'holy' Supernatural, and yet not throw away *reverence* for God as Absolute Goodness. It is not easy to do so. The Hebrews eventually got near the mark, but they did not perfectly attain it. 'Serve the Lord with gladness, come before His presence with singing', says one Psalmist. 'Serve the Lord with

[1] Cp. p. 66; and Snaith, *Distinctive Ideas of the O.T.* pp. 21–50.

fear, and rejoice with trembling', says another. When the modern irreligious attend a wedding in Church, not for them that sense of *holiness* which is the 'gold of obedience and incense of lowliness'. They can but condescendingly bow the knee to CUSTOM. But even the religious are apt to mix up some dread with their devotions, and not feel quite at home in 'our Father's house'. And all of us are ever in danger of holding apart the secular and the sacred—as though only some things were holy. 'The past is ever near us, not far off, and we do well to enjoy it, retaining its honey sweet, rejecting its poison-sting', counsels Abrahams. 'Know thyself', said Socrates.

There is a famous passage in Milton's *Areopagitica* concerning this problem:[1] 'Good and evil we know in this field of the world grow up together almost inseparably; and the knowledge of good is so involved and interwoven with the knowledge of evil, and in so many cunning resemblances hardly to be discerned, that those confused seeds, which were imposed on Psyche as an incessant labour to cull and sort asunder, were not more intermixt.' In Greek mythology *Psyche* stands for the likeness of the human soul, represented as a beautiful maiden with butterfly wings. The Platonic philosopher, Apuleius (A.D. 150), laid hold on the legend and retold it thus—How that Psyche (alas!) transgressed the limitations which God, her lover, had imposed; and how no way was left her to regain the happiness that should be hers, save by enduring tribulations and surmounting tasks that seemed insuperable. One of the tasks imposed on Psyche was to sort out, into separate heaps, a measureless mound of mingled seeds of barley and millet and beans. Poor Psyche! Poor *Soul*! The task seemed quite impossible. But lo! as she laboured seemingly in vain, the myriad ants were summoned to assist her, and they did the sorting. Let us turn the allegory to our use. God does not take vengeance on the erring human soul; nor is He indifferent to her distress. She does not face her desperate task without His providence for her need. All the resources of Nature she can call to her aid for rightful ends. God does not will that she should fail, but that she should succeed; and through trial find at last her rest in Him. 'The things which are impossible with men are possible *with* God.'

---

[1] Frazer uses it as text for his volume, *Psyche's Task*.

In what frame of mind should we of the modern world regard the ideas and customs of the Hebrew tribes of the desert, the Canaanites of the towns, and the eventual composite nation of Israel? With condescension? Or with realization that somehow even we are not using the resources of our civilization to the best advantage? Ignorant, early men! But you also were tempted like as we are and very sinful; groping your way towards wisdom, not without the aid of God.

Additional Note to Chapter V

The date of the Hebrew Conquest. The evidence, archaeological, literary and historical, that has had to be considered is intricate and fascinatingly interesting to those who are interested. A clear and thorough survey of the subject was published by H. H. Rowley in 1938 (*Rylands Library Bulletin*, vol. XXII, pp. 243–90), with special reference to Garstang's theory of the date as *c.* 1400 B.C. Rowley adheres to the view that the 'Pharaoh' of the oppression was Rameses II, and that the Exodus took place under his successor *c.* 1225; and in a footnote gives a long list of scholars who (*pace* Garstang) are also of that opinion. Garstang's 1400 date (see his volumes *Joshua-Judges* and *Foundations of Biblical History*) is open to grave objections. How comes it that the Hebrew memories in Judges preserved no indication of the turmoil in Canaan consequent on the Hebrew incursions (aided by Hittite intrigue) a generation after the supposed fall of Jericho in 1400? If it be said that the Habiru were the 'Joshua' Hebrews, the Egyptian account of the Habiru activity in the Tell-el-Amarna letters is radically different from the course of the invasion in the Biblical narratives, as S. A. Cook, Rowley and others insist. 'There are not any two facts in the two stories that agree', writes Baikie. Still more astonishing is the absence from Judges of any express indication that from 1350 to 1200 the Egyptians controlled Palestine, garrisoned its main centres, and from 1292 to 1272 were sending armies through Canaan to fight battles with the rival power of the Hittites. It is not enough to answer that the tent-dwelling Hebrews in the land were unconcerned with these major circumstances. Garstang, however, has a theory to meet the problem. He argues that the Egyptian control *is* dimly visible in Judges, disguised as the periods when the strong hand of Egypt enforced the king's peace between Hebrews and the Canaanites and also prevented Midianites and Ammonites from raiding Canaan. But this is much more clever than convincing. If it was the 'Mosaic' Hebrews who overthrew Jericho in 1400 and became masters of its plain, surely they must have attacked the hill country and its towns in the first flush of their initial success. But it now appears certain on archaeological grounds that those towns were captured about 1250–1230 B.C. For that reason the date of the Exodus (advocated in 1938 by Rowley and others as *c.* 1225) must be set back to *c.* 1275, and the attack on Canaan to *c.* 1240, allowing a period of some 30 years for the desert-wanderings and the occupation of Gilead east of Jordan prior to the crossing of the river.

This later dating of the 'Conquest' may explain an Egyptian inscription by Merneptah in 1230 in which, lauding the victories of his army against various peoples or places in Canaan, he records 'Israel is desolated, her seed is not'. Still earlier Egyptian records, however, refer to Israelitish names in Canaan—e.g. *Joseph-El, Jacob-El.* 'Asaru are mentioned by Sety I and Rameses II as resident in the district where the tribe of *Asher* is located in a Biblical reference. But those notices are explicable, provided it be correct that not all the 'Sons of Jacob' went down to Egypt and there had been in parts of Canaan from 1400 or even earlier an 'Israel' older than the time of Joshua—Aramaean clans akin to the later Hebrews.

In the later part of the 13th century the Egyptians were in no position to concern themselves closely with central Canaan. They were menaced by the vast migration of the Sea-Peoples referred to on p. 102. The period was opportune for determined tribesmen to establish themselves in Canaan's highlands.

CHAPTER VI

THE GOD OF THE HEBREWS

Constantly the desert influenced Canaan's history. The phrase, 'Behind Palestine stands Arabia, and beneath the Jew is the Arab', succinctly states the fact. In what ways does their arid habitation affect the thought and character of Arabia's migrant shepherd tribes—the Nomads—the Bedouin?

Life in the Arabian desert, blending great freedom with rigorous limitations, stimulates few ideas; but those few are graven deep in the mind of its inhabitants. 'Like human nature everywhere', says G. A. Smith, 'the nature of the Semite is a bundle of paradoxes; but his particular paradoxes are explained by the discipline of the desert, endured perhaps for millenia before the race broke into history.'[1]

It was the art of domesticating animals, and living upon their milk and superfluous young, that made it possible for men to sustain themselves in the wilderness. The desert-dwellers cannot 'stay put', living on the produce of their land; for the land simply will not produce. All they can do is—in the delightful phrase of Aristotle—to 'cultivate a migratory farm'. They must be able to roam over a wide region, seeking the scant pasturage, and watering their flocks at the occasional wells in the area. It is water, not gold, that the nomad covets, and to him wells are more precious than Klondyke. Immense stretches of the Arabian desert are so completely waterless as to be uninhabitable. Other tracts are such that they afford the barest possibility of supporting human and animal existence. Woe betide the tribe or family that (for its weakness) is compelled to make shift in such a region. Kinglake records meeting in the desert south of Palestine a Sheikh enduring that unhappy plight:

I discovered [he writes] that this man and his family lived habitually for nine months of the year without touching or seeing bread and water. The stunted shrub growing at intervals through the sand in this part of the desert enables the camel mares to yield a little milk, and this furnishes the sole food and drink of their owner and his people....

[1] *Early Poetry of Israel*, p. 33.

The Sheikh was not a good specimen of the effect produced by his way of living—a poor over-roasted snipe, a mere cinder of a man. I made him sit down by my side, and gave him a piece of bread and a cup of water from out of my goat-skins. This was not very tempting drink to look at, for it had become turbid...but it kept its sweetness, and tasted like a strong decoction of Russian leather. The Sheikh sipped this drop by drop with ineffable relish, and rolled his eyes solemnly round between every draught, as though the drink were the very drink of the Prophet, and had come from the seventh heaven.[1]

But vast Arabia also provides its children with vast areas in which sufficiency of water and pasture makes possible a mode of existence felt to be not merely tolerable, but of such merit that in normal circumstances the nomads scorn the softness of the towns-man, and would not exchange the freedom of their migratory farm for all the well-sprung beds and Public Utility Companies civilization has produced. For in such territory the nomads by the aid of their flocks and herds have, as Myres writes, 'solved the problem not only of living but of living as well as is possible under these exceptional conditions'. And, he continues:

It is mainly because they have solved the problem of existence as it is presented to them that purely pastoral societies are absent as they are from the historian's pages, and the regions where they exist are such blanks in the historical atlas. On the other hand, whenever any cause expels a pastoral population from its grasslands, the historical effects of its migration are as tremendous as they are, mainly because its mode of living and all the range of its ideas are so narrowly specialized, and so rigidly enforced on all its members.[2]

How can knowledge be found of the specialized ideas of men who lived in Arabian pastures (those 'blanks in the historical atlas') 3000 years ago? The task is not as difficult as it might appear. Physical conditions in Arabia are so unchanging that they impose on its inhabitants characteristics, and a social system, that are almost unalterable. Modern Arabian life is, very nearly, ancient Arabian life.[3] Much also has been learnt by study of Arabian

---

[1] *Eothen*, p. 186. [2] *The Dawn of History*, pp. 16, 22.

[3] The statement was true until (as it were) 'the day before yesterday'. But, writes Miss Freya Stark (*East is West*, p. xiii), 'the desert, with all its enchantment, no longer gives the essential picture of Arabian life.... The *To-day* of those who talk about Arabia is *Yesterday* to the Arabs them-selves.' Modern inventions are making the world one with a rapidity fraught alike with peril and advantage.

writers who lived before the time of Mohammed. And the Old Testament is a storehouse of information concerning desert ideas and ideals. The subject is here set out under *Religion—Psychology —Society—*and *Ideals.*

§1. *Religion: Demons and Deities*

In 1863 a French scholar, Renan, argued that men living in the uniformity of the Arabian desert tend to become monotheists: 'The Semitic genius', he wrote, 'consists in monotheism, the absence of philosophic and scientific culture, an almost complete absence of curiosity and feeling for fine shades of meaning.'[1] Renan was correct as to the absence of philosophic culture and of feeling for fine shades of meaning: 'The desert stimulates the nerves, but the mind starves. There is much to feed fancy, little to encourage discursive thought.'[2] But as for life in the desert naturally making monotheists, G. A. Smith replies: 'This thesis has been disproved by every fact discovered among the Semites since it was first promulgated.'[3]

The ancient desert-dwellers believed in the existence of countless supernatural Beings, almost all of them malignant and implacable—demons. It was said in the time of Christ that their name was *Legion*, 'A multitude'. This belief persisted and persists. G. A. Smith cites Musil's words: 'In the desert one must not whistle, for whoso whistles calls the demons together.' He adds:

> I once asked one of my servants, not a Bedawee, but a city-bred Syrian, to draw some water for me after dark from a cistern in the desert of Judaea. He excused himself, and when I insisted he trembled. When I said, 'What do you fear? You will see nothing there', he replied: 'It is not what I shall see, but what I cannot see, that I fear.' I knew what he was thinking: that the unseen spirits might crowd or, hustle him into the water, as he bent over to draw it.[4]

What are desert demons like? Answer may be given in W. R. Smith's words:

> In the belief of the heathen Arabs nature is full of living beings of superhuman kind, the *jinn* or demons. These *jinn* are not pure spirits

---

[1] *Histoire des Langues Sémitiques*, vol. I, ch. I.
[2] S. A. Cook in *C.A.H.* vol. I, p. 197.
[3] *Geography of the Holy Land*, p. 29.
[4] *Early Poetry of Israel*, p. 32.

but corporeal beings more like beasts than men, for they are ordinarily represented as hairy, or have some animal shape, as that of an ostrich or a snake. Their bodies are not phantasms, for if a *jinni* is killed a solid carcase remains; but they have certain mysterious powers of appearing and disappearing, or even of changing their aspect and temporarily assuming human form, and when they are offended they can avenge themselves in a supernatural way, e.g. by sending disease or madness. Like the wild beasts they are outside the pale of man's society, and frequent savage and deserted places far from the wonted tread of men.

How could a wandering Aramaean ancestor of Israel know whether he had to do with a beneficent God or a malignant demon?

A supernatural Being is not as such a god; he becomes a God only when he enters into stated relations with man, or rather with a community of men....Though there is no essential physical distinction between gods and demons, there is the fundamental moral difference that the *jinn* (demons) are strangers, and so, by the law of the desert, enemies, while the god, to the worshippers who frequent his sanctuary, is a known and friendly power.[1]

It is easy to understand why the demons were reckoned to be innumerable. The desert is a dangerous place to dwell in; for the area of pasturage and safe tracks is small compared to the immensities of untrodden waterless sands, into which if a man wanders and is lost, his wits are driven demented and his body perishes miserably of hunger and thirst: the demons have got him! The vast regions outside the known are their accursed abode; and enviously they are for ever seeking to invade the territory that nurtures life. How are they kept out? By the will and strength of the Gods, the kindly supernatural Powers to whom the good land belongs. The Semites called their life-giving, protective energy *The Blessing*; and its evil counterpart—all that weakens or destroys human health and prosperity—*The Curse*.[2] We say to ourselves that the nomads had a hard struggle against stern Nature. They felt their lives a battleground of spiritual antagonists, within them and without: everything turned on preserving the Blessing of the good Gods; forfeiting that, they would be overcome by the cunning of demonic Powers of evil. They thought there was a lot

---

[1] *Religion of the Semites*, pp. 119 f. Cp. Matt. xii. 43–45; Luke xi. 24.

[2] Deut. xxx. 15–20: 'I call heaven and earth to witness against you this day, that I have set before thee life and death, the blessing and the curse' (*v.* 19).

more to Life than the things that are visible. Being a good shepherd entailed more qualities than wisdom of scientific sheepbreeding (about which, to their loss, they knew little): he had also to be an upright man, whose ways with his neighbours the Gods could approve. After two devastating wars in half a century modern men might be wise to get a glimmering of the Bedouins' standpoint.

The sandy wilderness does not encourage belief that there are *very many* beneficent Supernaturals. 'The nomad lies between the bare stones and the clear stars. The only physical processes that excite his imagination are the dawn and the sunset, the passage of the planets, the shadows flung by great rocks, the rustle of the desert breeze, the mysterious crackle and whisper of the earth's surface when the night cold grips it; the rain and the thunderstorm.'[1] Few are the signs of the presence of *kindly* Gods—for rare are the wells and oases where the blessed marvel of living water flows to quench the thirst of man and beast, infrequent the great rock giving shadow in a weary land. Few are the *mighty* Gods. The stars evoke wonder but are so remote. The Evening and Morning Star, however, singled itself out as an especial marvel. The Sun in his glory is a terrific God. But what could the Arabians think of the Sun save that He was to be feared above all Gods? Nothing Man could do placated the flaming fury of his heat by day. Unquestionably the Deity most revered by the ancient Arabians was the Moon. 'Arabia from the beginning has been the home of moon-worship; moreover for similar reasons the cult prevailed in all the desert borders from Palmyra to Sinai.'[2] In desert life the principal occasions of worship were the seasons of the moon; the time of sheep-shearing; (most important of all) a spring-tide festival when the first-born of the flocks were sacrificed.[3] But let what further falls to be said about the God-in-the-Moon be held back for a moment.

There is important reason to think that desert-tribes addressed their worship to one God rather than to whatsoever Gods there be. G. A. Smith considers that 'the desert, bare and monotonous,

---

[1] G. A. Smith, op. cit. p. 31.

[2] Cp. Garstang (*Heritage of Solomon*, p. 159), who refers to Langdon, *Semitic Mythology*, pp. 86, 378. Regarding the importance of the planet Venus (the Evening and Morning Star) in Arabian and Semitic religion, see Chapter VII, p. 145.

[3] On the cult customs of the early nomads, see Lods, *Israel*, pp. 258–307.

conspired with this habit, which trained men to reduce all things under one cause and to fix their attention on one sovereign deity'.[1] The writer is of opinion that the habit arose from the inevitable nature of the sacrifices offered by the desert men. Arabians had no sheaves of golden grain, no luscious bunches of grapes wherewith to show their reverent thankfulness to the Giver of all good things. What could hunger-bitten, skin-clad Aramaeans (anxious to show their gratitude and to merit the fullness of Divine Blessing) offer, save one thing only? But that thing was their all-in-all. They sacrificed the most precious blood-life of the firstlings of their flocks. (Probably they felt that in theory they ought also to sacrifice their first-born children. But in that grim matter they called a halt to Logic, and so did better than the Canaanites.[2] Desert tribes could not afford the loss of man-power; and we may also believe that among them common sense or, may be, finer instinct triumphed over hard-and-fast reasoning.) In turn the Deity (it seemed to them obvious) showed recognition of their devotion by bestowing the Blessing of vital increase—births of men and animals. Thus through the interchange of the vitality (from God to Man, from Man to God) there came to exist between *this* God, *these* men and *these* flocks a psychic-physical Oneness.[3] The at-one-ment between God-Man-and-Creatures, maintained through the blood given and returned, must not be interpreted grossly, as if they thought that the shed blood worked the wonder automatically (Magic-Science). They regarded the necessity of sacrifice from a fundamentally religious and gentlemanly standpoint. Decent behaviour is not 'All taking and no giving'. Marvellous the gift bestowed by God; gratefully they received it; gladly (as was most due) they in turn made their gift to the Giver. They gave back the life they owed. The relationship was personal, and honourable to both sides. Further comment on the ideas implied in ancient sacrificial offerings (animal, vegetable and human) will be made in the following Chapter on the Gods of the Canaanites.

---

[1] *Geography of the Holy Land*, p. 30. (Smith's comment does not run counter to his insistence that desert life does not naturally lead to true monotheism: see p. 112.)

[2] See pp. 150f.

[3] Cp. the remarkable phrase in I Sam. xxv. 29: 'bound in the bundle of life with the Lord thy God.'

Here the immediate task is to point out the far-reaching importance, and value, inherent in the outlook on life implied in the desert men's mode of sacrifice. Giving back to the Super-natural the blood-vitality was their way of affirming (i) that our existence depends on something other and higher than physical Nature; and (ii) that the life each of us has is *not an individual possession*. They meant it realistically when they said: 'We are His people and the sheep of His pasture.' The tribesman neither thought nor said: '*I* am God's favourite; and these sheep are *mine*.' The desert attitude differed completely from Western materialistic Individualism. The tribesman could not blankly say to his neigh-bour in trouble (not even if the trouble was the man's own fault) —'What's that got to do with me? Stand on your own feet'. (This point has to be amplified later in the Chapter.) Suffice it to add that, if a tribesman did take a ruthlessly individualistic view of things, he was thrown out into the wilderness—like Cain—as totally unfit for human society. Ruthless Individualism is neither Christian nor scientific: the horrors it has produced, or failed to eradicate, support that claim. But we and our fathers have so long had to live, move, and have our being in the atmosphere of Western history that many decent people find it hard even to imagine any alternative between Democracy as it has been, and Communism as it may be (if it insists on a *finally* materialistic philosophy). Yet myriads of good people, democrats and com-munists, want to see 'a better world'; seeking for others and themselves a fair chance and a square deal. God may be very ready (as He is always willing) to give a fresh Blessing to mankind. But we may be in much need of copying the desert men, and being willing to make some sacrifices to obtain it. 'Our life is not our own', said the desert people in effect; and were convinced that human welfare depends on offering to the Highest the best we have to give.

Their conception of the relation between God and Man is shown by titles they used in addressing Deity. For a generic term they used *El* (plur. *Elohim*)—i.e. *God (the Gods)*.[1] They did not use the titles favoured by agricultural, town-dwelling Semites—

---

[1] Definition might be given by naming an attribute, such as 'the seeing God' (Gen. xvi. 13); or the locality of the place of worship, 'the God of Bethel' (Gen. xxxv. 7); or an event, 'the God of the Covenant' (Judges ix. 46).

namely, *Baal* (*Master* or *Owner*) or *Melek* (*King*): for they loathed and despised the social relationships indicated by those titles. They were free men, not anybody's slave, not even a God's. What is wholly significant is that they called upon their God as *Father* or *Brother*: so intimate, so personal, was the bond between Man and God. An immense advance had been achieved, when human beings ceased to concern themselves with Gods in general, and instead tried to worship *a* God, whom also they looked upon as *their* God; and felt (however dimly and perplexedly) that they lived in Him and He in them.

Did the early Arabians go further, and confer upon their chosen God a pet name, a personal designation? There is no substantial evidence to provide answer. In the ninth century the Moabites (but they were townsmen and agriculturalists as well as shepherds) invoked their God as *Chemosh*—a word for which no specific meaning is known.[1] One grand instance seems to prove the point —*Jehovah*, God of the Hebrews. But the Hebrews never called their God *Jehovah*! The word is a hybrid, being the vowels of one Hebrew word (*ĕdhōnāy* = *Lord*) attached in late Jewish manuscripts to four consonants Y (J)–H–V–H, which represent the ancient Hebrew invocation of their God, and which (we are reasonably sure) they pronounced as *Yāhvĕh*.[2] But further we know: (i) that the Hebrews of the northern kingdom ('Israel') held that Yahveh was not used before the time of Moses and had been due to his teaching;[3] and (ii) although the southern Hebrews (Judah) held that the Patriarchs had called upon God as Yahveh,

---

[1] See I Kings ii. 7. An inscription made by Mesha, King of Moab, also proves the fact. Mesha's inscription refers to the Israelite God as Y–H–V–H.

[2] For motives of reverence the Jews avoided uttering aloud the sacred name of God, substituting for it *Lord* (*ĕdhōnāy*). When therefore about the sixth century A.D. tiny signs to indicate vowels were added to the consonants in the text of the manuscripts, its letters were put with the consonants of the divine name, Y–H–V–H. The translators of the English versions naturally transliterated the amalgam—*Jehovah*. It would be pedantic in such a book as this to avoid writing *Jehovah*; but, on occasion, where there is some special reason for referring to the actual Hebrew word, *Yahveh* will be used.

[3] Accordingly the Israelite document (E) in Genesis consistently makes the pre-Mosaic Patriarchs refer to God as *El* (or *Elohim*—in their intention not the *Gods*, but a 'plural of majesty'). The late Priestly document, of course, follows the same tradition—cp. Gen. i. 1 (P) as compared with the Judaean verse Gen. iv. 1.

the form *Yahveh* is consequent on the influence of Moses, being a verbal expansion of *Ya* (*Yah*) (cf. p. 214).[1]

Our question narrows down to this: 'Was *Yah* a personal name for God?' To English ears *Yah* sounds like a term of abuse: it was certainly not that. Lord Curzon describes a Dervish religious dance at Kairwan in Tunisia, and relates how the participants rhythmically worked themselves into a frenzy of ecstatic devotion with reiterated cries in praise of Allah: 'Ya Allah', and sometimes: 'Ya Kakhar' (O avenging God!), 'Ya Hakk' (O just God!), while each burst of clamorous appeal ended in a shout: 'Ya Hu' (O He!). The writer believes *Ya* (*Yah*) was not a proper name but an ejaculation associated with the cult of the moon,[2] and that before the time of Moses the Aramaean ancestors of the Hebrews were moon-worshippers. The reader may feel that opinion startling. There is cumulative evidence to support it—some points are noted below.[3] If, however, he feels the possibility insults the intelligence

---

[1] On philological grounds G. R. Driver (*Old Testament Essays* (1927), p. 23) has shown that Ya (Yah) was not a contraction of Yahveh, but the more ancient form. Note the praise-exclamation *Hallelujah* ('Praise ye Yah!'); and compare Ps. lxviii. 4 ('Sing unto God...His name is Jah'). Conclusive is the fact that Hebrew compound proper names were never formed with Yahveh as part of the compound, whereas very many were with Yah, e.g. Elijah (Heb. *Eliyahu*). See Buchanan-Gray, *Hebrew Proper Names*, ch. iv. In Judah compound names with Yah began in the age of David (and then first in the royal family and court circles). In northern Israel they appear first in the reign of Ahab (ninth century). Earlier the Divine element used in Hebrew compound names was *El* or *Baal*.

[2] G. R. Driver (op. cit. p. 23) compares the ejaculations used in the worship of the Greek God *Dionysos* (=Latin *Bacchus*). See Euripides, *Bacchae*, passim.

[3] Ur and Harran, reputed starting points of Abraham's migration to Canaan, were focal centres in Mesopotamia for the cult of the moon under the name of *Sīn*. The names of the wife and sister-in-law of Abraham (Sarah and Milcah) are titles ascribed to the consort-Goddess of the Moon-God at Harran—as Skinner (*Genesis*, p. 237) points out. (Ur, it may be noted, was perhaps, like Harran, a place in northern Mesopotamia, not the famous, southern, 'Ur of the Chaldees'; see Lods, *Israel*, pp. 165 f.) *Sīn* appears in 'the Wilderness of Sin' (Exod. xvi. 1); as also in *Sinai*, the alternative name of the (Mosaic) Mount of God. For Hebrew worship in Canaan the time of new moon was a religious season; it is probable the Sabbath observance was originally a festival of the full moon, and that the springtime sacrifice of the firstlings of the flocks was originally observed in honour of the Moon-God. In Canaan, the moon was termed *Yareah* (not *Sīn*). Note thus Jericho ('City of the Moon'); and Jerahmeel (probably 'the Moon is God') as name

of pre-Mosaic Aramaeans, he should reflect that the moon was the only grand phenomenon in Nature that gently invited the adoration of nomads. The terrible heat of the sun is inimical to men and animals in the shadeless desert. The moon befriends the shepherds as they move their flocks in the coolness of the night hours. How much more sensible to have decided to concentrate adoration on that majestic beneficent and illuminating mystery, the Moon, rather than on Gods in general.[1] Were the ancients as unsophisticated as they seem? Who can say that there were not thoughtful Aramaeans who wondered whether the actual moon was manifestation of a Being more wonderful than the eye of man can perceive? 'Lead, kindly light.'

Desert tribes may have to leave the territory where their fathers offered sacrifice to their God—either driven out by violence of foes, or because increase in numbers made it necessary for part of the tribe to seek new wells and pasturage.[2] The silvery moon did not cease to shed its light upon the wanderers, and they could feel that the vitality of their God was present in the blood in their own bodies and in their animals. Still, separation from the ancestral holy place entailed strain, to meet which two devices helped. They might take with them a fragment of the soil or stone of the former sacred spot.[3] And, secondly, it became desert custom that tribes not in peaceful relationship could at the sacred seasons meet at a holy place they mutually revered and there worship under a truce

---

of an Aramaean-Kenite family; and the Kenites were associated with Hebrew efforts to penetrate Judah from Kadesh Barnea. (See Burney, *Judges*, pp. 242–53; Margoliouth, *Relations between Arabs and Israelites*, pp. 13, 20 f.; Lods, *Israel*, p. 237; Oesterley and Robinson, *Hebrew Religion*, pp. 92f.; and Garstang, op. cit. p. 160—who remarks: 'It cannot be fortuitous that the Israelite feasts which go back to the nomad period are connected with the phases of the moon.')

[1] One could not take liberties, however, with the beneficent Deity. In tropical zones the rays of the full moon can cause night-blindness; and on unbalanced temperaments may have other, very queer, effects.

[2] See Gen. xiii. 5 ff.

[3] The famous example is the tradition that the Ark which the Hebrews carried with them on the wilderness-journeyings and took over Jordan into Canaan had contained stone tablets from Mount Horeb (Sinai), inscribed—allegedly—with the Ten Commandments. We may feel sure it contained stones from the Sacred Mountain. Compare also the story of Naaman the Syrian whom Elisha healed of leprosy in the water of Jordan, how that he took back with him to Syria two baskets of the soil of Israel's land.

of God without risk of conflict. But now think of Hebrew shepherds in *Canaan*, who had moved out of the desert altogether. They could not go on pilgrimage back to Horeb-Sinai, the ancestral Mount of God, for it was 'forty days distant in the wilderness'! How did they feel about worship? Canaan was a goodly land for shepherds—how much better than the parched wilderness. The murmur of running water was in their ears; beneath their feet the grass grew green on the mountain pastures. Strong trees flourished in the forests, and on the terraced hillsides vines became laden. In valley and plain was the mystery of seeds ripening to harvest. From their uplands the nomads heard the Canaanites rejoicing at the High-Place where townsmen praised the Lords of wine and plenty; and they watched them take siesta under the pleasant shade of their vines and fig-trees. The Gods of this land were many and near. Surely the children of the shepherds would in time forget the austere ways of their fathers, and the very name of their fathers' God? Israel, astonishingly, did not forget.

§2. *Psychology*

(1) *The Nature of Man.* In ordinary speech we are heirs of Greek psychological terms, and in religion heirs of Jewish and Christian belief. The Greeks regarded the individual human being as a material body indwelt by an immaterial soul or spirit. Jewish and Christian theology holds that the soul may survive the death of the body, and means by *soul*, not a shadowy ghost, but the very Self or Personality—invaluable modern words which the ancients did not possess. But Jewish belief in personal survival of death did not emerge until two or three centuries before the time of Christ, and then did so under the stimulus of profound thought as to God's nature and the significance of moral choice. For that reason the hope could not have become general in valuable form much earlier than the second century B.C. (Jewish formulation of the belief was to some extent helped by contemporary Greek psychology with its idea of the immaterial soul). We find accordingly in the late, non-Biblical Jewish writings various expressions of the hope—such as the famous verse in the Wisdom of Solomon (its date about the time of Christ): 'The souls of the righteous are in the hand of God and no evil shall touch them.' This subject, however, is proper to the intended sequel to this volume, and is not

here pursued. We are here considering the normal Hebrew ideas about human nature found in the Old Testament; and its writings do not contain any allusions (save perhaps two or three, and those late in date) which express expectation of individual survival of death. A considerable number of its verses appear to do so, but that is because inadequately and misleadingly the Hebrew word *něphěsh* is translated as *soul* in our English versions, and the word *rūăch* as *spirit*. It is necessary to explain as clearly as possible what those two words meant. In the Old Testament the psychological and physiological conception of the nature of Man is very different from that of the Greeks, and is accurately summarized in this statement: 'The Hebrew idea of personality is an animated body, not an incarnated soul.'[1]

The chief of these all-important Hebrew words, *něphěsh*, is best translated as *Being* or *Entity*. Man is a human *něphěsh*; the ox is a cattle *něphěsh*. Hebrews could say that the soil has its own *něphěsh*: when Spring comes round and vegetation sprouts, the soil becomes a living (functioning) *něphěsh*, with its rights which man should respect.[2] Inanimate flesh and bones they called *něbhēlāh* ('carcase'). Man (they observed) is a *living* (human) *něphěsh* only when his body has blood in it and is able to breathe. What they thought about the vitalizing blood will be referred to in the next section concerning their social ideas. The other necessity for animation (the power of breath) they called *rūăch*, and regarded it as mysterious energy—manifested in gentler form as normal breath (which they sometimes called *něshāmāh*), but more impressively in the violent strength of the wind. God Himself, they shrewdly judged, cannot be any sort of flesh and bones, and is wholly *rūăch* (*Energy*)—superhuman, immeasurable power.[3]

The way in which the Hebrews thought that Man had become livingly existent is shown in Gen. ii. 7: 'And the Lord God formed man of the dust of the earth, and breathed into his nostrils the breath of life: and man became a living *Being*

---

[1] H. W. Robinson, *The People and the Book*, p. 362.
[2] Cp. Job xxxi. 38–40.
[3] Cp. Isa. xxxi. 3. Obviously *spirit* is not a suitable translation of *rūăch* in regard to the Hebrew idea of the Divine Being. Old Testament references to 'the spirit of God' (whether spelt in our Versions with or without a capital letter) mean simply 'God in active manifestation of His energy (*rūăch*)', e.g. Gen. i. 2.

(*nĕphĕsh*).'[1] Whenever a man displayed abnormal strength or capacity—such amazing physical might as Samson had, or power of prophetic utterance, or surpassing wisdom and skill[2]—the Hebrews ascribed his exceptional power to his having received from God a special inspiration of the divine energy.[3]

When a man dies, what happens? Obviously, for Hebrew thought his *nĕphĕsh* no longer exists; for that word signified only the Being caused by the coexistence of animating breath with flesh, bones and blood. His dead body of flesh and blood must be buried in the grave, and so returns to the dust of the earth.[4] His breath-vitality (*rūăch* or *nĕshāmāh*) returns to God who gave it. The returning *rūăch* (it must be emphasized) was in no wise deemed to be the Self or Personality. The old Hebrew view is exactly shown in the Psalmist's anguished cry for health, 'O spare me, that I may recover strength, before I go hence and be no more'.[5] Throughout the centuries covered by the Old Testament

[1] Our Versions translate '...became a living soul'. Misunderstanding of the real meaning is consequent. Much more familiar to English readers is the definition recorded in Gen. i. 27: 'And God created man in his own image, in the image of God created he him.' That verse belongs to the late Priestly document, and presents (in a poetic but profound way) the inference drawn by advanced Hebrew-Jewish thought from Man's unique, religious-moral, characteristics in contradistinction to all other creatures.

[2] Cp. Judges xiv. 6; I Sam. x. 10; Isa. xi. 2; Exod. xxxi. 2–5.

[3] Down to the sixth century the *normal* breath-energy imparted to men by God's superhuman energy (*rūăch*) is referred to as *nĕshāmāh*, never as *rūăch*. It is very interesting that after that date *rūăch* began to be used in allusion to Man's normal animation. This change was due to meditation on the superlative mental, and the unique moral, qualities of the human being in comparison with other creatures. *Man* receives from God his vitalizing power of breath (*nĕshāmāh*): he can be said to have special affinity with God; to him has been imparted *rūăch*. See H. W. Robinson, *The People and the Book*, pp. 360f. [4] Ps. xxxix. 13. Cp. Job xxxiv. 14, 15.

[5] It is difficult to outline this subject briefly. Account ought to be paid to the 'carry-over' in popular Hebrew thought of the really primitive, or savage, ideas concerning the persistence (for how long?) of a shadowy ghost-image of the dead—weak and wan, yet possibly dangerous to the living, as the necromantic and other usages noted in the Old Testament indicate. Further, it was vaguely thought (in popular religion) that the ghosts of the dead are congregated in a vast, dark, hollow (*Sheol*) beneath the earth, to which they 'go down'. The important matter is that the ghost-image was not regarded as man's living personality: its existence in relation to the dead body in the grave, or else in Sheol, was not *Life*. Cp. Isa. xxxviii. 9–19 (Hezekiah's prayer). See Langton, *Good and Evil Spirits*.

writings (apart from two or three, just possible, intuitions of immortality) it was not doubted that at death the individual's personal life ends. So much the more wonderful the courage of men who battled with the facts of life, and managed to find in them good and sustaining meaning—until 'the day broke' and a larger hope was seen. There is no questioning the vigour and valour of the Hebrews' attitude to life. Nevertheless it may be felt that their conception of Man's nature was basically, and drearily, material. The fact is that they regarded the capacities of the animated human body less materialistically than we do.

(2) *The Powers of Man.* The Hebrews were not aware of the functioning of the brain and the nervous system, or of the circulation of the blood in the veins. Reasonably enough, they consequently ascribed intelligence and volition to the heart, and emotions to the kidneys and bowels. But in their view the several parts of the body could exercise, independently, the psychic qualities of the individual's Being: ear, eye, mouth, even bones, were credited with psychic power for good and evil.[1] Qualities such as pride, enmity or pity, were deemed to be *in* the eye and sent forth by its glance. Potent above all were words spoken concerning another, whether with benevolent or malevolent intent. Our matter-of-fact minds assume that words are efficacious only when they are heard and comprehended. The Hebrew belief was that the spoken word had in it the entire power of the speaker; and the question whether its Blessing or its Curse would be effective depended not on its being heard by the person concerning whom it had been said, but on the relative psychic strength of the two parties. The goodwill or illwill would inevitably travel to the mark. 'When an Israelite pronounces blessings on another, these are not empty, though kindly words.'[2] A curse

---

[1] The liver (*Kebedh*), to which the Babylonians and others attached great importance in the art of divination, is strangely disregarded by the Hebrews. The consonants of the word are the same as those in Honour or Glory (*Kabodh*), and it has been argued that in certain passages the Hebrew text should be translated *liver* and not *honour*. Abrahams (*The Glory of God*, pp. 18–22) holds that these proposed emendations are mistaken.

[2] Cp. Pedersen, *Israel*, p. 167. Isaac (Gen. xxvii. 36, 38) could not recall the word by which he had bestowed on Jacob the blessing due to the first-born son. But Esau, irrevocably tricked out of his birthright, yet beseeches his father to utter a potent blessing on him also: 'Hast thou not reserved a blessing for me?...Hast thou but one blessing, my father?'

would glance off harmlessly (or even turn back on him that uttered it) provided the recipient's psychic armour—his measure of Divine Blessing—was adequate. If human words had such power, how immeasurably great the word of God to compass that which He pleases.[1] Further, the psychic quality in a man was deemed to extend beyond his body into all the material things that are his.[2] For example, the giant strength of Goliath was assumed to be in his sword; therefore David was eager to possess it: 'there is none like it.'[3] In the same manner the things that pertained to God, the Holy One, were deemed to have in them His divine force, and must be treated circumspectly as *holy*.

(3) *The Peril of Man.* Exactly as the individual was supposed to radiate psychic force, so his Being was held to be exposed to psychic influences from without. That was his peril, both from human and demonic foes. 'The horrible thing about the curse was that it could be put into the soul from without.'[4] Therefore ancient battles began with a shouted contest of cursing, for the will-power of the combatants' words (having in them the strength of the Blessing imparted by their respective Gods) would really decide the fight. Men's hope of wellbeing was to possess, to merit and to augment, such potency of Blessing that it would not be overcome. Whence came sickness and plague? Why did ventures fail, and crops wither? The inference was that for some reason (perhaps perceptible as conscious sin, but perhaps unguessable) the protective Blessing had weakened, and the illwill of human or demonic enemies had prevailed. Not until the great Prophets had done their work were there Jews who had learnt to say: 'Thou wilt keep him in perfect peace, whose mind is stayed on Thee.'[5]

When we examine this psychic concept of Divine Blessing which gave each individual his strength, the facts carry us into the heart of Hebrew social ideas. The Blessing was not the result of a man's own merit, nor simply his personal possession, but something he received and shared with others. It was the collective

---

[1] See Isa. lv. 11.

[2] 'All that a man possesses and that belongs to him is penetrated by his soul (*něphěsh*); this holds good of his tools, his house, his animals, the whole of his property' (Pedersen, op. cit. p. 170).

[3] I Sam. xxi. 9. Cp. also II Kings ii. 14 (the mantle of Elijah).

[4] Pedersen, op. cit. p. 441.   [5] Isa. xxvi. 3.

Blessing given by God to his People whose kindred blood flowed in his veins. It was like inherited capital held by each individual 'in trust' for all—capital which by his care and prudence might be augmented, or by swindling and folly be squandered to the trustee's disgrace and the loss of the beneficiaries. A man's Blessing came to him from his ancestors, having in it all their qualities and experiences. Its strength was what it was by reason of the favour of God, and all that his ancestors, himself and his contemporaries, did to merit the Divine regard. Wondrous great was the fullness of the Blessing inherited by an Israelite; for it was the Blessing God had bestowed on Abraham, His chosen one, His friend. All that Israel's men of outstanding courage, wisdom, virtue, could do was to conserve its amazing richness as it continued from generation to generation. 'We are the children of Abraham', proudly said the Jews; and meant by that much more than that they could trace back to him their physical descent.

§3. Society

The words *family—house—father's house*—are sprinkled over the Old Testament, and used in a curious way at times. For instance: 'And I will appoint over them four families: the sword to slay, and the dogs to tear, and the fowls of the heaven and the beasts of the earth to devour and to destroy.'[1] The sword a *family*? To Hebrew ears that did not seem strained metaphor. The men of the desert live in tents; in the Old Testament *house* is the Palestinian Hebrews' equivalent of the desert tent-dwellers' conception of *family*—as the following quaint examples illustrate. We possess houses, but they do not attend funerals. But in Judges xvi. 31 it is said concerning Samson dead that his brethren and all the house of his father came to Philistia in order to bury him. Portable houses are a modern invention; but Joseph in Egypt informed its king that: 'My brethren, and my father's house, which were in the land of Canaan, are come unto me.'[2] Of course, we understand what is meant; but to an extent we do not realize we have cashed and tamed to commercial and domestic uses the far-reaching significance of *house* or *father's house* on Hebrew lips. We speak of business firms as 'Houses'; and we say 'My house is in such and such a street'. Similarly we have so narrowed down the idea of *family* that the Hebrew usage is not understood. Ask a modern man whether he

[1] Jer. xv. 3.   [2] Gen. xlvi. 31.

has a family, and he may reply: 'Yes, two sons and a daughter.'
Press the question further, and another reply might be: 'Mine is a
very small family—an uncle and aunt are my only relatives.' Our
idea of family duty ('Blood is thicker than water') radiates from
strength at the centre (the single household) to weakness at a very
near circumference—shall we say?—as far as first cousins. Desert
fathers and mothers felt towards their children the same intimate
concern as should exist in a modern single household; but they
were also acutely conscious of being in a great *family* (or *father's
house*) which numbered hundreds, perhaps thousands, of persons
—all of whom counted one another to be *brethren of one blood*,
sharing mutual interests and obligations with an intensity we find
it difficult to grasp. The whole kindred group was conscious of
being *one flesh and one blood*; or, as we might put it, felt that it
existed as a corporate personality.[1] Each tribesman deemed himself to be living solely because there was in his body a share of the
blood (the vital energy) derived from him whom every individual
of the great family knew to be the ancestral 'father of them all',
whose Blessing was their common heritage. Israel was in Abraham, and Abraham's life continued in Israel—so the Hebrews
realistically believed. A fire and its flames may serve to illustrate:
for the Hebrews the continuing fire was the family, its present
members the momentary flames. 'The family or father's house',
writes Pedersen, 'was felt to extend back through time. The life of
the forefathers with all its substance, great achievements, wealth,
blessing, honour, everything which fills the name, lives on in the
descendants. Life is not something individual, to be shaped
according to the needs of each individual. Man is what he is only
as a link in a family.'[2] The stranger must declare his name as
So-and-so, the son of ..., *the son of*.... Only thus could it be
known to others what manner of man they had to deal with. So
efficient was the solidarity of obligation, created by the consciousness of vital unity, that if the weakest individual in a kindred
group suffered any injury at the hands of someone of another

---

[1] Cp. H. W. Robinson, *Christian Doctrine of Man*, pp. 27 ff.; *The Cross of
the Servant*, pp. 33–6.
[2] Op. cit. p. 254. Cp. Driberg, *The Savage as he really is*, p. 44: 'Every
savage is a thinking, rational, being, but he starts with the fundamental belief
that he is a member of a fraternity of the living and the dead as opposed to
other fraternities.'

tribe, the instant reaction of all its members would be 'Our blood is shed', followed by united effort to avenge the wrong. In Arabia the only individuals without a family are the few reckless rebels who have chosen flagrantly to ignore tribal (family) obligations, and therefore have been driven out of society—in which case their lone life is so impoverished and precarious as to be scarce worth living.[1]

Consider the formation of new kindred groups, and of very large social aggregations in the course of history. Men of pre-eminent greatness gave rise to a new 'father's house'. So marvellous was the strength of the Blessing seen in the shepherd-lad David, the son of Jesse, the son of Obed..., that after his death men spoke thenceforth of 'the house of David'.[2] As for the making of large-scale social unities, desert tribes that recognized no common ancestor and therefore counted one another foes, but wanted to be at peace and co-operate, could compass their purpose only by a rite—known as covenant-making (or more revealingly, *cutting a covenant*, by means of which realistically their blood was mingled); thereafter they could regard themselves as truly brethren of one blood, one family, one people.[3] The Hebrews employed the words *People* and *Nation* in reference to the large communities that shape in history.[4] But when we consider their use of those words, one fact of immense importance stands out—namely, the instinct and passion with which they held on to the

[1] Thus in the tradition of Cain and Abel, Cain's furious question: 'Am I my brother's keeper?' revealed in his nature a lunatic lack of the indispensable minimum of social instinct. He just had to be declared an accursed man, and driven forth to shift for himself in the accursed wilderness. Cain then cries out that his punishment is more than can be borne: 'Behold...I shall be a fugitive and a wanderer in the earth; and it shall come to pass that whosoever findeth me shall slay me' (Gen. iv. 1-15).

[2] Cp. I Sam. ix. 1. Saul in his youth was known as 'the son of Kish, the son of Abiel, the son of Zeror, the son of Becorath, the son of Aphiah, the son of a Benjamite'. After Saul's royal destiny was run, his descendants were called 'the house of Saul'.

[3] Participants in the covenant ritual bound themselves to one another by a solemn oath to their God or Gods, by walking between the severed halves of an animal slain as a sacrifice—touching its blood or having it sprinkled upon them as they passed—and afterwards eating its flesh. Cp. Jer. xxxiv. 18; and see W. R. Smith, *Religion of the Semites*, pp. 315 ff., with Cook's note, p. 481.

[4] *People*, however, could be used in reference to any group (large or small) having common interests, qualities, or experiences—e.g. particular classes in a nation, as well as the nation as a whole: such as, the unhappy, the faithful, or the ordinary folk as distinct from the rulers.

root-conception that, whenever any group of men—from the smallest to the largest numerically—lives and worships together, it is essentially a *family*; wherefore all its members, from the greatest unto the least, must stand to one another in the intense social obligations proper to a family—as brethren, men of one flesh and one blood—or else they will lose the sustaining Blessing. During the Hebrew monarchies the heirs of the desert tradition sturdily fought the pretensions of kings who proposed to treat them as subjects: they said the king was their father or brother, and spoke still of the house of Judah, the house of Israel. Struggle to prevent the individualism of monarchs, royal officials, land-owners and merchants, from destroying the family relationship as the bond of society became the supreme problem. Its issue was determined by the wonderful religious development we have to trace. The last of the great Prophets saw the Peoples of the whole world unified as one family, and foretold how God's purpose could be attained and made effective in the will of men.

The inspiring, lovable, obligations of family constitute for the Hebrew mind the sole basis on which human society can success-fully be constructed. And the clarity and tenacity with which Israel held that standpoint explain the power in the Bible's moral demands. 'It is here', writes Baeck, 'that we find the great social task grasped for the first time. The thought that human society is a community pervaded by human duties, a moral confederacy and solidarity, is here seen taking shape. And it is from the Bible that the social commandment has again and again gone forth into the world.'[1] Men must set themselves to treat one another not as things to be used, but as brethren whose welfare it is their joy and their pride to advantage. That thought was the key to the concept of Justice, the discernment of Right from Wrong, in the Religion of Israel. Western secular civilization, to its shame and misery, has fumbled the key, or refused to employ it.

In the light of what has been said, consider next *Character* and *Conduct*. The raw Semitic temperament was paradoxical, and un-compromising in the extreme—characteristics which probably reflect the strain of life as experienced in the desert under the glare of the sun and amid constant hardship of hunger and thirst. Since Judaism, Christianity, and Mohammedanism all originated in Semitic countries, one would expect the Semites to be exceptionally

[1] In *The Religions of the World* (ed. Clemen), p. 289.

pious men. Yet Sir Charles Lyall writes of the Arabs of the classical period (and their descendants the Bedouin of the present day) that they are 'one of the races most untouched by the solemnities of religious awe that have ever existed'. Paradoxically (as G. A. Smith observes) they combine 'strong sensual grossness with equally strong tempers of reverence and worship'. He instances Jacob, the father of the tribes of his people: 'a hardy, unscrupulous herdsman, yet capable of spiritual dreams and of wrestling with the unseen.' Smith further emphasizes their 'marvellous capacity for endurance and resignation, broken by fits of ferocity: the rugged patience usually bred by famine. We see it survive in the longsuffering, mingled by outbursts of implacable wrath, which characterizes so many Psalms. They are due to long periods of moral famine.'[1] The Semites were stiffly uncompromising—cause of weakness as well as strength: in the Semitic mind 'there are no half-tones—nothing between love and hate...and actions are *either* right *or* wrong.'[2] The social organization of desert life divided men into just two classes—either brethren or foes. Towards those not within its brotherly covenant the tribe recognized no moral obligation: Might constituted Right. Their lives, flocks, pastures and wells were there for the taking; and the victor felt that the spoil was justly his. Virility, pride, greed and boredom were forever inciting strife.[3] Only motives of prudence restrained: the slightest injury done to an individual of another tribe would be avenged by the whole of the man's kindred, and the grudge be cherished tenaciously to be wiped out sometime, somehow.[4]

[1] *Early Poetry of Israel*, Lecture II.
[2] S. A. Cook, in *C.A.H.* vol. I, p. 196.
[3] 'Famine and war are the annual curses of their life. The insufficiency of water and pasture; the strain of hunger and the jealousy of blood, all the heat and recklessness which are bred of poverty or pride; the constant temptation to raid the camels and cattle of other tribes; with the sacred obligation which binds a whole tribe to avenge the slaughter of one of its members—all these create a climate of feud.' (G. A. Smith, op. cit. p. 27.)
[4] Moreover, the effort was not 'to make the punishment fit the crime', but to exact vengeance commensurate with the offended tribe's unbounded opinion of its dignity. A very early poetic fragment in Gen. iv. 23f. illustrates the mind of the Bedouin chief: Said Lamech to his wives—'Ye wives of Lamech, hearken unto my speech: For I have slain a man for wounding me, and a young man for bruising me: If Cain shall be avenged sevenfold, truly Lamech seventy and sevenfold.'

We have indicated how radically different, on the other hand, was the standard of conduct amongst those who were brethren in covenant. Even so, early Hebrew justice was crudely realistic, taking too little account of motive and equity. Deeds were right or wrong, and men just or unjust. If an early Hebrew outwitted or wronged his fellow, and on trial somehow was acquitted, he was *ipso facto* the justified man. (Remember that we are considering only the raw material for the future religion. Early Arabians and Hebrews had infinitely much to learn about Right and Wrong; but they were on the open road to learning it; and eventually some of their descendants saw how to unify justice and mercy with unsurpassed wisdom of strength and gentleness.) When in Canaan administration of law and order became thoroughly corrupt, this ancient, too matter-of-fact, standpoint worked havoc. For long, however, in the settled land communal justice worked as an efficient deterrent to evil-doers; for the pronouncements given by the judgement of the elders at the gates (which sufficed for normal charges) powerfully upheld the exacting level of moral relationships demanded in a community of brethren. (Was it, or was it not, thus done in *Israel?*) [1] Very important is the severity with which the covenant-society reacted to flagrant crimes; such sins merited not only normal men's abhorrence and the punishment of the transgressor, but were guilt from which the entire community must purge itself, if it were not to lose the Blessing of God. A grim instance is recorded in Joshua vii: Achan greedily violated a solemn vow taken by the Hebrew warriors. When he was found guilty, it was judged that his immediate family and possessions as well as himself must be destroyed. What cruelty to the innocent relatives! The early view was that the household, being one with him in blood and therefore permeated by his character, was (so to say) diseased

---

[1] Some grave charges, and cases where lack of evidence made decision too hard for human decision, were brought 'before God', i.e. to the priests at the sanctuaries, where sometimes arbitrament was given by casting 'lots' (*Urim* and *Thummim*). Another method in such cases (still practised in the desert) was Trial by Ordeal (cp. Num. v. 16–31). Austin Kennett describes such an Ordeal by means of a fire-test, which he witnessed in the Sinaitic desert. It was carried out by 'a quaint little old Arab who inherited the post from his father, and who carries out his Ordeal all over Sinai'. Kennett (*Bedouin Justice*, pp. 107f.) relates that the accused (who protested his innocence) was required three times to lick a spoon taken red-hot from a charcoal fire; did so without injury to his tongue, and was therefore acquitted.

tissue in the body-politic requiring to be cut out by the surgeon's knife.[1]

Modern society exacts the death penalty for murder, and gives long imprisonment for various heinous crimes. For cruelty to children, black-marketing, and so forth, we impose fines or a mild term in gaol; whilst we simply do not know how to prevent much unbrotherly commercial ruthlessness from 'getting away with it' altogether. The early Hebrews would criticize Western civilization scathingly; for being often hard where we should be merciful, and more often soft where we should be stern. How weakly our civilization reacts to the deliberately selfish citizen!

§4. Hebrew Ideals

The invading Hebrew tribesmen carried across Jordan ideals which life in the desert had inscribed in their hearts. Possessions in Palestine enfeebled the force of those ideals, and partly transformed their nature for the worse.

(1) *Honour.* The great virtue in the desert social system was the immense incentive it provided that each should care for all, and

---

[1] One type of wrongdoing created a most difficult problem for a Hebrew family. If one of its members grievously injured one of his very own household, and a third member took it upon him to avenge the wrong, that would not set matters right. It only doubled the evil! Two sins against the covenantal harmony of brethren would but the more demonstrate how effectively the Curse had got into the 'house', destroying its Blessing. The classical instance is the trouble in David's family when Amnon violated his sister, Tamar. His brother, Absalom, thereupon slew Amnon, and the evil thus begun led on to Absalom's intriguing against David and finally leading a revolt against the king his father. Strong ruler that he was, David treated the danger to his throne and person with seeming incapacity. His servants were eager to fight; yet David tamely abandoned Jerusalem, and took to flight. The problem David wrestled with was not Absalom, but how to overcome the Curse which had invaded his house. If the next act of the tragedy had been that the father became the slayer of Absalom his son, that would but still more strengthen the Curse. David therefore would take no steps to bring about the death of his son. When at last battle was joined between the men who stood for David and those who were for Absalom, David's one concern was to command that no harm must be done to Absalom. Thus, when Absalom had been slain and the revolt crushed, it was clear to all Israel that the great King's sorrow for his dead child was genuine, and that in the whole dread sequence of events the Curse had not entered his own heart. David effectively triumphed, because his subjects could then believe the Curse had been cast out and the fullness of Blessing restored to his house.

all for each.[1] If the tribe was not to suffer defeat and dissolution, the tribesmen had to stand by one another to the utmost; and behold! they found zest and pride in doing so. What happened to the least of the brethren happened to them all. Prospering families in the tribe could not see others in distress without knowing that the loss affected them. The success of some advantaged all, and the misfortune of any was felt to be general loss.[2] It is not wide of the mark to label the desert attitude as *primitive socialism*; but our democratic minds must further understand that the system provided ample scope for individual enterprise and ambition—within the safeguard that the ambition was such that its realization benefited the community. There was strenuous effort on the part of the several families within the tribe, and of the several tribes comprising a large covenantal brotherhood, to acquire possessions and prestige; and assertions of superiority or right of leadership were weighed in completely realistic scales. If one family laid claim to be the greatest, its claim to have supremacy of *Honour* among them was acknowledged by the others only in so far as by actual prosperity and fighting-valour it could do, and did, most for the common welfare. If it weakened (no matter how undeserved its misfortunes) it sank in the balance of Honour, because its power to sustain others, to 'bless' them, had lessened. That was that! Desert families became great in Honour in various ways—by skilful management (or sheer good fortune) whereby their flocks and herds increased;[3] by conspicuously just dealings with their fellows;[4] by displaying wisdom in tribal debates; by giving 'strong' counsel (i.e. counsel which the event vindicated)[5] in serious issues such as war or peace; most of all by manifesting outstanding strength and doing heroic deeds in

[1] President Roosevelt, speaking at Vassar College concerning his reorganization policy ('the New Deal') put the principle mildly and negatively. 'No individual', he said, 'has a right to do things which hurt his neighbours', and 'the extension of the idea of not hurting your neighbour must be recognized as no infringement of the personal liberty of the individual'. The United States is not of one mind concerning 'the New Deal', but its public opinion seeks to remove the iniquity of 'raw deals'.

[2] The Levirate law of the old Hebrew codes was framed to ensure, if possible, that a family which had suffered the deaths of a father and his sons should not die out in the community. The lovely story of the Book of Ruth concerns such an occurrence.

[3] Gen. xxx. 27–30.   [4] Job xxix. 10–17.

[5] II Sam. xvii.

battle. 'An Arab of the old type knows nothing higher than to fight, and thus to gain honour as the first among his fellows. During the battle he seeks the most dangerous post, and shouts his name aloud so that everyone may know whom they have before them.'[1]

Among the desert men honour was accorded, not uncritically to those who had large possessions of flocks, but to those who had outstanding greatness of spirit, the inward force of Blessing, which was likely to achieve success or (if lost) to regain it. Amid the vicissitudes of desert feuds fortune easily had its ups-and-downs; but if the defeated was not crushed in will-power, his honour was still in him: all might yet be well. In the traditions of Gideon and of Samson, recorded in Judges, this heroic, desert, conception of honour still burns clear. Canaanite civilization damped down the fire, tending tamely to concede honour to those who had no more claim to it than that, being secure, they had riches. But the quite disastrous feature which besets Western civilization—namely, that men not only are tempted to profit at the expense of their fellow-citizens, but find it difficult to prosper without injuring others—that feature was not prominent in Hebrew life in Canaan for some considerable time. When eventually the rich and powerful freely and unscrupulously used their strength to the disadvantage of their neighbours, the ancient Hebrew concept of Honour or Greatness had been turned upside down. By contrast, the desert ideal had tremendous driving-force and moral potentiality.[2]

(2) *Peace.* It is the pallid, Canaanized, notion of *Peace* which has been handed down to us as its normal meaning. *The Oxford Dictionary* nicely expresses the modern idea as follows: 'Freedom from war or from civil commotion, from perturbation quarrels or dissension, from mental or spiritual disturbance arising from

---

[1] Pedersen, op. cit. p. 222.

[2] Pedersen (op. cit. pp. 215, 220) summarizes the ancient standpoint thus: 'He who communicates most has the authority and honour, because he upholds them all....Honour does not consist in being free of labour and trouble, but, on the contrary, in making the greatest effort; in being the one who carries the greatest burden; in giving most, in acting most. To be a chief does not imply ability to force something upon the community, to keep it down. His position depends on the acknowledgment of something underlying his actions, an actual greatness.' 'He that is greatest among you', said Jesus, 'shall be your servant.'

passion, sense of guilt, etc.; or absence of noise movement or activity.' In the Old Testament the ideal of Peace was positively, vigorously, valorously, different. What the early Hebrews meant by a peaceful life was a career in which all legitimate desires were satisfied—*Perfection* of Life. The literal signification of the word is *Wholeness* or *Completeness*. Emphatically, Hebrews did not mean by Peace 'Freedom from war', or 'from the risk of having to fight'. In their view a fighting man was in possession of Peace provided he was conquering his enemies, and not they him![1] A man lost Peace when his purposes were frustrated, or when he suffered some distress or humiliation that marred his contentment. Accidents of fortune, therefore, and qualities not ethically noble, might augment (or take away from) one's Peace in the early sense of the term. But the old idea had, at any rate, greater possibilities for individual and social good than the anaemic conception that peace equals freedom from trouble. Moreover, recognition that its attainment was bound up with righteousness was not far below the horizon, since it was believed that Blessing must depart from the evildoer: 'There is no peace, saith the Lord, unto the wicked'[2] —'Mark the perfect man, and behold the upright: for the latter end of that man is peace'[3]—'Mercy and truth are met together; righteousness and peace have kissed each other.'[4]

It is obvious that this positive conception of Peace as fullness of rightful life is closely connected with the great, and pervasive, Biblical idea of *Salvation*. In early Israel hope of Salvation, of course, was solely concerned with the issues that beset our present, 'earthly', life. When Hebrews successfully terminated a venture, or escaped a danger, so that their Peace had been increased or maintained, they said that they had experienced Salvation. After a victory they could say that they had been saved from their foes, and that their eyes had seen God's salvation. In Canaan the temptation was to let hope of Salvation become hope of not having to face perils, so that Peace tended to signify material prosperity enjoyed in security and without effort to maintain it. 'To be saved' was more and more construed as passive protection from every kind of trial. Only when the idea came into the stream

[1] Cp. Isa. xli. 3, where it is said of the victor that 'he pursued them and passed in peace'.
[2] Isa. xlviii. 22.
[3] Ps. xxxvii. 37.
[4] Ps. lxxxv. 10.

of Prophetic religion was full emphasis laid on Man's moral peril, and Salvation conceived essentially as victory over moral weakness. Then at last men learnt to pray for deliverance from wickedness in their own character, tempting to evil deeds that ruin what our life should ideally be. *The Oxford Dictionary* (rightly unconcerned with early Hebrew notions) does serious wrong to Christian theology by its stress on the other-worldly aspect of Salvation: 'The saving of the soul; the deliverance from sin, and admission to eternal bliss, wrought for man by the atonement of Christ.' The word has a far richer connotation in Christianity: it signifies deliverance from all manner of evil, in this world and the next. Salvation alike in the Old Testament and the New was not escapist theology. Collate the references in the Bible; predominant is the triumphant note of victorious strength achieved amidst the changes and chances of this fleeting world.

(3) *Freedom*. The invading Hebrews carried with them into Canaan a passion for Freedom. They also carried the social wisdom that leads to the finest Freedom, although this they did not fully understand. The tribesmen had much to learn about the demands imposed on human selfishness, if there is to be true liberty and not licence; but the root of the matter was in them. Unrestrained individualism would have been scorned as destructive madness by men the breath of whose life was the covenantal spirit, and who thought of their personal existence as due to a share in the vitality of their kindred family. No Hebrew that crossed Jordan was of opinion that he should try to be a law unto himself. What the Hebrew clung to tenaciously was the right of his brethren collectively—his family, his tribe, 'all Israel' (the covenant-unity of the several tribes)—freely to discuss and determine what they would, and would not, do.

The Arabians learnt their passionate love of freedom from the desert itself. Lawrence of Arabia makes the following memorable comment of the fact:

We who have gone out to discover the meaning of the desert have found only emptiness; nothing but sand, wind, soil and empty space. The Bedouin leave behind them every extraneous comfort and go to live in the desert, in the very arms of starvation, that they may be free. The desert exacts a price for its secret. It makes the Bedouin entirely useless to their fellowmen. There has never been a Bedouin prophet. On the other hand, there has never been a Semitic prophet who has not, before preaching his message, gone into the desert, and caught from the desert dwellers a reflection of their belief. The idea of the absolute worthlessness of the present world is a pure desert conception at the root of every Semitic religion, which must be filtered through the screen of a non-nomad prophet before it can be accepted by settled peoples.

So fierce the determination of the proud Arabian families and distinctive tribes to suffer dictation from no one to whom they have not voluntarily accorded leadership (for the time being), that they find it wholly uncongenial to plan and maintain large-scale operations. The following statement has the weight of Lawrence's authority: 'History is against the creation of an Arab Empire. The Semitic mind does not lean towards system or organization. It is practically impossible to fuse the diverse elements among the Semites into a close-knit State.'[1] Desert liberty, it would appear, lacked something which is necessary for a modern, 'planned', society; and the Hebrews when they crossed Jordan lacked it. In the next century the jealousies of their several tribes almost cost the liberty of them all; almost buried in the composite civilization of the Canaanite subjects of petty kings the treasure of unselfish Freedom which future Israel was to preserve for mankind. Treasure indeed it was—for 'Freedom is the essence of our personality. To act freely, not as the plaything of impulses, but according to an idea of law which our own reason has laid down for us, is to be a person, not a thing; is to rise into the realm of absolute purposes.'[2] In time, however, the Hebrews in Canaan mastered their initial incoherence; and then as the centuries passed they fought magnificently the battle of Freedom against despotic kings and selfish grandees; and they won the battle. Victory was gained because even in the early stages the tribesmen knew instinctively, and their descendants learnt definitely, that free men are *brethren*, who therefore use liberty not for 'a cloak of wickedness', nor for 'an occasion to the flesh', but (as the New

---

[1] L. Thomas, *Lawrence of Arabia*, p. 232. The tremendous Mohammedan conquest is the exception that proves the rule: and that was the work of civilized townsmen and traders (men who had the desert behind them) as well as of the fighting tribes. Miss Freya Stark (*East is West*, p. xiii) says regarding it: 'What the Arabs represent in history is the greatest commercial empire between the fall of Rome and the rise of Britain.'

[2] Oman, *The Problem of Faith and Freedom*, p. 176.

Testament insists) as power 'by love to serve one another'. Liberty is not licence. The great Prophets taught Israel the great secret— Resolve to obey God rather than Man.

It is claimed concerning the organization of the small but brilliant city-states of Greek civilization that 'the Greeks stand as the first protagonists of freedom'. The early Greeks (worshippers of the Sun-God, golden-haired Apollo) learnt their passion for freedom from bitter experience of autocratic rulers who in the sixth century B.C. dominated their towns. They overcame those *tyrants*, and by the magic of genius created instead *Democracy*. But the free Greek citizens became voters rather than brethren, and the city-states remained intransigently non-co-operative, refusing to see that changing circumstances required a more liberal and scientific concept of liberty. In the end Greek orators talked their 100 per cent democracies to death. The nomad ancestors of Israel loved Freedom much earlier than did the Greeks. But it is sensible to be thankful to both races, rather than to compare them as rivals: 'There is one glory of the sun and another glory of the moon.'

At the start of this chapter distinction was drawn between the waterless wastes where no man can live, and the spacious regions in Arabia where the nomads can roam with the flocks, and be satisfied with life. But *desert* nevertheless stands in our Western imagination for an appalling monotony of arid sand; and so frequently in the preceding pages has *desert* been written that perhaps the impression uppermost in the reader's mind is of sand, sand, and again sand. Let these words from a letter sent years ago to the writer serve as corrective, and also as conclusion to the chapter:

My memory of the deserts of Northern Arabia is rather of vast expanses of unwatered earth covered with the dry scrub that represents life asleep. Even where there is no water the camel must have at least some grass or scrub to live on, however dry. The nomad moves his tent from place to place to find water or sustenance. But when the occasional rain comes, what a change! The desert indeed blossoms like a rose. The dry earth is carpeted with green shoots in a day, and the flowers blaze out in great sheets of white and gold. Talking one day with a political officer who had visited an Arab sheikh in the early spring to persuade him to join forces with the British, or at least not to side with the Turks, he told me he had said to the Sheikh, 'My King will give you money.' 'Throw wide the tent flaps', the Sheikh replied, and waved his hand out towards the flowering desert—'There', he said, 'is all the gold and silver I want.' Is that answer a key to the nomad's mind? I think that no one who has seen the colour of the waking desert, and the sunset flaming on its rolling ridges, or even the soft lavender-blue of its receding levels in the dry season in the evening light—and what Eastern has not an eye for colour?—could fail to feel something of the beauty of Creation, which is surely one of the paths to God. Did the prophets go out from the degraded city-haunts of men to recover the *peace* and *beauty* of the desert, as well as the majesty of its open spaces?

CHAPTER VII

THE GODS OF CANAAN

The invading Hebrew shepherds carried across Jordan potent Ideals, and no doubt they were fierce fighters; but, for all that, they were culturally no better than a flock of innocents determined to find pasture in a land of wolves. That was true of the bulk of them, but not of them all. There were some on whose intelligence (as will be argued in later chapters) the genius of Moses had made an indelible mark; and that made a world of difference to our world-civilization. But if we are to appreciate the desperate odds against which the continuance of *genius* in the future nation of Israel triumphed and why it triumphed, then the immediate task is to try (in this Chapter) to realize what confronted the average Hebrew when he entered Canaan, and (in the next) the extent to which the popular religious beliefs of Israel became futility.

There were wellnigh 2000 years of civilization in Canaan before the Mosaic Hebrews entered it.[1] The ancient Canaanites thought themselves as wise as any other race, sophisticated men-of-the-world, who felt there really was not anything more for them to learn about how to keep on the right side of the Supernatural and how to deal with their fellow-men. Canaanite religion made no progress in getting down to root causes. Why? Before an answer can be offered, there is descriptive spadework to be done.

One way and another modern research has made it possible to give ample account of religious ideas and practices in ancient Palestine before the Hebrew period. We have discovered that international contacts throughout the Near East had occasioned at a very early age broad similarities of outlook on the Supernatural; the name and fame of great Gods worshipped in the several lands had spread abroad, and there came into vogue a system of worship so similar that it has usefully been termed a Cult-pattern.[2] We know that much that has been verified about the religious customs

[1] Possible traces of pre-historic, totemic ideas, and ancestor-worship, are antiquarian matters. See Langton, *Good and Evil Spirits*, chs. II, IV; Oesterley and Robinson, *Hebrew Religion*, ch. v.

[2] See *Myth and Ritual* (ed. S. H. Hooke).

of the major countries of the Near East applies also to early Palestinian worship, concerning which less is directly known.[1]

Next, it is clear that as regards Palestinian religion we must constantly (not merely in the very early centuries, but constantly) recognize the extent to which very different levels of thought coexisted. That was due partly to the physical diversities within the small land, partly to the complicated racial *strata* in its population. It had many small towns and agricultural areas, but also large tracts where shepherds continued their nomadic and semi-nomadic life. Anciently, considerable areas were afforested and inhabited by relatively backward people.[2] Wide were the differences of outlook as between townsmen, villagers, shepherds; between labourers and slaves and the owners of houses and vineyards; between merchants, priests and officials of the petty kings. Some Canaanites knew how to read and write. Hoary superstitions and naïve religious ideas could easily coexist with cultured opinions in the same town, nay, even in the same person; for intellectual consistency characterized the Semites much less than it does ourselves—and that is little enough.

§1. *Supernaturals, bad and good*

Like the men of the desert, Canaanites believed that there were very very many, bad Supernaturals—nasty unreasonable demons, chief among them the nightmare monster *Lilith*.[3] A few uncanny persons professed to have power to control a demon, or to evoke from Sheol the wraiths of the dead. Wizards and necromancers seem to have made a livelihood out of credulous individuals, unscrupulous or distressed. It is to be noted that strict Hebrew

[1] It is important neither to exaggerate nor to underestimate the broad resemblances. The early Amorite settlements in Syria influenced early Babylonia, but were also influenced by its still earlier Sumerian culture; and the Amorites again influenced Canaan. That, however, does not imply that the Amorites and Palestinians took up precisely the advanced theology and mythology of early Babylonia. The several Peoples made their own versions of the widely accepted myths, and in any detailed account regard must be paid to the subtle differences among the races who contributed to the civilization of Palestine. On the other hand, the similarities are sufficiently great to make it possible to do rough justice to the religion of the Canaanites.

[2] Notably, the northern part of the coast south of Carmel (the Plain of Sharon), and part of the Central Mountains.

[3] See Isa. xxxiv. 14; cp. Ps. xci. 5.

sentiment frowned on the nefarious business, and the great Prophets denounced it.[1] All this, however (important as it is to realize its persistence), was only the sinister underworld of personal superstition, not the open communal-religion of the land.

Unlike the men of the desert, the Canaanites believed that good Supernaturals were very many. With its golden sunshine and refreshing rain, its impressive mountains and fertile plains, its fountains of living water, its trees and crops, Palestine proclaimed itself a Holy Land, abode of many Gods. One can understand that running water was so precious that men wanted to thank and propitiate the life-giving Being that seemed to be manifested in its mystery. Some trees seemed to call for special attention and evoke reverence for the Being who caused their growth or perhaps was actually present in them;[2] trees of great size and age, or associated with some memorable event or occasion when their luxuriant whispering foliage had been deemed to convey supernatural guidance.[3] 'No one', writes G. A. Smith, 'can tell how many voices a tree has, who has not come up to it from the silence of the desert.'[4] Mountain-tops somehow suggest the near presence of God; and some remarkable rocks and stones seemed to be *holy*—in Canaanite opinion, at any rate. A famous example is the strange rock-formation at *Bethel* ('House of God'), which resembled a mighty ladder of stone reaching up to the sky-line.[5] Canaanites used the same general term as the desert men to denote worshipful and kindly Supernaturals—*El* (Hebrew plural, *Elohim*). But theirs was an experience of life in which there were masters and hirelings, lords and common folk, kings and subjects.

[1] See I Sam. xxviii (Saul and the witch of Endor); Isa. viii. 19.

[2] If it was the object itself (water, tree or rock) which was worshipped as a Supernatural, we term the attitude *Animatism*; if the object was regarded as a habitation or body wherein the supernatural spirit chose to be manifest, the term *Animism* is proper. As to Palestinian persistence (to the present time) of reverential attitude towards such objects, see Curtiss, *Primitive Semitic Religion To-day*.

[3] II Sam. v. 23, 24.

[4] *Geography of the Holy Land*, p. 88.

[5] See Gen. xxviii. 10–22. Peters (*The Psalms as Liturgies*, p. 296) writes: 'Bethel was a great nature-shrine, i.e. a sanctuary whose sanctity was originally derived from a striking natural phenomenon, a field of huge stone pillars, the result of erosion. These stand, or rather stood, for during the war [1914–18] they were broken up to construct a road-bed, on a sort of shelf above Bethel, on the side of the hill which rises in a crest northward.'

Therefore they showed their humble duty towards the Gods who owned and fructified the land, by addressing them as *Baal* ('Master, Owner'), or *Adon* ('Lord'), or *Melek* ('King').[1] Probably the shepherds disapproved, and sturdily called their God plain *El*, and in their hearts still thought of Him as 'Father' and 'Brother'.

Canaanite civilization was divided up into independent small towns (and neighbouring villages) which owned the immediate hills and valleys, vineyards and fields. Interest was concentrated on the productivity of the particular locality. Two ideas inevitably arose in the inhabitants' thoughts concerning the Supernatural Power that made it fruitful. One was that fertility in men and animals was consequent on the union of male and female. How could it be otherwise with the productivity of the soil? Surely there must be a Goddess as well as a God to be worshipped: beside *Baal* there reigns a *Baalath* (Mistress, Consort, Wife, Mother—in a longer term, Supernatural Femininity). Secondly, seed in Palestine (unlike Egypt) must have occasional rain.[2] Reason suggested that the God must have power in the skies to bestow the indispensable gift of rain; and that the Goddess was pre-eminently the Earth-Mother. But distinction of function between the two Deities must not be pressed. Canaanites were not

---

[1] Definition was sometimes given by adding place-name or special attribute. For instances—*El Bethel* ('God of the House of God'); *Baal Tamar* ('Master of the Palm-tree'); *Baal Zebub* ('Lord of Flies'—i.e. Averter of Disease). The last was the *El* worshipped at Ekron (II Kings i. 2). Macalister remarks concerning this God's title: 'This was no contemptible or insignificant lordship. A man who has passed a summer and autumn among the house-flies, sand-flies, gnats, mosquitoes, and all the other winged pests of the Shephelah will not feel any necessity to emend the text so as to give the Baal of Ekron a "lofty house" or "the planet Saturn" or anything else more worthy of divinity.' (Macalister, *The Philistines*, p. 92.)

[2] Robertson Smith (*Religion of the Semites*, pp. 102, 106) writes: 'The seats of the Gods were originally sought in spots of natural fertility, by springs and river-banks, in the groves and tangled thickets and green tree-shaded glades of mountain hollows and deep watercourses. All the Semites... attached a certain sanctity to such places quite apart from agriculture; and as agriculture must have begun in naturally productive spots, it is natural to infer that agricultural religion took its starting point from the sanctity already attaching to water-groves and meadows....As husbandry spread from those centres and gradually covered the whole land, the worship of the Baals spread with it; the gods of the springs extended their domain over the land watered by the sky, and gradually added to their old attributes the new character of "lords of rain".'

THE GODS OF CANAAN

so severely logical. It seems certain that in their minds the *Baal* and the *Baalath* were revered as Lord and Lady of Earth *and* Sky.

When Canaanites lifted their eyes to the skies, like other men they beheld the sun, moon, and stars; and marvelled. As for the stars it is a safe inference that they worshipped the Evening-and-Morning Star ('Venus'); for the cult was widespread throughout the Semitic lands,[1] and seems to have been equated with the adoration of the great Goddess, called in Babylonia *Ishtar* and in Syria-Palestine *Ashtarte* (*Asherah*). Evidence of direct sun and Moon worship in Canaan is less than might be expected. Albright suggested what may be the explanation: 'In part this situation is perhaps due to the fact that solar and lunar aspects were attributed to other divinities.'[1] The moon is not beneficial to agriculturalists as it is to the desert nomads. But the sun was indispensable for prosperity in Palestine. Its flaming majesty was God manifest— Deity good and glorious, yet also terrible. For its warmth and light grew the crops, but its scorching heat in the late summer withered the precious vegetation. This was a God who slays and makes alive again.[1]

Canaan (on compulsion) imported various famous Gods— Deities bearing the names which its recurrent conquerors were accustomed to give to their Gods. Thus into Canaan in the early Amorite Age came the great Gods—*Amon, Ramman* (later called *Rimmon*),[3] *Addu* (later, *Adad* or *Hadad*), *Dagan,* and *Resheph.* The Hittites about 1750 B.C. brought *Teshub,* their national God, and *Hipa* (or *Khiba*) their Goddess. From 1500 to 1200 B.C. the Egyptian garrisons fostered the honour of Egyptian Gods—*Amon-Ra, Isis* and *Osiris, Ptah,* the Goddess *Hathor*; and also a quaint dwarf God, *Bes* (many seals and figurines of *Bes* have been excavated in

---

[1] Especially in certain of the cities in Mesopotamia, and outstandingly in those of southern Arabia. See Sayce, *Religions of Ancient Egypt and Babylonia,* p. 482; and Langdon, *Semitic Mythology.*

[2] Its mysterious power of transferring itself back from the west to the east during the night was a standing puzzle. Egyptian records refer to the sun as one of the great Deities of the Palestinians, and there is also the evidence of various ancient place-names, e.g. *Beth Shemesh,* 'House of the Sun'. See Albright, *Archaeology and the Religion of Israel,* p. 82. Solomon's temple had solar alignment. There is a Rabbinic saying somewhat to this effect— 'Our fathers worshipped in this place facing the East, but we turn our backs to the Sun and worship the LORD.'

[3] See II Kings v. 18.

Palestine).¹ The religion of the Philistines is inadequately known. At Ashdod and Gaza they worshipped *Dagon* (probably fusing the cult with that of the ancient Semitic Corn-God, *Dagan*).² *Gad* and *Asher* (names of two of the Hebrew tribes settled in Canaan) were certainly also Semitic Deities.³ A hitherto unknown divine named M–K–L has recently been disclosed by excavations at Bethshan.⁴ There was an important Goddess *Anath*,⁵ and another called *Kadesh*; and everywhere and always the great Goddess *Ashtarte* was adored.⁶ Who knows how many more Gods and Goddesses further information might reveal? What a list! And what a muddle!⁷ Might not three words have served our purpose —*Canaanites were polytheists*? It is important to realize that the Canaanites were readily hospitable to new Gods. When into their midst came certain Mosaic tribesmen, insistent on worshipping none save Jehovah their special God, the Canaanites must have been puzzled by the intolerance—much as certain Roman

¹ The Egyptians were patronizingly tolerant in religious matters. In Egypt itself they had allowed the multitudes of immigrant Asiatics to continue their native cults. In Palestine therefore they did not seek to suppress native Deities; instead, in cultured fashion, they choose to regard them as but variant names for their own Gods. Thus the Egyptian Sun-God *Amon-Ra* was equated with the Semitic *Shemesh*; *Sutekh*, their God of battle, they recognized in the Canaanites' *Adad*, or *Rimmon*, or *Teshub*.

² See Macalister, *The Philistines*, pp. 94–9; and cp. Judges xvi. 23; I Sam. v. 1–5. The opinion that the Philistine *Dagon* was a Merman-God is due to misinterpretation of a Philistine word, combined with a Hebrew play-upon-words (in Hebrew, *Dag = Fish*).

³ Cp. Isa. lxv. 11.

⁴ An unknown Deity, *Salm*, may possibly be inferred in *Jerusalem*.

⁵ Her name is found in Anathoth, a village close to Jerusalem. In a fifth-century papyrus, concerning a Jewish temple in Egypt, *Anath* is (surprisingly) mentioned in a way which implies that she was one of two female Deities there associated with the worship of Jehovah.

⁶ Variant forms are *Ishtar–Atar—Ashirat—Ashtarte—Asherah—Ashto-reth*. The last should properly be pronounced *Ashtereth*—the Jewish scribes substituted the vowels *o* and *e* of the Hebrew word *Bosheth*, which means *Shame*.

⁷ An interesting illustration is a seal found at Taanach on which Egyptian hieroglyphs are combined with an inscription in cuneiform to read 'Atanahili, son of Habsi, servant of Nergal'. 'No more typical example', observes Lods (*Israel*, p. 63), 'could be imagined of the mixture of influences prevailing in this country than this Canaanite, who declares himself in the Babylonian tongue worshipper of a Babylonian god, and adorns his seal with Egyptian symbols.'

philosophers and men-of-the-world were puzzled by Christians who insisted that God in Christ must alone be worshipped.

Our subject, however, suddenly seems simple when we note that these Gods of many names overlap in character, and together cover the few, fundamental interests, hopes and fears—the perennial need for food; the mystery of male and female; birth, marriage and death; the violence of Nature (storm and tempest) and the violence of foes (war); the goodness of Nature and the joys in human life; the necessity and difficulty of doing the right thing the right way; the ease with which passionately or weakly we do wrong, and the terrible consequences of misdeeds.[1] But what a tangle the Canaanites continued to make of the issues in life, century after century. Europeans have long walked in the confused ways of the Canaanites: they should give far greater heed to the Christian Faith, and to Science.

§2. The Worship of the Gods

(1) *Places, Persons and Seasons.* Worship in Canaan was offered in the open air. The towns were built on defensible hill-sites, and the communal place of worship (the *High-Place*) was normally on or near the top of the hill—literally a *high* place. Low walls were built to form a spacious court, or system of courts, enclosing the holy ground, wherein the worshippers assembled.[2] The place of

---

[1] In detail—the male Deities were Lords of the Elements—sun and rain; thunder and lightning; sources of fertility; conquerors in battle. Resheph was especially, it seems, God of lightning and fire. Adad's emblems were the thunderbolt and the bull. Dagan was the immemorial Corn-Spirit deified. Gad and Asher were Gods of Good Fortune. As regards the Goddesses, Ashtarte (as has been said above) was Mother-Nature, Woman deified—wife, consort, sister, mother—the loving and the beloved. Anath and Kadesh were Goddesses of the passion and mystery of love, but they were also credited with martial power. The same is true of Ashtarte; and in some Semitic lands (but not in Canaan) the great Goddess seems to have changed gender and been worshipped as a warlike God. (Cp. W. R. Smith, op. cit. pp. 58f.) Traces of a matriarchal stage in prehistoric times are inferred by some scholars. See, in general, S. A. Cook, *Religion of Ancient Palestine.*

[2] The sacred precincts might contain various simple buildings—rooms for priests, and a temple or 'house of the God'. These embryo temples were not ambitious erections like the large temples of later antiquity. They were small, unlighted, structures in which an image or specially sacred object of the cult would be placed. 'The temple in Canaan, as in Greece, originally existed only when there was an idol to be kept in it.' (W. R. Smith, op. cit. p. 147.)

sacrifice was sometimes a natural outcrop of rough rock, but normally the Canaanites built a large altar (or altars) of stone or brick on which animals could be slain or their carcasses burnt entire.[1] A huge standingstone (*Massebah*), or an alinement of such stones, symbolized the God; whilst a wooden pole (*Asherah*)[2]— perhaps set in a stone socket, and obviously substitute for a living tree—denoted the Goddess.[3]

Canaanite religion, of course, had its *quota* of sacred persons. The Priests, who were guardians of the sanctuaries, conducted the sacrificing. There were Seers, gifted with psychic powers of insight—and Diviners skilled in reading omens. But it had also a class of persons, male and female, in our thought very dreadful. Those were the 'Servants of the God'; but that discreet title, whilst it no doubt implies that its bearers had various duties, covers the fact that they were set apart ('consecrated') to show God the need of fertility by imitative sexual relations with the worshippers. Further comment on this will be made. And, lastly, it is most likely (although we have no direct evidence before the Hebrew period) that Canaanite cult included a peculiar class of persons—devotees of the God, who (singly at times, but usually acting collectively) used to work themselves into a hypnotic frenzy which the onlookers took as proof that the power (*ruach*) of the God had entered the men, and were impressed by any utterance to which they might give vent. Such persons were called *Nĕbhiim* ('prophets').[4] It is likely that their relation to the

---

[1] In the desert a single stone, or heap of unhewn stones, had to serve as altar.

[2] The word is used in the Old Testament also to denote the Goddess, i.e. the ubiquitous *Ashtarte*, symbolized by the pole or sacred tree. *Asherah* occurs in the Amarna tablets as a variant designation of the Goddess. (See Burney, *Judges*, pp. 195–8.)

[3] A splendid example of a Canaanite High-Place was unearthed by Macalister at Gezer. One of its eight (originally ten) great standingstones showed that it had been regarded as the special abode of the God, where his presence should be reverenced by oil-anointing and kissing. Cp. Gen. xxviii. 18; Isa. lvii. 6.

[4] It is probable that the phenomenon spread from Anatolian (Hittite) religion into Syria, Phoenicia, and (presumably) early Palestine also. (Cp. T. H. Robinson, *The Classical Review*, October 1917.) A remarkable Egyptian record relates that an Egyptian envoy, visiting Byblos (a port in northern Syria) in the eleventh century, was unable to obtain what he required until prophetic ecstasy seized a young nobleman of Byblos, who declared that its *Baal* had granted the desire of *Amon*, the Egyptian's God.

priests of the sanctuaries was closer and more formal than used to be supposed.

The sequences of Nature in the Palestinian year gave rise to three principal holy seasons: (i) The Springtide Festival, when the agriculturalists were able to offer the first-fruits of ripe corn, and the shepherds the firstlings of their animals. Then also, we must infer, men felt bound to offer—or to commute their duty to offer—the first-born of their children. (ii) Seven weeks later, when the harvest of wheat and barley had been gathered, came the Mid-summer Feast.[1] (iii) The third great occasion of communal worship took place in autumn when the harvest of the grapes was gathered; and this was a Feast of drunken jubilation—significantly called 'Shoutings' (Hillulim).[2] It is written, 'wine that maketh glad the heart of man'[3]: one understands what Palestinians meant by the idea.

(2) *Pleasing the Gods*. Canaanites considered that Gods are touchy persons, standing very much on their dignity.[4] Ritual must be carried out punctiliously: it was not for priests and worshippers to ask why these things should be done, but to do them. Palestinian Gods seemed worse than touchy; there was an unaccountable streak in them; for, when the rites had been carried out scrupulously, lavishly, and enthusiastically, sometimes the rain did not fall and the crops withered, and sometimes pestilence broke out, and sometimes the warriors were beaten in battle and towns besieged and taken. Piety did not seem always to reward. Canaanites reasoned that in normal circumstances the Gods were (and should be) well pleased, if ungrudgingly men offered of their substance by gifts of fruit and animals. Naïve Canaanites thought that the Gods enjoyed the savour of burning flesh, the reek of the life-blood that they absorbed, and the sweeter (expensive) scent of incense. Wiser Canaanites reckoned that Gods demanded great deference from their worshippers. Do not kings and great men expect the same? On Man's side, however, it was reasonable to expect fair play from the Gods; a response to the

---

[1] In the later Jewish calendar known as 'the Feast of Weeks', and (since it commenced on the 50th day) in Greek-Christian circles as 'Pentecost'.

[2] See Judges ix. 27.   [3] Psalm civ. 15.

[4] The custom of burying a human sacrifice in the foundations of an important building implies anxiety to avert the jealousy of the Gods against human achievement. Cp. I Kings xvi. 34.

gifts, a return for the outlay. What was to be done when, notwithstanding all the normal offerings, things went amiss, and the Gods seemed unreasonably angry or negligent? What *could* be done except offer (if resources permitted) yet more sacrifices, make loud lamentation, confess sins known or unknown, and beseech the mercy of the Gods by presenting special expiatory sacrifices ('whole burnt-offerings')?[1] One thing more, however, was possible—to offer up a human sacrifice. And that (II Kings iii. 27) was done to meet desperate emergency, or some especially solemn need.

There is also a wider, awful, possibility. Did Canaanites normally sacrifice their first-born children? If so, it is certain they did it by burning the infants in honour of their God as *King*— *Melek*, the Lord of Fire. Evidence is forthcoming from an unexpected quarter. The city of Carthage, on the Tunisian coast of North Africa, was a great Phoenician colony; and Phoenicians and

---

[1] '*Theory' in Ancient Sacrifice.* Worship in the desert was relatively simple, although its men may have had more than one notion about the efficacy of animal sacrifices. The essential matter undoubtedly is that their sacrifices (whereby the vitalizing blood was returned to God and the flesh of the animal consumed by the worshippers as a sacred meal) can be viewed as primarily a feast of communion (sharing) which united God with men, and men with God, and the participants with one another. Robertson Smith (*Religion of the Semites*), with very persuasive erudition, argued that this was the oldest theory of Sacrifice, whereas the *gift* theory was a later development ensuing on agricultural life. His famous study had the utmost importance in bringing out the necessity of realizing desert psychological ideas. But the antithesis he drew was too sharply set. The desert attitude to sacrifices was both 'communion' and 'gift': so it was argued in the previous Chapter. When the agriculturalists offered their animals, they too may have felt much the same. But in their case considerations arise which go to show that the 'gift to the Gods' notion became disastrously dominant in their minds. Their problem was complicated. They had to face the mystery that the seed must be buried before it can come to life, and the necessity that sun and rain should work together until the harvest. No wonder they were often anxious and sore perplexed. When men eat bread or boil vegetables they do not feel that they are shedding the green *blood* of the cabbage or that corn has been *slaughtered* to provide the loaf. Therefore, as regards all their cereal and fruit offerings, it was obviously easy for the agriculturalists to view them as gifts to the God (naïvely, as *food* for the Gods). What was wrong with that? Only that it is so close to the precipice of inferring that the favour of the Gods must be bought, and can be bought. And over that precipice the Canaanites were constantly tumbling. What gives them away is that they were not content to offer a token of gratitude, but felt it wise to multiply sacrifices. In time of prosperity they plumed themselves on doing so, and in time of disaster felt it was the only thing to do—the Gods must be pleased and appeased.

Canaanites were men of the same racial origin and culture. When Carthage in 146 B.C. was on the verge of capture in its last war against the Romans, we know that its citizens judged their God (*Baal-Ammon* or *Melek*) was angry with them because the rich had been buying children from the poor to sacrifice instead of their own first-born.[1] (The children for sacrifice were placed in the arms of a huge statue of the God from which they slid into a furnace.) Since this custom was evidently regarded as right by Phoenician (Semitic) citizens in 146 B.C., it seems impossible to doubt that the Semitic Canaanites practised it, at least occasionally, during the 2000 years of their civilization down to the Age of the Hebrew kingdoms. One would like to think that they did so only under the shadow of fear; and that in fair-weather years they commuted the child's life by a material offering. Surely (it may be argued) the tax on man-power entailed by regular sacrifice of the first-born would have caused its discontinuance? The Mosaic tradition in Hebrew religion was appalled, and counted the custom utterly repugnant: an 'abomination of the Canaanites'—and the fact seems irrefutable evidence that it *was* custom in early Canaan.[2] The writer is reluctantly of opinion that for the Canaanites it met the problem of keeping down intolerable increase of population in their overcrowded fortress-towns. Further, we know that under certain of the Hebrew kings (and at a late date too) it was practised in honour of Jehovah—probably by Ahaz *c.* 735; certainly by Manasseh *c.* 650 B.C.

Besides the fundamental method of pleasing the Gods by sacrificial investments from which a good yield might reasonably be expected, Canaanites worked another line of approach—they *showed* the Gods what ought to happen by means of dramatic ritual ceremonies.[3] Men needed that Order should prevail over

---

[1] Diodorus Siculus, xx. 14, 65. Tertullian (*Apol.* cix) says that these horrible offerings persisted secretly even after the destruction of Carthage, even down to his own time, *c.* A.D. 200.

[2] Infant bodies buried in pots were found in excavating the sanctuary at Gezer. If these had been first-born sacrifices, the numbers would assuredly be far greater, and they would be found at other sanctuaries also. Besides, they were buried, not burnt.

[3] These imitative rites stand on the borderline between Magic (Science) and Religion (Faith). Where the intention of the ritual was to force the desired result to come to pass, there was Magic. Where the hope was to deserve that the Gods would set in motion their power to bless, the attitude was religious, however naïvely so.

Chaos, Light over Darkness, Summer over Winter, Birth over Death. Year by year, the withering of the vegetation and the cold of winter prompted fear lest the miracle of fertility should fail. And was there not deep significance in the fact that the seed must first be buried in the cold earth and seem to die, in order that it might rise triumphant from the grave? Did not the visible process imply that even the invisible Life-Giver must Himself first go down into death to the end that he might return in freshness of youthful vigour? But what power could resurrect him from the grasp of the grave? Surely the power of the sorrowing love of the Goddess—the faithful Earth-Mother![1] These thoughts gave rise to the enactment annually of two, most moving, ceremonials. One—probably at the Midsummer Festival[2]—dramatized the death and resurrection of the God, to ensure the revival of the seed when next it should be sown. But who was to play the part (realistically) of the slain God? The king embodied the Divine Blessing for his People. Obviously *he* must die—in theory. The monarchs no doubt objected to the logic, and even their subjects did not want to change their ruler every year. Provided that one man died for the People, a human substitute for His Majesty would serve. At the autumn Festival the thought that Order is triumphant over Chaos,[3] that Heaven and Earth are united, was given dramatic form in an annual jubilant procession symbolizing the enthronement of the God and his sacred marriage to the Goddess.[4]

---

[1] Celebrated in Babylonia and Syria as the mourning of Ishtar (Ashtarte) for Tammuz—in Asia Minor, of Cybele for Attis; (later) of Venus for Adonis. Allusion to the Tammuz ritual probably underlies Amos viii. 10; Isa. xvii. 10; Zech. xii. 10; Jer. xxii. 18; and also the tradition concerning Jephthah's daughter. See the Commentaries on Judges xi. 40.

[2] In Babylonia the occasion was the Springtime Festival.

[3] Cp. the enthronement Psalms, e.g. Ps. xcix.

[4] In Hebrew religion, as the Old Testament presents it, the symbolic marriage was completely expunged from the ritual. Trace of the custom possibly survives unrecognized in the metaphor of Yahveh as Israel's husband; possibly also in the dwelling in booths at the Autumn Festival. (See Hooke, op. cit. pp. 85, 139f.) Dramatizing the sacred marriage may have originated in Asia Minor in Hittite worship. There is also no real evidence that an 'Enthronement of God' ceremony took place in Hebrew worship (see Snaith, *The Jewish New Year Festival*).

§3. *Verdict*

Sentence may now be delivered on the ways of the Canaanites, and it may be pronounced in these severe words about the civilized Semites in general: 'The ritual tended to stir up in the worshippers a wild excitement; maddened by the cries, the dances, the wine, they gave themselves up by turns to unbridled merriment and to the bloody practices we have just alluded to, cutting themselves or offering to the gods whatever they held most dear. For the same reason ecstatic phenomena and sexual excesses played a large part in the religious life of the inhabitants of Palestine.'[1] Nevertheless, seeds of good as well as evil were subtly intermixed in their religion. The mischief was that for 2000 years the Canaanites were too incompetent, or too guiltily indifferent, to try to sort them out and plant 'the good seed of the Word'. Wherefore tares grew rankly, and wheat sparsely, in the religious and moral fields of ancient Canaan. Tares have flourished in the fields of Europe for 1900 years, and Europeans have less excuse for the unprofitable fact.

If we are to read a lesson for ourselves in all this, we should first be very fair to the Canaanites' good intentions, which they failed to disentangle from base and foolish ways. The horrible custom of sex license with the servants of the God at the sanctuaries was not guilty behaviour. These men and women were regarded as consecrated, holy, persons; set apart from normal family life not for their own gain, but to promote the necessity of fertility. At the root of the custom was the illusion that (through imitative dramatizing) physical means would induce the supernatural end desired to come to pass: the material action caused or assisted the Gods to impart the Blessing. The custom gratified sensuality; yet there was more to it than sex-emotion. It touched the deep sentiments of parentage, and offered a door of hope to childless women in a society which was very cruel to the childless wife.

Fine ideas were latent in the sacrifices of first-fruits and animals. The system asserted belief that human welfare is not obtained by having regard only to the visible world, but requires in us certain profoundly ethical qualities. The man who does not give to God will not receive; and he must give of his best. (The animal he

---

[1] Lods, *Israel*, p. 102.

selects for his sacrifice must be 'without spot or blemish'—God must not be treated as a salvage dump for what we no longer want and shall not miss.) Only by reality of willing and generous giving, only in integrity of purpose, could the vital bond between Man and the Supernatural be established and sustained. The *peace offerings* —where the flesh of the beast was returned by the priest to the worshipper that he and his family and friends might eat of its meat together 'before God'—asserted that religion was occasion for happiness. The expiatory *burnt offerings*—whether on behalf of the community or of an individual—testified that men must have solemn and costly consciousness of guilt and of need for pardon and reconciliation to one another and to God. But what a muddle the Canaanites were making of these fine instincts! No theorizing can make animal sacrifice other than a gross and grotesque expression of spiritual feelings. Imagine the cries of the driven animals, the stench of blood and burning flesh. Frankincense was a desirable accompaniment of ancient worship. Far worse was the basic fact that the system came not far short of being an attempt to commercialize the relations of God and Man. Continually it tempted to suppose that the favour of the Gods could be bought, if one paid high enough price: now and again it might need to be even a human life, but *that* would surely do the trick. Normally, however, a quite reasonable outlay should secure a very profitable return. In good years the investment might yield 100 per cent. But the stock was not gilt-edged, despite its solar colouring. The variable climate of Palestine saw to that. When the celestial company paid no dividend, Canaanites could not understand what had gone wrong between them and the Gods.

The Gods were deemed to be, very vigilantly, on the side of social righteousness. But the Justice which the Gods were supposed to uphold was the traditional usages of the community. It is quite a safe inference that Canaanites were not racking their brains about problems of equity, or reflecting deeply about motives, and certainly were not forcing their conscience to confront an ideal of Absolute Goodness.

It has often been charged against the Canaanites that, as compared with the nomads who boldly called their God their Father, they *localized* their Deities, counting them Lords of places and things. That is not correct. The Canaanite Deities were adored also in terms of personal relationship—Lords both of places and of the persons resident therein.[1] It is sometimes argued that, as compared with the nomads, the Palestinians were following a lower level of religious thought because they styled God *Master* and themselves His *servants* or *slaves*, instead of His *sons*. In feudal England men were not abject, because they acknowledged themselves to be (say) the servants of the King, or of the Earl of Surrey. Fortunate and honourable was the Canaanite who knew himself the subject of a good and great king, the servant of a mighty Baal. The Master-Servant relation ought not automatically to be disparaged: it was capable of development into the Prophetic conception of the faithful 'servant of the Lord'. Neither the Canaanite acknowledgement that service is due, nor the desert claim to Sonship, were of any real value until both were sublimated by the genius of the great Hebrew Prophets.

Finally, Canaanites believed that, whatsoever they did religiously, they should do with all their might. The great seasons of Palestinian worship can justly be stigmatized as licentious orgies. But at any ràte the Canaanites did not relinquish religion to the special attention of a handful of earnest people in the body politic. Nor did they regard its practice as an individual affair, but as the very bond of society. All gave it their serious concern, which is more than can be said of Western civilization.

§4. *Significance*

Canaanite religion and sociology progressed up to a point, and no further. How far did they travel? To be unkind, one can stress that they lacked sense to shake off even the chains of ridiculous, gross superstitions. Taking the most charitable view, it is plain that they were polytheists. But it may be urged in their favour that their belief in many Gods amounted in practice to adoration of just *the* God and *the* Goddess approachable at their own High-Place, Benefactors of their little community: one might call the theology 'Duo-theism'. Some scholars have thought that at times (and in very early times) theologically-minded Canaanites had advanced to belief that the God (*El*) worshipped at the many places was really one and the same supreme, solar, Deity. The

---

[1] Baudissin's exhaustive examination of the designation 'Lord' (*Baal*) has proved the point (Κύριος, vol. III); cp. S. A. Cook's review in *J.T.S.* (April, 1931), p. 234.

writer thinks the scant evidence is misconstrued.[1] And it is indisputable that the Canaanites lapsed back into polytheism—the advance, if it occurred, was not held and clarified. Even if the theory be correct, worship of a supreme *El* amounted to *numerical* monotheism. The crucial issue is not whether there be one God, but what is the character of the One God in relation to Man, and how does Man rightly serve His will. Towards *ethical* monotheism neither the religion of the Canaanites, nor (as we have next to indicate) that of the vast majority of the Israelites, was making any vestige of progress. There is no evidence that they were on the way towards surmounting belief in the Goddess alongside of the God, nor to learning higher thoughts concerning what the Supernatural requires from Man, nor to treating one another as brethren. They were of divided and doubtful mind.

Jesus said: 'Seek ye first the kingdom of God, and all other things shall be added unto you.' The Canaanites, for all their

---

[1] Attention is called to the use of the honorific titles *El Shammaim* ('God of the heavens'), *El Elyon* ('God exalted'). *El Shaddai* (Exod. vi. 3) is a philological puzzle, but the meaning is now generally regarded to be 'God of the mountain.' See S. A. Cook, *Religion of Ancient Palestine*, pp. 141, 160. Garstang (citing Dussaud) stresses a phrase in the Ras Shamra tablets alluding to Canaan as 'the land of *El* absolutely', wherein nothing is done without his order. The Ras Shamra phrase may be no more than diplomatic politeness —the Amorite-Syrians' recognition that Canaan is a land enjoying to the full the benefit of divine protection. Garstang, however, thinks that prior to the fifteenth century there was, in some quarters, widespread worship of a common Deity, implying a one-time unity, political, racial and religious, which disintegrated in the Egyptian period with the result that 'El, like Teshub among the Hittite confederated cities, thus became a Baal, adapted to the local needs and customs of individual cities'. He does not consider that the many Baals were ever regarded as localized worship of one supreme Baal: 'Among the Canaanites there is nothing to suggest that all the worshippers of Baal were united by a common religion: the local Baal seems to have remained for each district an individual and even jealous god, an element of separation rather than a bond.' (See *Heritage of Solomon*, pp. 118–21.) In a different connexion, S. A. Cook, on the basis of an Egyptian document, points out that: 'To the Egyptians Baal was perhaps the best known Semitic deity, a war-god whose roaring spread terror.' *Baal*, however, is an epithet, '*Master*', and Canaanites of diverse racial allegiances worshipping *Amor*, or *Teshub*, or *Adad*, or *Resheph*, could each invoke the God as *Baal*. The Egyptians did not grasp to which God precisely Canaanitish warriors addressed their confidence, but they were impressed by the roaring. (As to so-called 'Primitive Monotheism' see p. 365. It is doubtful if even *numerical* monotheism obtained among the early Babylonians.)

genuine piety and anxiety to please the Gods, approached the problem of life from the other end. They were set on getting all other things, and were baffled to understand why they received them only spasmodically, and found that war and pestilence and hunger and cruelty continued. They did not see the values in life in the right order, and were mystified because it seemed that the Gods were only semi-good. Europe for 1900 weary years, and America for a hectic century or two, have been plagued by fighting scrambling and longing for things that do not belong to our peace; by besotted and dogged determination to worship Mammon first and (perhaps) God second; and by perplexity when affairs do not work well. What was wrong with the Canaanites religiously was that they had a squint, and did not understand why facts were hard to focus.

CHAPTER VIII

JEHOVAH: GOD OF ISRAEL

When the Hebrews who had been with Moses (probably less than 10,000 in number) entered Canaan about 1175 B.C., it was expectable that in the course of centuries their thoughts and customs would merge into the general culture of the ancient population. If that be doubted on the ground that they brought with them matchless memories of extraordinary events befallen them under the leadership of an extraordinary man, reflect how hard it is to enable later generations to realize the Past with the vividness that alone makes it influential. Modern children are no longer stirred to patriotic enthusiasm by the struggle against Napoleon, or by the American War of Independence. A Hebrew grandfather would find that 'How I crossed the Red Sea' was no more to his grandson than a bed-time story, and that his sons were much more concerned whether anything could be done about the latest insolence from the Canaanites. The purpose of this chapter is to consider not the achievement of a few remarkable Hebrews, but 'the Mind of the Many'—to trace how insidiously the influences of life in Canaan moulded the religious ideas of the majority. Our present aim is to understand how their naïve trust in the God of the desert mountain developed eventually into worship of Jehovah as the *national* God of the two Hebrew kingdoms. For that popular or official religion of Israel is the sombre background against which the faith of the great Prophets shines. The survey has to cover a period of six centuries, from the crossing of Jordan to the Fall of Jerusalem in 586 B.C. Since this study is not a political History of Israel, only the phases and episodes which profoundly affected the course of religion and morals will be emphasized.

§ 1. *Jehovah Conquers*

(i) *The Gods of Battles.* The average Hebrew when he entered Canaan was imbued with one religious conviction—Jehovah was a warrior-God, mighty in battle, Lord of fire and storm. That swept the tribesmen up to the highlands and the capture of Bethel and Ai. But there (more or less) the tide of victory ebbed, leaving them high and dry on the mountains, envying the riches of the fortress-towns but quite unable to drive out the Canaanites who (provokingly) 'would dwell in the land'.

(*a*) *Victory over Sisera*. The decades passed. The tribes became increasingly weak and disunited, and had to be content that they had not been driven out of the land. What use was distant Jehovah now?—the shepherds asked themselves. Their God dwelt remote at Mount Horeb, or somewhere else in the *desert*. But there came an amazing victory over Sisera and his horsemen and chariots in the Plain of Esdraelon beside the river Kishon. And it was due to a terrific storm causing the river to overflow until the soil was a morass in which were bogged chariots and floundering horsemen. Jehovah had shown the reality of His power and purpose to be with them even in Canaan; and the Hebrews sang—

> Yahveh, in thy path from Seir,
> In thy march from the field of Edom,
> Earth quaked, yea, heaven rocked,
> Yea, the clouds dropped water.
> The mountains shook before Yahveh,
> Before Yahveh, God of Israel.[1]

It was like the triumph of the Exodus over again, when Moses and the children of Israel exulted, saying: 'Yahveh is a man of war: Yahveh is his name. Pharaoh's chariots and his host hath he cast into the sea: his chosen captains also are drowned in the Red Sea.'[2] Nevertheless, the victors over Sisera found that the Canaanites still 'would dwell in the land'. Things, however, were not quite so bad, and some Hebrew families were able to combine the task of pasturing flocks with cultivation of the soil (not grape-growing— that was beyond their skill) in places unwanted by the Canaanites.[3] In time they were suffered to occupy villages of their own, where the nearby townsmen were reasonable. And *now* what use was Jehovah? What they needed was not a God of battles, but a God

[1] See Judges v. 4. (Cp. Smith, *Early Poetry of Israel*, pp. 85 f.)
[2] Exod. xv. 1–4.
[3] At first the system would be for the group of families to work the sown area in common, each receiving its appropriate share of the harvest. Garstang (*Heritage of Solomon*, p. 269) points out that 'It was only in the later history of land-tenure, when the development of agriculture and the monarchical system with its social changes had led to the subdividing of the soil, that the inalienable right of each citizen to the ownership of his hereditary parcel of ground was recognized'. (Cp. Naboth's vineyard, I Kings xxi.)

of bargaining. They had to barter the fleeces of their flocks for a few luxuries at exorbitant prices; for in the transactions the Canaanites had the upper hand and pointed out that they were business-men, not philanthropists.

(*b*) '*The Troops of Midian.*' There came a succession of large-scale raids into Canaan made by the Hebrews' first cousins from the desert—Midianites and Amalekites and Ammonites. The brunt of it fell on the Hebrews with their unwalled villages and exposed crops, their flocks and herds in the open pastures—easy booty. The attacks were marauding ventures, not serious attempts at permanent settlement; and the Canaanites in their strong towns could view the temporary inundation without much concern. From their vantage-ground on the battlements they could comfortably 'see the troops of Midian prowl and prowl around' (as the Victorian version of a Greek hymn phrases it). If there was to be courageous resistance, it had to be made by the Hebrews. Resist they did! The peril evoked 'Heroes of Jehovah'.[1] Jephthah of Gilead fought the Ammonites.[2] Gideon, of the tribe of Manasseh in central Canaan, with a few ardent followers dramatically routed the Midianites and drove them in confusion back across Jordan.[3] His personal triumph had a fascinating, significant sequel. Some Hebrews, much impressed, felt it was time for a social revolution in order to obtain systematic arrangement for defence. They wanted to make him *king*: 'Then the men of Israel said unto Gideon, Rule thou over us, both thou and thy son, and thy son's son also.'[4] Gideon, true to the desert instinct that free men do not rule over one another, refused. But his son, Abimelech, a reckless scamp, coveted what his father would not take. Married to a Canaanite woman, he persuaded the Canaanites of Shechem to make him their king; proceeded (with the aid of a ruffian bodyguard whom he hired) to massacre his now indignant Hebrew kinsfolk in the vicinity; next quarrelled with his Canaanite subjects, and in revenge managed to burn Shechem itself; and finally had his pretensions ended at Thebez by a woman who with

---

[1] I.e. outstanding men, valorous and successful, whose leadership in battle others were willing to accept, and to whose arbitrament they might bring their disputes in time of peace. Such a man the Hebrews termed *Shôphet* (Hero, Judge). The gathered traditions of the leaders in this period were therefore entitled *The Book of Judges*.

[2] Judges xi.   [3] Judges vii, viii.   [4] Judges viii. 22.

excellent aim and unusual strength threw a millstone down on his head. One Abimelech was enough to make Hebrews dubious for a long while about hereditary rule by kings.

(c) *The Armies of the Philistines.* The Philistines occupying the southern coastal plain were very strong. Their cities, organized on a partly democratic basis, were capable of taking united action, and their iron weapons were far superior to those of the bronze-armed Canaanites and still worse-armed Hebrews. They could have overrun the inland hills at any time, but—like the Hanoverian Government long reluctant to have to police the Scottish clans— they had the sense to know that it may be easy to defeat mountain-men in a fight, but much more difficult to keep them permanently pacified. It sufficed the Philistines that the Judaean highlanders knew who could be their masters. The next traditions in the Book of Judges tell how a youthful Hebrew called Samson carried out a series of bold exploits, single-handed, against the Philistines.[1] The important point is Samson's radiant certainty that his tremendous strength, and his successes, were due to Jehovah, who filled him with His divine energy (*ruach*). Eventually the Philistines got hold of daring Samson, and tortured him to death. These happenings were no more than irritant pin-pricks to the Philistines. About 1050–1025 B.C. the Philistines resolved on thorough action, struck into the heart of the country, scattered the Hebrews, smashed up their one temple of Jehovah at Shiloh, and got control of a sufficient number of strategic Canaanite towns wherein they established garrisons to dominate the mountains. That was the end of the Canaanites, *qua* Canaanites, in opposition to Hebrews. They vanish as such out of history; and the reason is that it was the Hebrews who opened up a new chapter in history. The Philistine onslaught had momentarily broken the tribesmen, but did not quite quench their spirit. Surprisingly they rallied; and rallied because they believed that their God could, and would, come to their aid, if they would respond to His *inspiration* and fight against the daunting Philistines. Bands of prophetic devotees started to fan the flame of faith in Jehovah's might. Influenced by the Seer-Prophet Samuel, who called upon them to concede *kingly* authority to Saul and fight under his leadership and that of

---

[1] To the annoyance of the men of Judah, who saw that Samson was merely stirring up trouble and did not like it: 'Knowest thou not', they said to him, 'that the Lords of the Philistines are rulers over us?' (Judges xv. 11.)

his valorous son Jonathan, a considerable number of the tribesmen vowed to do so. Little was effected for some time. Then heroism and good fortune enabled Jonathan to overthrow one of the Philistine garrisons, and for a short while Hebrew control of the highlands was restored.[1] Came Tragedy—both Saul and Jonathan were slain in a disastrous battle on Mount Gilboa overlooking the Plain of Esdraelon.[2] But the immediate sequel was the meteoric career of David, whom jealous Saul had driven out of Judah, and who had won the confidence of the Philistine ruler of Gath. When therefore after Saul's death David became leader of the Judaeans and they declared him their king at Hebron, the Philistines probably thought the situation was to their own interest. Too late they discovered that a Master of Men had arisen: warrior, statesman, magnetic personality.

For the first time in Canaan's history, David created a united and strong State in the central mountains; the Philistines were eclipsed; David's control spread far; and his reign was followed by the glories of Solomon's kingdom. David wrested Jerusalem ('Zion'), the fortress of the Jebusites, out of their grasp to be his royal residence and capital of the kingdom he meant to make.[3] When its gates had opened to the challenge of Jehovah—'the King of glory, the Lord strong and mighty, the Lord mighty in battle'[4] —indisputably the Hebrews' God had conquered Canaan. Its ancient war-Gods, *Adad, Teshub, Resheph* and the rest, faded into oblivion. Henceforth *Jehovah* was the great God of the Hebrew realm, so long as it should endure.

(ii) *The Price of Victory.* The victory had its sinister aspect— which may be summed up by saying that Jehovah, the desert

[1] There is evidence that Saul's actions and merits were unduly depreciated by the Hebrew historians, in order to point the contrast with David. But it is clear that Saul's position was precarious, and his kingship probably more nominal than real. Only his own Benjamite region, and the territory east of Jordan where he had delivered the town of Jabesh-Gilead from the Ammonites, were strongly attached to him; and his career darkened through his finally insane jealousy of the prowess of youthful David. The Philistines remained strong as ever on the coast, and controlled the vital Plain of Esdraelon with its key-town of Bethshan near the Jordan. See further, Chapter XI, pp. 230 f.

[2] See the famous poem lamenting their death (II Sam. i. 19–27). Its verses, no doubt composed by David, are one of the oldest passages in the Bible.

[3] II Sam. v. 6–10.

[4] Ps. xxiv. 7–10.

God, was now revered as mighty *Baal* of Canaan. He had become its *Master*, its *Owner*. The multitude of Canaanite subjects of David were perfectly willing to admit the fact. The claim did not disturb their religious equanimity. Canaan had adored some martial Deity as its great Baal time out of mind. *Amor, Teshub, Resheph, Adad, Sutekh, Jehovah*—'What's in a name?' And the Hebrews, as they to their joy began to consolidate their mastery, innocently and proudly annexed the title for Jehovah. Indeed the fashion had set that way as early as the time of Gideon's exploits against the Midianite marauders; for Hebrews began to use *Baal* in forming compound names to bestow on their children. (An alternative name for Gideon was Jerubbaal; Saul had a son called Ishbaal, and a grandson Meribbaal; and David called a son Baal-yada.[1])

(*a*) *The Social Cost.* It seems a pleasing matter that a wandering shepherd should decide to settle down, plough up a plot of land, plant some vegetables and build a humble dwelling for his family. But a change which transformed him in body mind and soul had occurred. Very soon his wife would be furious because someone had touched 'her things', and his children's children would say that, of course, there are always 'Masters and Men', and 'Riches and Poverty'. To guard against giving impression of crude exaggeration, be it said that the argument is not that all virtues belonged to the nomads and all vices to the townsmen. The pattern of life is too exquisitely complex for such easy analysis. Nevertheless, the social transformation here indicated is immense. Something revolutionizing takes place in the depths of our being when there are things that we can count our own, and we can say to a fellowman 'Go' and he goeth, and to another 'Come' and he cometh. The Western World has been so immersed in that way of life century after century that we can scarce imagine another outlook. But here it is in the words of Miss Freya Stark:

[1] Kittel thinks that it may become usual to give the eldest son a name embodying *Ya* (*Yahu*), and the second a name compounded with *Baal*—symptomatic of the fusing of Hebrew with Canaanite ideas. See I Chron. viii. 33, 34; xiv. 7; etc. (Lods, *Israel*, p. 408, notes that *Ostraka* of Ahab's time, found in Samaria, show the prevalence of names compounded with *Baal*.) The copyists of later times substituted *Bosheth* (*Shame!*) in such names for motives of reverence in public reading. Thus in the text of II Sam. ii. 8 Saul's son is termed *Ishbosheth*, not *Ishbaal* as in I Chron. (the correct pronunciation).

Even in the modern town [Aden] the Past has a way of jostling you off the pavement in the shape of some blue-painted Bedu [Arab], naked-torsoed, ballet-skirted, his hair matted under a fillet, and waist broad-belted and jewelled with a dagger—who leads his camel by a rope in the space reserved for walking and looks at the ousted passengers as if they were a column of ants in the dust. I have often wondered what gives the nomad Arab that superb and arrogant poise which he loses as soon as he enters our modern world as a townsman or a tiller of the soil. It is, I believe, his feeling of equality. Not American equality, which depends on equal justice, equal opportunity, equal motor cars, frigidaires, permanent waves, equal comforts and movies. Your Bedu, if he could bring himself to envisage it at all, would call this Captivity. What he feels is something independent of possessions or even of rights; it is the innate equality of human beings, implied in their subservience to God. If he wants a radio set, or a gun, or an education, he wants them for themselves, but not with the idea of being somebody else's equal: that he is already by the inalienable right of his manhood. This gives him his unselfconsciousness, his dignity, his easy courtesy and careless walk, whatever his contrast of rags may be with others' kingly garments....And I am sure that the West is doing the East no service by destroying it in the mind of the Young Effendi: an Equality which inspires you to meet your neighbour without envy and your death without fear is not to be despised.[1]

In Canaan very swiftly Hebrew owners of property became like-minded with the Canaanites. The desert ideals wilted. Thoughts turned anxiously inwards upon things, lest they should be taken away. To lose one's riches was to lose one's *Honour*, and be broken in spirit. *Peace* meant security: the absence of war, the safety of one's person and goods—undisputed possession without need to maintain it. In Canaan it was difficult not to covet a neighbour's goods. Wealth could be acquired, and exploited, for the selfish interests of the owner. A man might profit by the downfall of a brother. In Canaan what could the impoverished and the weak (the widow and the orphan) do, save hire themselves out to labour for the fortunate or become his slave?

(*b*) *The Religious Cost.* 'Canaanized' Hebrews began to make God in the image of their changed outlook on life. Jehovah as *Baal* became the Divine Possessor and Master. Then, as with the Canaanites, Hebrew religion began to be a muddle. (Remember that from the time of David onwards we are thinking about an

---

[1] *East is West*, p. 16.

amalgamated population: Hebrew families held leadership and dominance in the Monarchic Period, but those of Canaanitish descent were preponderant in numbers. Remember also the allowance we have to make for the co-existence of different levels of thought.) There were three ways of thinking what exactly one meant by hailing Jehovah as *Baal*; and the subjects of the Hebrew kings followed all three of them. (i) It might mean that Jehovah had not destroyed the ancient Supernatural Beings who had always made the land fertile, but had *mastered* them and reduced them to serve His will for His favoured People. That seemed a reasonable view; they themselves had not exterminated the former inhabitants, but were being very successful in making them labour for successful Hebrews. Long before Hebrews crossed Jordan Canaan was a holy land, where Supernatural Beings, its Baals, caused fountains to rise and streams to run, cattle to live, and seeds to ripen. That process had not stopped. The inference was that the Land was 'Under New Management', but the *personnel* of 'the Old Firm' had been retained. The Canaanites knew all about the exact way to propitiate the divine Beings that blessed the corn and the vines and the olives in each locality; and were positive all would go wrong unless the wonted rites were carried out carefully year by year. Very many Hebrews agreed with them, and judged that the right thing was to honour Jehovah as the national Deity (supreme Baal of the Land, Lord of Victory, Lord of Justice), and also to propitiate His obedient servants, the ancient Baals, at each and every local sanctuary. Proof that this attitude was prevalent as late as 750 B.C. (two centuries after the time of David and Solomon) is furnished by a verse in Hosea which voices the Prophet's protest.[1] (ii) Dull-witted, and very parochial, Canaanites were not interested in academic theological questions, and did not worry whether the Baal to whom they paid their dues was asserted by the priest to be the *Sun* or *Resheph* or *Adad*. All they cared about was their fixed opinion that their own local *Baal* and his *Baalath* were different from, and more efficient than, the *Baal* and *Baalath* worshipped by the next town. Dull-witted Hebrews may have followed suit, and been in danger of degrading the national Jehovah into the notion that there were many rival Jehovah-Baals—of this place and of that. At any rate it has been suggested that the notable urgency in the Command-

---

[1] Hos. ii. 10.

ment, 'Hear, O Israel, the Lord, thy God, is *one* God', may imply need to combat that foolishness. (iii) There was latent possibility of a great advance in thought and morals when the Hebrews brought faith in the God of Moses (however dimly the essence of it may have been grasped by them) into the civilization of Canaan, and when (the Hebrews having gained the leadership) belief in the ancient Deities had waned and might now be replaced by worship of but one God. The frightful calamity that occurred in course of time was that the popular and official conception of Jehovah adopted as proper for His worship the orgiastic paraphernalia of the ancient Canaanite religious system, rejoiced and persisted in it. Skinner sums up the position as regards the general attitude of the Hebrews in these words: 'The gain was more than neutralized by the degradation of Yahweh to the level of a nature-deity, and by the absorption of the old Canaanite ritual with all its repellent features into the public cultus of Israel.'[1]

§2. *Jehovah Reigns*

David and Solomon caused Jehovah, already *Baal*, to become *King*. Ordinary men construed the divine kingship after the pattern of the earthly one laid down by David, Solomon, and their successors. Judah and Israel experienced two or three worthy kings; the rest were average despots or worse. If God is toward Man as a Palestinian monarch towards his subjects, then Divine commandments are promulgated not for free assent to their rightfulness, but for servile obedience. What the priest enjoins and the State maintains, that do, and ask not *Why*. The path to kings was difficult. Royal officials saw to that. Judicious gifts, however, will smooth the way; and the greater the boon desired, the larger surely should be the token of respect. If a suppliant reach the Presence, let him bow down to the soles of the monarch's feet. How should it be otherwise with God, the King of kings? Men reasoned that none should come before Him without an offering, and should worship in fear and trembling. Seeds of good were mixed up in that opinion, but for the most part the notion consisted of deep-rooting seeds of evil.

David and Solomon first showed the Hebrew what it is to be a king indeed. They had the usual three problems to solve, and a

---

[1] *Prophecy and Religion*, p. 60.

special one of their own. First, they had to enlist a trustworthy bodyguard and arrange for an efficient army in time of war. Second, to fill a treasury, in order to pay the soldiers' wages and meet the heavy expenses of a court befitting royal dignity. Third, some officials were needed (an embryo Civil Service) to watch the king's interest—to deter powerful families from taking such revenge as to upset the general welfare; and to keep a very vigilant eye on possible rebels. David and Solomon, in addition, had also somehow to make Zion-Jerusalem a capital acceptable both to the Judaeans and the Israelites: a place of strength, and worthy of veneration by all their subjects.

David hired a 'Foreign-Legion' bodyguard;[1] as nucleus of the army he formed a Hebrew *corps d'élite*—the 'mighty men of valour'. In his early reign popularity and victories (spoils for all) no doubt gave him voluntarily all the other warriors he needed on occasion. It is likely that the range of his kingdom may have extended to part of Syria, and (much more important) he controlled Edom and the lucrative caravan route to the Gulf of Elath. As for revenue, booty from the wars and tolls on caravans were in general enough. We infer that he had the dignity of simple personal wants. He attempted no large buildings. It may be true (as tradition believed) that he gathered material resources to serve more ambitious plans his successor might carry out.[2] As for Justice, it was his duty, as king, to be Court of Appeal, provided the litigant could bring the matter to his notice. In later years his rebel son, Absalom, accused (or slandered) him for negligence in this respect.[3] David exalted the religious honour of Zion by bringing into it, as soon as he could, the sacred Ark of the Lord.

Solomon inherited an opportunity, and took it with consummate skill by a mixture of diplomatic, military and commercial measures.[4] He made a firm alliance with Hiram, King of Phoenicia. He recognized that foot-soldiers were behind the times, and set

[1] The 'Cherethites and Pelethites'. It seems certain that the Pelethites were Philistine recruits, and until recently much the same interpretation was placed on the Cherethites. It is now probable that the latter were men from the desert region of the Negeb south of Gaza, known as the land of Keret.

[2] The census of the population which (to the disgust of his People) he made in later years was probably a step towards arrangements for general taxation. (II Sam. xxiv.)

[3] See II Sam. xiv, xv. 1–6.

[4] See Garstang's graphic description. (*Heritage of Solomon*, pp. 334–94.)

himself to multiply cavalry and chariots—until he was reputed to have 'a thousand and four hundred chariots and twelve thousand horsemen'.[1] (In his hey-day he even ran an armaments trade, selling horsed chariots, price about £100, to the Egyptians and petty kings of Syria.) Thus he was able to station swift-striking forces at strategic places dominating the great trade-routes, so that he and Hiram could levy toll on the immense volume of trade from the Phoenician ports to Egypt on the one hand and to southern Arabia (the Queen of Sheba's realm) on the other. Immense wealth resulted. Solomon is the first instance of Hebrew commercial genius on the breath-taking scale. He and Hiram set up a private Joint-Stock Company to run a sea-trade down the Red Sea to India and Africa; Solomon building the ships at the port of Elath, and Hiram's Phoenician seamen sailing them. Exotic rarities poured in to Jerusalem—ivory and apes and peacocks. And riches—gold and silver! 'Silver was nothing accounted of in the days of Solomon.' Then the Hebrew Croesus proceeded to overstrain even those resources by building on a scale truly magnificent, and staggering to the imagination of his subjects.[2] He fortified Jerusalem with an immensely strong wall, enclosing a far greater area than David's Zion, within which the expelled former Jebusite (Amorite-Hittite) population, and others attracted to the royal city, could reside. Then he really got going —on a positively amazing scheme of royal buildings to serve as palace and temple. David may be said to have contributed at least its magnificent site—the present temple-area of Jerusalem. But alas! what an edifice Solomon built thereon—a super-extravagant palace and a Phoenician-designed temple. Millionaire monarchs do not do their own architecting and building: they pay experts. Solomon hired skilled Phoenician architects and craftsmen. Huge quantities of cedars of Lebanon had to be imported over the difficult mountain tracks. So many the workmen required that he imposed forced labour on his astonished but indignant subjects. As for the palace—there was a splendid state-hall and throne-room, called 'the House of the Lebanon and Porch of

---

[1] Excavations at several places, notably Megiddo, have disclosed extensive stables of the Solomonic period.

[2] The financial inference is drawn from his having ceded to Hiram a large tract of Hebrew territory (the region of Asher) south of Phoenicia. It looks like a case of selling property to foot the bill.

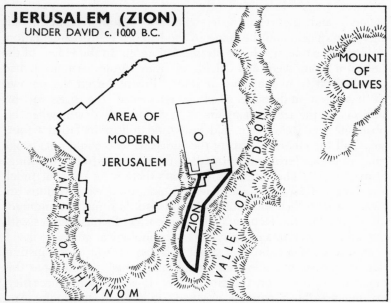

JERUSALEM (ZION)
UNDER DAVID c. 1000 B.C.

AREA OF
MODERN
JERUSALEM

MOUNT
OF
OLIVES

VALLEY OF HINNOM

ZION

VALLEY OF KIDRON

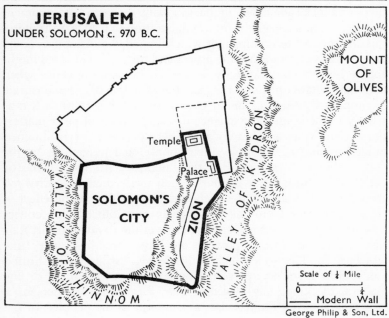

JERUSALEM
UNDER SOLOMON c. 970 B.C.

MOUNT
OF
OLIVES

Temple

Palace

SOLOMON'S
CITY

ZION

VALLEY OF HINNOM

VALLEY OF KIDRON

Scale of ¼ Mile
0   ¼
—— Modern Wall

George Philip & Son, Ltd.

Pillars', and the regal apartments for Solomon himself, his Egyptian queen, and the ladies of the harem. For ornamentation, gold was the one metal that pleased Solomon. In the House of the Lebanon alone were 600 shields of beaten gold. Ambition had travelled far from the days of tents. But not even the renown of having a millionaire as king reconciled the mass of his subjects to the trend of affairs. On Solomon's death, when his obstinate son Rehoboam said he would follow in father's footsteps, all the Hebrews (except the Judaeans who could not) broke off, and under Jeroboam formed, to the north of Judah, the kingdom of Israel. Thereafter for 300 years there were kings of Judah and kings of Israel. Candidates for Scriptural examinations are aware of it to their vexation; scholars also, burning the midnight oil to correlate the Hebrew dates, and correct inconsistencies with the aid of Assyrian and Babylonian chronological tables.

A balance-sheet showing profit and loss as regards the institution of monarchic rule over Judah and Israel would have this much to set down on the credit side. It was political necessity, making possible a national existence, culture and outlook. And there was social advantage in that gradually the central government had to seek to supervise some administration of justice, restraining the disruptive 'desert' instinct which impelled an irate person to exact whatever vengeance the power and fury of his kindred might enable him to take. Morally, it was an immense advance when national welfare upheld as the *ideal* the principle of commensurate recompense: 'An eye for an eye, a tooth for a tooth.' It was wholly to the kings' convenience that in the mass of petty matters the ancient system, whereby the elders of localities maintained public opinion of Right by their counsel and judgement 'at the Gate', should continue. But the kings saw to their own (or national) interests by a method which made their authority *felt* throughout the land, but which had far-reaching tragic effect— either they sent from the court their own officials (to collect revenue, supervise justice, and watch over the royal authority), or they conferred special powers on local 'worthies' (or 'unworthies'!). These men (called the *Sarim*, 'Nobles') constituted a new class in society: persons whose fortunes were made or unmade as the kings might please. They formed, says Pedersen, 'a new aristocracy, a limited class as opposed to the people. In the small towns this new aristocracy may not have made itself felt.

But in the large cities, and above all in Jerusalem, the new class dissolved the power of the old families....The King could raise new men who pleased him, and the old order of property was not respected....The *Sarim* of the new class were dependent on the King, the ties connecting them with their poor fellow-citizens were broken, and so they crushed them instead of upholding them.'[1] As for furtherance of True Religion, monarchy did not help. If it be suggested that kings taught the Hebrews to think majestically of their God—reverence for ultimate verities of Truth, Goodness and Beauty is respect not for grandeur but for virtue, not for wealth but for wisdom. Consider the influences that spread from Solomon's magnifical temple, built to be 'an house meet for God to dwell in'.[2] Take a glance at its layout.

Phoenician architects designed it. Naturally they planned it like the temples in Tyre and Sidon wherein was worshipped *Melkart* their God, the sort of Deity in whose honour first-born children were sacrificed by fire. The alinement of its courts, the chief altar and the sanctuary itself were laid out with mathematical exactitude to suit worship of the Sun.[3] Within the temple was the dark chamber holding the sacred Ark, watched over by two winged figures (the Cherubim), like the Guardian-images found in Egyptian and Babylonian temples. There is no evidence of standingstones (*Maẓẓeboth*) to denote the male Deity; but—if not from the start, soon afterwards—a wooden pole (*Asherah*) to symbolize the Goddess was set up. Phoenician craftsmen wrought the decorations—the golden vessels and the carvings. Profuse (palm-tree) ornamentation emphasized the fertility cult. And international Solomon had not been narrow-minded; he built altars for sacrifice to the Gods of other lands. These are said to have been in the vicinity of Jerusalem, but analogies in other countries suggest that at the festival seasons symbols or images of these Gods would be brought into the temple as visiting Deities come to pay their respects to Jehovah. No doubt the magnificent temple and palace made a vast impression on the Hebrews. But what ideas did they take back home of how God wanted to be worshipped? Did the resplendent vessels, and the robes of the royal priests, suggest belief that the pious should feed the hungry and clothe the naked? Did the emblems of the fertility cult

[1] *Israel*, p. 39.   [2] I Kings v. 5; viii. 12, 13.
[3] See Hollis, *Archaeology of Herod's Temple*, pp. 132f.

suggest that worshippers of God should 'visit the widow and the fatherless in their distress'?

Finally, take some snap-shots of monarchic notions on propagation of the popular 'Gospel' of Jehovah during the 250 years from Solomon onwards. As for conditions in Judah—about fifty years after Solomon died Maacah (Queen-Mother at the time) ordered the erection in the temple of 'an abominable image for an Asherah' (i.e. symbol or idol of the Goddess).[1] So horrible, however, was it that her royal son, Asa, cut it down, burnt it and deposed the Queen-Mother from her dignity! The episode calls up thought of Polynesian totem-poles. About 850 B.C. the Phoenician Baal (*Melkart*) was worshipped along with Jehovah both in Jerusalem and Samaria, the northern capital. Down to Isaiah's time, *c.* 725 (when Hezekiah had it destroyed), a bronze serpent was worshipped in Jerusalem.[2] That the Jerusalem temple often, if not normally, had its retinue of male and female persons dedicated to sacred prostitution is put beyond doubt by the notices that this and that king suppressed the custom.

As regards the new kingdom of *Israel*, what a start was made by its first king, Jeroboam! Concerned to show his zeal for the Hebrew God, he selected two ancient holy places, Dan and Bethel —the one in the north of his realm, the other in the south—and there set up to the glory of Jehovah two, gold-plated, images of a Bull.[3] Shorter cut there could not be towards helping his subjects to regard Jehovah as lineal descendant of *Adad* and *Resheph*, whose symbol had likewise been the bull. In 850 B.C. King Ahab and his Phoenician Queen, Jezebel, were determined that the great Baal of Phoenicia should be honoured together with Jehovah in their land. What the great Prophets have to say about the official

[1] I Kings xv. 13.
[2] The Jewish historians said it had been a memorial of an episode in the Wilderness wanderings. Possibly so—but it had become an object of worship. Serpent cult, we know, existed in pre-Israelite Canaan, and was prominent and widespread in the western Mediterranean civilization. This image may have been continuation of a Jebusite custom, or conceivably introduced by David's Philistine bodyguard. See II Kings xviii. 4.
[3] The word is misleadingly translated *Calf* in the English versions. Cp. Babylonian references to their God Marduk as 'Overpowering Ox', and the huge Assyrian statues of winged Bulls. (Two examples are preserved in the British Museum.) The 'Golden Calves' were probably stripped of their gold and destroyed by the Assyrians when they conquered Israel in 721 B.C.

and popular worship down to the end of the kingdom of Israel in 721 B.C. makes it impossible to doubt that adoration of the Great Goddess (*Ashtarte*) was continued. In general, the cult practised at all the sanctuaries, whilst offered nominally to Jehovah, in form was scarcely distinguishable from the ancient Canaanitish mode— orgiastic drunken licentious worship; and yet (so complex is human nature) also most earnest and well meaning.

§3. The Reign of Terror

The 200 years from 784 to 586 B.C. may fittingly be styled a 'Reign of Terror'. The affairs of those two centuries, in all their vivid tragedy, have to be reviewed in dealing with the great Prophets, and therefore only briefest indication is here in place to show the general religious and moral degeneration. The period opened with a forty-year phase which *we* can see to have been a 'Reign of Terror' morally, but which the prosperous alike in Israel and Judah regarded as 'the best-time-ever'—safety and luxury such as had not been known since the days of Solomon; and in his time wealth had been mostly concentrated in his own sagacious royal grasp. During those forty years (from 784 to 740 B.C.) there was a large number of very rich people (officials, landowners, merchants), and a larger number of families satisfyingly well-to-do—fathers and mothers, young men and maidens, all very merry and bright. When, however, we take a closer survey of the period, both kingdoms were like unto a whited sepulchre inwardly full of corruption and dead men's bones. Thirty years of war, preceding 784 B.C., had killed and injured great numbers of the peasant-proprietors. Men weakened by wounds, and widows and orphans, were in sore difficulties, of which large landowners and money-lenders took full advantage. Commerce had boomed, and currency (the 'almighty shekel') had come into general use. There was flagrant cheating, and corrupt administration of Justice. Contrast of great luxury and grim poverty became glaring. Amos accuses the rich of 'panting after the dust on the head of the poor'; calls the ladies of Samaria overfed 'cows of Bashan'. Isaiah speaks of 'the daughters of Zion with wanton eyes and mincing gait'; and of drunken, vomiting, banquets. A pitiless period! Now, in face of all this, the official representatives of the worship of Jehovah raised no protest. The priests cashed in on the lavish maintenance of the sacrifices. The ordinary prophets had only smooth words to utter. All was well, thought they. For Jehovah was defending His People and blessing them with wealth? Isaiah looked at his land of Judah, and loathed the sensual worship offered at its temple and High-Places. In Jerusalem he saw abundance of silver and gold, but what poverty and misery! The courts of the temple were thronged with worshippers. He said that the hands they raised in prayer were in God's sight dripping with the blood of the innocent.

After 745 B.C. the storm broke. Assyria was ready to conquer the world. In 732 it destroyed the kingdom of Syria and ravaged Galilee. Eleven years later Samaria was captured and the kingdom of Israel became an Assyrian province. Jerusalem was only fifteen miles south of its border. From 690 Judah, nominally independent, was a puppet State at the mercy of the Assyrians. In 586 it was sacked by the Babylonians (who replaced Assyria in 612 as the World Power), and the kingdom of Judah came to an end.

Here are some facts concerning 'religion' during those last terrifying decades. In 735 B.C. Ahaz, King of Judah, was in peril from a threatened joint attack on Jerusalem by the kings of Israel and Syria. The method he adopted to secure Jehovah's full assistance was to sacrifice his son as a burnt offering. He got out of his difficulties by purchasing promise of support from the Assyrians, but one aspect of the bargain was that he had to set up an altar for sacrifice to the great God of Assyria in his temple, relegating Jehovah's to second place. From 693 Manasseh reigned for 55 years. Manasseh was a most willing polytheist. He promoted the Assyrian astral cult; altars and emblems of sun, moon and star worship were multiplied in Jerusalem, and at the Judaean High-Places. Adoration of the Goddess-fertility cult with its sacred prostitutes had full scope in his temple. Worse still, Manasseh saw to it that child-sacrifices by fire were offered to the King-God (i.e. Jehovah) in the valley of Hinnom outside Jerusalem. One would like to lay the guilt of it all on Manasseh and his trusted favourites. But the bulk of the citizens cannot be acquitted. Not until eighteen years after Manasseh was dead, when the young King Josiah was on the throne, was action taken to undo what Manasseh had done.

§4. *The End*

Josiah's Reform in 621 B.C. was a genuinely felt repentance, supported by priestly and popular opinion. But we have Jeremiah's eyewitness realization that, in respect of deep religious understanding, it went no more than skin deep. 'The sin of Judah', he said, 'is written with a pen of iron, and...graven upon the table of their heart.' 'Religion of the heart' was still to seek in the streets of Jerusalem: ritual reform did not make men and women kind and true. The men feared lest the might of the Babylonian Gods would prove too much for Jehovah, even if He secured the assistance of the Egyptian Gods to help Him defend Jerusalem and Judah. The women were miserably certain that everything would go wrong, because (after Josiah's Reform) they had been ordered to stop baking cakes in honour of the Great Goddess.

The sorry tale of popular thought about Jehovah may conclude. True, the ordinary Hebrews in Canaan had not forgotten their ancestors' Deity. But they had transformed the God of Moses into Jehovah, God of the Hebrew *Nation*: and they represented Him in character as similar to any other Semitic Deity as is one pin to another. Both intellectually and morally the end thereof was Death.

Additional Note to Chapter VIII

The above drastic remarks need qualification. *The end thereof was Death*. But the Hebrews did not perish when Jerusalem fell. Becoming known to other nations as the Jews, they continued to exist in Palestine, and elsewhere multiplied amazingly. But what they had believed about God (Jehovah) foolishly, *that* died. The religion held by *the Jews* in general, even as soon as 50 years later, was a transfigured Faith—wonderful fact which lies outside the scope of this book. *The sorry tale of popular thought about Jehovah.* Is a populace ever completely of one opinion? *The ordinary Hebrews.* Is there an ordinary man? Are we not all extra-ordinary individuals, more or less eccentric?

We may fairly deem that, when the Judean Monarchy perished, many of the Hebrews either from sheer stupidity or from absorption in worldly matters were religiously *incorrigible*, their minds sealed against any other idea of their God than that which had manifestly failed them. They had trusted in the Unreal; intellectually and morally their Faith was worthless.[1] Their notions were like a site so bombed that complete demolition precedes the erection of a different edifice. All the prominent citizens of Jerusalem were removed into exile. But the mass of the Hebrews were left in the land. Most of these were simple folk who had tamely assented to what 'their betters' told them they ought to believe and do regarding Jehovah and religious rites. Picture them as not theologians, but ordinary people principally concerned about the weather and the crops, their own family affairs and the burden of domestic chores—sheep who had been without a trustworthy shepherd. Given a lead in the right direction they were capable of responding. It follows that they were religiously *teachable*. Now great disaster constrains even simple men to try to think, and it stimulates thoughtful men to perceive what can be believed and should be taught—as life in the present terrible century is demonstrating.

Furthermore, originating from the influence of Moses, there had all along been in the nation a core of 'puritan' abhorrence of religious and social enormities practised by ruthless kings and wicked priests. Those recalcitrants could view the disaster as deserved, and could remember that true Prophets had foretold its coming. For, above all, there had been in Hebrew history the few supremely great Prophets who in the name of the real God had spoken words that to most—but not to all— of their hearers had seemed incomprehensible and incredible, but which now had come to pass.

With those regenerative factors in the calamity the remaining chapters of this book are concerned.

[1] Cp. Skinner, *Prophecy and Religion*, chap. iv, 'The Two Religions of Israel'.

Part III
THE FAITH OF THE PROPHETS

TABLE OF DATES

1275*	The Exodus from Egypt—Covenant at Mount Horeb [MOSES]	
1240–1025	The Entry into Canaan—Settlement Period ('The Judges')	
1075–1025	Philistine Oppression (Shiloh destroyed)—Saul made King [SAMUEL]	
1002–922	Reigns of David and Solomon—Revolt of Northern Tribes	

	KINGS OF JUDAH	KINGS OF ISRAEL
922	Rehoboam	Jeroboam
869	—	Ahab and Jezebel [ELIJAH]
842	Amaziah, *m.* to	
841	Athaliah, *d.* of Ahab	Jehu's revolt and reign, followed by disastrous (30 years) war with Syria
785–740	Uzziah (Period of Prosperity)	
782–742	—	Jeroboam II [AMOS, 750–742] [HOSEA, 745–734]
733	—	*The ASSYRIANS conquered Syria*
721	—	*The ASSYRIANS conquered Israel*
740	Jotham [ISAIAH, 740–701]	**End of the Kingdom of Israel**
735	Ahaz	
715	Hezekiah	
687	Manasseh (Judah tributary to Assyria—polytheism in Jerusalem)	
640	Josiah (Reform of worship, 621) [JEREMIAH, 626–585] *The BABYLONIANS conquered Assyria in 612—defeated Egyptian army (Battle of Carchemish) 605—and thereafter could dominate Palestine*	
608	Jehoahaz	
607	Jehoiakim	
597	Jehoiakin (Babylonians enter Jerusalem; Jehoiakin and many citizens taken to Babylon)	
597	Zedekiah, last King of Judah	
588–586	Babylonians besiege capture and devastate Jerusalem, taking some thousands of captives to Babylon **End of the Kingdom of Judah**	
538	*The PERSIANS (under Cyrus) conquered Babylon, and ruled Palestine to 331*	
520–516	The 'second' temple built at Jerusalem	
445 (?)	Jerusalem's walls repaired by Nehemiah	
331	*GREEKS, led by Alexander the Great, conquered the Persians*	
331–198	Palestine ruled by Greek Kings of Egypt	
198–167	Palestine ruled by Greek Kings of Syria	
167	*The Maccabaean Rebellion*	
142	*Jerusalem (under Hasmonaean Kings) independent until the ROMAN Period, from 65 B.C.*	

* For the pre-monarchic period the dates given are approximate.

CHAPTER IX

HEBREW PURITANS

Our Faith did not come to us from the popular religion of the Hebrews. Its development was due to a feature omitted from the preceding survey because it was not congruous with the ordinary Hebrew ideas of Jehovah, but antagonistic to it, and unique in religious history. That feature forms the subject of the Third Part of this study under the title 'The Faith of the Prophets'; and to it the present chapter serves as introduction.

Throughout Hebrew history in Canaan there was a tough core of resistance to being completely 'Canaanized'. The evidence is found in considerations affecting persons, classes, and institutions of the State, and sometimes concerns the early period only, sometimes runs through the whole course of the history; so that it is not easy to set forth the subject in a well-ordered sequence. But it is hoped the picture will build itself up.

§ 1. Shepherd Puritans

Obviously antagonism to the ways of the Palestinians would continue strong in such of the Hebrews as wanted not to become townsmen and agriculturalists, but preferred to remain shepherds. Those families would be acutely conscious that they were Hebrews of the Hebrews, not Canaanites—whose Gods were not their God, whose aims in life they did not share. The shepherds of early Israel lived in tents as free men 'under the wide and starry sky';[1] and they loved and reverenced their way of existence.[2] Canaanites

[1] Even when, later, they resided in villages, or in the small towns, we have to think of them as men whose interest was in the open country where they shepherded their flocks.

[2] There is interesting evidence showing how tenaciously one such family held to the old ways, and was respected for its anti-Canaanite stand by Hebrews who had accepted civilization. From II Kings x. 15–18 we learn that at the time of Jehu's rebellion (c. 840 B.C.) the family of Jonadab ben Rechab lived under vow to dwell in tents and build no house, to plant no vines and drink no wine. Cultivation of vines drew men into veneration of the old Gods of the soil, the *Baals*. Jonadab would have no truck with them: his God was Jehovah; and the rebel captain Jehu counted it important to enlist the support of this zealot for Jehovah. Descendants of Jonadab were living near Jerusalem in 600 B.C. still obedient to the family vow. (Lods cites a parallel case, *Israel*, p. 399.)

wanted to sleep securely and stuffily under a roof protected by city-walls, with their thoughts penned up in its jostling, feverish, life. Let them do so. The Hebrew chroniclers were concerned to set down what was necessary to tell about the busy life of the towns—the affairs of great men and kings; national policy and perils: so that the presence of the shepherds in the land did not write itself upon the pages of history. But they were there—along the southern fringe of Judah, east of the Jordan in Gilead and Bashan, but also in large tracts of the central mountains of Judah, Samaria, Galilee, and in the great Plain of Esdraelon. And they were there not just for a short while after Israel had won its entry, but continuously.[1] Were there not shepherds in the 'Field' of Bethlehem on Christmas Eve? City men and women do not often give a thought to the shepherds in their country, even when lamb happens to be on the menu; and, if they do, think of them as lonely individuals quite out of the swim of things. Townsmen are apt to be too busy to think; but the shepherd has long leisure, and far-seeing eyes (houses do not get in the way of the view). If he happens to have a first-class intellect, he can use it to great discernment concerning the things that belong to our peace. That was doubly true of the ancient East, which lacked libraries, newspapers and films. Twice in Hebrew history in Canaan (three times, if we include David, who in his youth kept the sheep of Jesse his father) a man from the open country, where the flocks find pasture, brought piercing intelligence and sterling character to bear on Hebrew civilization, with results which altered its course and left permanent effects.

§2. *Old-fashioned Gentlemen*

The 'pull' of Canaanism was at its maximum in the two royal cities, and very strong in towns which, lying on or near the main thoroughfares, were exposed to the march of events and the interests of commerce. But there were very many villages, and a

---

[1] There was always peaceful penetration into the edges of the sown land by nomadic families drifting in from the desert proper, and there are indications of a considerable incoming of such families during the disturbed conditions in north Israel consequent on Jehu's revolt against Ahab in the ninth century, as well as after the fall of the Israelite Kingdom (721 B.C.); and quite certainly into Judah after the sack of Jerusalem in 586 B.C. (See S. A. Cook, in *C.A.H.* vol. ii, pp. 370 f.)

number of less important small towns, where good men were much more likely to cherish old-fashioned good manners and the traditions of desert-brotherhood—subject of course to the inevitable modification that they now had possessions of their own in property and houses. Such men of the Hebrew 'Old School Tie' or Family Inheritance (unlike the Bedouin chieftains) no longer thought that perfect life (in their phrase, *peace*) must include the thrill and challenge of an occasional fight. They wanted to dwell in safety and be prosperous; but they could be proudly content with little; and, if they had much, then they sought honour from others by deserving to be reputed a strength to the community of their brethren. A perfect illustration of the type is provided in the Book of Job;[1] for Job, hero of its poem, is represented as exceeding rich in flocks and herds and owner of house and servants, dwelling however in a community close enough to the desert to be in danger of raids by the nomads. Out of the agony of his unmerited misfortunes, thus speaks Job concerning the ideals he had cherished in the days of his prosperity:

Oh that I were as in the months of old, As in the days when God watched over me....When the Almighty was yet with me, And my children were about me; When my steps were washed with butter, And the rock poured me out rivers of oil! When I went forth to the gate unto the city, When I prepared my seat in the street, The young men saw me and hid themselves, And the aged rose up and stood....For when the ear heard me, then it blessed me; And when the eye saw me, it gave witness unto me; Because I delivered the poor that cried, The fatherless also, that had none to help him. The blessing of him that was ready to perish came upon me: And I caused the widow's heart to sing for joy. I put on righteousness, and it clothed me: My justice was as a robe and a diadem. I was eyes to the blind, And feet was I to the lame. I was a father to the needy: And the cause of him that I knew not I searched out. And I brake the jaws of the unrighteous, And plucked the prey out of his teeth.[2]

Mark the contrast with the desert-warrior whose blessing and honour may still be strong in him provided he is resolute to

[1] Surprisingly; for the poem about Job probably must be dated not earlier than 400 B.C. Despite that fact, it is indisputable that the author has portrayed in Job the outlook intermediate between that of the powerful, prosperous, desert-chieftain and that of the thoroughly urbanized Palestinian townsman.

[2] See Job xxix. 2–17.

avenge his defeat. Job's attitude to disaster is resignation: 'The Lord hath given, and the Lord hath taken away: blessed be the name of the Lord.' But mark still more that Job feels his honour is lost because he no longer has *power to be one who upholds others*.[1]

It may be said that the Book of Job is literature, not life. Here then is life—Naboth of Jezreel, owner of a little plot of land inherited from his fathers, which powerful King Ahab wanted to take over as a convenient kitchen garden for the adjacent royal residence in the little town. No offer of money or of compensation in better land elsewhere, nor yet fear of royal displeasure, would induce him to part with it. The king, he feels, was foolish so much as to imagine that he would, and must take 'No' for answer from a free brother man. What a glimpse the story gives of staunch maintenance of the old conception of equal human rights. (On the other hand, the subservience of Naboth's neighbours to Queen Jezebel's resolve to compass Naboth's death shows how fully Canaanism had seized their spirits.) Jezreel, moreover, was on the line of march, almost under the eyes of Samaria. Its Naboth is therefore good evidence that there were many men of substance in the towns and villages whose standards approximated to the desert ideal of brotherhood.

§3. *Jehovah's Stalwarts*

There were Hebrews who, given the stimulus of perilous circumstance, showed themselves to be of no uncertain mind, but men whose faith and hope were rooted and grounded in loyalty to Jehovah, God of the Hebrews. With all their might they responded to challenge, and the infection of their courage, the fire of their zeal, must have been (we know it was) a potent influence in conserving and clarifying and strengthening the Hebrews' consciousness that they were not Canaanites, and had their very own God to trust and to obey. The author of the Epistle to the Hebrews called them 'men of faith', and said that the roll of their number was too great for full recital. Call them *Jehovah's Heroes* —Barak and Deborah stirring the tribesmen in Jehovah's name to dare to fight Sisera; Gideon and Jephthah routing Midianites and Ammonites because the God they served was Jehovah; Samson, filled with His might, goading the Philistines; and in the great struggle against the Philistines resolute Samuel, brave Saul

[1] Cf. Pedersen, *Israel*, p. 215.

and Jonathan, victorious David—all inspired to their task and led to achievement because of their zeal for the Lord God of Israel!

Mention of Samson brings up a fresh point, for he was under the vow of a *Nazir*. There were in the early period Hebrews dedicated to Jehovah by a permanent vow, to the end that, filled with divine energy, they should be able to fight in battle with supernatural power and courage. Call them *Jehovah's Champions*.[1] Their obligation and their feats impressed the people: 300 years later they were reckoned a gift which Jehovah had in past times bestowed; for Amos (reproaching thankless Israel as having tried to corrupt them) says: 'And I raised up of your sons for prophets, and of your young men for Nazirites...but ye gave the Nazirites wine to drink; and commanded the prophets, saying, Prophesy not.'[2]

Allusion has been made in Chapter VII to the likelihood that a feature in Canaanite religion was the actions and words of men who—perhaps singly but usually collectively—worked themselves up to an ecstasy of enthusiasm in honour of the God. These psychic persons were called *prophets* ('spokesmen for God'), because their shouts and utterances when in the hypnotic state were deemed to be supernaturally imparted by the God whose energy (*ruach*) had possessed them, or because (restored to their normal senses) they were able to tell others about a vision they had seen or a divine message they had heard whilst in the trance. (It is essential to differentiate them from the men of highest religious genius in Israel's life—the supreme Prophets; and to that end the latter are designated in this volume by the capital letter.) The ordinary, ecstatical prophets—call them *Jehovah's Devotees* —are first mentioned in Hebrew history at the terrible time when Samuel the Seer was rallying the tribes against sub-

---

[1] The external signs of the obligation were that the *Nazir* must drink no wine and must not cut his hair. See Judges xiii. 1–5; xvi. 17. An allusion to *Nazirites* in battle array may lie beneath Judges v. 2, for the original text was probably: 'When locks of hair were worn loose.' Lods (*Israel*, p. 305) cites Janssen and Savignac, *Coutumes des Fugara*: 'Even now when the Fugara Bedouin undertake a campaign or a raid, they undo their hair; it is said of everyone who is preparing to take part in an expedition "he has untied his hair".' (Num. vi, which describes the vows of a Nazir as temporary in character and unrelated to war, is a passage much later than the Age of the 'Judges'.)

[2] Amos ii. 11, 12.

mission to the victorious Philistines, and probably it really was that desperate situation which first evoked the phenomenon among the Hebrews.[1] But, the Philistine crisis surmounted, prophets did not cease to be. On the contrary they became a regular class in the community, an expression of special zeal for Jehovah, and a means of obtaining His guidance.[2] It appears that in an informal way they were associated with the priests of important sanctuaries such as Bethel, Gilgal, Samaria. Kings and priests took them under their supervision. Eventually a retinue of men, whose function it was to fall into ecstasy and prophesy when required,[3] became a regularized part of the staff of the Jerusalem temple and principal sanctuaries: prophets of Jehovah were numbered by hundreds in Ahab's reign and were persecuted by his Queen, Jezebel, whose prophets of the Phoenician *Baal* also numbered hundreds at his court. Their function was occasional, not constant; and in the earlier period it seems likely they were sustained partly by their own labour, and partly by official support and by gifts of the people who respected their uncanny powers, and felt their inspired utterances needed in time of danger. The physical capacities of the human body when under deep ecstatic frenzy, with normal consciousness completely submerged, are astounding, both as respects feats of strength and as regards self-inflicted wounds which scarcely bleed and heal at the touch of a leader bringing the devotees out of hypnosis. We do not need the Old Testament for evidence, but only present-day *dervish* dances. No wonder that Hebrew kings and commoners believed such men to be possessed by supernatural power and to convey supernatural messages.[4]

Consider their values and deficiencies. Surely such men cannot be ranked as Hebrew Puritans. In one way yes, emphatically.

[1] The allusion, in Num. xi. 25, to 70 elders prophesying before Moses in the desert period is an anachronism. See the Commentaries.

[2] The phrase 'Schools of the Prophets' formerly in vogue in allusion to this matter (see Cruden's *Concordance*, s.v. 'School') is a misnomer; and '*Sons* of the prophets' does not imply a hereditary calling: it is equivalent in Hebrew idiom simply to *prophets*, just as *the children* (or *sons*) *of Israel* means *Israelites*.

[3] Cf. Jeremiah's words, spoken in irony (xviii. 18): 'Then said they, Come, and let us devise devices against Jeremiah; for the law shall not perish from the priest, nor counsel from the wise, nor the word from the prophet.'

[4] King Ahab got assurance from 400 of the prophets that, if he went to war against Syria, he would be victorious; yet when one prophet—Micaiah ben Imlah—resolutely foretold defeat, the king was in utter trepidation.

They were zealots for *Jehovah*, fanatically sure that from Him came Israel's strength and from Him must guidance be sought. But otherwise they are just a feature in that pathetic futile tragedy— the popular religion, devoid of value for us. Grave responsibility was upon them at critical moments in relation to peace or war, and so forth. But they had no means of meeting the demand to give divine guidance save by stimulating themselves to frenzy and uttering ejaculatory words; and the fatal thing is that they always predicted what people wanted to hear, because they thought of national welfare in terms of material prosperity. Therefore their subconsciousness echoed back only 'smooth things': Jehovah, in whom they trusted, was 'the Giver of Victory'. These men had no eyes for the moral corruption that was rotting the heart of their People. We may believe most of these prophets were sincere, but many were not; and, as time passed, undoubtedly they de- generated as a class. Ordinary men recognized that madness and ecstatic prophecy were akin, and (significantly) used the same term for both. Practice of phrenetic excitement exposed them to danger of mental and moral derangement; and there was temptation also in the fact that their capacity was a means of livelihood. It has, however, been justly said that they opened the eyes of the people to a mode of seeking to learn the Will of God which was distinct on the one side from the priests' function in maintaining the rites of sacrifice, and on the other from the mechanical art of divination.[1]

§4. *Men of Insight ('Seers')*

The Puritan tradition in Hebrew religion set its face against wizards and necromancers seeking power or direction from demons and the dead. To its influence also is due the comparatively slight interest taken by the official Hebrew cult in a class of persons upon whose arts all other ancient nations set great store—*diviners*, interpreters of 'omens' and 'signs' drawn from inspection of the entrails of animals or observation of the flight of birds. It is clear that to a remarkable extent the Hebrews became averse to mechani- cal methods of ascertaining the Divine Will—fact vastly to their credit; for 'resort to an external event artificially linked to some power beyond itself is really an escape from moral responsibility'.[2] Hebrew instinct tended to seek guidance from God through those

[1] G. A. Smith, *The Twelve Prophets*, vol. I, pp. 23, 24.
[2] H. W. Robinson, *Redemption and Revelation*, p. 118.

persons who were deemed to have good right to assert that supernatural truth and wisdom had been imparted to them. Compared
with the importance of that principle, it is small matter that the
people were mistaken in thinking the ecstatic prophets to be (in
fact) such persons. A different type of man might appear who had
the highest intellectual and moral right to claim that light from
on High had shined in his heart. Like other nations the Hebrews
produced individuals gifted with peculiar psychic sensitiveness—
call it 'the sixth sense', or what one will—and found they had at
times extraordinary insight and foresight far exceeding normal
human powers.[1] These individuals they termed *Seers* or *Vision-
aries*. One such man is famous in their history—Samuel, the *Seer*
of Ramah: respected as a 'man of God', not only for his abnormal
psychic powers but also for his normal qualities. At Ramah's
High-Place he acted as priest offering the sacrifices, and the
Hebrews (rightly) came to think of him as Prophet as well as
Seer;[2] for in Samuel there was quality that numbers him among the
builders of the great Faith (as a later chapter will state)—capacity
in a complex situation to judge by moral principle as well as
psychic sensitiveness.

§5. *Faithful Priests*

It is easy to collect a damning indictment of the priests of Israel
from the pages of the Old Testament. What manner of men were
they who were wont to administer the gross rites practised in
honour of Jehovah (and the Goddess) under the monarchy, and

---

[1] I Sam. ix. 5–9.

[2] Not that all who professed to be Seers were truly 'men of God'. A verse
in Zechariah (xiii. 3—perhaps fifth century) refers to them as a public nuisance
in Jerusalem. Cp. Aristophanes' ridicule of the Greek oracle-mongers (*The
Birds*, ll. 950ff.). In passing it should be remarked that 'in early times Seer,
Prophet and Priest were not sharply differentiated'. The priests had not then
established an exclusive right to carry out the ritual slaughter of the sacrificial
animals. Illustration is provided by the narrative (Num. xxii–xxiv) concerning
the non-Israelite Seer, Balaam, who (as G. A. Smith expresses it) was
'essentially an Arab *Kahin* or Seer of that early type which combined the
priest's offices of ritual and sacrifice, the diviner's reliance on omens and lots,
and the prophet's experience of ecstasy and dreams' (*Early Poetry of Israel*,
p. 63). Gaster (*P.E.F. Quarterly*, July 1934) notes concerning the Syrian
sanctuary at Ras Shamra (*c*. 1400 B.C.) that it was administered by two
guardians: 'a priest (*Kohen*) who was probably more of a soothsayer than a
priest', and 'a man of God who was the sacristan proper'.

who staffed Manasseh's temple of many Gods and sacred prostitution, and who served child-sacrifices in the valley of Gehinnom?
The Hebrew priests were ever in danger of supporting conventional ideas, and at their worst were tools of the State authorities,
with vested interests in abuses that corroded the morals of the
people. But beneath the surface of the records there is a different
aspect to be inferred. Obviously at the start in Canaan the
Hebrews sacrificed to their own God, not to Canaan's Deities.
They built a temple at Shiloh to His glory; and, as they gained
mastery in different parts of the country, surely the priest-
guardians of their sanctuaries must have been Hebrews—not
Canaanites—men who knew the mode of the desert worship and
knew the specific tradition of Moses.[1]

Now priests are, above all else, conservers of tradition, of the
way things used to be done. When the elaboration into typical
Canaanitish ritual gradually had occurred, we may judge that not
a few of the priests had an uneasy conscience about its excesses. It
is significant that on the two occasions when the cult of Jerusalem
was purged, a prominent priest took a leading part in effecting
the reform. The priests had superlative opportunity to do good,
if they would. It is a misconception to suppose that the range of

[1] From the curious tale in Judges xvii–xix about an unquestionably
'Hebrew' Hebrew, Micah of Ephraim—who proudly had 'an house of gods'
(equipped with graven image and ephod and teraphim!), and who first of all
made one of his sons its priest-guardian, but later was, to his delight, able to
secure a young Levite to take charge—we have evidence that men claiming
descent from Levi were held in special estimation for priestly functions. Why
that should have been the case raises most intricate questions. It is, of course,
clear that in the early period there was no *organized* priesthood. Tradition
related that in distant pre-Mosaic times the Levites were a fierce, fighting
tribe (Gen. xlix. 5, 6), which together with the Simeonites met with such a
defeat at the hands of the Canaanites of Shechem that it lost tribal cohesion;
its surviving families becoming dispersed amongst the other Hebrew clans. If
(it has been suggested) it happened that Levites were the priests of the cult
of Jehovah at Kadesh during the years when Kadesh was the place of assembly
for the Hebrew tribes preceding the invasion, it would be natural that Levites,
rather than others, should be chosen to have charge of the first Hebrew altars
in Canaan, with the consequence that the dispersed Levite families tended to
be sought out for like purpose as Hebrew control in Canaan extended.
Eventually (*not earlier* than Josiah's Reform in 621 B.C.) exclusive right to
offer the sacrifices was won by men who claimed descent from Levi through
the families of Aaron and *Zadok*. (After that principle had been established
all temple-ministrants in theory were of Levitical descent. Actually

their duties was guarding the holy things, sacrificing the animals
and receiving due payment. They had to teach 'the manner of the
God'. In the old days they enjoined the Hebrew to repeat the
words: 'My father was a wandering Aramaean...', i.e. not a
Canaanite. Ancient sacrifice required that appropriate words be
spoken as well as the deed of slaughter performed. The individual
bringing his animal to pay a vow of confession or thanksgiving
had to be instructed what he ought solemnly to declare; and the
concourse of worshippers likewise. Psalmody therefore was an
accompaniment of sacrifice. What golden opportunity those
chants presented to teach the true traditions of the Faith! The
priests explained why their sanctuary was holy ground for
Israel. We may be sure that the splendid form which the tales
about the Patriarchs, Moses, the Exodus and the Mount of God
eventually assumed was due to the efforts of Puritan priests as well
as Puritan prophets. 'They were the most continuous and
recognized teachers in the country, not always so negligent and
lacking in discernment as Hosea portrays them.'[1] 'The antagonism
between the priests and the prophets can easily be overstated.'[2]
And yet, and yet—how deep and wide the gulf between their
mind and the inspiration of the supreme Prophets: the ordinary
priests could not endure *their* words. Wide and deep it was, as the
gulf which opened between Jesus of Nazareth and the recognized
religious leaders of His time. But in final justice to the good
Hebrew priests note that the formulation of the law of Jehovah in
Deuteronomy presents a wonderful fusion of most truly Prophetic

name-lists of the lower ranks of the temple servants show that some were not
even of Israelitish origin.) Just how and when the Zadokites acquired their
exclusive prerogative is obscure. The rigid distinction between Zadokites and
other Levites did not exist earlier than 621 B.C.: 'Down to the Reformation
of Josiah all Levites were priests: after the Exile not all Levites were priests.
That important fact stands sure.' (Buchanan-Gray, *Sacrifice in the Old Testament*, p. 233.) Earlier than 621 a very different attitude had obtained. Not
only Hebrews who were Levites, but also uncircumcised aliens, had been
freely employed in the service of the temple and High-places (Ezek. xliv. 7,
11). Moreover, Hebrews other than Levites had been *priests* without contemporary scandal to public opinion, both in Israel (down to the fall of its
Kingdom in 721), and among the Judaeans (the sons of David, for instance,
II Sam. xx. 26). The late compilers of the historical Books could but record
their almost incredulous disapproval (I Kings xii. 31).

[1] Buchanan-Gray, *Sacrifice in the Old Testament*, p. 223.
[2] A. C. Welch, *Prophet and Priest in Old Israel*, pp. 62, 72 ff.

aims with priestly conservation of the ancient rites. Deuteronomy embodies the Hebrew Puritan spirit—insistence that Israel has no God save Jehovah, that the abominations of the Canaanites are utterly alien to His worship, and that Hebrews must deal with one another as brethren and preserve themselves a distinct people.

§6. *'Democrats'*

There were no Hebrew Democrats or Republicans, or Conservatives, Liberals or Labour, or Marxists and Communists. But there were very very many Hebrews who indomitably held to it that the Hebrew monarchy was a kingship differing from the usual Oriental form of royal rule in a way that made all the difference. At its commencement acceptance of Saul as king was conceded on a basis that we may fairly regard as of the essence of democratic principle. Saul did not force his rule on the Hebrews; neither did David. The tribesmen decided to make Saul king. David had to wait until events seemed to make it evident that the Blessing had departed from Saul's house and had rested on him; so that men felt *he* was the man whom God had chosen because he was worthy to be entrusted with the duty. Then, when leaders of the tribes came to Hebron to invite him to be king, David *made a covenant with them in Hebron before the Lord.*[1] The standpoint was that the ruler held his office under judgement of God to do right for his People, and in relation to his fellows never ceased to be one of the brethren although consecrated to most solemn responsibility to ensure the nation's welfare. As the history moves on, again and again we mark insistent efforts on the part of the Hebrews to demand from their kings recognition of that attitude.[2] The horrible plots and assassinations that blackened the last twenty years of the kingdom of Israel gave rise to a view that the institution of a monarchy had been an entire mistake—a sin of religious mistrust: Israel needed nothing to guide its way save the Word of

---

[1] Despotic actions by David on two occasions were denounced by a Prophet, and vehemently resented by his people, although he was at the height of his power.

[2] Covenant-promise was exacted when the child-king Josiah was placed on the throne of Judah, and was given by Josiah prior to the Reform in 621 B.C. We can account for Ahab's scruples in dealing with the peasant Naboth only by inferring that he felt himself not at all in the position of autocratic authority that his Phoenician queen assumed he ought to have.

the Lord which Jehovah would not fail to give by the mouth
of faithful Prophets. There was also an interesting compromise
view—The wish of the tribesmen to make Saul king had been a
sin of mistrust; but Jehovah had made concession to the weakness
of their faith[1] ('Behold, the Lord hath set a king over you'),
provided one condition was observed—'Both ye, and also the
king that reigneth over you must be followers of the Lord, your
God.'[2] In general, the Hebrew, Puritan-democratic, conception
of the only right relation between government and governed—
the indispensable condition for social welfare—is an astonishing
achievement, unparalleled in antiquity. 'In Israel monarchy was a
unique phenomenon. Elsewhere the king was absolute: a limited
monarchy is, to the oriental, a contradiction in terms.'[3] The
Hebrew conception lays down the best means, in any age and under
any system of civilized administration, of conserving the dignity
and value of the individual in the structure of organized society.

§7. *The Supreme Prophets*

Had the foregoing features been the sum total that falls to be said
about resistance to Canaanization, calamity would have been
complete, and the religion of Israel of no more interest to the
modern world than the religion of Phoenicia or Moab. Collectively these deterrents do not constitute even what might be called
'a resistance movement'; since the several elements were not a
system of thought clearly held by a body of men, convinced of
their purpose, organized and determined to achieve it. The
suspicious and even sharp antagonism with which the ways of
the Canaanites were regarded by some Hebrews did not avail

[1] When the divine choice had been indicated and the trust conferred, the
Hebrews regarded the person of the king as sacrosanct; for he had become
the psychic channel of the Blessing, the Life and Light of his People. The men
of Israel sought to restrain David from risking his life in battle: 'Thou shalt
go no more out with us to battle, that thou quench not the lamp of Israel'
(II Sam. xxi. 17).

• [2] I Sam. viii. 10–22; xii. 12–25. This intermediate position was very neatly
formulated in Deuteronomy (xvii. 14–20)—Only the man whom Jehovah
chooses shall be acclaimed king; one from amongst his brethren (not an
alien); he must not (like Solomon!) maintain a harem and heap up for himself
riches in gold and silver. (Lods, *Israel*, p. 385, regards these rules as *late*,
Judaean, theorizing; but see Welch's criticism of that opinion, *Code of Deuteronomy*, pp. 117–32.)

[3] T. H. Robinson, *Palestine in General History*, pp. 42–4.

to prevent the religion of the ordinary Hebrews from becoming indistinguishable from the usual 'Old Oriental' conception of God. Singly and collectively the features named amount to 'all that was good in the ancient simple ways of the desert fighting a losing battle with Oriental Civilization'. The Puritan factors in Hebrew life in Canaan would never of themselves have given rise to the flame of moral Monotheistic Faith which enabled the Jews to maintain their racial identity through the centuries, and which was the prelude of Christianity. That achievement was due to the creative and lasting influence of eight individuals—*the Supreme Prophets*. It would have been better if they were known by the simpler term 'Men of God'. What they said and did revolutionized the world of conventional thought. The debt which we owe to the Hebrew Puritans is that, if they had not existed in Israel's life, the gulf between the popular outlook and the mind of the supreme Prophets would have been too wide to bridge. Or, we may say, Hebrew Puritanism was good soil in which the seed of the great Prophetic Faith was able to germinate.

The eight individuals were: Moses, Samuel, Elijah, Amos, Hosea, Isaiah, Jeremiah, and a Poet-Prophet of the sixth or fifth century B.C. whose name is unknown and whose utterances are recorded in the latter part of the Book of Isaiah.[1] If we ask concerning each of them in turn: 'What, in sum, was the impression he made?'—the proper reply is not vaguely to say that he was a conspicuously good person, but to recognize the fact that the historical influence of his life and words established—for the first time, in an unforgettable way—*one* cardinal principle of belief concerning Supernatural Reality and the consequent nature

[1] The omission of Ezekiel from the list may be surprising. The writer is of opinion that the material in the Book of Ezekiel is very far from being the product of one man; that much of it belongs to the consideration of post-exilic Judaism; and that while certain of its oracular passages are of pre-exilic date, these do not add any development of thought not covered by the eight great personalities. The Old Testament mentions a number of individuals concerning whom actions or utterances are recorded which have, or come near to having, the quality of the supreme Prophets. But incidental allusions to them must suffice for the purpose of this work. They had not anything approaching the magnitude of importance, spiritual or historical, that attaches to the eight men named above. The most notable were Nathan (in David's reign), Elisha, Micaiah ben Imlah, and Micah, and Zephaniah. Several of the short Books known as 'the Minor Prophets' are either negligible for our purpose (e.g. Nahum), or are post-exilic in date (e.g. Zechariah, Joel).

of human duty. The specific principle in each case is therefore made the title of the following Chapters in this work. One by one these 'living' principles were taken up by the intelligence of the successive great individuals; until, woven together in coherent unity, the eight principles constituted a universal, 'timeless', interpretation of the mystery of existence and of the spiritual-moral character of human personality.

In the first Chapter brief reference was made to the disastrous narrowing-down of the significance of the term *Prophet* from meaning 'One who declares what he believes to be God's truth' (truth which it is vitally important that men should believe and obey), to 'One who, inspired by God and without any personal responsibility for the validity of what he said, uttered predictions of future events'.[1] So dominant has been the impression that the latter, restricted, meaning states the substance of the matter that the fact that these eight individuals were called *Prophets*, together with another obvious fact about them, causes modern, non-Biblical, humanity (if it so much as knows their names!) to assume that ancient persons of that type have no bearing on present world-problems or individuals. Human life is chock-a-block with predictions. Where the basis is the regularities of the physical world we call them calculations. The chemist can foretell that, if certain substances are mixed, of a dead certainty there will be an explosion. In the less monotonous realm of human behaviour we predict that, unless Connie controls her temper and Tom is less selfish, there will be trouble. We foresee world-disaster unless the Great Powers sufficiently work together to prevent it. When a modern is blazingly certain about what seems to him to be right and urgently important, he may say: 'It's God's truth I'm telling you!' When the supreme Hebrew Prophets were filled with similar imperative certitude, and imperative sense of duty to make others understand and be convinced, they said: 'The Lord God shewed me'—'Thus saith the Lord'. If they had been asked why they considered their view to be better than purely subjective opinion, they would (in their way of speech) have answered that 'The Lord laid his hand upon me', or that they spoke not of themselves but as 'the messenger of him that sent me'.[2] When

---

[1] See p. 13.

[2] Incidentally it may be mentioned that the supreme Prophets made their responsibility a vocation, not a profession. Amos (vii. 14) rapped that point home to Amaziah, King Jeroboam's priest at Bethel—saying: 'I was no

other prophets contradicted them, saying also 'Thus saith the Lord', they had this answer to give—that, if men cleared their minds from prejudice and their hearts from love of wickedness, they would rightly judge where the truth lay; and that events would in the end sustain their message. There they were on very strong ground, for essentially they were speaking about Right and Wrong, and predicting the issues that follow on moral choice.

But, secondly, the great Hebrew Prophets were men of abnormal psychic sensitiveness, to a degree that is comparatively rare in Western civilization; a fact that made their contemporaries call them *Seer*, as well as *Prophet*. It is indisputable that sometimes they experienced trances. We possess from two of them brief, extremely vivid, accounts of a trance-experience which first convinced them that God required them to speak in His name, and would not fail to reveal to them His truth. This characteristic of trance-experiences has evoked curiously diverse reactions in the course of the last hundred years. During the dignified reign of Queen Victoria psychical research and the phenomena of subconscious mind were looked at askance. In the nineteenth century students of the Bible concentrated on every other aspect of the great Prophets. They were approved for their theological wisdom and their political acumen and their literary ability, but above all for their forcefulness as social reformers. During the present century the pendulum has swung violently the other way,[1] and we have been urged to appreciate the great Prophets by fixing attention on their abnormal psychic experiences. The phrase has been flung out: 'the Prophets as Ecstatics.'[2] The Phoenician

prophet, neither was I a prophet's son; but I was an herdsman...and the Lord took me from following the flock, and the Lord said unto me, Go, prophesy unto my people Israel.' When Isaiah had become the outstanding Seer in Jerusalem and King Hezekiah, with the Assyrians at the gates of the city, besought him to seek guidance from Jehovah, nobody supposes that Isaiah asked or received a handsome fee for his services.

[1] Especially since the publication of Hölscher's *Die Profeten* in 1914. A valuable survey of the development of this subject was made by T. H. Robinson in *The Church Quarterly Review*, January 1923.

[2] Some writers are open to the charge of torturing what evidence there is for abnormal psychic states in the great Prophets until every syllable of it is made to shriek *ecstasy*, and of manufacturing evidence where there is really none. See N. Micklem's trenchant criticism of the extreme contentions (*Prophecy and Eschatology*, 1926). The eccentricities ascribed to Ezekiel furnished the most striking points of evidence, but recent criticism of the Book of Ezekiel has disposed of that seeming evidence.

prophets of Baal, the ordinary Hebrew devotees of Jehovah *were* ecstatics, and tried to experience ecstasy. We may well note that significantly their oracular utterances expressed the wishes of minds uncontrolled by deep religious and moral principles, and seem the product of mass-suggestion operating on suppressed fears and expressed hopes; and it is necessary to mark the radical contrasts between the characteristics of those fanatical zealots and the psychic experiences and positive teaching of the supreme Prophets. It is reckless and reprehensible to call the great Prophets 'Ecstatics', because the term is bound to convey to most readers an impression of morbidity which is fundamentally unjustified by the evidence.

The first duty is fully to recognize that ecstasy is properly used to denote the extreme phenomena of frenzy or catalepsy, and that between ecstasy and normal consciousness there are very many gradations.[1] Every thoughtful person in intent meditation becomes correspondingly unaware of environment or other objects of thought; the greater the power of concentration the more 'rapt' the experience. In many persons of disciplined intelligence and well-balanced character mental intensity deepens to a condition for which we need a special word—*trance*.[2] The fact is abundantly illustrated in the literature concerning poets, musicians, writers, philosophers, scientists and saints.[3] Ideas received in trance may

[1] *Ecstasy* is a Greek word. It is wise to forget ancient Greek psychology, and remember the ideas of the nature of man that obtained in Semitic lands, as outlined in Chapter VI. 'The prophet could believe that Yahweh gave new capacity of vision to his eye, or of audition to his ear, without in any way interfering with the rest of his bodily functions....Because we have lifted the phenomena of consciousness into the psychical realm, we have to invent a whole new vocabulary of "sub-liminals" and "complexes" to explain them.' (H. W. Robinson, *Redemption and Revelation*, pp. 142f.)

[2] 'It is a fact that under strong emotion religious ideas and convictions do sometimes give rise to visual and audible representations hardly distinguishable from sense impressions; and there is ample evidence in Christian biography that this is compatible with perfect sanity of mind and balance of judgement. Of this nature we take the visions of the Prophets to be.' (Skinner, *Prophecy and Religion*, p. 12.) A notable recent instance is the Sadhu Sundar Singh, for whom trance became a constantly recurring experience. Yet the Sadhu, 'who began his Christian life with a vision like that of St Paul on the Damascus road, united his mystical raptures with a life of devoted Christian evangelism'. (Cited by H. W. Robinson, op. cit. p. 147, from Streeter and Appasamy, *The Sadhu*.)

[3] See W. James, *Varieties of Religious Experience*.

be very wonderful. Often the experient reports an awareness of Reality so convincing that the impressions of his normal consciousness, far from persuading him that the things known in his trance were illusions, instead leave him unshakably sure that he has returned from light into shadow. Micklem cites Wordsworth's statement (*The Prelude*, Book XIII) that for three consecutive days, which the poet spent in walking over Salisbury Plain, he found himself in a trance-condition involving both visions and auditions. 'Nevertheless', Micklem comments, 'there is no reason to think that the poet refused his meals during that period, or that he failed to return home at night and converse reasonably with his companions, and fall asleep in the normal manner.' St Paul spoke of having a trance-experience so intense that he knew not whether he was in the body or out of the body. Neither Wordsworth's nor St Paul's state of mind is going to be illuminated by studying the dancing devotees whom Saul the Hebrew encountered in the days of Samuel.[1] The great Prophets declared that the initiative came from a Reality infinitely greater than themselves, and we find that the convictions they received in trance and reported afterwards dealt with the profoundest conceivable issues touching God and Man. The right way to understand the Hebrew Prophets, and why they sometimes had trances, and why the thoughts that came in those trances were what they were—is to begin by thinking about what manner of men they were in their normal hours and normal senses.[2]

We do not know how often the several great 'Men of God' experienced the intellectual and emotional stress best described as trance. Once at least—in an initial experience which convinced them beyond all doubt that God called them to be selflessly vigilant to hear what God the Lord would say unto His People, and to be willing to declare it. Did they have visions once a day, or once a month, or once a year? Or was it, perhaps, three times in a fortnight, and not again for years? At most, the terrific moments of trance amounted to an infinitesimal fraction of the years of their lives. It would be huge exaggeration to suggest that those moments of exaltation amounted to 1 in 1000 hours of their ordinary existence! Still, take it at that. What were the great Prophets like in the other 999 hours? From all that we know about

[1] Cp. Porteous, 'Prophecy' (*Record and Revelation*, p. 228).
[2] See further, Chapter XVII, p. 365.

them it is certain as certain can be that they were wholly earnest and honest men, capable of reasoning and of drawing conclusions. Granting that convictions about supernatural Reality and the inflexible operation of the divine purpose of righteousness were from time to time burnt in upon their souls by the white light of Vision, the crucial matter is what use they made of those impressions when afterwards they confronted the complex problems and conditions of life around them. They did not then fumble about in perplexity. They went straight to the mark. They did not see facts 'without *seeing*'; they both saw and felt, and reflected on what they saw. Amos had certain, terrible, trance-visions concerning God and Israel. But he was not in a frenzy and slashing himself with a knife, when he told the men and women of Samaria that deeds have consequences, and said: 'God hath shewed me what will befall this city. Thus saith the Lord....'

But the point can be followed up more definitely. The first characteristic of the great Prophets is that they were morally alert to the possibilities of good and evil in human life. They loved its possible good qualities of courage, devotion and tenderness; they were touched by its sufferings and sorrows, and were moved by the shame and tragedy of vice. That is why their words are so vivid that we cannot fail to see what they saw and hear what they heard —the open violence and cruelty, the lust and petty meanness, in a thoroughly corrupt society; the sorrows of the oppressed— defenceless cheated peasantry in north Israel, ragged and hungry widows and children in the streets of prosperous Jerusalem. They were sensitive to actualities as those are sensitive who to-day live close to the poor. For such persons *Destitution* is not merely an economic problem, but also thought of known individuals beset by misery and helplessness. And the great Prophets believed that God is righteous and real, and requires us to help one another to the utmost.

The second characteristic is their unflinching courage in facing the truth that deeds have consequences. Amos 'saw the raw facts ...he had no illusions: he knew a mirage when he saw one'. In their treatment of human beings Judah and Israel were violating elemental obligations inherent in a bond between God and Man, if God be Justice and Mercy. The Prophets allowed no patriotic bias, and no antique assumption that a God would not wholly cease to defend His People, to deter them from drawing dire conclusions.

And, thirdly, to their moral and intellectual integrity there was added capacity for intense emotion. Unlike our ultra-individualistic selves, the Prophets, as Hebrews, thought of their personal existence as literally an integral part of the life-blood of their kindred. It was impossible for them to stand apart, and view the spectacle and prospects detachedly. On the one hand, they were emotionally part of their People, hurrying itself to its doom. On the other, they were emotionally one with the sorrow of God in His frustrated good purpose, so completely had they given themselves to His service. It would be strange indeed if, in men of such resolute mind, moral sensitiveness and tender imagination, normal consciousness had not at times been exalted into trance.

But these qualities in conjunction illuminate why the outcome of their trance-experiences was a body of beliefs that interlock and supplement one another. The consistency of meaning in the visions and auditions which came to the great Prophets is explicable by and congruous with the fact that in their normal senses they sought to control their personalities by great principles and not be at the mercy of random inclinations and mundane wishes. Therefore the working of their subconscious (or superconscious) mind produced not incoherent phantasies which only the psycho-analyst could wisely unravel, but constructive insight and foresight that cut through the perplexities, not only of their own times, but of ours also, concerning the things that belong to our peace. How did that marvel come to pass? Was it not because they were men in whom desire had become longing to do that which is right, whose will it was to do the Will of God, who wanted to face truth whatever might be the cost of knowing it? It has been said that 'the pure in heart shall see God'.

CHAPTER X

'GOD WITH US'

In 1860, for the English-speaking public, battle was joined around Moses and the Pentateuch. Bishop Colenso in South Africa published a work on the subject; and, if facts are facts, he had made it clear that Moses had not written the first five Books of the Bible. If Moses had been master of all the learning of Egypt and had written five-and-twenty books, he had not written those five Books. Therefore, he was not the author, at God's dictation, of the mass of 'commandments, statutes and judgements' in Exodus, Numbers, Leviticus and Deuteronomy. After a considerable period the religious public (except in out-of-the-way places) realized that God was still in His heaven, and ceased to feel perturbed about the sources of the Pentateuch. That battle was won. But private, tolerably polite, war had to continue among the critics, seeking exactly to define and date the four main documents in the Pentateuch, to detect minor sources[1] within the main ones, to weigh their value as evidence for the times when they were composed, *and* to consider what reliable evidence (if any) they provide concerning Moses and the events associated with his name. This last question ought to interest anyone to whom it matters whether he has a Faith; for principles of belief about life are ascribed to Moses which deeply concern the nature of *our* Faith and how it came to exist.

The earliest of the chief sources must be dated hundreds of years after the death of Moses, and the latest (and most impressive)—the Priests' Code—perhaps 800 years after his time. It is this latest document which depicts Moses as having been 80 years old at the time of the Exodus; as assisted by Aaron the priest, his elder brother;[2] and as having promulgated to the tribes in the wilderness

---

[1] Conspicuous are 'the Book of the Covenant', 'the Ten *Ritual* Commandments' (not the Decalogue), and 'the Law of Holiness'.

[2] The presence and position of Aaron in the story arose, it is generally agreed, from his being regarded as the great ancestor of the guild of priests which eventually obtained pre-eminence, and certain exclusive rights, in the temple of Jerusalem. 'The prominence of Aaron as the agent and representative of Moses is one of the most easily recognizable characteristics of the latest and least trustworthy redaction.' (Phythian-Adams, *Call of Israel*, p. 51.)

all the Rules and Regulations. Most people have a ponderous idea of Moses in their minds. They derive it from passages in the Priests' Code source; aided perhaps by having seen a photograph of Michelangelo's magnificent statue of Moses in the Church of S. Pietro in Vincoli at Rome: 'The prophet, supposed to have just come down from Mount Sinai and found the Israelites worshipping the golden calf, sits, heavily bearded and draped... his right hand grasping the tables of the law—an incarnation of majestic indignation and menace.' The idea of Moses derived from the Priests' Code has been styled 'the most influential and the least historical' of the documents; and it is pure gain that we can dismiss that conception. When we turn to the great Prophets, we find a portrait of Moses robed in the dignity and simple greatness of the 'man of God'.[1]

It is beyond question that in Exodus to Deuteronomy we possess only traditions about Moses which have been 'recast, idealized and enlarged in the course of centuries, as each successive generation of historians referred back to the founder those principles, laws or institutions, which they considered essential to the national religion'.[2] From sources so clearly shaped to emphasize ideas and interests of their own times (centuries after the Age of the Exodus about 1200 B.C.) can anything at all be safely inferred concerning Moses and his work? Some extreme opinions have been argued. On the depressing side it has been asserted that 'Moses is merely a mythical figure', or that 'It is to the age of Amos and Hosea c. 750 B.C. that we must look for the first signs of distinctively lofty principles in the religion of Israel'.[3] On the optimistic side some scholars detect details about Moses of which the compilers of the documents were quite unconscious.[4] The

[1] Cp. Hos. xii. 13; Jer. vii. 22, 23.

[2] Lods, *Israel*, p. 308.

[3] Budde (*Religion of Israel*, Lecture I) advanced an ingenious, curious, theory (which in the form he gave it does not now carry weight) to the effect that a religious-ethical principle of importance was brought about through a covenant between Kenite tribes and the Hebrews from Egypt, since the Kenite God was unknown or alien to the Hebrews. But he further argued that, as regards Moses himself, 'all attempts to find the germ of the ethical development of the Yahveh religion in the material content of the conception of God as represented by Moses have completely failed'.

[4] E.g. Sellin's contention that Moses met a martyr's death at the hands of Levitical priests. (*Mose und seine Bedeutung*.)

author of a College Essay pronounced a sensible verdict when he wrote: 'Between the two extremes wisdom, and probably Moses, lies.' A recent expression of this middle attitude puts it thus: 'That a mass of sacred legend has been attached to his name is a fact which must be obvious to any candid student of the documents; that Moses himself was less than the greatest of religious leaders is an unproved assumption, which effects nothing save to render the problem insoluble.'[1] Most scholars now feel it is not reasonably disputable that a solid historical basis underlies the tradition of Moses' greatness. The present writer does not take a depressing view of the available evidence. He holds that we can see through the towering smoke of tradition to an elemental fire which is its heart. He proposes to state his conclusions straightforwardly in the text, leaving argument and qualifications to footnotes.

§1. The Making of Moses

In ancient Egypt a frontier wall, running south from the Mediterranean to where the Red Sea then terminated in shallow waters and marshes, prevented the wild men of the desert from entering the rich country. Between this wall and the mouths of the Nile (the Delta region) there was excellent grazing for sheep. In it Aramaean (Hebrew) pastoral tribes had been allowed to live: some of them held that their ancestors had been there for some 200 years, having originally come down to Egypt from Canaan. It suited the Egyptians to keep the uncouth shepherds in that 'Land of Goshen' (as it was called). Many useful articles can be made from wool, and mutton makes good eating. The shepherds found it a pleasant land; for, besides good grazing for their sheep, it grew vegetables prolifically—cucumbers, melons, leeks, onions and garlic, and there was fish in abundance to be had from the Nile waters.[2] They would have felt content to be for ever there, were it not for one or two very irksome things. In the marrow of their bones they reckoned themselves men of the desert, who ought to be free to go anywhere they pleased, whereas they were not allowed to leave Egypt if they wanted to. That made their Arab souls feel in prison. Also the Egyptians were abominably rude: they said 'Shepherds were an abomination to them'.[3] However,

---

[1] Phythian-Adams, The Call of Israel, p. 43.
[2] Num. xi. 5.   [3] Gen. xliii. 32.

Aramaeans could silently give back contempt for contempt. They thought to themselves that the Egyptian towns were astonishing in luxury, and their temples breath-taking—stupendous in size with no end of Gods all sumptuously worshipped. But in Egyptian towns everybody cringed to somebody—from the slaves up to the king's vizier. Then, a terrible thing happened to them. A king of Egypt (Rameses II) had such a mania for building that even he ran short of slave-labour, and he rounded up the shepherds to make and lay bricks. That was insult unspeakable! They gave trouble. Egyptian overseers saw to that. The trouble-makers were flogged, and their task redoubled.[1]

Tradition related that a royal Egyptian lady took one of the Hebrew shepherds' babies into her home.[2] The boy was given an Egyptian name ('Moses'), and grew up in the splendour of a wealthy, possibly a royal, household. He learnt to have Egyptian haughtiness, but there ran in his veins Aramaean blood; and he came to know about his Hebrew parentage. The narrative continues that, grown to man's estate, he slew an Egyptian overseer who was lashing a Hebrew. That action revealed in Moses 'the youth as father of the man'—hating cruelty, regardless of self-interest, passionate, authoritative. The deed altered his life. He had to forsake Egypt for the desert, where eventually (a long way from Egypt) he settled with a nomadic Midianite family, whose encampments (so the writer thinks) were in the neighbourhood of the Gulf of Elath, not very remote from the volcanic mountain which Moses was later to make for ever famous in history. Aramaean Midianites were moon-worshippers accustomed to shout *Ya! Ya!* as they invoked the blessing of its celestial Being. It has been suggested that Moses, now married to a Midianite woman,[3] was converted *to* the religion of the Midianites.

[1] This feature of the tradition is, in its essence, historical: 'No people would ever have invented a tale that their ancestors had been slaves, if the bondage had not ended to their glory.'

[2] Late Jewish writers embroidered the tale of the infant Moses' rescue from the basket floating on the Nile (see Driver on Exod. ii. 10). There are close parallels in the folk-lore of other nations. Because the story of Moses in the bulrushes may be fiction, it does not follow that its hero was a figment of the imagination.

[3] Her father is variously named as Jethro the priest of Midian, or as Reuel, or Hobab. What is related concerning Jethro is probably devoid of historical basis, and due to an etiological motive. (Cp. Phythian-Adams, op. cit. pp. 72–7.)

Not so—unless Moses was a very simple-witted man. Why should one who had witnessed the splendour of Egyptian sun-worship be awed by nomads adoring the moon? Test this alternative suggestion—that Moses was an extraordinary man; one of those very rare intelligences capable of independent thinking about the mystery of life. Suppose, further, that he was in no need of being converted *from* the religion of Egypt, having in his early manhood seen through the mumbo-jumbo of its many Gods —the magical spells, the mummification of the wealthy dead, the grotesque half-animal Deities, and even the royal cult of the Sun.[1] Just conceivably he had heard tell about the commotion in Egypt 200 years before, when the 'heretic', Ikhnaton, had tried to do away with polytheism and bade men worship the Disk of the Sun as symbol of one, invisible, beneficent Reality. But if Moses had never so much as heard of Ikhnaton's name, what occurs to one man of genius may occur to another—namely, that polytheism is unconvincing, and that the problem of Existence calls for better explanation. At least consider that Moses may have carried into the desert a thoughtful mind, and used wearisome leisure to meditate, neither upon the glory of the sun or the moon, nor on this God nor on that God, but on Life-in-general and on the Mystery-of-all-things. Moses in the desert was assuredly a man drinking the dregs of the cup of bitterness. What had the ardour of his youth achieved? Complete failure to alleviate his kinsmen's lot; complete ruin of his own career. Piping to the flocks did not satisfy Moses. His spirit was 'kicking against the pricks'.

There follows the account of the sight which transformed *Moses the Failure* into *Moses the Man of God*.[2] Wandering far afield with his sheep—absorbed in thought, angry with his futility, baffled—he became aware of a desert shrub which at a distance seemed aflame with fire. Approaching it, he saw the light

---

[1] On the question of possible traces of Egyptian influence on early Hebrew religion, see the careful note in Lods, *Israel*, pp. 318–20. Ezek. xx. 5–8 declares that the Hebrews in Goshen trusted in the idols of Egypt, but in so late a passage the belief may be no more than a general inference. No more is likely than that the shepherds occasionally saw, as spectators rather than participants, the worship of the native Egyptians. 'It does not appear that the cults of Egypt had any deep influence on the half-nomad Hebrew tribes of Goshen at the time when their national religion took shape: the divergence between the two peoples was too great.' (Lods, op. cit. p. 319.)

[2] Exod. iii. 1–14.

vanish, but the bush stood unconsumed.[1] Suddenly there flashed into his soul its meaning *for him*. The passion of his youth to see his kinsfolk free from Egyptian arrogance and cruelty ought not to have been consumed. If the impression had been no more than rekindled longing, the wild hope would soon have been extinguished in common sense. But there came upon Moses conviction that a Reality greater than his own mind was calling him back to duty, and had enabled him to see that his life should be an abiding determination. For Moses the place had indeed become holy ground. Here is just such a transforming intuition as has been the making of other great religious personalities.[2] The instant of insight cannot have removed from his mind the seeming impossibility of his task. But he was a changed man. As he turned his steps back to Egypt, fear was overborne in assurance that the Being from beyond the visible, Who had called him, would uphold him. Henceforth to him God was not a Question-mark but an illuminating Reality. It was as if a Voice spake over and over again, saying: *I will be with thee, I will be with thee*. That experience (not the moon-worship of the Midianites) created the faith of Moses. *He will be with me! He will be with us!* The question has been debated whether Moses' conviction can possibly be construed as belief that only One God exists (*Monotheism*), or was merely belief that only this particular God he, and his people, should henceforth worship (*Monolatry*). Genius has a way of over-leaping the boundaries we prescribe for it. Moreover, the issue is wrongly posed as a sharp antithesis. Moses was not wrestling with metaphysical problems. But the crucial fact is that between the Supernatural and his finite soul a relation had been established so personal, so purposeful, so noble, that it amounted to the initiation, not merely of implicit monotheism, but of what is vastly more important—ethical monotheism.

[1] The Commentaries quote comparable occurrences from modern records of desert life.

[2] Exactly as, 600 years later, the sight of an almond tree first gave certainty to Jeremiah that God was watching over His word to perform it. Just as the account of Christ's temptation derives from what Jesus afterwards told His disciples, so also the narrative of the burning bush has its source in what Moses told about his experience. 'The true origin of Moses' work must be sought...in an inward illumination, which tradition, and perhaps Moses himself, first depicted in the form of the vision of the burning bush.' (Lods, *Israel*, p. 325.)

§2. *The Achievement of Moses*

(1) *Victory over Egypt.* Moses found his kinsfolk in Egypt so furious about the forced labour, so enraged by the cruelties of the Egyptian taskmasters, that they were ready to exchange the lush pastures, the plentiful water, the unrationed fish and vegetables, of the Land of Goshen for thirst and hardship in the desert; ready to risk their lives in a desperate venture to assail the frontier wall, if only they could get out. But they failed to overwhelm the frontier garrison; and then they knew that a punitive force would swiftly be on its way to deal with them. Their position was desperate. The only faint hope was the fact that, where the wall ceased at the marsh in which the shallows of the Red Sea ended, the bog (under very exceptional circumstances of wind and tide)[1] could be crossed by men and by the animals without which tribes cannot possibly subsist in the desert. The place was known as the 'Sea of Reeds' (*Yăm Sūph*).[2] It is a misfortune that our versions translated 'the Red Sea'; for the impression was given that it was the wide deep waters of the Red Sea itself that were crossed by the Hebrews. The heart of Israel's story of the Exodus from Egypt insists, however, that the tribes' escape across the shallows took place in unprecedented circumstances which were a veritable Act of God —so astounding was the drying-up of the ground at the crucial moment, so overwhelming the return of the waters that drowned the pursuing Egyptians. This tradition is historical; for nothing else properly explains the note of marvelling triumph that resounds in the memory of the deliverance. The physical occurrence that

---

[1] See the evidence quoted by Driver, *Exodus*, p. 125. 'And the Lord caused the sea to go back by a strong east wind all the night, and made sea dry land.' (Exod. xiv. 21.)

[2] Other similar places had the same designation—notably the marshy shallows in which the Gulf of Akaba near Elath terminated (see I Kings ix. 26; cp. Jer. xlix. 21), which some scholars have considered to be the place of the marvellous crossing. But the northern end of the Gulf of Akaba descends into the Valley of the Arabah across which the tribesmen could have continued their way on dry land. Why should they have needlessly plunged into its bog? As Phythian-Adams dryly points out there was no reason for them to stand gazing in despair at the terminal waters of the Gulf! (Op. cit. p. 169.) Further, it seems incredible that a pursuing Egyptian force of cavalry and chariots would not have overtaken the slow-moving shepherds long before they reached the Gulf of Akaba 150 miles distant from the Nile Delta.

would occasion such an outflow and subsequent tidal wave is a seismic disturbance farther south affecting the bed of the Red Sea. That view is not conjuring up volcanoes to explain miracles. The conjecture is perfectly permissible, and is strengthened very greatly by other features in the general narrative, especially its assertion that the sacred Mountain which they reached 'burned with fire'.[1] The Red Sea crosses one of the principal geological 'faults' in the crust of the earth: comment is further made in the note below.[2]

(2) *The Journey in the Wilderness.* Moses succeeded in bringing about 6000 persons into the freedom of the desert. That really is the probable total![3] If the reader will charter a camel, or fly an aeroplane, from the Nile Delta, and will direct his course eastwards right across the Peninsula of Sinai (the Wilderness of Paran) to the top of the great arm of the Red Sea known as the Gulf of Elath, he will be on the route of the escaped Hebrews.[4] From

---

[1] Cp. Gressmann, *Mose*, p. 444; Oesterley and Robinson, *Hebrew Religion*, pp. 104f.

[2] The deep rift in the earth's surface, which forms the Valley of the Jordan to the Dead Sea, extends as the Wadi Arabah to the Gulf of Elath, passes under the Red Sea and then continues far south into Africa; and its line is bordered by extinct or dormant volcanoes. In Africa native tribes in the neighbourhood of the rift have their own legends of eruptions and changes in the configuration of the country. Eruption and earthquake near the sources of the Nile might temporarily pollute its stream in ways that could give rise to certain of the plagues alleged to have beset Egypt.

[3] The total present population of the entire peninsula of Sinai is approximately 5000 persons. The numeration in Exod. xii. 37f.; Numb. i, xi. 21; states that the total of male Hebrews over twenty who escaped from Egypt was 600,000: that is to say, the assertion envisages about 2,000,000 people living for forty years in the desert! See Gray, *Numbers (I.C.C.)*, pp. 12ff.; McNeile, *Numbers*, pp. 4f.

[4] C. S. Jarvis (for some years Governor of the Sinaitic Peninsula) has argued that the fugitives were forced to follow a narrow neck of land that for some fifty miles has the Mediterranean on its left and the *Sirbonian Lake* or *Bog* on its right. Overtaken, they might attempt to escape the Egyptian chariots by trying to cross the clay-pan of the Lake. Jervis was able interestingly to show that occasionally flooding of the Bog takes place with a rapidity that might have caused disaster to the Egyptians (*Blackwood's Magazine*, February 1931). The theory involves great difficulties regarding the Hebrews' subsequent line of march and the location of the Mount of God. Jervis felt his case to be decisively strengthened by the tradition that the fugitives were fed by *manna* (a deposit by a small insect that feeds on tamarisk bushes) and by *quails*. In southern Sinai, he observes, the quail is never seen and tamarisk

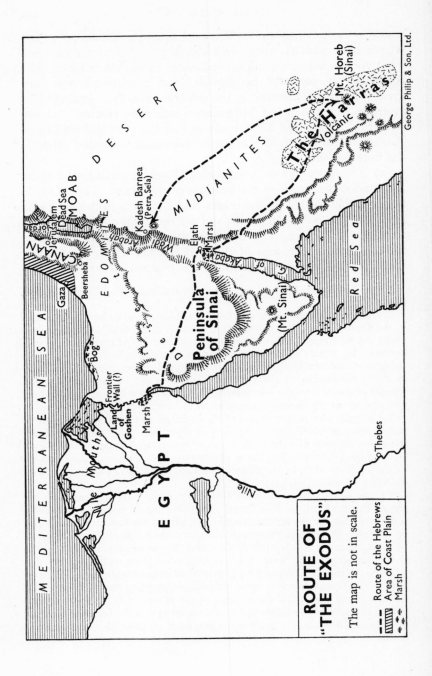

ROUTE OF
"THE EXODUS"

The map is not in scale.

- - - - Route of the Hebrews
||||| Area of Coast Plain
≈≈≈ Marsh

George Philip & Son, Ltd.

Elath if he rides (or flies) along the present caravan-track to Mecca close to the coast of Arabia, and leaves it about 100–150 miles south of Elath to strike inland up to the high plateau that runs parallel to the Red Sea, he will find himself in the *Harras*, truly 'a great and terrible wilderness'—anciently in Midianite territory. Therein he will find a volcanic mountain, called by the Arabs to-day *Tadra* or *el-Bedr*. The writer believes that was the burning Mount of God to which Moses led his followers. They called it *Mount Horeb*; but in much later times uncertainty arose about its location and it was eventually supposed to have been in the southern part of the peninsula of Sinai, and therefore in the later Hebrew documents is called *Mount Sinai*.[1] The location of the sacred Mount at *Tadra* is due to Dr A. Musil's recent investigations in the Harras region.[2] The surrounding tract is nearly impassable, but in the vicinity of Mount Tadra there is a plain affording water and scant pasturage; and from Bedouin in this district Musil heard legends regarding the sacredness of *Tadra* curiously apposite in relation to the Hebrew tradition. When Israel came out of Egypt, Mount Tadra was active. As they journeyed across the desert its volcano became visible, so that (as tradition put it) they were led 'by a pillar of cloud by day and of fire by night'. When they reached its neighbourhood, how awe-inspiring would be the impression made on their minds by its occasional titanic energy, the roar and shaking of the rocks, the flame and lightnings around its peak.[3]

bushes are very few; whereas to this day migrating swarms of quails 'pitch exhausted on the Mediterranean shores and nowhere else; and manna is sometimes found on the tamarisks of this region'. But in later times travellers' tales about manna and quails on this route from Egypt might be the source of both these features in the tradition, in order to answer the question—How were the people fed in the desert?

[1] Unquestionably, in the older Hebrew documents the name was *Horeb*, and it was understood to be far distant, 'forty days and nights from Canaan'. (Cp. Deut. i. 2; Num. xxxiii. 16–36; I Kings xix. 8.) Only after the sixth century B.C. was the name *Sinai* given to it. (See Phythian-Adams, op. cit. pp. 131–3.) And it is only subsequent to the fourth century A.D. that Mount Sinai was regarded as being the mountain called *Serbal* or *Musa* in the south of the Sinaitic peninsula.

[2] See Musil, *The Northern Hejaz*, 1926; Phythian-Adams, in *P.E.F.* July and October 1930, and subsequently his *Call of Israel*, pp. 140–54 and Appendices. Also Lods, *Israel*, pp. 179, 180.

[3] 'And mount Sinai was altogether on smoke...and the smoke thereof ascended as the smoke of a furnace, and the whole mount quaked greatly'

What could have persuaded the hard-headed shepherds to leave the safe and easy places of the desert and enter so fearsome a region? Nothing would, except the constraint of an extraordinary dominant personality—Moses. Men and women died on the march. He told them that God had not delivered them from the lash of the Egyptian overseers in order that they might follow their inclinations, but that they should worship Him; and the place where they would be taught to do that acceptably was *at this mountain*. They cursed and they grumbled: 'We remember the fleshpots in Egypt, the fish and the cucumbers, the leeks, the onions and the garlic. Why hast thou brought us forth that we may perish in this waste wilderness wherein are only serpents and hunger and thirst?' Moses went forward; and they followed.

—(3) *Israel's Pledge*. If the aim of Moses had been merely to liberate his kinsfolk, the physical deliverance at the Sea of Reeds might have occurred, but the result would have been to diminish the brick-makers of Egypt and augment the population of Arabia by a few thousand shepherds—just that and nothing more. In making for Mount Horeb the object of Moses was not that the Hebrews should reach a geographical point. He was subjecting them to a stern discipline. Nor was Moses anxious to set these men free so that they might worship the moon and invoke its Deity with a loud voice saying, *Ya, Ya*: as probably they believed their Aramaean ancestors had done. If he had desired to see a concourse of simple men ecstatically baying the moon, then his path was quite easy and there was not the slightest need to struggle to reach Mount Horeb. The moon sails serenely in the skies. But if his aim was so to stir their conscience that the crowning mercy they had received would, generation after generation, evoke gratitude and determination to obey their redeeming God, that task was more difficult than crossing the Sea of Reeds. If his longing was to impart to them his own profound faith about the nature of God, the task before him was almost superhuman. Moses was a genius.[1] Therefore, he did not begin by a frontal

(Exod. xix. 18). It is not tolerable to tone down the tradition of the burning mountain into a damp squib—as that the story arose from a custom of carrying 'a brazier at the head of a caravan proceeding by night', or was due to 'violent thunderstorms breaking on the mountain-summit'.

[1] Ikhnaton had been king absolute in Egypt, and addressed his new theology to a cultured people. He too was a genius; yet, for all his brilliance and royal authority, his hopes failed completely.

attack on the obtuse minds of his followers, arguing with them that the *Ya*-theology of their ancestors was out-of-date. His own spiritual experience taught him that what matters is not *that God is* but *what God is*. Moses took the efficacious way of persuading the Hebrews to think; to think what God had done for them, and what God required from them.

He made the awe-inspiring scene at the sacred mountain occasion for momentous choice. There he called upon the tribes to acknowledge their deliverance and its significance, telling them that the God whose power over Nature they beheld in the burning Mount, whose power over Man they had witnessed in their rescue from the Egyptians, willed to bless them and be their God. Would they pledge themselves to be His People and to live as He would demand of them? In the name of God he proclaimed: 'Now therefore, if ye will obey my voice indeed, and keep my covenant, then ye shall be a peculiar treasure unto me.' 'And all the people answered...and said, *All that the Lord hath spoken we will do*.'[1] By that solemn assent the men of Israel had taken upon themselves their obligation towards God and towards one another. What they called, and we call, a relation of *Covenant* was now recognized to exist; but what they meant by 'being in covenant', and what we mean by 'making a covenant', are apt to be two, very different, things. And whensoever in theology the Hebrew (religious-social) idea of Covenant is not understood in its fullness, and instead the Western (legal-commercial)[2] notion is read into Israel's covenant with its God, then the devil gets into the Church decorously but sardonically.

This matter is of vital importance, if we are to hold a religion worth calling a religion. In technical terms it concerns the relation between Divine grace and human personality.[3] Is that relationship mechanical or personal? Does God deal with us as sons or merely as a balance-sheet? If we come short, does He exact His 'pound of flesh', or does He will to forgive and always seek to raise up the fallen? Does He compel or persuade? It has made a

[1] Exod. xix. 5–8.

[2] In our normal usage *Covenant* means a business agreement, a binding contract assented to between *A* and *B* at a certain date on certain terms. (See *The Oxford Dictionary*.) One recalls legal documents to which anxiously we 'set to our hand and seal'. We reflect sadly on the fate that overtook 'the Covenant of the League of Nations', with its Constitution framed in constituent Articles.   [3] Cp. Oman, *Grace and Personality*.

vast difference in religious history which way men answered those questions. In so far as persons not deeply religious give a thought to religion, they seem (unconsciously beset by Western legalism and commercialism) to answer them off-hand the wrong way; and they dismiss 'religion' as something in which they really could not bring themselves to believe, and feel it not worth attempting to do so. Unless men firmly conceive the Author of our being to be ceaselessly the 'friend' of the souls that He hath made, they bring into their thoughts of God and Christ features suitable for the portrait of a business-man putting through deals from time to time on the basis of a *quid pro quo* for his money.

Desert tribes understood thoroughly that *being in covenant* with other men meant that a state of friendship *existed* between them, so that they were brethren of one blood through vital unity with the God or Gods who blessed them all.[1] So far, so good. If two tribes hitherto hostile to one another decided to be friends, they made ('cut') covenant between them before God at a time and place, whereupon a new phase of their existence began for them both. What happened for Israel at Mount Horeb was radically different and unprecedented: and every Hebrew present understood. This event did not signalize that a hitherto hostile God had changed His mind and, having decided to be different from what He was before, intimated that He was willing to begin to be friendly, if they cared to strike a bargain with Him.[2] The Hebrew People's Pledge at Horeb declared *their* confession that this God had never ceased to be faithful to His covenant with their fathers, and to the forgetful children of those fathers had manifested His abiding mercy. The Pledge was *their* acknowledgement of God's continuing grace—to which *they* now responded, vowing themselves to be faithful, willing now to trust in His guidance and henceforth to walk in His ways. (And, of course, on the human side, the promise, as with any ordinary covenant into which men entered, involved that those who pledged themselves would be brethren

---

[1] Hebrews could say that they were 'in covenant' concerning circumstances where no initiating agreement could have occurred. (See Kennett, *The Church of Israel*, pp. 143–5.) Cp. also Kurt-Galling, quoted by H. W. Robinson in *The Companion to the Bible* (ed. Manson), p. 320.

[2] Kennett (op. cit. p. 145) rightly emphasizes: 'That God should bind Himself by a covenant to do that which He would not do of His own eternal unchanging righteousness is unthinkable....Those who speak of the uncovenanted mercies of God as distinct from the covenanted "darken counsel by words without knowledge".'

one to another.) Then—to the penitent, the thankful, the willing
—God, whose mercy never faileth, could impart the gift that He
could not sooner give, *knowledge how to live aright*: God's marvellous gift for the freedom of their spirit, even as the liberation from
Egypt had set free their bodies. If they were truly willing to obey
His will, God could bless them, as His mercy everlastingly desires
to do. *Divine grace—human acknowledgement—Divine teaching*:
that is the sequence then and ever.

In Hebrew tradition the giving of the Law followed Israel's
promise.[1] The narrators made no mistake about the cardinal fact,
and they did not represent the Commandments, Statutes and
Judgements, as God's terms in a bargain on acceptance of which He
would cease to be hostile and become friendly! The Law is the
gift of God; wisdom for the welfare of human life.[2] And the
great Prophets (unlike some theologians) did not equate the
letter of the Law with the realities of its spirit. They did not so
much as mention that a Covenant was made at Mount Horeb.[3]
They did not solemnly summon their hearers to remember that
the customary ritual for cutting a covenant was duly carried out by
slicing an animal in two, walking between its severed halves and
having drops of its blood sprinkled on the people.[4] The Prophets

[1] It is very important to appreciate that the Hebrew word *Torah* (which
our versions translate as *Law*) means *Teaching, Instruction, Guidance*.

[2] Brilliantly the narrators of Israel's story from the Call of Abraham to the
death of Moses present the great conception: Abraham set forth in trust and
walked in covenant with God, believing that his children would serve the
divine purpose. Fugitive Jacob dreamed of God at Bethel, and his chequered
life was guided to its rightful end. But Jacob's descendants forgot. God did
not forget. He manifests His faithful mercy at the Exodus. Then the climax—
the Mount of God—Israel's promise—the giving of the Law.

[3] The earliest allusions to the covenant-making at Sinai are in fact the
passage in Exodus (part of the J-E document) and references in Deuteronomy;
i.e. not earlier than about 650 B.C. and perhaps later than the Fall of Jerusalem.
Unquestionably the Hebrews of the Monarchic Age claimed that from the
time of Moses Israel became the people that worships Yahveh. It has been
argued that the graphic scene at Sinai is only a reading-back into the time of
Moses of the later belief, much as the narrative of Aaron's making of the
golden calf in the desert reflects the 'Sin' of Jeroboam's Bull-images set up
at Bethel and Dan after Solomon's death. The writer considers that there is
no substance at all in that argument, and that a great decision was asked by
Moses and given by the people at the sacred Mount.

[4] No doubt the ritual act, which would disgust us, impressed the tribesmen. In
their *naïveté* they may even have thought it necessary, because they supposed
that unity in the physical blood was part and parcel of the psychical bond.

fastened upon the supreme matter—What God is, What God does. They besought men to bethink them, not of a Pact made between equals, but of the immeasurable grace of God.[1] Other nations were wont to take for granted the relation between them and the Deities, as in the nature of things. To Israel alone it was given to conceive the way of life as the joy and duty of response to the changeless grace of God. Upon that rock our theology and our understanding of duty should be built.

(4) *Making a Nation.* The good possibilities for the future of Hebrew religious thought latent in this unique conception of the relation between God and Man cannot be overstated. But all too easily inherent possibilities may come to naught. Men in the mass have a way of grasping a truth vividly at a dramatic moment and forgetting all about it 24 hours later. At Horeb the tribes thanked their God with all their might for all the blessings of this life. All too easily they might soon have been complaining that their sacrifices to merit God's favours were not working properly: the goods were not being delivered with regularity. That tragedy did not happen, because Moses long continued to be the resolute leader of his people. From the Mount of God the tribes turned towards Canaan, and at last reached the desert-country over against its south-eastern borders, where Petra (Kadesh-Barnea) became their rallying point. Moses was in their midst during this period—perhaps many years—until his death. He had opportunity to impress his faith and character. Why should we suppose he lacked the will to do so? Sojourn at the Mount of God concluded, did Moses fold his hands as though his life-work had been accomplished? Did the dominance of his personality cease, or thenceforth count for naught? Surely he set himself to the most necessary task of being the interpreter of covenantal relationship. When Moses and his people turned from the Mount of God there remained the third, and not the least, part of his life-work— consolidation of what had been achieved.

[1] A clear general statement on the attitude of the several documents to the Law, and of the Prophetic standpoint, is given in the article 'Covenant' by A. B. Davidson in Hastings' *Dictionary of the Bible*, vol. I, pp. 509 ff. ('The prophetic idea of the relation of God and man differs from the idea of a covenant as *real* differs from *formal*; the assurance of redemption reposes, not on the divine promise, but on the divine nature, on God Himself as men have historically found Him in His acts of redemption already done, and as He is known in the hearts of men.')

Moses held his followers together, welding their jealous tribes into a coherent people. It is almost impossible for large nomad groups not to disintegrate, in consequence of the proud independence of the tribesmen and the feuds that break out between families, and because, as men and animals increase, wells and pasturage become inadequate and some of the component tribes must seek new grounds. 'There never was a nation in Arabia till Mohammed fused the tribes for a time by the fierce heat of his religion and the passion for spoil.'[1] An illustration of failure to maintain tribal coherence, despite favouring circumstances and obvious fighting advantage, can be cited from modern times. In A.D. 1922 the Riffs of North Africa, despite the prestige of their leaders Bukkeish and Abd-el-Krim, were unable to maintain unity in their defiance of the French and Spanish Forces. As a personal witness of the struggle phrased it: 'All the efforts of Bukkeish and Abd-el-Krim failed to hold the tribes together. Bukkeish was a wild barbarian whose overweening truculence roused the resentment of the proud chiefs, and Abd-el-Krim, infinitely more capable, was suspect by reason of his Spanish education and wider outlook.' Moses succeeded, notwithstanding his imperious temperament, his Egyptian upbringing and his wider outlook. He succeeded not because he was a man born to command, but because in his youth defeat had not embittered him but had led to that vision of God which makes men both humble and great. 'The great changes in the past', writes S. A. Cook, 'can be ascribed to men who, by their superior personality, have wielded an authority which was above local rivalry.'[2] Moses gave the tribes unity by basing their will to be a People on something far more wonderful than desire to eat and drink in the land of milk and honey.

§3. The Legacy of Moses

The greater the genius of Moses, the greater must have been the distance between his mind and the minds of his followers. The question presses whether he could communicate to others his deep thoughts of God in such wise that recollection, and in some measure understanding, would be transmitted to future generations.

(1) *The Name of God.* Moses urged and persuaded the Hebrews to do something better, when they worshipped, than shout *Ya!*

[1] G. A. Smith, *Early Poetry of Israel*, p. 35.
[2] See his note on W. R. Smith, *Religion of the Semites* (3rd ed.), p. 524.

Ya! till the heavens rang. Assuredly they found the custom magnificent and thrilling, and felt that God or the Moon just must have heard them, so loud and united was the yell. But, however often one exclaims *Hallelujah!* (*Praise ye Ya!*), the exercise after all tells one nothing *about* ' *Ya(h)*'. Moses taught them that, whensoever they called upon God to give His blessing and send His help, they must cry, *Ya be WITH US*. Translate that in-vocation into their language—'With us' is *immanu*, and the ancient Aramaic for 'be thou' is *hvĕh*: *Ya-hveh-immanu*.[1] So shouted the Hebrew warriors in battle, and their foes came to think of Israel's God as *Yāhvĕh*.[2] Moses also taught them that they were constantly to say to themselves 'WITH US is God'; to believe it and think about it, morning and evening, when they journeyed and when they encamped, at the rising of the moon and at the going down of the same. *El* means *God*: wherefore in Hebrew 'With us is God' is *Immanuel*. *Immanuel* became the *watchword* of Israel; *Yahveh-immanu* was its *invocation*.[3] And since in Hebrew *Name* is virtually equivalent to *Character*,

[1] Just why the ancient invocation *Ya(h)* should have been transmuted into *Yahveh* has been a standing puzzle. The view which the writer here offers rests on the following argument. In Hebrew 'He will be' (see Exod. iii. 14: 'I will be that I will be') is *Yihyeh*, not *Yahveh*. But the Hebrews learnt to speak the Semitic dialect classed as Hebrew after they entered Canaan; much as Englishmen migrating to Scotland might in time learn to speak Scottish. Previously, in the desert, their Aramaean fathers spoke an ancient form of the dialect known as Aramaic. Now in Aramaic 'Be thou' is *hvĕh*: that united to *Ya* would give the sound *Yahveh*. Moses told them 'Our God is with us' (*Immanuel*); and confidently they called upon His help, saying ' *Ya*, be with us!' (*Ya-hveh-immanu*). *Hveh* occurs six times in the Hebrew Bible. Five of these instances are in post-exilic passages, late Aramaisms; but one (Gen. xxvii. 29) is in a fragment of early poetry embodied in a later prose passage.

[2] There is the interesting fact that Mesha, King of Moab (*c.* 850 B.C.), inscribed the name of Israel's God as Y–H–V–H.

[3] Amos v. 14 (*c.* 750 B.C.) proves that the phrase was habitually used: the Prophet urges, 'Seek good, and not evil...and so the Lord...shall be with you, as ye say.' Isa. vii. 14 (cp. viii. 8) evidences the importance of *Immanuel* (Emmanuel) in the national thought. The tradition of the revelation of the Name to Moses came to be formulated in the famous words in Exod. iii. 12–14. Note the emphasis in *v.* 12, 'Certainly I will be with thee'. In *v.* 14 the A.V. and the R.V. texts render, 'And God said unto Moses, I AM THAT I AM'. The R.V. (margin) translates 'I will be that I will be'; and that is the preferable translation: 'I am' and 'I will be' are the same in Hebrew. In English *I am that I am* may easily be construed as a metaphysical assertion about

Moses gave his People more than a noisy battlecry. He had given them a thought about God, an idea of inestimable value—'God is *with us*'. Thus by a stroke of genius—for the effect was created by so simple a means—Moses instilled into the minds of simple men capacity to conceive of the Deity to whom they prayed as an accompanying Reality, *The Living God*. To do that was to lay the foundation for the temple of a higher Faith.

(2) *The Compassion of God*. The genius of Moses did not allow the Hebrews to go upon their way comfortably (and quite vaguely) believing 'God is with us'. He constrained them to think about the character of the God they had vowed themselves to worship. He had his chance; for there was one road open to their conscience. All of them knew what life had been like when Egypt's press-gangs darkened their tent-doors. But none could contend that Freedom was earned recompense for sacrifices made to Yahveh in Egypt, for in Egypt they had not offered them. Here was fact that touched the interests of every man and woman among them, prompting reflection the simplest could comprehend. Why should we not believe that with persistence, and skill, Moses pressed home the consciousness and the duty: their God was a God of wondrous compassion, as well as wondrous power. Moses constrained the Hebrews to *think*. It had been in mercy and pity that God had saved them from the land of bondage! Could they refuse gratitude, who now dwelt in liberty? 'The Lord is merciful and gracious, slow to anger, and plenteous in mercy.... He hath not dealt with us after our sins, nor rewarded us according to our iniquities....Like as a father pitieth his children, so the Lord pitieth them that fear him.' The Psalmist's words are pure 'Mosaism'.

(3) *The Will of God*. In the name of 'Him that sent me unto you', Moses commanded that the mercy the liberated Hebrew had received from God he should show to his fellows. That brethren of one blood must fight for one another, and not too outrageously fight with one another, was a commonplace of desert-life; bedrock, social necessity. Moses insisted that these covenanted tribes were the People of *Yahveh*, the God whose mercy is high as the

Absolute Being; and it is certain that notion was not intended by the Hebrew. As Driver (*Exodus*, p. 40) says: 'The phrase is no prediction regarding God's essential nature, but one regarding what He will show Himself to be to those in covenant with Him.'

heaven is above the earth. Therefore they had to try to live up to His divine standard, and be such a brotherhood of real goodness and willing mutual help as the desert and the world had never seen.

Did Moses inscribe on stone tablets, or parchments (where would he get those?), Rules and Regulations for the conduct of that brotherhood? We may count it gain that we are sure Moses did not record the huge amalgam of laws found in Exodus to Deuteronomy. It is good to believe that Moses left no rigid system of ordinances to choke and fetter his people, and showed genius in what he abstained from doing as well as in what he did. Even the earliest parts of the Pentateuchal Codes concern the requirements of Canaanite agricultural life, blending with nomadic custom. But from that general finding one possibility stands out —Did Moses declare 'The Ten Commandments'? The writer considers that Moses did declare those ten fundamental principles of welfare for the brotherhood of Yahveh's People. But there are very strong reasons against that opinion, as well as strong reasons favouring it.[1] Confident conclusion either way is rash. But

[1] THE DECALOGUE. 'The Ten Commandments', or the Decalogue, is given in two passages—Exod. xx. 1–17 and Deut. v. 1–21. In present form they reflect settled life in Canaan—note the references to houses, cattle and servants. But these details may well be later expansions of ten concise commands suited for oral transmission. As for the tradition that the Ark (which was certainly brought into Canaan by the invading Hebrews) contained tablets inscribed with the Ten Commandments, that may be no more than later belief, and its original contents two uninscribed stones which were taken from the sacred Mountain. Probably the majority of scholars regard the Decalogue as the product of much later times than the Age of Moses. To quote a somewhat extreme example of that view—Lods (*Israel*, p. 315) writes: 'The Decalogue, like Deuteronomy, is a faint echo of the message of the prophets of the eighth and seventh centuries.' Many feel very non-committal (e.g. Oesterley and Robinson, *Hebrew Religion*, p. 141, and *History of Israel*, i. 96; Lofthouse in *The People and the Book*, p. 235). Others, however, definitely incline to accept its Mosaic origin, e.g. Volz; Gressmann; Kittel; McFadyen in *The Expositor*, 1916; Charles, *The Decalogue*. Of especial interest is the argument in favour put forward by Welch (*Deuteronomy, The Framework to the Code*, esp. pp. 19–22), who urges that the long sojourn of the Hebrews at Kadesh gave them experience of semi-agricultural life, and holds that 'it is to this period we can date the first form of the Decalogue and can measure through that dating its immense significance and its specific purpose'. He urges that, in contrast with the contents of the Codes which presuppose life *in* Canaan, the injunctions of the Decalogue 'were intended for Israel under all conditions and in all periods of its life....It could not supply the positive regulations which were to guide Israel's wor-

dubiety on that score should deter no one from trying to trace why it was that in later times Moses was revered as the inspired revealer of Justice and Right, whose authority was claimed for all that came to be approved in Israel.

Human nature being what it is, men may agree that they are in covenant together, but that will not prevent quarrels—wrongs perpetrated, claims made—requiring to be weighed and settled. Moses' pre-eminence must have made him judge of his people in such matters, to whose wisdom willingly they referred their troubles.[1] Surely Moses brought to that difficult task the qualities which the discipline of life had given him—resolute righteousness, hatred of cruelty, wonderful loving-kindness, longing to aid the distressed. We may believe that the example of his personal integrity and compassion was the human source of the qualities which eventually made Israel's Law so wonderful. He, first of all men, showed how to translate into act profound belief that God is

ship and to regulate the details of its life. . . .What it supplied was the norm or necessary conditions to which that religion in all its further development must conform'. The chief difficulty in the way of accepting Mosaic author-ship turns on the Commandment, 'Thou shalt not make unto thee a graven image'. But loyal Hebrews did so in Canaan during the period of the Judges, and also during the Monarchy down to 721 B.C. at least—apparently without any consciousness that they were violating a fundamental Commandment. (Micah's images, Judges xvii; the Teraphim in David's house, I Sam. xix. 13; the Brazen Serpent to which incense was offered until c. 725, II Kings xviii. 4.) Above all, we have to consider that Jeroboam, the first King of Israel, anxious to demonstrate his zeal for Yahveh, erected to His honour the golden Bull-images at Bethel and Dan. There is a narrow way through this difficulty. It is arguable that the Ten Commandments were known, but that the prohibition of images was construed as forbidding the making of them to honour other Gods than Yahveh. (See Welch, op. cit. ch. III.) Peters (*Religion of the Hebrews*, p. 104) adduces a parallel from early Christian custom: 'In contact with image-worshipping peoples, the Christians, while condemning those images as idols when worshipped as representations of other Gods, did not regard them in the same light when adopted as repre-sentations of their own God or their saints.'

[1] Robertson Smith (*Religion of the Semites*, p. 70) notes the parallel with Mohammed: 'In his quality of Prophet, Mohammed became a judge, law-giver, and captain, not of his own initiative, but because the Arabs of different clans were willing to refer to a divine authority questions of right and pre-cedence in which they would not yield to one another. They brought their difficulties to the prophet, as the Israelites did to Moses, and his decisions became the law of Islam, as those of Moses were the foundation of the Hebrew *Torah*.'

measurelessly merciful and just. Imagine that a dispute had broken out between the proud, large, tribe of Ephraim and the fiercely proud, small, tribe of Benjamin; dispute so furious as to threaten the peace of all. The one tribe claimed that they were much the more numerous and great; the Father of their 'House' having been Ephraim, on whom Jacob had bestowed the Blessing of the First-born. The other tribe said that quality not numbers counts; and that the Father of *their* 'House' had been Benjamin, the youngest but the truly beloved son. They brought their fury to Moses. To their surprise he answered nothing about their contention. He spoke about God, the Father of them all; and reminded them about Jacob, who in his hot and greedy youth had quarrelled with Esau his brother and deceived him, but who had dreamed a dream that God would be with him whithersoever he went, if only he would be a different sort of man. And then Moses spoke about the compassion of God, who had brought them one and all out of Egypt. They went away shamefaced and quiet—to think.

(4) *The Faith of Moses.* The tribesmen were perplexed about Moses, especially as regards his religion. In our ecclesiastical language, they were uncertain if he were quite 'sound' about the doctrine of the Moon. Indeed, they themselves, the more they thought about it, felt that it did not seem as if it had been the Moon that brought them out of Egypt. Did he perhaps want them to worship the Supernatural Being whose power was in this fiery mountain? He never said so; but always that they were to worship God *at* this mountain. If they ever asked him point-blank which God he meant, we may be sure he replied by talking about *God.*

Moses often left the camp, and went apart by himself alone. It was told that, when he returned, there had been a light in his face which others could see, but of which he himself was not aware. The people used to come together for him to speak to them. He told them that when they worshipped and prayed they ought not to be thinking about the mountain or the moon, but about God, the Father of them all. Some of the tribesmen said they would never forget the words of Moses the Man of God, and that they must teach them to their children. (On the surface the Bible appears to have been written entirely by men. That is not so. There were women listening to Moses. The faith and love of the generations of the women of Israel is written into the '*Word of*

God'. For it was they who for the most part taught the children: and the children grew up to write the Books.) During the time that the Hebrews were encamped near the awe-inspiring mountain, Moses did not seem to be afraid of it. Sometimes, when it was quiet, in the cool of the evening hours or at the dawning of the day, they had seen him going up into its rocks alone. When he came down from the Mount, Moses taught the people: He taught them, 'Blessed are the merciful'. Over and over again he said to them: 'You are the People of God. Therefore you must seek to be as merciful as God, your Father, has shown Himself. Then God will be with you.'

Moses taught: 'Blessed are the peace-makers.' He said that they must not take away from the welfare of one another, but must desire to make their brother's life more perfect. God is with those who extend peace. The greatest honour, he said, belonged to those who did most to help their brethren.

Moses taught that they must not be proud in the wrong way— conceited, selfish, domineering. Dimly they understood, because they were all too apt to be that, and also because they were awed and perplexed by the gentleness in Moses himself. For Moses was the greatest of men; they knew that only the tremendous force of his determination had driven them through that terrible wilderness and brought them to safety. And yet, astonished, they realized that he was also humble.[1] Moses explained that no man could be otherwise if ever God had drawn nigh unto him.

They asked him: 'How near had he been to God?'—'Had he

[1] Cp. Num. xii. 3. 'Now the man Moses was very meek, above all the men which were upon the face of the earth.' There is no good translation in English for the Hebrew word translated *meek*, and there ought to be. It is the characteristic of a man who is a man indeed, but does not regard others as worms; who, if great, has no thought that he is a superman and others beneath him. Persons with this kind of humility are usually towers of strength in whatever walk of life they may be. It does not mean weakly meek, or abjectly humble. It is tragic that we have no adequate positive term; for this Hebrew word and idea underlie the Greek in some very important New Testament verses—'Blessed are the *humble* in *spirit*....Blessed are the *meek*....Take my yoke upon you, for I am *lowly* and *humble in spirit*.'

That the ascription of this quality to Moses is truth of history is the more certain in that the records so frankly relate that at times he was in deadly danger of losing it. What is said of him in this respect has a note of singular beauty and reverence—that a man so powerful could be so dominant, and yet so self-abnegating. (Cp. Exod. xxxii. 32.)

seen anything when he was alone in the Mountain?'—'What did
he mean by speaking about the Presence of God, about God being
in their midst?' Moses answered that, so long as they truly lived
as brethren caring one for another, the Glory of God was in their
midst and His Presence would go with them. That was very
difficult to understand. But again and again he said it; and that
they must strive to understand.

At one time they were in desperate straits for water, and there
was tumult of appeal that they should turn and get back to the
wells they had left. Moses said God was with them, and ahead
there was a place with rocks where God would give them water.
They must go on. But there were frantic women, who heard God's
call to *them* on the parched lips of their exhausted babes and
children. And the multitude in the Hebrew tents were not all
docile pietists. There were very many bad men for whom Moses'
incessant *God with us* was nonsense. They were brewing revolt
—'This Moses would be the death of them all! Did he think that
a heap of corpses could conquer Canaan, and who wanted to
anyway?' They yelled at him, *Water* not *God*; and the multitude
took up the cry. Moses knew that, if their nerve broke, there
would be no Israel in Canaan; and they would never do more than
roam the desert. Silent for once about God, Moses met the challenge
with the full force of his own dominance; and his imperious
personality turned the scales. Some of the families turned back,
and were swallowed up in the spaces of the desert that knows no
history. The rest went on, and dragged themselves to the place he
meant. Moses was wise in the ways of the desert, for he had lived
there a long time. He sought for a certain rock, and struck at its
base with his staff; the rock flaked off, and water gushed out.[1]
When the agony of their need was satisfied, and they were rested
and refreshed, Moses said he had something to tell them which
they did not yet understand and must learn; *must* learn before
they entered Canaan where men worshipped Gods of corn and
wine, in a Land of water in abundance and food without stint. If
they bowed down to the Gods of Plenty and worshipped according
to the evil ways of that land, they would assuredly cease to be a

[1] Num. xvi. 12 ff.; xx. 1–11. Modern parallel is recorded from the Sinaitic
Peninsula. A desert-wise Sergeant of the Egyptian Camel Corps obtained
water for his Company by flaking the base of a porous rock, whereupon his
men joyously and irreverently shouted, 'Hail! the prophet Moses!'

People. Often (he said) they had hungered on the desert marches. Now they knew, and would never forget, what it is to thirst. But God wanted them to learn something that would enable them to remain His Nation even when they were in the Land of Canaan. Then Moses taught the people: 'Blessed are they which do hunger and thirst after *righteousness*, for they shall be filled.' He said also that he had done wrong to have urged them in his own name to follow him. God was their leader, and always they must seek His guidance by doing right.

It must have been Moses who fired his followers with intense determination to force their way into Canaan, and expectation that they would succeed, although the feat was as formidable as getting out of Egypt. Perhaps we should trace Moses' conviction in this matter to an intuition, or a psychic vision, which had reasoning at its heart. Did thought arise in his mind and grow to certitude that this moral knowledge of God ought not for ever to remain in the desert, but should be carried into the cities of men? Civilization, as he remembered it in the days of his youth in Egypt, needed this God. Would he have explained his intuition to our modern minds by saying: 'In vision God showed me these men passing over Jordan; for it is His purpose that all should know *Right*, and that those who serve Him after this manner become as the grains of sand that are upon the face of the desert, which cannot be counted for multitude.'[1] The tribesmen asked Moses to tell them why he was certain they would enter Canaan. How had God revealed to him the future? Moses gave an answer which was the source of the singular expectancy that developed in the religion of Israel. He met their questioning by saying that he had not always felt sure. But, when he had once been near despair, he had seen God's glory visible in the Past; that he knew God was with

---

[1] Cp. Exod. xxxiii. 12 ff. Recall Num. xxiii, xxiv—the Vision of Balaam the Arabian Seer, whom Balak, king of Moab, hired in order to get him to fall into trance and pronounce a curse upon Israel so as to turn it from its object. The poem dates, no doubt, from the monarchic period in Hebrew history. The essence of what it relates is that Balaam in his Vision became aware that irresistible energy of purpose was in this People, a force of Blessing so great that it was impossible for him to speak against it. If an alien seer had that psychic intuition about these Hebrews, is it unlikely that the same psychic conviction that their destiny was not endlessly to roam the desert may have been in their leader's mind—arising perhaps in normal thought, perhaps in a visionary experience?

them in the Present; and, after he was dead, God would raise up other men who in the Future would make plain to them His truth and will. He said they must not be troubled in heart and of anxious mind, but must believe in God. The light, that others could see and he could not, came into his face; and they heard him say: 'He showed me all His glory, and He spake unto me, saying, "My Presence shall go with thee, and I will give thee rest".' It is not credible that traditions of this quality originated in any less exalted source than a wonderful personality.

All these things Moses spoke in his own way, and we may not know his very words. But the traditions are filled with assurance that Moses was a man like that; one whose life was sustained by trust in the reality of God—God requiring justice and mercy in His worshippers, *the Living God*. Israel must believe that, after Moses was gone, others would be inspired to take his place.[1] Moses was sure he had spoken truly—but also sure that the last word of Truth had not been spoken. Therefore he gave Israel a religion stable in its principles, but capable of growing in the knowledge of truth. He bequeathed to the future a treasure that was hidden from the unthinking and the evil, but could be found by the sensitive mind and the pure heart.

§4. *Success and Death*

Moses succeeded. There is the tremendous fact that the whole story was told so as to exalt the work of God, not the glory of Moses. Who but Moses instilled conviction that Hebrews were to look to their God for salvation, and to think of himself only as the

---

[1] The point comes out most interestingly in the attitude of the framers of the Code of Deuteronomy to the problem of divine guidance. They viewed 'the Ten Commandments' as immutable principles of Israel's religion; the 'Statutes and Judgements' as application of those principles to the manifold, social and ritual, affairs of the life of the nation. And the Deuteronomists were also sure that genuinely inspired Prophets are sent of God and must declare whatsoever God wills to reveal by them. (See Deut. xiii. 1–5; xviii. 14–22.) But the Deuteronomists also recognized need to differentiate true from false prophetic utterances, and laid down this rule: Any professed 'Word of the Lord' that ran counter to the basic principles of the Decalogue must be repudiated, no matter how positive its spokesman may be or how sincere he seems. The Prophets whose words were to be trusted would be men like unto Moses. (Cp. Welch, *Framework to the Code of Deuteronomy*, ch. 11.)

servant of God? Surely that is authentic memory of a great man
seen to be living for an end greater than himself? Moses succeeded
in his *essential* task. When the Hebrews crossed over Jordan, there
were some who had understood that to worship *Yahveh* as God
was to worship One whose amazing might was actuated by
amazing mercy. In the great literature that Israel in later times
created—in Histories, Prophets, Psalms,[1] the theme rang out like
a peal of bells rejoicing together: JUBILANT! THANKFUL!
calling their music down the Ages—*Marvellous things did he
in the sight of their fathers, In the land of Egypt, in the field of
Zoan—We will not hide them from their children; Telling to the
generation to come the praises of the Lord*—JUBILANT!
THANKFUL! In the splendour of those Psalms of gratitude we
listen to the teaching of a great soul, who, being dead, yet
speaketh.

As a wise and humble man Moses realized there was a future for
his People he could not live to share. Men said that at the end of
his life, knowing it was not for him to enter Canaan, he went up
from the plain of Moab to the summit of Mount Nebo, and gazed
thence across the Jordan to the mountains of the Promised Land.
The tale may be read as a parable of his permanent significance for
religion. His intelligence stood very high above the desert-level
on which his followers lived. But the real greatness of Moses was
that from the height of insight he himself had reached he had the
courage to look beyond himself, beyond the Present, towards the
hills of a future Faith not yet attained. Moses did not pass over
the River Jordan. Nevertheless, for him 'the trumpets sounded on
the other side'.

[1] Cp. Ps. lxxviii, esp. *v.* 12.

CHAPTER XI

CONSCIENCE AND REASON

The ripe fruit of the Prophetic Faith will not be found on the next page of history following the death of Moses. The events which unforgettably fixed the authority of *Conscience* as a principle in the growing structure of the Faith occurred a century and a half later (1025–1010 B.C.), and it was about 860 B.C. that the relation of *Reason* to Conscience was imperiously declared. The first of these achievements was due to Samuel, the second to Elijah; and with the genius of these two men the present chapter is concerned.[1] In both cases we shall find the decisive circumstances entangled with barbarities of the Age—ferociously so as regards Samuel. The seed of the strength and gentleness of Moses had to spring to life in rough and stony soil.

I. CONSCIENCE

Hebrew tradition solemnly related that the tribesmen had carried with them into Canaan a portable box of acacia wood (the Ark of Jehovah) containing two stone tablets, on which had been inscribed the Ten Commandments that summed up the duties of Israel's brotherhood. Fortunately, some of the Hebrews carried in their minds the thought of Moses, a less vulnerable treasure. But most of them more and more came to suppose that hope of receiving the help of their God in Canaan was somehow involved in having in their midst the wondrous stones in the Ark. They placed the Ark in the little temple they built at Shiloh and entrusted its care to Eli, a good and stupid man. No prophetic protest on Eli's part is recorded when in time the Hebrews adopted the Canaanitish vintage festival, and were wont to get drunk at Shiloh in honour of Jehovah.[2] Eli drifted on the tide of popular usage.

---

[1] It is not implied that, except for Samuel and Elijah, no Hebrews had been either conscientious or intelligent between the death of Moses (*c.* 1175) and 860 B.C. For evidence, it would suffice to refer to Nathan's rebuke of David (II Sam. xii).

[2] See I Sam. i. 12–15.

In old age he became blind; his sons were scamps, and there were scandals at Shiloh. It appeared that Eli had been a more faithful custodian of the Ark than competent father of his family. When, c. 1050 B.C., the Philistines subdued the highlands, the ill-armed Hebrews put up a desperate but superstitious resistance. Their master-stroke was to take the Ark from its resting-place into battle, so as to ensure that Jehovah would be 'with them'.[1] Eli they left behind at Shiloh, trembling for its safety: a man who really believed that the help of God was inextricably bound up with a couple of stones from Mount Horeb in the desert. So too thought the Hebrew warriors when they met the Philistine army at Aphek. They were utterly defeated, and the Ark captured: *Ichabod, Ichabod*—'The glory is departed!' When the news reached Shiloh, the sightless old man fell from his seat by the gate and died. That is the last word about Eli. The fire of Prophetic Faith was not in him. But it was burning at Ramah not many miles distant, in the mind of Samuel, who was respected there and in its neighbourhood as a man of psychic power—a *Seer* or *Visionary* or *Prophet*. We do not know the stages by which his influence extended among the Hebrew tribes in general, but there are no good grounds for doubting that the Seer of Ramah became the focus of his People's reviving courage—courage which eventually under David's leadership snapped the iron fetters of the Philistines.[2]

---

[1] I Sam. iv.

[2] The Book of I Samuel, which relates the capture of the Ark, and the history of Eli, Samuel, Saul and David up to the death of Saul, is due to Compilers (living some 400 years after the time of Samuel) who, making their own comments, utilized for the purpose selections from two principal documents. (These main sources are themselves composite in some measure; but for close analysis and for discussion of Eissfeldt's three-document theory reference must be made to the Commentaries.) Of the two documents one (assuredly later than the Fall of Samaria in 721 B.C.) is anti-monarchical in that it views the Hebrews' demand for a king as a sin of flagrant mistrust of the guidance of Jehovah. The other (which is on the whole earlier and more reliable, but by no means approaches contemporary record) favours the monarchy in the sense that it views its institution as having been in accordance with the will of God, who guided Samuel to choose the man and to call upon the tribes to accept his royal authority. It is the blending of these two comparatively late documents, together with the interspersed observations of the Compilers, that explains puzzling and sometimes grotesque features which are evident to an observant reader of I Samuel. Obvious are a number of closely similar episodes—these are parallel accounts of the same incident seen from

§ 1. *Men, not stones*

The Philistines saw to it that the Hebrews were kept as good as disarmed. The situation was remediable only by a man of indomitable courage. That quality was in Samuel of Ramah. But courage does not of itself cause a man's name to be inscribed in the history of Religion. Samuel's courage rose out of a religious intuition of the highest order. We learn that in the neighbourhood of Ramah devotees (prophets) were seeking to revive trust in the power of their God by collective manifestations of ecstatic fervour, which the onlookers felt to be proof that His supernatural strength had actually entered their minds and bodies. Patriotic demonstrations could not be conducted under the noses of Philistine garrisons, but the noses of Philistines could not be everywhere. These 'bands of the prophets' were an excellent means of stimulating hope. Who set the movement on foot? It is a fair conjecture that Samuel did so; it is quite certain that whole-heartedly he approved the prophets' zeal, and utilized it for his own wiser instinct as to the real need.[1] Samuel realistically discerned that the men of Israel could, and must, actualize *in themselves* the will of their God. He called for stout hearts and strong arms. The Ark and its stones had been captured by their foes. To Samuel that mattered nothing. Plague broke out in the cities of Philistia, and the superstitious Philistines yoked cows to a new cart and let them drag the Ark of the Hebrews' offended God back again to the hills of Judah— perhaps hopeful that the angered Deity would give the plague also to His incompetent warriors. Samuel was not jubilant over its

the differing standpoints of the makers of the two main documents or the Compilers. Again (after a pleasing tale of Samuel's boyhood at Shiloh, and the story of the capture of the Ark) in chs. vii, viii, Samuel is presented as an ageing or aged Prophet, famous throughout the entire Hebrew land, at whose command all Israel assembled at Mizpah to fight the Philistines, and in answer to whose prayer such miraculous victory was won that Israel's territory was wrested from its foes, whereafter Samuel judged Israel all the days of his life, and only towards its close, on Israel's insistence and with rebuke of their sin, did he present Saul as their chosen king. [This narrative continues at ch. x. 17 ff.] But, suddenly, at ch. ix. 1 [here is the older document woven in] Samuel is spoken of as a Seer at Ramah, respected by its inhabitants but so little known elsewhere that a young Benjamite named Saul, whose home is not many miles distant, has not even heard of him!

[1] Cf. I Sam. x. 5–7, 9–13.

return.[1] Everything depended on the way Hebrews faced adversity. God would be with them, if they remained undaunted, and willing to obey the guidance His Prophet would give.

'Hebrew versus Philistine' 3000 years ago seems inexpressibly remote from modern affairs. But Samuel was asserting a distinction as vital for good or evil now as then. For it was essentially the difference between treating Religion as conventional piety dependent on material things, and Religion as resolve to live and die for the ends we feel to be right. Samuel stood for trust in spirit, not in superstition; for reliance on men, not on stones. Let us suppose that the stones in the Ark were inscribed with the profound Ten Commandments. Samuel knew that the principles of divine wisdom ought to be written in men's minds. Then it would not matter how often Philistines captured stones and, if they chose, smashed them up. The Law could be rewritten! Israel eventually learnt that great lesson thoroughly. Eight hundred years later a Greek-Syrian king destroyed all the Jewish sacred Books he could lay hands on. The Jews had men who knew the Law by heart, and could write out the whole of it at any time. And thus it has happened that thousands and thousands of times

[1] What did the Hebrews do with their recovered treasure? There was a notable holy place of Nob (some two miles from Jerusalem). Why did they not place it there? They deposited it a few miles away from Nob in a house in a small town, Kiriath-Jearim; and there it remained until David (with utmost rejoicing and reverence for its sanctity) was able to bring it to his new capital, Zion—Jerusalem. Phythian-Adams (*The Call of Israel*, pp. 84 ff., 134, 150) thinks that its two sacred stones had been uninscribed rocks from Mount Horeb, and that the Philistines in derision had removed them and smashed them up, so that what came back was (so to say) 'the ring without the pearl'; and argues that the Ark was left at Kiriath in shamed neglect—*its* glory had departed. But this theory does not seem to accord with David's eagerness and respect when it was brought to Jerusalem. There was no temple at Nob in which to keep it safely. Who can say that the Hebrews did not transport it from Kiriath to Nob when required for their seasons of worship? (It has also been suggested that Kiriath was still in Philistine control, and the Ark not really surrendered to the Hebrews.) Phythian-Adams conjectures that glory was restored to the Ark in Solomon's reign, when two tablets which were inscribed with the Ten Commandments were placed in it, and connects the matter with the transfer of priestly pre-eminence from Abiathar (of the House of Eli) to the Zadokite Levites. But the tale of the breaking and rewriting of the Ten Commandments is bound up with the 'sin' of the Golden Calf, and that surely is related historically to Jeroboam's action after the *death* of Solomon. The whole subject bristles with difficulties.

those Ten Commandments have been written on parchments, printed on millions of pages, spoken and obeyed by myriads of human beings. If the Philistines were to remove Mount Horeb itself until their Plain was strewn with its boulders, *and cart* them all up again to the Hebrew hills, Samuel saw that it would matter nothing. Much is not being made of a small affair. Jesus said that, if men will have even as much faith as a grain of mustard seed, mountains can be removed. Samuel removed the mountain of Israel's despair, and his courage is in the lineage of our Faith.

§2. *Commonsense*

It was characteristic of the really great Hebrew 'men of God' that they urgently sought to relate their beliefs to affairs, with the result that the Prophetic Faith became a supremely practical religion— not merely a system of thought provocative of debate, but an incentive to action. Nations tend to be either intellectualist in their attitude, or else practical. The former type is so intrigued by an idea that it is apt to be inattentive to the problems of application; the latter tries to tackle the obvious problem with inadequate realization that men are set on fire by ideas. One may venture to say that the logical, mercurial, French belong rather to the first category, the stolid British to the latter. The French view of Samuel's situation would have been to concentrate on devising a first-class marching tune, and blazoning banners with *La Liberté*. The British would have told the Hebrews to suspend their tribal jealousies, form an All-Party Government to meet the crisis, train an army and do some staff-work.

The Hebrews could not make headway unless they could recover confidence in God, and unless they would accept a 'Commander-in-Chief' and support his plans unitedly. Samuel sought to meet both necessities. His genius saw that the fundamental, social change would work to their welfare on one condition: King they needed, but the rightful king must be a man who would unswervingly seek to be ruled himself by the righteousness of God. In terms of our own Age, a 'Planned Society' in relation to individual freedom may be not a short-cut to prison but the road to liberty, if only the planning is for the highest ends. The Prophetic principle, initiated by Samuel, was that Government will prove in the deepest sense democratic provided it is *theocratic*. But it was very difficult for the tribes to admit that the defiant independence, which had been the breath of their life in the desert, had become effete; and to trust that under a different organization suited to changed conditions they would not be turned into slaves. It is easy for us scornfully to consider that they were stupidly slow to see the obvious need. But it is not very long ago since Mr Wendell Willkie, in urgent anxiety to persuade us to face the obvious, wrote a book entitled *One World*. Present circumstances suggest that the modern world could do with several Samuels.

§3. *The Authority of Conscience*

Samuel's insight had in it the constraint of a great responsibility: it was laid upon him to discover the man born to be Israel's king. An interesting narrative tells how, impelled by divine guidance, he thought that man to be Saul, the son of Kish, a Benjamite—exceptionally tall, and in the prime of life[1]—and how he disclosed to Saul his destiny. No doubt thereafter he did his utmost to impress on the tribesmen that this Saul should be their king: for thus had God shown him. Men with the blood of the desert in their ancestry would not accept even a Seer's Vision without good evidence for its truth. By such an exploit as was Gideon's victory over the Midianites Saul must first give proof that the force of God's Blessing was really in him. Then they would know that the Seer had 'seen' truly. It is told that soon Saul's chance came, and that large numbers followed him as leader in an expedition to rescue the town of Jabesh (across Jordan in Gilead) from besieging Ammonites, who had mockingly offered to spare its inhabitants' lives on pain of having their right eyes put out.[2] The venture succeeded, and Saul was acclaimed king by those who chose to think so and to say so. Probably that happened in 1025 B.C. Philistines were sterner metal than Ammonites. It is likely that for some years young Saul could do little against them except sit on a nominal throne. Not until his son, Jonathan, was adult, did the time come when a pin-prick could be gallingly pressed

---

[1] Cf. I Sam. ix. 1, 2; x. 21–24.

[2] See I Sam. xi. 1–12. As to the number of Saul's followers the text (*v.* 8) says 330,000! Perhaps the fantastic figure shows how remote the written tradition was from contemporary fact. On the other hand, the documents sometimes name reasonable figures, e.g. 600 men, I Sam. xiv. 2. Perhaps Hebrew readers interpreted this 330,000 as an idiomatic way of saying 'A quite surprisingly large number'.

home. A bold exploit on Jonathan's part overcame a Philistine
garrison at Michmash, and a punitive effort by the Philistines to
avenge the defeat met with disaster.[1] About 1015 Saul's reign
ended in a battle with the Philistines on Mount Gilboa (overlooking the Plain of Esdraelon), in which both Saul and Jonathan
were slain and the warriors of Israel utterly routed.[2] A good deal
else about Saul is related in the interwoven documents which
form our present text. But the episodes are worked up chiefly to
tell the prowess and goodness of youthful David, the true friendship between him and Jonathan, and the darkening of Saul's mind
towards insanity through his jealous fear that David, and not
Jonathan, would be king in his stead. It is possible that in some
respects the traditions obscured Saul's difficulties with continuing
tribal jealousies, and undervalued persistent minor efforts to lead
the Hebrews to success. History forgets or belittles men who fail.
Saul was Defeat, David Victory. One episode (probably of Saul's
mid-career) seems to be in its essence a reliable memory; for it
explains the tragedy of his distracted mind in the closing years. Its
story brings us back to Samuel and the history of religion.

Raids inflicted by their desert-cousins on the weakened
Hebrews were bitterly resented. A reprisal attack directed
against the Amalekites was declared to be a *holy* war: that is to say,
the Hebrews vowed to obtain no personal profit from a victory;
no booty must be retained, and any men, women and children
captured must be slain as sacrifices to Jehovah. Saul and his
warriors won the fight, and broke the vow—bringing back with
them the choicest part of the booty, and Agag the Amalekite king.
When Samuel received the news, he went to meet Saul, declared
to him that Jehovah had rejected him from being king over Israel,
and the Prophet himself 'hewed Agag in pieces before the Lord'.[3]

---

[1] See I Sam. xiv. 1–46.

[2] See I Sam. xxxi; and the fascinating narrative (II Sam. i), concerning the
bringing of the news to David, which in its closing verses (19–27) preserves
one of the most ancient passages in the Old Testament—a Poem of Lamentation for Saul and Jonathan, undoubtedly the composition of David and contemporary with the event.

[3] See I Sam. xv. A parallel account of Saul's rejection, but on the ground
that faint-heartedly he himself offered a sacrifice for victory instead of waiting
for Samuel to arrive and do so, is found in I Sam. xiii. 2–14. But it is
generally agreed that ch. xv gives the historical actuality, and is the earlier
document.

Pass for a moment the barbarity, and mark these implications. Samuel was vindicating that in this kingdom its Ruler must obey a higher law than his own inclinations and calculations. Saul pleaded that he was only postponing his religious obligation. By bringing Agag back the people at home would be heartened by witnessing the execution of their foe. An interesting rhythmic verse (embedded in the later prose narrative) may preserve the very words of Samuel's oracular reply—'Hath the Lord as great delight in burnt offerings and sacrifices, as in obeying the voice of the Lord?...Because thou hast rejected the word of the Lord, He hath also rejected thee from being king.'[1] Concerning this G. A. Smith writes: 'It must not be overlooked in any appreciation of the religious distinction of Israel; it holds in germ one of the main principles of later prophecy.'[2] Saul could also argue that his loot-hungry soldiers forced his hand, constraining him to concede something to them in the flush of victory; and Samuel may have longed to give to the man, whom he had felt guided by God to choose, a reprimand and a second chance. But Samuel conceded nothing to the weakness in Saul's character: men of that stamp must not rule over, because they could not serve, the Kingdom of God's purpose. Saul had taken the vow, and knew his obligation. Thus (in savage circumstances) emerged assertion of the principle of the paramount authority of Conscience. It is no venial fault in Kings or Commons to play fast and loose with the sense of duty, and imagine that the imperative in which Conscience speaks can safely be transmuted into the optative mood. Conscience is not one amongst other legitimate claims on our attention; it is not rightly understood as one motive in competition with others; but is a basic endowment in the nature of Man. In the words of Bishop Butler's famous sermon 200 years ago: 'Conscience is placed within us to be our proper governor; to

---

[1] I Sam. xv. 22, 23. The middle words of the fragment (omitted above) are obscure in meaning, due in part to some textual corruption. They are perhaps a later addition to the ancient oracle.

[2] 'The great words "To obey is better than sacrifice"', writes Kennedy, 'bring to a luminous point the whole ethical teaching of the great prophets from Amos downwards.' Kennedy, however (*Samuel* in the *Century Bible*)—and also Smith (*Samuel*, in the *I.C.C.*)—ascribe these verses to the *author* of the chapter. The writer strongly disagrees. Late historians did not compose fragments in verse to form part of their prose, didactic, treatment of traditions.

direct and regulate all other principles, passions and motives of action. That is its right and office: thus sacred its authority.'[1]

§4. *Learning from Experience*

Saul could not bring himself to accept the verdict. He felt penitent, resolved not to sin against conscience a second time, hopeful that he would yet lead Israel to victory. He did not know how deep in his nature was personal ambition that he should be king and his son reign after him. Hence the mental tragedy of the passing of his early affection for David into suspicion and black hatred. He could not contemplate that another might increase, and he and his house decrease. Jealousy ever finds our human nature dry tinder for conflagration. Saul learnt his lesson about the authority of Conscience too late and too literalistically. It befell that, when Jonathan achieved the success against the Philistine garrison, quite unknowingly he and his armour-bearer broke a vow which the rest of the Hebrew fighters had taken in their absence.[2] Saul resolved not to flinch: he must obey Conscience, and put his loved and valiant son to death; and he was only prevented by his sensible expostulating soldiers! This time his weakness was failure to see any difference between deliberate and unintentional trespass. He ought to have applied Reason to discover what his conscience would then say to him. Saul died defeated on Mount Gilboa. Poor, confused, Saul.

David learned much from Saul's jealousy and tragedy. When his own son, Absalom, revolted against him, David did not seek by violence to keep his throne and compass Absalom's death. Instead he followed the realistic virtue of ancient Israel, humbly accepting that, if through his faults the Blessing had left him, he must abide the fact. Whereas, if the greater sin were in Absalom events would vindicate him and turn to the praise of God.

Samuel learnt his lesson—hard lesson for a man of God—namely, that, although he had felt inspired when he chose Saul to be king, he had made a mistake. His danger was injured pride, disillusionment, temptation to count psychic convictions foolish dreams. Samuel had the humility to judge that he had not erred about God's will that Israel should have a king, and the courage to be ready, if God would use him, to seek again for the man born

---

[1] Sermon II: *Upon Human Nature.*   [2] I Sam. xiv. 1–46.

to be king. This time, so the tradition tells, he wisely found him
in David.

§5. The Inadequacy of Conscience

Conscience of itself is not sufficient guide. Blind obedience to its
supposed dictates is the stuff whereof fanatics, not saints, are made.
We are rightly revolted that Samuel counted it his duty to hew
Agag to pieces before the Lord. How many other atrocities have
been perpetuated in the name of religion; how many vicious
hatreds and perverse misunderstandings cherished 'conscientiously'? Yet all those dark deeds do not refute the vital importance of the principle Samuel upheld, but with inadequate
wisdom. The point is that along with willingness at whatever cost
to themselves to obey constraint of Conscience, there is required
of men uttermost intelligent effort to discern what really is right
'before the Lord'. That effort was made in Israel's subsequent
history. Therefore the time came when Hebrews were led by their
conscience to obey the voice of God not by destroying other
men's lives and property, but by themselves accepting the
loss of all things and enduring martyrdom: 'For thy sake are
we killed all the day long.'[1] In the story of the Book of Daniel
there is a great sentence concerning three Jews who refused to
worship the idol set up by Nebuchadnezzar: 'Our God whom we
serve is able to deliver us from the burning fiery furnace; and he
will deliver us.... But *if not*, be it known unto thee, O king, that we
will not serve thy gods, nor worship the golden image which thou
hast set up.'[2]

II. REASON

One hundred and fifty years after the lifetime of Samuel a Prophet
intervened in the affairs of the northern Kingdom of Israel with
consequences so impressive and enduring that 'he is to be ranked
as the greatest religious personality that had been raised up in
Israel since Moses'.[3] Apart from his name, Elijah, and that he
lived in Gilead east of Jordan, nothing is known of his circumstances. All that is related about him suggests a lonely man, and
the absence of personal information enhances fittingly the rugged

[1] Ps. xliv. 22.   [2] Dan. iii. 17, 18.
[3] Skinner, *Kings* (*Century Bible*), p. 222.

strength of his individuality. 'In solitary grandeur', writes
Wellhausen, 'did this Prophet tower conspicuously over his
time. Legend, and not history alone, could preserve the memory
of his figure.' The phrase 'Legend, and not history alone' has
reference to the fact that the narratives about Elijah are not
contemporary, and in them the 'poetry' of momentous events is
impaired by the 'prose' of extravagant miracles. Fortunately, the
traditions seem to have been written down not later than a century
after his death, and there is virtually convincing reason for
judging that 'the biography of the Prophet must have taken shape
in an age for which the work of Elijah was a living memory'.[1] The
deeds, words, and character of Elijah have tensely dramatic quality.
Hebrew narrative-art did justice to that fact, as these pages cannot;
but let the thought that a great drama was enacted in history shape
this statement. We have first to set the stage for Elijah's entrance.

After the death of Samuel and Saul, David reigned at Zion
(Jerusalem). To David succeeded Solomon, who enlarged the
capital and built a wondrous temple and palace. On his death
the northern tribes revolted, and under Jeroboam formed the
kingdom of Israel, leaving Solomon's son, Rehoboam, to play
'King of the Castle' in Jerusalem and be Ruler of Judah's stony
soil. The split reduced Solomon's grand realm to impotence:
Judah was very weak, except for the strength of Jerusalem.[2] For
nearly half a century there is nothing important to record—
kinglet succeeded kinglet. In Israel in 886 B.C. King Elah was
murdered by Zimri. 'Had Zimri peace who slew his master?' No;
for seven days later Zimri was slain by the commander of the army,
Omri. Omri, however (after a struggle with a rival called

[1] Skinner, op. cit. p. 223. S. A. Cook (*C.A.H.* vol. III, pp. 364–79), in a
searching analysis of subtle inconsistencies in the sources, urges that they
point to social changes and movements of population at this time greater than
the Biblical historians realized; and remarks: 'Undoubtedly we have a land-
mark in the history of Israel: Elijah himself stands for some far-reaching
changes.' The view that the Elijah of tradition is little more than a personalizing
of a much later struggle in favour of the exclusive worship of Jehovah (so,
in general, Kuenen, Stade, Hölscher) presents a phase of criticism which
insists on making the worst of both worlds—extreme caution and rash
conjecture.

[2] In Rehoboam's fifth year Shishak, king of Egypt, entered and plundered
Jerusalem, carrying off the 600 shields of gold which Solomon had made to
adorn his palace. Rehoboam made brass ones in their stead (I Kings xiv.
25–8). That left him the consolation of a glitter.

Timri), began a long reign in which (though Hebrew history almost ignores his achievements) he showed himself the strongest of all the rulers of Israel. By building Samaria he gave the northern kingdom a capital as strongly fortified as Jerusalem. He was able to exact heavy annual tribute from the king of Moab. Judah was no danger, for Israel had far greater man-power and wealth. Omri's master-stroke was (like Solomon's) to establish full understanding with the king of Phoenicia, the alliance (formal or informal) being sealed by the marriage of Omri's son, Ahab, to Jezebel, daughter of the Phoenician king. This arrangement enabled Omri to impose at his ease profitable taxation on the caravan-trade from Arabia through Esdraelon and Galilee to the Phoenician ports. Riches poured into his coffers and trade into his capital. Moreover, firm Phoenician friendship was a bulwark against the potential danger that existed in the ambitions of the Syrians with their capital at Damascus in the desert. It is likely that from this time sacrifices to the God of the Phoenicians (*Melcart*, the Baal of Tyre) were offered in Samaria, and corresponding respect paid to Jehovah in Tyre, much as in the modern world the flags of allied nations fly side by side. Certainly the Tyrian Baal was worshipped in Samaria when Ahab was on the throne (about 876–855 B.C.), and Jezebel his Queen. Jezebel was one of the women who have affected history. Of stronger will than her husband, she took her ideas of religion from the God of Tyre, and of royal rights from her father, Ethbaal—who, by the way, had murdered his brother in becoming king of Phoenicia. Jezebel was fanatical in devotion to the Phoenician God, maintained large numbers of priests and prophets to serve her Baal at Samaria; and, when to her surprise and indignation antagonism was aroused, Jezebel 'persecuted the prophets of Jehovah'. Probably there was negligible resentment in Samaria itself, but Jezebel may have attempted to extend sacrifice to her God elsewhere in the land. The conscientious objectors perhaps were not numerous, but they were obstinate; and the Queen was angry. Jezebel did not understand the fuss. To her all Gods were alike, morally. She felt she was asking only that Hebrews would render to Baal the things that were Baal's, and to Jehovah the things that were His. If, however, no further grave factor had arisen, discontent might have come to naught. That is the background against which the figure of Elijah appeared; and these are the

Persons in the meaningful drama—Ahab, son of Omri, king of Israel; Jezebel, his queen, princess of Phoenicia; the Priests of the Phoenician Baal; the People of Israel; Naboth, a Hebrew citizen of Jezreel; Elijah, Prophet of Jehovah.

SCENE I. *The Hammer of God*

Adjoining a royal residence at Jezreel there was a vineyard belonging to a Hebrew called Naboth, which Ahab desired to add to the royal garden.[1] When Naboth refused on any terms to cede the heritage of his fathers, Ahab desisted and returned sulkily to Samaria. How remarkable! An oriental king, who did not assume that he could deal as he pleased with his subjects' property. Jezebel was astonished at Ahab's feebleness. Jezebel acted: she browbeat the elders of Jezreel to have Naboth condemned on a false charge. They yielded to her will, and stoned the life out of Naboth. Told that her demand had been met, Jezebel scornfully bade Ahab go and take possession, 'for Naboth is dead and not alive'. *Her* conscience was not ill at ease; for there was nothing in the character of the Great Baal of Phoenicia, whom she worshipped, to forbid kings overriding the wishes of a mere subject. Royal lady, she saw the Naboth affair as a matter of royal rights: 'Fool of a peasant, he had got what he deserved.' News of the outrage passed over Jordan into the hills of Gilead, and reached Elijah. Elijah acted. He went to Jezreel, confronted Ahab in the vineyard of the murdered man; and there, as the Prophet of Jehovah, told him in the name of Israel's God that for that foul deed he and his dynasty would be brought to disaster—'where dogs had licked the blood of Naboth, dogs would lick the blood of Ahab and of Jezebel'.[2]

Elijah's action and words proclaimed to the whole nation the moral difference between the Baal of Tyre and Jehovah, God of Israel. The Prophet's anger against the tyrannous deed was not due either to his being a Social-Democrat, or an Arabian chieftain truculently intolerant of kings. All Israel knew that he

[1] Jezreel, twenty miles north of Samaria, stood in a commanding position above the plain of Esdraelon and the valley of Jezreel.

[2] In order of time this incident (I Kings xxi) must have preceded Elijah's contest with the prophets of Baal on Mount Carmel (ch. xviii), for after the event on Carmel the Prophet was driven out of the land.

had uttered no mild protest, but struck like the hammer of God that breaketh the rocks in pieces. It was doom that he had pronounced on Ahab and on Jezebel, and all Israel knew he had spoken as a man of God, in the name of Jehovah. The God of Israel had not been asleep or negligent, whilst the Queen plotted and the cruel stones were flung. Elijah's intervention for the sake of peasant Naboth touched elemental concerns of human life. He struck at Covetousness—pervasive poison that excites those who have much to want more: for King Ahab in Naboth's little vineyard exemplifies for ever that evil in the soul. He struck at Cowardice—the Elders of Jezreel condoning and abetting a shameless wrong; by contrast Elijah showed utter fearlessness in the cause of right. The circumstances made his boldness far more significant than when Samuel had rebuked King Saul, and Nathan King David; for Ahab and Jezebel were incomparably less amenable royalties! It was the first dramatic manifestation that faithful Prophets of Jehovah would not silently tolerate Rulers (however autocratic) using power to do just as they pleased. The murder of Naboth was indubitable evil—no decent man could argue that Jezebel was partly justified, and Ahab excusable. Elijah was the voice of Ultimate Righteousness; and he had declared to all Israel that Jehovah, its God, is that Righteousness. Startlingly and gloriously, he had brought faith in Jehovah down out of the region of Ideas into everyday affairs. It has been well said that 'the nature of Him whom Israel reverenced would in the end determine the life that was lived in every hamlet in Israel'. Generation after generation what Elijah said to Ahab at Jezreel was remembered. It has never ceased to be remembered; and there is no one in the world who does not stand in constant need to remember 'Naboth's vineyard'.

SCENE II. *The Mountain of Decision*

The curtain falls on Jezreel. It rises to show the crest of Mount Carmel. Ahab is there, and a great concourse of Hebrews. The ministrants of Jezebel's Baal are there, standing beside an altar on which a sacrifice lies ready to be consumed. Over against them, and alone, beside an ancient altar rebuilt in honour of Jehovah, stands Elijah. For over a year no rain had fallen in Phoenicia or Israel, and in the pitiless drought the springs ran dry, the cattle

died, the seeds lay dead in the iron soil and no fruit was on the
vines. It was Elijah who had brought about this gathering. It is
related that he forewarned Ahab of the oncoming of the drought
—sign of God's anger—and that when it lay heavy on the land
Ahab had sought for him in vain, hoping no doubt to cajole him
by fair words or open threats into uttering a prophecy of mercy.
When premonition of the ending of the drought came upon the
Prophet, he caused Ahab to come and meet him. The king
addressed him as 'Thou troubler of Israel',[1] but none the less
obeyed when Elijah told him to assemble the people at a place
high on Mount Carmel. There and then it would be seen whether
the Queen's Baal or the God of Israel would respond to their need
of rain. The wonderfully dramatic narrative in I Kings xviii
(written perhaps a century later) relates what befell that day. It
tells how in the evening (in answer to Elijah's supplication) fire
miraculously fell from heaven on Jehovah's altar and 'consumed
the burnt-offering, and the wood, and the stones, and licked up
the water that was in the trench'; how next the prophets of Baal
were seized and slain, and how *thereafter* Elijah went up to the
summit of the mountain to pray, and how at the seventh time
of his praying a cloud appeared and rain ensued. Those who
consider that precisely thus it happened are free to do so. Those
who think that the tale grew in the telling may surmise that the
order of events was different—the outcome not less providential:
for assuredly rain came, and the deliverance was ascribed to the
people's vow that they would worship Jehovah, and to Elijah's
prayer on their behalf. Was the sequence of events this—

Through the hours of the day of decision, the servants of Baal
in vain besought their God—ecstatically dancing and shouting,
slashing their bodies with knives; whilst Elijah mocked their zeal,
urging greater effort, since perhaps their Baal was asleep or gone
hunting or otherwise occupied. That was talk the multitude could
follow, not theology above their heads; and shrewdly it drove
home the folly of men who could conceive that possibly their God
was capable of such behaviour. In the evening of the day Elijah

---

[1] Recall that the Naboth incident had preceded, leaving the King troubled
in conscience, anxious and angry. Further, it is a legitimate conjecture that
Elijah may have been outstanding even earlier among the prophets of
Jehovah who opposed the Queen's insistence on worship of her Baal along
with Jehovah.

put his belief to the test. He began by compelling the people to *think*—to think about the difference between Baal and Jehovah. We may suppose that in words of burning sincerity he called them to reflect on the God of their fathers, bidding them remember that not Baal of Tyre, but Jehovah, God of mercy as well as power, had saved the Hebrews from the grasp of Egypt. Not Baal, but Jehovah had saved them from thirst in the desert; not Baal, but Jehovah had brought them into this their land. Jehovah only they ought to worship. Therefore choose they must—either Baal, or Jehovah; *but not both!* They shouted—'Jehovah, He is God!' When the people had given decisive answer that they would put their trust in Jehovah, Elijah (so the writer thinks) *then* went up to the summit of Carmel, and prayed on their behalf, again and again and again—sending his servant to the very crest to gaze westwards over the sea for sign of rain. At the seventh time the man ran to him: 'Behold, there riseth a little cloud out of the midst of the sea like a man's hand.' In Canaan such a cloud was certainty of fast-approaching deluge.[1] *Just what did Elijah pray?*—that is the unrecorded heart of the matter. Was he beseeching God for rain, in order that the remaining riches, cattle, comfort in the country might not further be diminished? Surely (in his own way) he was praying for answer in order that men in Israel should no longer bow down to that caricature of Deity called the Baal of Tyre, and that instead there might be a Land where men believed that justice and mercy are the foundation of the throne of the only God there is—a Land therefore where justice and mercy would be practised in their lives.[2]

Elijah returned from the summit to announce to the king and waiting people that his prayer had been granted; he had seen the rising of the cloud, which meant certainty of fast-approaching rain. Fire was then kindled on Jehovah's altar, and, amid wild rejoicing, the vanquished prophets of the Baal were seized and slain. Did Elijah command that slaughter, or not disapprove it? We cannot tell. He lived in an iron Age, and was a man of iron

[1] An interestingly parallel account of the breaking of storm after drought in Syria was given in *The Times*, 2 November 1937.

[2] Was it not because the tension of that spiritual-moral longing was in his soul, that subconscious premonition of the onset of the great drought was given him, and premonition likewise of its ending: so that he was impelled to choose that day for the test on Carmel?

will. Ask not too much of him. He was unaware how much more needed to be learnt about what God actually desires of us; unaware also how much he was going to learn about weakness in his own character. But at Naboth's vineyard and on Carmel, this rugged Prophet, at the hazard of his life, vindicated profound principles of true religion.

First—by denouncing the murder of Naboth Elijah had asserted the absolute concern of God with human conduct. Second—at Carmel he raised the issue of patriotism and religion; in a way, moreover, which has everlasting significance for religion. Hitherto the influence of the Hebrew prophets had coincided with the ordinary political interests of the Nation. But Elijah's un-qualified opposition to reverence being paid also to the Tyrian Baal cut right across military and commercial advantage, power-fully undermining the useful 'entente' with Phoenicia.[1] Indeed one may say that whilst the insult to Jezebel concerning Naboth had been serious affront to her royal father, Ethbaal, as well as to herself, Carmel and the slaughter of her prophets was mortal insult and gave notice unmistakable to the Phoenician king that Ahab had not got his subjects in subjection

Patriotism is a virtue—standing in great need of receiving definition in our minds. For at times sharpest conflict may arise between the religious-moral quality of a nation and its material advantage—as nations of the modern world, threatened or enticed by the Nazis to make terms with sheer evil, have recently had to see, and decide their choice. Elijah (and the great Prophets who came after him) was pellucidly sure that Israel must seek first 'the kingdom of God and His righteousness'. Above all, he asserted this claim by momentous insistence that men must use their intelligence to discover what they ought to believe religiously. Large numbers of Hebrews were not defying the dictates of their conscience when they offered reverence to Jezebel's God as well as to Jehovah. For they did not consider that thereby they were dishonouring their own national God. Their fatal error was that, in face of cogent moral facts, they were keeping Conscience and

---

[1] After Ahab's death long and disastrous fighting against the Syrians began, and it does not appear that the Phoenicians gave any support to Israel. Sometime in Ahab's reign the king of Moab successfully ceased to pay the tribute Omri had exacted and defeated a Hebrew army. That may be evidence of Ahab's weakened authority.

Reason in separate compartments.[1] They had not set themselves to think clearly what it was about the character of Jehovah that should command their devotion. If they had, they would have realized they could not adore the Baal: for rational men cannot simultaneously worship good and evil. Elijah saw that it had to be 'EITHER...OR'. And memorably he put the point: 'How long halt ye between two opinions? If Jehovah be God, follow Him; but, if Baal, follow Him.' Elijah in derision urged the prophets of Baal to shout more loudly; to his own People he said in effect: 'Less shouting and more thinking.' That was a very great contribution towards sound doctrine.[2] The subsequent great Prophets claimed that Hebrews had no excuse for unintelligent failure to relate their religion to their conduct.[3]

SCENE III. *The Depths of Despair*

From Carmel Elijah ran beside the king's chariot all the way back to Jezreel: exaltation gave wings to his feet. But at Jezreel his hard lesson began. Ahab was once more with his Jezebel, and the multitude melted away. The next move lay with the Queen, and she gave the Prophet a day's notice to clear out of the land on pain of death. Elijah found he was impotent, and the shock of disappointment following the moment of victory broke his spirit. It is written that 'he arose and fled for his life to Beersheba'—that is, south of Judah into the desert. The sequel is told in one of the most perfect passages in the Old Testament (I Kings xix); indeed, it is literary sacrilege to abbreviate its story in other words. It describes a transformation that took place in Elijah's thoughts, and its intimacy of knowledge is beyond what a later age might imaginatively construct. It must derive from what he himself

---

[1] The history of religion in ancient Egypt shows paralysingly foolish efforts to amalgamate, or conserve side by side, incompatible ideas.

[2] Wellhausen's fine summary of the profound importance of Elijah's intelligence should be noted: 'To Elijah Baal and Yahveh represented, so to speak, a contrast of principles, of profound and ultimate practical convictions; both could not be right, nor could they exist side by side. For him there existed no plurality of Divine Powers, operating with equal authority in different spheres, but everywhere One Holy and Mighty Being, who revealed Himself, not in the life of nature, but in those laws by which alone human society is held together in the ethical demands of the spirit.' (*Israelitische und Jüdische Geschichte* (5th ed.), p. 78.)

[3] Cp. Hos. iv. 1; Mic. vi. 1, 2; Isai. i. 2–4.

said about his experience to Elisha, who afterwards became his companion and disciple. The Prophet went on from Beersheba deeper into the desert, alone and unprovisioned, purposing to die in its sands. But there passed by that way 'a messenger of God' —one of those all too rare visitants to this selfish world, a 'Good Samaritan'—who took pity on the fallen man sleeping the sleep of utter exhaustion, and left beside him food and water. Revived in body, the greatness in Elijah lent to his desolate mind courage to choose the right direction. He did not creep back to safety in Judah, but resolved to make for distant Horeb, the mountain of the ancient covenant. We may assume that he was not far off a desert route; that he joined a caravan on its way to southern Arabia; and that Bedouin families, making for Horeb, took the holy man with them to the Sacred Mount. There he made his dwelling in a cavern, and tried to think things out—in the bitterness of his soul, in the unconscious pride of his self-imposed loneliness. He reasoned that none but he in all Israel had proved loyal to the ancient faith. An inner voice rebuked, and told him how far that was from true. He argued next that he had given God a magnificent chance, and God had completely failed to seize it: He had sent rain on the fields of Samaria, but not ruin on Ahab and Jezebel! As Elijah stood by the mouth of his cave, baffled in mind and wellnigh faithless, a terrific storm broke on the mountain. When it had passed, the strong silent world of Nature remained. In its stillness, following the raging of the storm, suddenly Elijah heard God's parable for him.—He had imagined that God was active only when the cloud appeared, and the multitude yelled its joy. In reality, when the tumult and the shouting died, God and His purpose continued. He must return to do whatsoever he could, patiently, in the quiet of seemingly disappointing years. There was one thing above all else that he must do—find someone who vould share his thoughts and be Prophet of Truth when he was dead. Elijah returned to Canaan a humbler and a greater man. He found 'Elisha the son of Shaphat...and cast his mantle upon him...'; and Elisha 'went after him and ministered unto him'. These things, as they stand written in the translucent Hebrew narrative, have meaning for whosoever has done his utmost for good, and come very nigh to believing that he has laboured in vain. *De profundis clamavi, ad te, Domine.*

SCENE IV. *Beyond Death*

In a similarly exquisite narrative (II Kings ii) there is an account of a last journey made by Elijah and his disciple Elisha from Gilgal through Bethel and Jericho, across Jordan and on into the mountains of Gilead or Moab.[1] There Elijah died, and (as with Moses) it was not known where he died. The inference is that he told Elisha not to disclose what he alone could tell. When Elisha returned to the prophets at Jericho, he must have spoken perplexingly; for the closing verses of this chapter are most remarkable. Some of his hearers understood him to imply that Elijah was still alive amidst the mountains: eagerly they said that fifty strong men would search and find him. Others understood that Elijah was dead: they urged that they should seek his body for honoured burial. To one and all Elisha replied: 'Ye shall not send.' And some gathered that Elijah had passed out of life, but not in the ordinary way; and from these spread belief that Elijah had been caught up to heaven in a whirlwind by a chariot and horses of fire. Some wonderful and strange words of Elijah must underlie this record of bewilderment. Jewish belief in the possibility of individual survival of death arose only centuries later; so late, indeed, that there is scarce a trace of it in the period of the Old Testament writings. Can it be that these two men (as other intimate friends have done) had talked together about death—the loneliness of the survivor when human souls have deeply loved one another; the 'wrongness' of it that death should not only sunder man from man, but man from God, ending the loyal service and uplifting of the heart to Him? Had they meditated on the marvel of human

[1] The hour had come when Elisha must finally decide whether or not to accept the burden of being Prophet in his Master's stead. When he refused to 'turn back', Elijah solemnly asked what parting gift he would ask from him, and Elisha answered: 'Let a double portion of thy spirit be upon me.' The request is liable to be misunderstood as presumptuous. The phrase signifies the inheritance of an eldest son on whom falls the responsibility for the family. Elisha asked simply: 'Make me worthy to be thy son.' History had nothing to tell of Elisha comparable to the greatness of Elijah. But, in different circumstances, he too was faithful, and was gratefully remembered as upholding the courage of the nation in the calamitous wars with the Syrians that followed on Ahab's death; so that, when he died, it was said of him, as of Elijah, that he had been 'the chariots of Israel and the horsemen thereof'.

memory, which can be so vivid as almost to yield an unseen, guiding, Presence? At the moment when Elisha in the mountains beyond the river saw that the flame of life had left his master's body, can it be that conviction flamed within him that somehow Elijah was not parted from God, whom he had served so faithfully? Certainly it seems that Elisha gave some of the prophets that impression—Elijah had been taken from him, from them; but what mattered was power 'to see him' even so. Elisha knew that of a certainty Elijah in his life had been *with God*.

The curtain drops upon the final scene. But the last words spoken in this drama suggest that death is not the end of the human soul.

CHAPTER XII

MERCY

'The mountains of Judah', to which foothills ascend from the coastal plain, are not separate peaks but a lofty tableland of exceedingly stony moors some 3000 ft. above sea-level. Where, however, its rolling surface breaks in ridges and shallow vales, cultivation of vine and olive and crops was possible. Of these more fertile tracts the most notable were at Bethany, Bethlehem, Hebron, and the vale of Eshcol. Judah had but one strong city, Jerusalem. Twelve miles south of Jerusalem and six miles from Bethlehem, on the eastern edge of the tableland where it overhangs the chasm of the Dead Sea, there was a village called Tekoa, enclosed north, south and west by a low ridge of limestone hills. The territory of Judah was as a watch-tower from which men could see distant prospects. Let a man of Tekoa walk northwards from his village to the near crest of its enclosing hills, and beyond Bethlehem the towers of Jerusalem were just visible on the horizon. Let him travel west some fifteen miles, and he stood on the fringe of the highlands of Judah, whence his eyes could follow the downward sweep of the hills falling to the broad plain where lay the ancient Philistine cities and in the distance the waters of the Mediterranean. Southwards, at much the same distance from Tekoa, was the small but famous town of Hebron. At that point the level of the highlands begins to fall away. Another twelve miles south, and the keen-eyed Judaean looked towards the desert-borders of the 'sown' country and the spaces of the true desert—strange home of nomad Amalekites and Edomites. *East* of Tekoa, as also east of Bethlehem, the prospect lies open; and how dauntingly formidable! The ground drops to form a great shelf of moorland, 35 miles long by 15 wide. Over its rocky expanse sheep have to wander far and wide for their pasture. From the border of this shelf the mountain-height of Judah plunges down in a cascade of ferocious rocks (aptly named *Devastation*) to the Dead Sea 4000 ft. below. Eastwards beyond the Dead Sea rises the barrier-wall of the mountains of Moab; but such is the elevation of the crest of Judah that its shepherds looked down upon the tops of the distant hills. The tract of rugged, dangerous moorland on the edge of the terrific descent was known as *The Field*—The Field of Bethlehem and Tekoa. (Recall Luke ii. 8, concerning Christmas Eve at Bethlehem: 'And there were shepherds in the same country abiding in the field.') *Field* in the Old Testament does not signify a hedge-enclosed meadow, but, although it sometimes refers to an area of cultivated land, usually denotes 'the rough uncultivated, but not wholly barren, bulk of the hill-country where the beasts of the field [that is, *wild* beasts] found room to breed and became a serious hindrance, from first to last, in Israel's conquest of its land'.[1] In that majestic and austere setting the task of caring for the flock called for a strong and vigilant man, persistent to seek the animal strayed and lost, ready to encounter wild beasts come up from the torrid depths below through the tangled rocks to seek their prey.[2] G. A. Smith writes:

I do not remember ever to have seen in the East a flock of sheep without a shepherd....On some high moor across which at night the hyenas howl, when you meet him, sleepless, far-sighted, weather-beaten, armed, leaning on his staff, and looking over his scattered sheep, every one of them on his heart, you understand why the shepherd of Judah sprang to the front in his people's history; why they gave his name to their king, and made him the symbol of Providence; why Christ took him as the type of self-sacrifice.[3]

One hundred years after the time of Elijah, there was a shepherd of Tekoa named Amos. So great was his insight into the meaning of life that it has been said of him: 'Amos is one of the most wonderful and inexplicable phenomena in the history of the human spirit.' Yet it is only in respect of the final mystery of his conviction that *God* had apprehended him and made him see truth that we touch the inexplicable. All else about Amos is explicable, as what may happen when a humane and fearless spirit faces terrible evils and allows no illusions to confuse his judgement. How do we know what this shepherd saw and thought? We know, not by effort to dissect a core of history from an overlay of tradition, but by the preservation of his own words in the Book of

---

[1] G. A. Smith, *Historical Geography of the Holy Land*, pp. 79, 80.
[2] Cp. Amos iii. 12: 'As the shepherd rescueth out of the mouth of the lion two legs, or a piece of an ear.'
[3] Op. cit. p. 312.

Amos.[1] Similarly, we possess in the Book of Hosea direct knowledge of the thoughts and utterances of a contemporary great
Prophet, Hosea, in north Israel. It is significant that these two
men (or their close friends) must have felt it had been given them
to declare such immutable truths that their words, scorned or
uncomprehended by the mass of their hearers, ought to be set on
record and not allowed to perish in the speaking.

One hundred years after Elijah—much had happened in that
century, a chain of events giving rise to a situation closely paralleled by the confident civilization and moral blindness of Europe
and America during 1918–39. Broadly speaking, we mark the
same general sequence—devastating war; then peace and prosperity; a disconcerting interlude of 'slump'; renewed optimism
and reckless selfishness; crazy refusal to foresee a rising tempest.
The awful tax of war on the man-power of Israel began with the
great battle of Karkar in 853 B.C., when King Ahab with all the
resources he could muster was part of a confederate Palestinian-
Syrian host and fought a mighty Assyrian army. The battle halted
its southward advance, but at a terrible cost in life. The Allies
celebrated their narrow escape from Assyrian subjugation by
counting themselves free to develop their local 'hates', and expend
what was left of their strength in petty conflicts with one another.
The Syrians turned on Israel; King Ahab was mortally wounded
in battle against them at Ramoth Gilead.[2] Before long, within

[1] The last verses in the Book (ix. 11–15) are assuredly not from Amos, but
an addition provided (in the light of later history) to mollify by a cheering
conclusion the dread declaration of Divine retribution which Amos felt called
to pronounce to a heedless and debauched people. These verses stand in stark
contradiction to what precedes them, and the general effect is to reduce the
stern Prophet to a weakling who lacked the courage to adhere to his real
convictions and instead 'let milk and honey flow from the cup of the wrath
of Yahweh'. Otherwise the authenticity of only a few verses has been
questioned. Three allusions to God and Nature (iv. 13; v. 8–9; ix. 5–6) sit
loose to their context. But these may be actual words of Amos, their original
context lost. Especially in this so as regards the magnificent iv. 13 ('He that
formeth the mountains, and createth the wind, and declareth unto man what
is his thought, that maketh the morning darkness, and treadeth upon the high
places of the earth, the Lord, the God of hosts, is his name'), and v. 8, 9
('...that maketh the Pleiades and Orion, and turneth the shadow of death
into the morning, and maketh the day dark with night...the Lord is his
name'). So, indeed, might a great man speak, who kept watch by day and
night from the height of the wilderness of Tekoa.
[2] I Kings xxii. 29–35.

Israel, Elijah's insistence that the dynasty of Ahab and Jezebel ought to be overthrown came to fulfilment about 842 B.C. in Jehu's revolution and wholesale massacre of the royal household. Israel had grown weak: for Phoenicia was now indifferent, the powerful Syrians a dread menace, Judah able to reassert its independence. From the time of Jehu for some 30 years the Syrians launched repeated attacks on Israel's land, defeating its unaided armies, and harried its territory of Gilead (east of the Jordan) with ferocity, finding it a pleasant, profitable, pastime to give Israel 'merry hell'.[1] Brother Edom took its chance to attack enfeebled Brother Israel, 'casting off all pity'. The Ammonites, as well as the Syrians, ravaged hapless Gilead, enjoyed themselves 'ripping up the women with child', and annexed certain districts. Moabites attacked the Edomites and, having captured their king, jokingly decided to deny his spirit the rest of decent burial by burning his bones to lime. Raiders from the strong towns of the Philistine plain swept up to Judaean villages, seized every man, woman and child they could lay hands on and sold them as slaves to the Edomites. The small nations had learnt nothing from deliverance in the great battle that had stopped the Assyrians. On the contrary, a sort of unprecedented brutality was in the air. The ancients had been cruel, but not quite in the same way. The world ought to be wiser, but men grew more vile—as if a sub-bestial delight in cruelty was working loose in human nature. Just as the holocaust of war in Europe in 1914–18 left its aftermath of wounded men, and families mourning and weakened, so after Elijah's death protracted warfare with the Syrians during the last half of the ninth century branded its hideous mark on Israel's population; filling the earth with the graves of the young; leaving its trail of disabled men, of widows, fatherless children, and impoverished homes.

At the very end of the ninth century, however, the tide turned in favour of Israel. About 805 B.C. Assyrian armies assailed the Syrians, and in 802 B.C. captured their capital, Damascus, and broke their power. Israel recovered the territory it had lost to the

---

[1] See Amos i; ii. 1–4; and II Kings vi. 24; xiii. 1–7. The Hebrew historians were in difficulties concerning the dates of this period, and set forth the order of events confusedly. Assyrian records have helped to straighten out the tangles to some extent. It seems certain that the crippling attacks by the Syrians fell in the thirty years after Jehu's revolt.

Syrians. And (to complete the reversal) Assyria, after conquering
Damascus, surprisingly stayed its hand—internal weakness had
developed, and for over forty years its terrible armies left Palestine
alone. Thus the one great fear did not materialize. Fortune had
smiled, and went on smiling for forty years. Between approximately 785–740 B.C., Israel under Jeroboam II and Judah under
Uzziah (or Azariah)—note that both kings reigned for the same
long period—were secure and prosperous. Once again they could
control and levy tax on the rich trade-route from Elath on the Red
Sea along the Transjordan border of Canaan across, through
Esdraelon and Galilee, to the Phoenician ports. Came of a sudden
then—Security after Peril, Wealth after Destruction. As in
Europe and America after the defeat of Germany in 1918, the
successful felt safe to turn their thoughts to peace without effort,
prosperity without limit. And in Israel they did! For all in Israel
(and Judah) who had not been killed, disabled, or impoverished by
the wars there was golden opportunity to get rich quick, always
provided that a man was not so silly and sentimental as to consider
himself his brother's keeper. The king and his great men, the
owners of strong houses and fertile fields, priests of the royal
sanctuaries, merchants and traders, leaped at the chances with alert
minds and greedy hands. As for commerce, if merchants cheat the
unwary and small traders use false weights, at any rate the strong
see to it they do not play tricks on them; as for the common folk,
caveat emptor.[1] The royal priests had a chance, if they were conscienceless enough to take it. Jehovah was a bountiful Jehovah,
and the court was all in favour of honouring the national Deity
bountifully. There was no tension 'twixt Church and State in
Jeroboam's Israel. The priests had legitimate dues, and there were
ways of twisting their rights unlawfully. Some priests were
evil men. The contemporary Prophet, Hosea, accuses them in a
startling verse (vi. 9) of violence as well as villainy: 'As troops of
robbers wait for a man, so the company of priests murder in the
way toward Schechem; Yea, they have committed lewdness.' But
never had the national worship been practised on so lavish a
scale—rivers of oil and streams of blood; animals sacrificed by the
thousand; shouting and music; dancing and revelry. How pleased
Jehovah must be to see such unstinted devotion! As for Justice, if
the poor man fancied he had a grievance, by all means let him state

[1] Amos viii, 5.

a case. In the ancient East it was custom that litigants before a Judge might indicate their respect, and the importance of their matter, by a suitable present. In Jeroboam's Israel ('Stood to reason!') the rich were wise to out-gift the poor. And Hebrew law of the time was clear on one issue—loans were loans and must be repaid. The creditor could seize the defaulting debtor's land, or his person and his children to keep or sell as slaves: 'the Court awards it, and the Law doth give it.' As for the economic position, numbers of the peasant-proprietors, especially if husband or sons had died, were drifting into dire straits. Well, let them give up the struggle for independence, and hire out their labour for wages. But they were apt to make a last struggle to tide over difficulties, by recourse to a loan. Grand times for the lenders of money upon interest and security. Perfect nuisance these widows and orphans, whining, begging, getting into debt. Best way was to 'sell 'em up', and let large landowners cultivate the soil properly, using hired and slave employees. Following the European War of 1914–18 there was a terrible slump. In Britain the unemployed got the dole, and there and elsewhere the strong weathered the storm not too badly. In ancient Israel the forty years of prosperity had now and again disconcerting breaks. An awful plague occurred one year; at another time there was a consuming visitation of locusts; at another a fearful drought. However, the adroit can turn other people's losses to their profit, 'making good come out of evil', as they would say. In Israel there was no dole for the impoverished. After the drought, the holders of grain in Jeroboam's realm astutely saw they could agree to make a corner in the commodity, and then the cost of bread soared to an unheard-of level; the dealers found they could sell the merest refuse of the wheat to the starving at fancy prices.[1] One way and another, but especially at such heaven-sent moments of calamity, the land of the Hebrews became a profiteers' paradise.

Which things the eyes of Amos beheld. For he did not spend all his days in the wilderness of Tekoa. At times he journeyed north to dispose of the fleeces of his sheep, or to sell the increase of his flock to townsmen who must needs buy an animal for their intended sacrifice at the Festivals. Sometimes he went beyond Jerusalem; past Ramah where had lived Samuel, who had said in

[1] Amos viii. 5, 6.

God's name that what a man knows to be his duty that must he at all costs do. He went to Bethel, the great sanctuary of Israel's kingdom, administered by Amaziah as its chief priest. We know from his vivid words that, once at least, he went to Samaria, the capital, proud and rich and strong. As he went, he watched; marking on the one hand the sufferings of the poor, and on the other the luxuries and vices of the powerful—those lords and ladies of Samaria (fat discontented tyrannous women)[1] inhabiting great houses equipped with rich divans, silken cushions and rare ivory ornaments.[2] How he scorned the drunken banqueting of the wealthy, and loathed their smug inhumanity: 'unfeeling men, incapable of pity and void of any dram of mercy.' He returned to Tekoa with his soul shocked by the bitter wrongs, and his heart pierced by the miseries of the oppressed. The time came when this man, who knew life in its honest simplicities with its demand on him for vigilance, care and courage, set down what he had seen in brief burning words that never depart from their reader's memory. Let us attempt to picture a scene that could give rise to one such of his phrases: 'They have sold the righteous for silver, and the needy for ⟨the worth of⟩ a pair of shoes.'[3]

Amos was in Samaria. Beside one of its great houses he saw a woman waiting, with a girl and two younger boys beside her, ragged and wan and frail. Amos also waited. From its door came Simeon its owner, and the woman flung herself at his feet. 'Woman,' he said, 'keep thy filth at a distance! What have I to do with thee?' 'Lord, have mercy,' she moaned, 'Lord, have mercy upon us. We owe thee thirty pieces of silver, a debt on our land. My husband is dead; his elder brother was wounded in battle near the king's chariot and the wheels went over his legs. He is a cripple. Master, I and the children have toiled; we are famished, and we cannot pay.' 'Why so great a debt?' said Simeon. 'Master! it was for new vines and seeds after the locusts had consumed all; and then again after the great drought. Have mercy, Master; for thy Steward demands the debt, and we cannot pay.' 'Woman,' answered Simeon, 'I am known to be an upright man. I will think what should be done with thee, and I will speak with the Steward of my lands. Thou shalt have—well, justice; yes, justice. Return at sunset, thou and thy children.' So Simeon

[1] Amos iv. 1.   [2] Amos iii. 12, 15; vi. 1–6.
[3] Amos ii. 6; viii. 6.

consulted his Steward, and said: 'Why have you lent so much to such incompetents?' 'Sir,' he answered, 'I foresaw what would happen. Nothing will be lost to us. Hers is a fruitful plot of ground, if rightly worked. Thou hast but to add her heritage to thy fields, and to seize the daughter as a slave. The girl alone will sell for more than thirty silver pieces. The Phoenician dealers are ravenous for women slaves. They use them up first in Phoenicia, and then can ship them overseas to sell again in their colonies.' At sunset the woman was there with her children. Amos also was there; leaning upon his staff, watching. Simeon appeared, and two friends (dining with him that night), and the Steward. The woman bowed her head to the dust. The Steward spoke: 'Daughter, my lord is resolved to be gracious to thee. The debt is due; but thou shalt not starve. First he bids me say to thee (since thou art hungry now) that, after he has dined, scraps from his table will be sent out. As for thy plight, thou art not able to manage thy land, and the loan and interest are overdue. Wherefore for half the debt my lord will take over the land and add it to his own.' 'Sir, Sir,' the woman cried, 'the heritage of my fathers!' 'And, Sir, didst thou say, "*Half* the debt"?' 'What! A complaint?' rang the man's voice, 'Dost thou dare to complain? Then take thy cause to the judge. Be careful to show him thy respect by offering a worthy gift. Foolish one and ungrateful, understand that my Master will hire thee and thy sons to work for him: so shalt thou be fed. Now as for the other half of the debt, for that my lord must seize this thy daughter as a slave.' A cry broke from the mother's lips, and she fell fainting. Quickly the Steward gave a sign, and a slave wrenched the wailing girl from her mother's body and carried her off. Then Amos spake. 'Simeon,' he called, 'Simeon, I have somewhat to say unto thee. As I passed through Ramah there was a rich man in like case. But he had compassion, and the people were calling him *Blessed*, because *he* had raised up a desolate heritage in Israel. Cursed be thou, who devourest the portion of the widow and the fatherless! The Lord God of Israel curse thee, and all that thou hast!' Angry and discomposed, Simeon turned to go in. The Steward hastened to say, 'Master, heed not his curse. It cannot harm thee, for he speaks not as a *prophet*. 'Tis but a pestilent shepherd from Judah, known for his impudence. The authorities should deal with him.' One of Simeon's friends added, 'Most just, Simeon, most just. Thou hast done only what is necessary. Hard cases make bad laws. These ill-worked patches of ground are useless nowadays. The time has come for large holdings and hired labour: only so are results good and the country prosperous. Forget it, my friend. Come, let us dine.'

Back in Tekoa, with his mind afire with anger, his heart aching with compassion, Amos reflected. Everywhere *cruelty*. Those ruthless Phoenician-Philistine slave-traders, hardened beyond a trace of feeling. Syrians, Ammonites, Edomites, Moabites—each perpetrating horrible atrocities. And the men of Judah and Israel most of all; for they wreaked their cruelty on brethren; and they sinned against knowledge, against the commandment of their God. It has been rightly said that 'Amos was the first to realize that the sins of civilization—abuse of justice, oppression of the poor, corruption of the innocent, selfish luxury and sensual vice—are worse than all the barbarities of savage warfare'. Amos reflected: That mother! That girl! Never had Amos dreamed he could feel so deeply moved by pity. Why such cruelty? Not mere injustice, but wanton sneering cruelty as well. Why do not men long to be kind? Why do not the strong desire to protect the weak, as a shepherd his sheep? Do they never search for the lost until they find it and bring it back to safety? Justice is not enough, not what men call justice. Simeon—standing there for justice and his rights!—had done unspeakable wrong. Israel in Egypt had had no just claim upon its God; and God had redeemed His people from slavery. God's justice had been *compassion*. God had been *merciful*. Amos meditated on his own impotence. He could not rescue that girl from enslavement. (Where was she now?) He could not pay the widow's debt. (Think of her anguish for the child she loved in slavers' hands.) He could do nothing, nothing. Tend the sheep, feed the lambs—that was his life— watching sheep, watching sheep, his sheep. There was absolutely nothing else he could do, a mere shepherd of Tekoa.... He says that it was like the sudden roar of a lion when the voice rang in his consciousness—THUS SAITH THE LORD, *Go, prophesy, unto my people Israel.*[1]

Everything in the Book of Amos reads like a record of actual utterances.[2] True, in chapters i, ii, it is effective literary treatment whereby the indictment of other nations is made to

---

[1] Amos iii. 8; vii. 14,15.
[2] Excepting ix. 11–15. See p. 247.

culminate in the arraignment of Judah and Israel, but the order is
equally art of the *speaker*. How gleefully would Hebrew hearers
lap up his denunciation of foreigners! How shocked when their
own turn came! In chapters vii, viii, ix, 1–10, five *Visions*
seen in trance are related. The verses preserve what had passed in
the intimacies of the Prophet's superconscious mind, but are not
notes set down for his own interest. The Visions concerned God
and Israel, and it was for him to make known their forewarnings.
The words which we read Amos spoke to the people—and
how many more beside? Amos mentions but one specific incident
concerning his prophetic activity—when at royal Bethel he confronted Amaziah its priest, and in the name of God pronounced
sentence of death upon King Jeroboam and of exile upon the nation
of Israel. He tells us that Amaziah, in reporting the matter to
Jeroboam, used the phrase 'the land is not able to bear all his
words'. *All*—we may surmise from the priest's remark that there
were many unrecorded occasions when Amos had endeavoured to
make the men of Israel hear his 'Word of the Lord'. Presumably
the occasion at Bethel was the last time, but by no means the first
time, when Amos spoke prophetically within the realm of Israel.
Amaziah, scornful and irate, ordered him henceforth to confine his
mouthings to the territory of Judah, and there earn his keep as a
prophet! Our task must be restricted to discerning the principles
that inspired the Prophet's oracular utterances, to appreciating
their incisive relevance for his own Age, and to valuing their
significance for our belief to-day.

From the very moment of his Call the thoughts of Amos rose
out of, and rested on, certitude that the feelings which the sights
in Israel had awakened in himself—anguish of pitying mercy, fire
of righteous indignation—exist likewise in the mind of God. He
was sure that the emotion of his soul was in this at one with the
changeless nature of the Deity. The loathing and anger that hideous
misdeeds had roused in his conscience were how much more felt
by Jehovah, the Altogether-Righteous. The wave of compassion
for wronged and suffering men, women and children that had
flooded his heart—God, Creator of the World and them that
dwell therein, felt compassion for them how much more than he;
God who (as Elijah had declared) cares for the life of the humblest
of the souls that He has made. Was Amos's unargued assumption
—that, as a good man feels and thinks, so much more God—

a guess in the dark, a wishful assertion? On the contrary, it was philosophical wisdom and common sense. *Philosophical wisdom*—because in that basic belief Amos is in line with those philosophers who, since Plato, have stressed the metaphysical significance of moral values. *Common sense*—because, although Amos's certitude can be regarded as intuition rather than reasoning, it may with at least equal propriety be regarded as lightning logic. Of course, if we take our stand on the opinion that the totality of Existence is nothing save manifestation of a wholly unconscious and therefore non-moral Force (unintelligent and finally unintelligible), we shall draw no such conclusion about the metaphysical significance of Virtue; but we have then to turn a blind eye on the fact that the Universe does include in Man intelligent moral consciousness. If, however, we seek to understand the significance of human consciousness, with its innate and developing sense of Right and Wrong, on the hypothesis that the marvel of Existence is not finally irrational and non-moral but derives from a super-material and super-human, purposeful, Intelligence (in brief, from *God*), for whom therefore distinction of Good and Evil must be real—*then* it is sense to conclude that God cannot be less good than the best of men. And if human nature be capable (as it is) of the noble emotion of mercy, God must be infinitely more merciful: 'The Everlasting Mercy.'

Amos in the depths of his mind was utterly certain that God would give him guidance. He was heir to the great conception of Jehovah as the God who had revealed His will to Moses, and had had compassion on Israel in Egypt, making covenant with His people to the end that they should honour Right and be brethren one to another: that is to say, he regarded the intercourse of men as not devoid of meaning but morally intelligible. Therefore Amos became very sure that, if he centred his mind on God and sought to see all things in the light of the Divine character, what God purposed to do would be revealed to him; his duty would be made plain, and the word that he should speak in God's name be given him. 'Surely,' he said, 'the Lord God will do nothing, but he revealeth his secret unto his servants the prophets.'[1] It followed that Amos believed things do not happen irrationally. Therein he was the heir of Elijah, insistent that men must bethink them what they do, and reason that

[1] Amos iii. 7.

they cannot sow evil and reap good. They cannot fall asleep at the post of duty and prevent the wolf from seizing the sheep. Consequences have causes. Amos's calling taught him that. For as G. A. Smith has memorably written of the wilderness of Tekoa:

It is a very empty and a very silent world, yet every stir of life upon it excites, therefore, the greater vigilance, and man's faculties, relieved from the rush and confusion of events, form the instinct of marking, and reflecting upon, every single phenomenon. . . .Every shadow, every noise, the shepherd must know what is behind it and be warned. . . . Such a vigilance Amos would have Israel apply to his own message and the events of their history. . . .Certainly there is no habit which, so much as this of watching facts with a single eye and a responsible mind, is indispensable alike in the humblest duties and in the highest speculations of life. . . .Israel sweltered with optimism. The glare of wealth, the fulsome love of country, the rank incense of a religion that was without morality—these thickened all the air, and neither the people nor their rulers had any vision. But Amos carried with him his clear desert atmosphere and his desert eyes. He saw the raw facts: the poverty, the cruel negligence of the rich, the injustice of the rulers, the immorality of the priests. The meaning of these things he questioned with as much persistence as he questioned every suspicious sound or sight upon those pastures of Tekoa.[1]

A simple thought was the foundation of Amos's greatness. (It is ever the greatness of simple truths which lesser men fail to grasp.) He believed that in the sphere of human conduct effect follows on cause with the same subtlety and rigorousness as in the realm of Nature, and that evil begets evil and leads to disaster. He would assuredly have said that history had offered no such plain evidence of the working of this principle as the twentieth century A.D. has furnished. Prior to 1914 in all the great nations moral incapacity was perverting the resources of patriotism, science, finance and industry, in ways that led straight to the European War. What use was made of the respite of peace after 1918? Radical amendment of our ways? Awed consciousness that the continuance of our life had been purchased by the blood, suffering and sorrow of millions? How like our civilization has been on the great scale to ninth-century Israel on the small! Cruelty and stupidity continued, turning prodigious power to the uses of

---

[1] *The Twelve Prophets*, vol. I, pp. 75, 82, 84. See Amos iii. 3–8.

damnation, overwhelming the will of good men for better things. The end thereof was world-war.

Amos recognized that nations other than Israel were cruel, and did not acquit them of guilt on the score that they worshipped cruel Gods. The interesting implication is that he was rightly assuming there is in human nature an elemental sense of Right, a capacity for kindness, and therefore Man as Man has moral duty whereof none may plead ignorance. The novel and startling fact, however, is that he said it was *Jehovah* who, as God, would bring upon these other nations the terrible retribution that was justly due to their persistent, flagrant wickedness. But in Israel Amos recognized guilt unparalleled. To Israel had come a unique conception of God, and therewith unique opportunity to perceive what truly is good. To Israel also had come abounding material reason for thankfulness. But the men of Judah and Israel had answered their blessings with black ingratitude—learning in Canaan to revere other Gods and practise horrid rites, utilizing the riches of their country for oppression and debauchery, hating and silencing those who rebuked.[1] Finally, in his own day unequalled prosperity had produced unequalled wrongs. He saw the faces of hard men— the greed of some of them so insatiable that they seemed to pant after the very dust on the head of the poor.[2] Certainty grew upon Amos that these men had lost capacity to repent: he knew the utter contempt with which they met his own remonstrance, pleading and warning. Hence the logic of his mind impelled him to think that coming calamity must match the frightfulness of the iniquity. What shape would it take? His imagination pictured an Assyrian army storming Samaria.[3] What would that entail for luxurious lords and ladies? Assyrians had a custom of driving hooks into the faces of their captives, and dragging them along on a rope. But the 'How' was neither here nor there. Of one thing alone Amos was convinced—the inexorable operation of God's righteousness. He felt Israel had sunk beyond power to repent. He knew that (for grave, but far less grave, cause) Samuel and Elijah had predicted and called for the downfall of the reigning dynasty. From the surpassing present evils he inferred calamity exceeding all previous imagining, and was led to a conclusion dumbfoundering and incredible to those who heard him utter it.

[1] Amos ii. 11, 12.   [2] Amos ii. 7.
[3] Amos iii. 15; iv. 2, 3

Not for such bitter fruit had Jehovah planted Israel in its fertile land: therefore Jehovah would now uproot it and cast it out of the land. He went to the royal sanctuary at Bethel, and in the name of God prophesied, not merely that King Jeroboam would fall by the sword, but that *Israel would be led captive out of its land*.[1]

So far we have written of Amos as 'reaching convictions', 'drawing conclusions'. And rightly so. This shepherd did *reason*, on the basis of his certainty of the reality of God and His moral purpose. But let it not be imagined that the reasoning of Amos was cold reasoning. We know (for he tells us) that at times in the furnace of his spirit the metal of thought became the molten experience of trance. Visions came to him, terrible Visions[2]— Vision of the virgin-daughter of Israel fallen to the ground, never to rise again: prostrate upon the earth with none to lift her up. Scenes and sounds of devastation—great houses sacked and ruined, corpses strewing the streets, voices of wailing women; for the feasts had been turned into mourning and the songs to lamentations. Vision of God standing beside an altar built for His honour, commanding its utter destruction: for 'the high places of Isaac shall be desolate, and the sanctuaries of Israel shall be laid waste'. Vision of men and women fleeing from the swords of their foe, supplicating God to stop this war and have mercy on their desperation: but 'there shall not one of them escape'. These had been men and women whose aim in life had been, not to deliver others from affliction, but only themselves to be delivered. 'How should men hope for mercy, showing none?'

Amos marvelled that Hebrews could be so recusant to face what was entailed by being in covenant with the God whom Moses had declared to be power, righteousness and compassion. He was led to perceive illusions that misled their minds; mirages that they allowed to dazzle their sight. The first of these illusions was misconstruction of the belief that Jehovah had chosen Israel to be His people. They interpreted the idea as implying that Jehovah would do His utmost to favour them, lavishing such material

[1] Amos vii. 11.

[2] See Amos vii. 1–9; ix. 1–6; viii. 1, 2. (To appreciate the force of this last-named passage an assonance between two Hebrew words *Kaitz* and *Ketz* has to be known—as follows: 'Thus the Lord God showed me : and behold, a basket of summer fruit. And he said, Amos, what seest thou? And I said, A basket of summer fruit (*Kaitz*). Then said the Lord unto me, The end (*Ketz*) is come upon my people Israel.')

benefits as He could confer, exerting all His power to give victory
or (better still) to keep them immune from attack. Voicing their
military optimism, they were wont to make use of a notable phrase
The day of the Lord, meaning thereby that in battle signal triumph
was sure to be won by the support of Jehovah's might. If fighting
there should be, they were wholly confident of its issue. So to say,
'We don't want to fight, but by jingo! if we do, we've got the men,
we've got the arms, we've got Jehovah, too.' Accordingly they
professed themselves eager to witness God's activity in history on
their behalf. Amos answered them: 'The day of the Lord cometh,
but it will be darkness and not light.'[1] Their foes would defeat
them, because God is righteous. In equally famous words he
declared also the great principle that to whom much is given,
of him shall much be required.[2] For the first time explicitly it was
thus asserted that Israel's claim to unique relationship with God
must be understood as unique opportunity and unique obligation
to learn, and assent to, God's Self-revelation as moral demand. The
Prophet was saying: 'God *is* active in history; but to the end that
His people shall pre-eminently bring forth the fruits of righteousness.' Further, there is the highest significance in Amos's declaration (ix. 7) that all nations, not Israel alone, are under the
control of Jehovah, their movements and settlements in divers
lands are His ordaining—'Are ye not as the children of the Ethio-
pians unto me,...saith the Lord? Have not I brought up Israel
out of Egypt, and the Philistines from Caphtor, and the Syrians
from Kir?' To that add the Prophet's assertion (referred to
earlier) that it was Jehovah who would bring retribution upon
other nations for their cruelties one to another. Obviously the
mind of Amos had completely broken with the otherwise unquestioned, immemorial notion that there exist many Gods, each
having his own 'pet' people; Jehovah, for instance, happening to
be the private God of Israel, whom Israel (as it were) keeps in its
pocket, a benevolent yet not quite reliable *Genie*, who if he gets his
expected material dues and noisy praises can be counted on usually
to respond to the treatment by delivering the goods. So thought
Amos's contemporaries. When Amos referred to Jehovah as God
of Israel, the thought in his mind was the only God there is, Maker
of Heaven and Earth and Man. His faith had reached the level of
monotheism, as lucidly as any need require who do not insist that

[1] See Amos v. 18–20.   [2] Amos iii. 2; cp. Luke xii. 48.

religious belief cannot effectively be expressed except in the terminology of metaphysics.

The second illusion was sustained by popular assumption that the gross forms of ancient worship were well-pleasing in God's sight and efficacious. Nothing could more vividly reveal the people's deep incomprehension of the nature of worship acceptable to God than their reaction to uncomfortable national events. They regarded the trouble as a passing cloud over the assured sunshine of their God's favour, to be met not by amendment of their conduct, but by increasing the stench of burning flesh and reeking blood as they multiplied propitiatory sacrifices. The wise intelligence of Amos was aghast at the absurdity of these animal-sacrifices wherein they deemed God took pleasure, and supposed themselves to be doing their duty towards Him who made Orion and the Pleiades. His clean spirit revolted at the drunkenness, sensuality and excitement at the sacred Festivals—'Worship' (in expectation of a bountiful return for their Services) addressed to their own particular Fairy-Godfather! Amos uttered the first of the Prophetic series of categorical denunciations of the traditional ritual—when, as the voice of God, he said: 'I hate, I despise your feasts, and I will take no delight in your solemn assemblies. Yea, though ye offer me your burnt offerings and your meal offerings, I will not accept them.... Take thou away from me the noise of thy songs; for I will not hear the melody of thy viols. But let justice roll down as waters, and righteousness as a mighty stream.'[1]

Some modern writers have expressed perplexities, hesitancies and even timorous protests, about those forthright words, as well as the other equally trenchant attacks on Hebrew ritual made by later Prophets. They pose the questions, 'Did Amos really wish that the ritual worship of his time should be swept away, leaving—a blank? Was his meaning as drastic as it seems? Perhaps the intention of his words was only to utter rebuke of "*your* feasts" (*You* being such bad men!), whereas if only *you* had been good men God would have had no serious criticism to make of your mode of worship? In any case *ought* not that to have been his counsel—Reform, not Abolition, of the sacrificial system?[2] This surrender to God of the animal's life—might not the

[1] Amos v. 21–24.
[2] Cp. pp. 278, 324.

worshippers have construed it as beautifully symbolic of that offering of our souls and bodies which is our rational sacrifice? Should we perhaps go further, and (to be on the safe side) think that mysteriously sacrifices or other rites are *per se* efficacious with God, things material and external being *automatically* sacramental?' Amos would have answered that such dubieties, however well-intentioned, show no proper apprehension of the illumination God had granted him to receive concerning the nature and range of what does constitute effective reverence towards God. He would have said to his contemporaries that he meant exactly what he said; and to us that, if our eyes had seen what his eyes beheld, we would have had no doubt that to consign the whole bloody bestial business to the nethermost pit was the first step towards hope of discovering spiritually sensible ways and means of adoring Him who must be worshipped in spirit and in truth. *That* for only the start of Amos's answer. For this Prophet had clearly grasped a profound principle which should warn us that no matter how refined a ritual form may be, or how exquisite its symbolism, it is in vain unless it evokes the heart's genuine reverence, illuminates the mind and quickens conscience. Perhaps it is worse than in vain; since observation of a rite is apt to beget self-righteousness. It has proved almost insuperably difficult for men whole-heartedly to abandon the illusion that acts of worship, as distinct from their spiritual-moral effects on the worshipper, have in themselves value in God's sight. But it is essential to grasp the radical distinction, if the sound instinct that men need to get together to lift up their hearts unto God is to be revitalized in modern life.

Consider the central, constructive insight of Amos concerning the nature of worship acceptable unto God. The last part of his answer would be to repeat those words: 'Let justice roll down as waters, and righteousness as a mighty stream'; and to bid us reflect deeply. With absolute explicitness he declared the two-fold truth—that authentic worship creates the will to do right, *and* equally that every merciful deed is authentic adoration of God.[1] Two neighbouring sentences in the Book of Amos concentrate

---

[1] Cp. G. B. Gray, *Sacrifice in the Old Testament*, p. 44. ('The tenour of their [the Prophets'] teaching was, not gifts, but fellowship; but the way to fellowship which they pointed out was not through the existing sacrificial system re-interpreted, but through conduct.')

the Prophet's meaning: 'Seek the Lord, and ye shall live'—'Seek good, and not evil; and so the Lord shall be with you, as ye say.' [1] That was finally to ground Ethics in Religion, and to give Conduct the guidance and inspiration of a boundless standard of Right. It was like sunlight on the face of life; since everything that falls to us to do and say takes on a lovely, but most challenging, aspect. When acts of helpful goodness between man and man are sensed as worship, the range of our spiritual approach to God is immeasurably enlarged. For the times and seasons that should bring our spirits consciously into living fellowship with God are not just the occasions of collective profession of our faith, but the ceaseless contacts with one another in daily life. Such worship falls to be offered in the days of prosperity; but it is in the dark and cloudy days of adversity that men can find the greatest opportunity of drawing nigh to God by aiding one another in sorrows and sufferings. Amos's helpfulness in thus perceiving the nature and expression of reverential trust in God can scarcely be overstated. Religion becomes master of circumstance, and not its slave, when the practice of devotion to God is thus conceived. Altars can be destroyed, but not the will to do good.

Amos was great also because resolutely he looked down into the deep abyss of Evil in human nature. He understood how tough and interwoven are the roots of wickedness in the vigour of man's self-will; understood how seemingly impossible it is to make bad men good or stop them from wrecking social welfare, their own and their neighbours'. For vice grows not only from our heritage of primeval ignorance and savagery; it battens on the fatness of the land, and flourishes in the hot-house of sophistication. Civilization is apt to progress by leaps and bounds in the wrong direction. With Amos the faith of the great Hebrew Prophets began properly to realize the severity of the problem, and to grapple with it.

And Amos was very great because he looked up, and saw *Mercy* in the high heaven of God enthroned above Justice. In the history of religion Amos is the Apostle of Mercy. His function in the development of Hebrew thought of God was to turn a searchlight on to that aspect of the Mosaic tradition which recognized in the liberation of Israel from bondage in Egypt an act of divine compassion. All normally respectable people accept that Mercy is one of the virtues. Amos, by becoming a merciful man, put actuality

[1] See Amos v. 6, 14.

into an abstraction. That makes a world of difference. To illustrate the point—there is a saying in the Book of Psalms: 'Eyes have they but they see not.' Any decent citizen or motherly woman (if her horizon is not quite confined to the four walls of her residence, the doings of her sons and daughters and the strict circle of her closest friends) is sorry that there should be a housing problem. *The Housing Problem* is seen in a different light, if the man has intimate and extensive acquaintance with the state of 'slum' property, and if the woman knows personally a good mother struggling to do her utmost for a family in one room with no sink, or if she has affectionate concern for a young couple with a baby and no home. Amos had travelled to Samaria an upright and fair-minded man. He came back appalled by men's notion of their rights—those corn-dealers in the year of the famine dangling bread before the eyes of the starving, exercising the right of free-trade in accordance with the law of supply and demand! He came back longing that *God's* righteousness were at work. He went to Samaria a latently kind man. He returned conscious of the imperative need for mercy. Simeon's *justice*! Amos could never forget the haggard woman and the sobbing girl. Think of the transformation on her face there would have been, if rich Simeon had come to her rescue, used the merest fraction of his power and wealth to aid her and her crippled brother, and by his aid made it possible to work her heritage, keep her home and bring the boys to manhood. Ah! twice-blessed quality of Mercy. Only love of mercy can teach men what their duty is. Amos derived his convictions about human life from his belief that

> Mercy is an attribute to God Himself,
> And earthly power doth then show likest God's
> When mercy seasons justice.

What would this merciful Prophet have thought of the slums of our mighty civilization in contrast with its goodly houses? What warning would he have given to the peoples of Europe and America in 1919–39, dancing down the years to the World War, worshipping those great twin-gods—Confusion and Almighty Cash? What message would be broadcast to this our world, if the voice of Amos, abiding in the Field and keeping watch by night over his flock, could be heard from Tekoa—calling the nations on Christmas Eve?

CHAPTER XIII

LOVE

In the years when the shepherd of Tekoa spoke to pitiless men concerning Mercy and Judgement, there lived in the kingdom of Israel a man, by name Hosea, who grew in knowledge of the length and breadth and height and depth of the most exacting, most ennobling and most enduring of all human qualities—Love. English speech uses the word *love* in the slackest way, applying it to any degree of liking for persons or for things. Languages need, and lack, a term reserved for the self-giving tireless longing to aid the highest well-being of others, which *love* should properly denote.[1] Love takes ceaseless thought to see and to contrive whatsoever it can do to help. Its intensity is most fully felt between individuals; and it is in the nature of things that constantly it arises between man and woman. But it must not be identified with bodily attraction, which it transcends. It is seen at times in friendships between men. The Hebrews remembered the love of David and Jonathan ('passing the love of women', said David); how that these two eager youths so cared for one another that it mattered naught to them that the crown would rest on the head of one and not of the other. Whoever has in him the quality of Love

[1] The disciples of Jesus, seeking to make known the quality of love which they had seen in Him, set aside the usual Greek term *Eros*, and used instead in reference to the Love of Christ a very rare word, *Agape*. Only one instance (and that questionable) can be adduced in evidence of its use in secular Greek literature. (See Moulton and Milligan, *Vocabulary of the Greek Testament*, p.2.) Hebert—translating Nygren's *Agape and Eros*, Part I, pp. xi f.—rightly lays emphasis on 'the fatal confusion between *Agape* and *Eros* which now obscures the meaning of Christianity'. In the marvellous passage written by St Paul concerning Agape (I Cor. xiii) the R.V. and the American Standard Version rightly translate Agape as *Love*. It was a disaster that the A.V. rendered it as *Charity*—since in present-day English charity has been narrowed down in meaning to denote 'assistance to the poor'. In Hebrew also there was no specific, adequate, word. Hosea, striving to body forth his sense of the ideal relationship, deepened the significance of the word *Hĕsĕd*, which meant essentially 'fidelity to covenantal duty': on God's part therefore it signified 'the grace of God', His constant, unmerited, generous goodness; on Israel's part response of grateful eager loyalty; and as between men the kindness, justice, sincerity of those who esteem and care for one another.

in its greatness is concerned for all others, for Love has in it, on the one hand, recognition of an immeasurable sacredness in human personality as such, and on the other hand is characterized by humility—awareness of need oneself to be given, not bare justice, but generous sustaining love. Capacity to love (in this noblest sense) is the most wonderful fact in existence.

Like Conscience, Love is an inclusive, controlling disposition. Under its guidance the several virtues are refined and strengthened. Bare justice may be satisfied by legal equivalent: 'an eye for an eye, a tooth for a tooth.' But Justice inspired by Love is not resolve to uphold law or exact retribution. Love vindicates Right not punitively, but as necessity in a process which seeks only that the unjust, realizing what is right, may be delivered from the evil that has been in his soul. Love includes and transcends the quality of Mercy, for the compassion of those who do not truly love is evoked only in regard to sorrows such as seem to *merit* pity, or goodness that *deserves* reward. Love reaches out to the undeserving and the ungrateful: 'While we were yet sinners', said the disciples of Jesus, 'Christ loved us.'[1]

In the Bible to *know* denotes not surface-acquaintance, but an intimate awareness wherein intelligence comprehends, emotion is stirred and the will responds. That is what the Prophets intended when they called upon men to *know the Lord*. In English an intonation of the voice may convey this richer meaning: as when one in great pain or grief, speaking of his suffering to a friend, is answered 'Yes, I *know*; I have been through it'. Amos came to *know* Mercy by reason of the pity which the sufferings of others quickened in him. Hosea learnt to *know* Love by enduring the anguish of a personal tragedy. Only the unselfish can know Love, and only the sensitive can experience the agony it may entail, and discover its sustaining power.

An abnormal number of mistakes mar the text of the Book of Hosea to such an extent that very many verses are meaningless in the English translation. Indeed, a reader without access to the detailed discussions available in the Commentaries may be at a loss

---

[1] Again the New Testament writers gave prominence to a specific word, *Charis* (Grace)—as in 'The grace of the Lord Jesus Christ', 'The grace of God'. The basic meaning of *Charis* is *Charm, Loveliness*. Its extended usage denoted *Goodwill, Lovingkindness*; and, in especial, *Kindness shown to the undeserving*. In Elizabethan English *Charity* had that significance.

to see how the outline of the Prophet's witness and faith here to be presented is justified.[1] A few lovely phrases strike home at once, but for the rest specialist interpretation is necessary to disentangle certain later intrusions that stultify the context, and to elucidate perplexing phrases and metaphors. Another difficulty is that themes are touched only in briefest fashion, and that the Prophet's thoughts and pleadings stand in no order whatsoever either of time or subject. We possess in the Book of Hosea, as it were, a casket of unset gems—or fragments of a beautiful stained-glass window which we would fain complete and set in order. It is beyond the compass of these pages to offer a survey of the Prophet's words. The aim is instead to appreciate his pain, the wisdom he reached because he endured, the use he made of his central conviction and its lasting significance. The daunting obscurities in the Book of Hosea have, however, in a strange way aesthetic propriety. It is as though the broken text reflects the anguish of the Prophet's broken heart. As Robertson Smith expressed it: 'The swift transitions, the fragmentary unbalanced utterances, the half-developed allusions, that make Hosea's prophecy so difficult to the commentator, express the agony of this inward conflict.'[2]

The Book of Hosea is the sole place where the Prophet is mentioned, and even there nothing explicit is said about where he lived, or where and when he 'prophesied'. Inferences from his words seem conclusively to show that, like Jesus of Nazareth, he was a Galilaean.

Hosea's love steals across his whole land like the dew, evoking every separate scent and colour, till all Galilee lies before us, lustrous and fragrant as nowhere else outside the parables of Jesus. . . . Throughout

[1] The stimulating, general, expositions given by A. C. Welch (*Religion of Israel under the Kingdom*) and G. A. Smith (*The Twelve Prophets*, vol. I) should be consulted. Harper's large Commentary (*I.C.C.* 1905) suffers from excessive doubt of the authenticity of the text on metrical and other grounds.

[2] *The Prophets of Israel*, p. 157. Smith's reference to 'half-developed allusions' concerns the interesting fact that Hosea makes passing references to events of which we have otherwise no knowledge. He speaks of priests who were a snare at Mizpah and spread a net at Tabor (v. 1); of priests on the way to Shechem guilty of conduct which was actual or moral murder (vi. 9); of the princes making themselves sick with wine on 'the day of our king' (vii. 5); of a place where Ephraim dealt treacherously with Jehovah (vi. 7). Hosea spoke to men who vividly knew just what were these events and scandals in the national life.

Galilee Lebanon [i.e. Mount Hermon] dominates the landscape. You cannot lift your eyes from any spot in northern Israel without resting them upon the vast mountain. From the unhealthy jungles of the Upper Jordan, the pilgrim lifts his heart to the cool air above, to the evergreen cedars and firs, to the streams and waterfalls that drop like silver chains off the great breastplate of snow....Hosea's sacraments are the open air, the mountain breeze and lilies, the pines; and what God asks of men are not rites nor sacrifices, but life and health, fragrance and fruitfulness, beneath the shadow and the dew of His Presence.[1]

But beautiful Galilee was the environment of a very sad man, who made his grief a healing sacrament for others.

By inference we can conclude that Hosea's prophetic activity began shortly before the death of Jeroboam II about 745 B.C. and ended before the fall of Samaria in 721: it has been suggested that he may have been killed or deported when an Assyrian army ravaged Galilee in 734. It is important to realize how terrifying were those few years, 745–721 B.C. Soon after 745 mighty Assyria was stirring, and bent on conquests. Public policy in Israel rapidly became distracted—'Perhaps there was really no need to fear; perhaps security could be purchased by tribute; perhaps the Assyrians would rest content with attacks on Syria; perhaps with the aid of Egypt their army could be defeated.' Anyway the powerful in Israel did not allow dread to prick their conscience, and induce them to cease their oppressions or reflect on their mode of worship and purge its uncleanness. Hosea beheld the selfsame religious and social evils as had horrified Amos. The nation had basked in prosperity and safety throughout the forty years of Jeroboam's reign. But on his death within the next seven months two kings were enthroned and murdered in Samaria. The successful murderer of the second managed to die a natural death in 737. The next two kings were assassinated, and the murderer of no. 2 (Hoshea) was Israel's last king, ruling for five years but as a puppet of Assyria. In 738 the Assyrians invaded Syria and Palestine—at which time the then king of Israel (Menahem) paid huge tribute in order to be left on his shaking throne. In 734 they captured the Syrian capital, Damascus, and made Syria a province of their empire; and the fall of Samaria in 721, after a protracted siege, put an end to Israel's kingdom.

[1] G. A. Smith, op. cit. pp. 233, 312.

One fact alone the Book of Hosea states concerning the Prophet's life. Hosea married a woman named Gomer, and three children were born in his home—a son, a daughter, and a son. About six years after the marriage Gomer left her husband for another man. So far the tale is one with many parallels—although (be it noted) more often it has been the man who deserted wife and children. This tale, however, had a sequel presumably without any parallel in antiquity, and with few since. Gomer's paramour abandoned her (or she left him), and in time she sank into some sort of servitude, for she was purchasable—at no very great price. Hosea came to feel it was veritably God's call to him that he should continue to do the utmost possible to care for and protect her. Accordingly he bought her from her owner, and, not renewing their marital relation, gave her again the shelter of his house and the reality of his care.

Now in the impact of this tragedy on his spirit, and in the way he dealt with it, he found the essence of his faith in God and the particular Prophetic message which he gave to his People. Therefore he had to make bare mention of his personal grief, but did so with such proper reticence that we are left to conjecture what Gomer's natural disposition may have been, and to imagine how intense was his agony of mind as the tragedy developed. This effort of imagination ought to be made; otherwise the power and poignancy of Hosea's faith may be perceived only superficially. We are not wholly without guidance in essaying the conjecture, for Hosea drew a comparison between his wife's attitude to him and Israel's to its God; and, although it is precarious to insist on exact correspondence in analogies (as study of the Parables of Jesus shows), there is in this analogy an important, general clue to what happened between this man and wife. Nothing, however, is harder than to appreciate with deep feeling a form of suffering through which one has not personally passed, and there is no phase in the development of the Prophetic Faith so difficult adequately to describe as the spiritual achievement of suffering Hosea. Nevertheless, sympathy should of itself enable us, in relation to any kind of suffering, to do better than murmur 'I'm so sorry', or 'Now, isn't that just too bad'.

No one doubts that Hosea was a good and kind man. The Prophet did not treat Gomer brutally, giving her great cause to desert him. But a good man is not inevitably an infallibly wise husband. As for Gomer, the view that she was all along a thoroughly bad woman, of dissolute disposition, and (may be) a shrew who made her home a hell, cannot be categorically ruled out. But if that view be correct, observe that it was relatively easy for Hosea's affection to decrease instead of to deepen, and he did not suffer the subtle agonies of bewilderment, horror and hope that he must have endured if his profound affection saw that in Gomer seeds of good as well as evil were subtly intermixed.[1] If she was bad as bad can be, he would the more readily have 'got over' his disappointment. Moreover, anyone who is confident that the harshest view of Gomer is the right view, blandly ignores that human life is complex. Other possibilities are open to us to consider; for there is no cogent reason to decide that from her youth up Gomer was a wicked woman, and there are strong reasons to the contrary.[2] Let us follow a kinder interpretation—

[1] What he said concerning Israel in relation to its God supports that opinion, as will be made clear later.

[2] Despite the statement in i. 2 ('And the Lord said to Hosea, Go, take unto thee a wife of whoredoms, and children of whoredoms'). (i) Most scholars have been, and almost all now are, of firm opinion (based on cumulative reasons) that this is an instance of a not infrequent, curious, Hebrew idiom which states an initial action in a train of events as having been *intended* to produce the result which was its ultimate outcome. In such cases literal rendering is inadequate and misleading. Comparable instances are Isa. vi. 10 (on which see the excellent note in Skinner's *Isaiah*, p. 50), or Luke viii. 10, on which Abrahams (*Pharisaism and the Gospels* (1st ser.), p. 106) remarks: 'the supposition that Jesus taught in Parable *in order* that men might misunderstand is preposterous. This is to mistake an Oriental process of thought by which consequences are often confused with motives.' On this view the meaning of Hos. i. 2 is, at the utmost, that Hosea may have been aware of dangerous traits in Gomer's youthful character, but emphatically NOT that he knew beforehand she would not conquer the dangers. Almost certainly we have an instance of Hebrew idiom; and the implication in 'And the Lord said to Hosea' is simply that, looking back on his life, Hosea realized that God had enabled him to turn his sorrow to the service of truth, and therefore he could feel that the good hand of God had been with him from the start, despite the personal tragedy for Gomer and for him. (It should be noted that Hos. i is cast in the third person whereas the further reference in iii. 1–3 is impressively in the first person: 'Then said the Lord unto *me*, Go yet, love....' Accordingly i. 2ff. may be narration by someone (other than Hosea himself) who knew the whole story and what Hosea had said regarding the meaning of the names given to his children. But no great importance attaches to the change of person.) (ii) It has been held by some that i. 2 may carry a more literal meaning, if perhaps Hosea felt impelled to marry one of the women serving

This bridegroom was unquestionably a good man, and wedded the woman of his choice. But what was Gomer's view of the matter? Marriages were *arranged* for Hebrew girls. Suppose, however, that she was a normal Hebrew bride, who might have developed into a happy wife and mother. Suppose then that Gomer had her own golden hopes on the wedding day, expecting and wanting to love her husband. But there is such a thing as 'incompatibility of temperament', and concerning even minor vexations there runs a too facile but comprehensible saying: 'Enough to try the patience of a saint'. It is no easy thing to be married to a genius, even if he be a theological genius. Allow that Gomer was not in the least of wanton disposition, yet equally not preternaturally good. Suppose that she took the ordinary view of the national religion, seeing nothing amiss in general, and enjoying the solemnities and fun of the Festivals as a pleasant, thrilling interlude in household drudgery. In her home she found herself confronted with *extraordinary* religion; her husband's mind preoccupied with thoughts of God and dire forebodings about Israel.[1] In that alone was one tragic cause for incomprehension

the sex-cult at the sanctuaries. Were it so, remember that such women were not profligate, and were regarded in the community as 'consecrated'. Consider also that in all likelihood they were there not by their own will but by their parents' decision. The Prophet, loathing the cult, may just possibly have felt moved to give to one such woman the sanctuary of a normal home. (iii) Most unlikely of all is it (for a different Hebrew word should have been used) that Hosea married a harlot. Were it so, what should be our reaction? Sometimes men and women have been able to do things physically repellent, because they felt it to be God's will—e.g. Father Damien's self-sacrifice in going to live with the lepers. What sort of women were harlots in Jeroboam's Israel? Some no doubt were degenerates. Far more were widows and orphan girls driven to desperation in that hard world. Some were voluntarily sensual. Were these last all unpitiable and irredeemable? It should not be forgotten that in a later century one such woman in the same beautiful Galilee was moved to tears and purity by the holy influence of Jesus, and that concerning her He said: 'Her sins, which were many, are forgiven.'

[1] It is likely that even before his marriage Hosea had felt it laid upon him to speak as a Prophet in the name of Jehovah concerning the wrongs rife in the land and the evil in its worship of Jehovah and the Baals. It is as good as certain that from his youth up his mind (like Jeremiah's) had been religiously and morally outraged by what he saw. Since he called his first child by a symbolic name that embodied a specific, 'prophetic' judgement and warning, it is quite certain that soon after the marriage terrible tension of religious concern was upon him.

between this pair. Hosea (in Prophet-manner)[1] called his first-born
son by a symbolic name, *Jezreel*. The name means 'God sows'—
i.e. 'Land made fertile by divine blessing.' But the actual town,
Jezreel, had been the scene of Naboth's murder, place of Queen
Jezebel's bloody death when rebel Jehu arrived, and whence
he drove on to Samaria to commence his reign by treacherous
massacre of King Ahab's household. Hosea explained that he
called his son *Jezreel* in order to signify that Israel's king and army
would there be bloodily shattered in a defeat which would be
God's retribution for the bloody deeds perpetrated a century
before. He called his daughter *Lo-ruhamah* ('Unpitied')—i.e.
'Jehovah's favour ended'; and his second son *Lo-ammi* ('Not my
People') to signify Jehovah's repudiation of Israel. Did Gomer,
a normal mother, like it when he insisted on those outlandish names;
or did she, infuriated, tell him that, if he believed such horrid
things, he ought to preach about them himself, but not turn her
innocent children into dismal 'walking-sermons'? We may judge
that Hosea could not fathom her moods, the sudden gusts of
temper and shrill words; and that bewilderment and agony beset
his great affection. The coming of the first child would help for a
moment to bridge the widening gulf. In speaking later of God and
Israel, Hosea used the simile of a father teaching a little child to
walk. That is a window through which we may see a day in his and
Gomer's life; for surely the mother, laughing and loving, assisted with him the valiant tottering steps. But such sunshine as
there may have been in the home was fitful. Gomer was married to
a man outside the range of her intelligence and tastes. These two
were ill-matched, and in the end she may have become a woman
nervously distraught. Seldom does a woman who has not suffered
agony of disappointment or ill-use decide to leave home and
children and safety, venturing her all for a lover's promises and
risking the horrible fate that in fact overtook Gomer. Vexation of
spirit grew too much for her; and then came temptation beyond
her power to endure. As for Hosea, he endured finding his
devotion and care less and less reciprocated, patience and tenderness
flouted—until it seemed he could do nothing right in his wife's
eyes. But the tragic discipline was testing and refining the reality of
his affection: it is no easy thing to learn to *know* that 'Love is not
provoked, hopeth all things, endureth all things'.

[1] So also Isaiah: see note 2 on p. 294.

Obviously the departure of Gomer brought the trial of his character to climax. We may guess that his neighbours did not assist him to master final bitterness. Their notion of helping would be to inform him they had long ago realized what manner of woman she was, to assure him that he was well rid of her, and to urge him to forget the worthless wretch.[1] They did not understand how horribly their counsel hurt: piteously and deeply he had cared. But were they not right about his present duty? Again and again he may have felt that he ought to cast off all pity, that Gomer's future and her fate were nothing to him now. 'Forget, forget!' He began to discover that he could not forget. He was conscious not only of his own misery, but also perplexed by the vividness of his concern for her. One simple reflection proved his salvation, because it turned his mind outwards from himself. Perhaps the comparison had long been rising in his thoughts; now it came in intensity—*As Gomer had treated him, so Israel had treated Jehovah*. If the Prophet had been a self-centred and not a humble man, this easy analogy would have been a snare to him; for it would sub-consciously have completed itself in proud thought, 'And *I* have been as good as God—as patient with Gomer as He with Israel!' Hosea drew no such disastrous conclusion.

The similes of *Father* and *Husband*, that came so lightly and loosely on the lips of men concerning God and People, flowed in his reflecting mind. To God—to Jehovah—Israel owed its very existence. In Egypt the Hebrews had been no nation, and knew him not. 'Out of Egypt have I called my son'—that was God's gift of life itself to this Nation, His gift of freedom. Truly the years in the desert had been like the experience of Childhood's innocent receiving, from the wisdom and love of a father's protection, nurture, teaching, discipline: given freely, joyously; received in half-conscious gratitude—until with Youth came comprehension and fresh eager affection responding to love. The simile changed in the Prophet's mind—youthful Israel had reached maturity, and became the Bride of Jehovah. (Hosea was idealizing the Hebrews

---

[1] It is usual to deduce from ii. 1, 2 that Hosea was aware that another than he was father of the third, and perhaps of the second, child. The writer is not at all convinced that this interpretation is justified—compare ii. 4ff., where plainly the significance is Israel's worship of the Baals, and 'her children' means the Israelites. All three names are essentially symbolic 'prophecies' about Israel, and may be completely so, having no relation to Gomer and the actual child.

whom Moses had led and taught, but for his purpose was justified; for in contrast with the sequel the Israel of the desert had been thankful and innocent, aware that it owed its all to Jehovah, responding in gratitude and trust.)

Canaan was given to that bride to be her home. Oh, wondrous, lovely, home of Israel! Every sensitive Galilaean saw its beauty. The hair-cloth tents of the passing Bedouin were too frequent in the vale of Esdraelon, and the parched monotonous sand of the desert itself too near, for a Galilaean to miss the contrast. In Israel's homeland, eyes rested on the sweep of hills and mountains up to the snowy summit of Mount Hermon; forests and trees were there, and fountains of water pouring their lavish vitalizing streams day and night; there was sunshine and blessed rain and freshening dew—gifts of God to Land and People. 'Thou waterest her furrows abundantly; Thou settlest the ridges thereof: Thou makest it soft with showers; . . . Thou crownest the year with thy goodness. . . .And the hills are girded with joy. The pastures are clothed with flocks: The valleys also are covered over with corn.'[1] Nature in Galilee sang for joy. Israel, bride of Jehovah, entered that home. How swift and terrible had been the change in her. She thanked the *Baals* for the corn and the wine and the oil, and exulted in their ugly rites. Jehovah she remembered now and then, especially in any time of trouble: then she fawned upon him. But the love of the Baals corrupted her soul, until she hoped to please Jehovah by the same sensual rites. And her heart grew hard: kindness and brotherhood were vanished virtues. Cruel, dissolute Israel! For centuries past the 'marriage' between Jehovah and Israel had been unreal—a matter of name—because the heart of the People was not given lovingly to its God. When the crash came, it would be but to make outwardly visible what had long been inwardly fact. And the tragedy had not been due to God's impatience with wayward men. Hosea began to be conscious of a divine constancy in goodness passing the patience of human beings, a ceaseless forbearance which also was not indulgence. Generation after generation God had given great and faithful men to save and to guide, to rebuke and to enlighten. But Israel had been incorrigible, and the Prophet did not shut his eyes to the black truth that now his People did not *know* the only real God, and that their ignorance was of their own making. Their eyes were

[1] Ps. lxv. 10–13.

blind, because they had made their hearts adamant. The root of the manifold wickedness in their thoughts and deeds was the deep sin of thanklessness. 'To Hosea,' says Welch, 'it was a mystery that men could take everything from affection and give nothing in return. Perhaps it does remain the final test of our strange nature, the answer men make to the things they get for nothing.' [1]

Hosea was saved from introspective self-pity, and from negative bitterness regarding the iniquity of Israel, because he perceived how far the forbearance of God surpassed the power of human character. He had been patient with Gomer for six years, the Deity with Israel for six hundred. When he so considered, the moment of illumination was near. We may surmise that it came through some such train of thought as this—Those six years had felt like an eternity. Why had he persisted so long in hope, or indeed sought to do anything for Gomer? Was it simply because he pitied her and felt merciful? No! everything had been due to a greater reality in him than pity or mercy. He had, humanly, loved her. The light shone in his soul concerning God and Israel. God's eternal Being *loves* the souls that He hath made, and the purpose of God is the ineffable purpose of *loving* goodness: that there should be a People living in righteousness and tender mercy because similar Love abides in them. Provocation does not alter the mind of God. God superhumanly loves; therefore in Him is undeviating will to cause men to *know* Himself—to know what Love is. Suddenly his own immediate spiritual error must have dawned upon him. He was trying to be very unlike God—trying to hate Gomer and forget her! 'Then said the Lord unto me, *Continue to care for Gomer.*' [2] One wonders whether, in the revulsion of feeling, for a blessed moment he laughed with joy. He could not hate, because there had been in him a gleam of the eternal Mind; a quality other than and wholly surpassing mere affection. He understood why he was unable to take his neighbours' advice; why it was sheer misery when they told him her lover had cast her off and that 'he had the laugh over her now'; why, when they brought the latest news of her increasing degradation, their words excruciated him. (How little they understood, loveless men and women!) Normal affection, which men too lightly term love, had ceased to be between Gomer and him;

[1] *Preparation for Christ in the Old Testament*, pp. 108 f.
[2] So understand iii. 1.

for that can perish and die in tragic circumstance. Hosea was beginning to discern the nature of God's love, which remains imperishable in concern and care, in infinite desire to bless. He knew now that that should be in his soul, and saw what it demanded from him.

The shock of the great truth was the Prophet's awakening call to his national duty, even as Amos in the Field of Tekoa had heard the Voice: 'Go, prophesy unto my people Israel.' But it also came upon Hosea as revelation of his individual task, which he accepted. He freed Gomer, and brought her to the security of his protection and house; not as the Righteous condescending to the Unworthy, but in longing to help her. Was all then well? The hopes of their wedding-day were gone beyond recall, 'years that the locust had eaten'. But were they now on the road to happiness, so that we may believe that 'All came right in the end' (as the fairy-tales require)? He is an optimist who fancies that. Is it probable that purchased Gomer returned home overflowing with gratitude and in peace of mind? More likely she told Hosea that she hated him more than ever, but his bread was better than beggary. The words were agony to him. But she had her share of agony also. The neighbours (to be sure) did not kill fatted calves to welcome the prodigal-wife. When Gomer went out of doors she met the sneering looks of men and the tossed heads of successful women. As for Hosea, he found his erstwhile friends wholly contemptuous of his sentimental folly. Yet he did not refuse to go on learning that Divine Love may be pierced with the nails of scorn and thrust through with the spear of contempt; but *it does not die*. Therefore, when he translated God's word to Israel, he was very great— incomparably greater than Amos, to whom it seemed that God's mercy was exhausted and it remained only to proclaim THE END. Believing that the love of God endures, Hosea knew hope that does not perish.

As we pass to certain aspects of his thought regarding Israel, it is important to recognize that, although Hosea concentrated upon Israel, the significance of what he said is not less universal than the words of Amos, who was conscious of the one God in relation to other nations also. What Hosea declared to be truth concerned the deep meaning in all human life; and ingratitude—the sin against knowledge—of which he accused Israel lies to the charge of every nation that walks not by the light it has. When Hosea speaks about Israel, we may mentally substitute 'Our World'.

So gross and materialistic were the ideas the Hebrews attached to the conventional allusions to Jehovah as *Father, Husband, Master* (*Baal*), or *King* of His People, that it is remarkable Hosea did not discard the popular terminology.[1] It was the particular quality of his genius to discern transcendental value in good relationships of human lives. So he took his hearers at their own level, and sought to make them see that they misunderstood what they thought they perfectly well understood. In consequence he achieved a miracle of insight, not only making clear the spiritual conception of the relation between God and Man, but illuminating the proper nature of the human institutions that were serving as analogies— *Marriage, Property, Government.* Often his words are as drastic and trenchant as those of Amos; but in general it is true that Amos fought evil by denunciation, Hosea by showing the beauty of whatsoever things are pure, whatsoever things are lovely.

The Hebrews thought of Marriage legalistically and carnally, the wife being a possession of her husband over whom he had right of dominance as *Baal* (*Owner* or *Master*). Hosea declared marriage relationship to be sacred just in so far as there exists reality of mutual unselfish love.[2] Jehovah is not Israel's Baal. It is because of Jehovah's fidelity in righteousness and loving-kindness and tender mercy that men may call Him Husband of His People; and that is the spirit which should unify and bless the homes of Israel. Skinner somewhere has said: 'It was an entirely new departure in the idea of marriage, and this man's amazing thought of God was born not out of the usages of society, but out of the depths of his own soul.'

Readily with their lips the Hebrews acclaimed Jehovah as the Divine *Father* of Israel; but in their lives they regarded His paternal benevolence as that of an Autocrat lavishing *largesse* on his favourites when he felt in a good mood. And so it followed that in all too many of their homes Paternity was another name for vehement authority and spasmodic interest. Like a wise, wise, man Hosea spoke in pictures. He told them that Jehovah was their Father because 'When Israel was a child, then I loved him, and

---

[1] 'Instead of rejecting the current symbolism, Hosea appropriates it; but does so in a way that lifts it wholly out of the sphere of natural religion, and makes it the vehicle of the profoundest spiritual truths.' (W. R. Smith, *Prophets of Israel*, p. 174.)

[2] See ii. 19, 20.

called my son out of Egypt...yea, I taught my child to walk, and
carried him in my arms.' The reality of fatherhood is not begetting,
but caring. And God, their Father, knew how to give good gifts
to His children. Hosea besought them to believe that none of the
produce of Canaan was the work of Baals, but all the richness of
its fertility the gift of Jehovah.[1] But how terribly they misconceived the Giver, and therefore misused His gifts. The bounties of
Nature are not flung out by God for this lucky child and that to
snatch and to hug to himself, but are the Father's provision for the
whole household in order that none of His children may lack and
suffer want. We do not realize how fundamentally possessions
test our character to the core, and that our attitude to what we
have is the immanent Judge and Revealer of our souls. 'Freely ye
have received, freely give' is an order easily unheeded or unheard.
Everything comes back to the presence or absence in us of the
loving heart, outward-looking, caring for others, finding joy in
their welfare.

The pernicious attitude to possessions vitiated Hebrew *worship*;
for the fine moral and mystical ideas our Science of Religion
perceives in ancient ritual was gold paint (worn thin) on the raw
wood of material hopes. The Hebrew High-Place was 'Stock Exchange' for a system of barter. Men offered bullocks for bounties,
reckoning that God ought to give them a square deal on the transaction. Unloving men could not conceive the ways of Love, how
that it longs to give, and its gifts are not counters in a bargain.
Wrong ideas of the nature of Deity give rise to grotesque and
coarse rites, and in turn the ritual debases the worshippers, and
then coarsened minds see nothing to criticize in the ritual.[2] It is
true that religious conviction needs to find some forms to
express reverence. But it is a deep and deadly error to gloss
over the ritual situation that confronted Hosea, search for excuses
and stress that the poor dear early Hebrews meant well. Hosea
attacked the ritual kissing of the Golden Bulls that symbolized
Jehovah at the two royal sanctuaries, and did so with unmitigated
scorn. No matter how sincerely the worshippers meant to show
reverence for their national Deity, they ought to know that such
carnal veneration of man-made images (Hos. viii. 5, 6) had no

[1] Cp. Hos. ii. 5, 8.
[2] Hos. iv. 11, 'Whoredom and wine and new wine take away the understanding'.

relation to right thought about God.[1] Amos, Hosea, Isaiah, and Jeremiah beheld Hebrew ritual (we have not done so), and they were appalled—not merely by excesses of drunkenness and license, but by animal-sacrifice itself. Flesh of bulls and blood of rams acceptable to Jehovah! Amos had thundered: 'God loathes your offerings and singing! Be done with it all! Offer justice and mercy!' His fierce uncompromising words were invaluable, but did not indicate how religious feeling should find expression. It is very interesting that Hosea (likewise declaring that Jehovah desires mercy and not sacrifice) continues 'and the knowledge of God more than burnt-offerings'. The significance of his *more than* has been much discussed. Does it mean that a reform of this sort of ritual was in his mind? Would he have been content if only the Hebrews had held Temperance Festivals, at which respectable worshippers would have witnessed honest priests slitting the throats of domestic beasts in a more refined manner? In the writer's opinion that is an absolute misjudgement of the man. When God sends a great Prophet into this world, He sends genius.[2] Unlike the writer in the Book of Ezekiel, Hosea visualized no temple in the midst of the Ideal Life he longed to behold. But (as a single revealing sentence shows, xiv. 2) he did foresee therein a Holy Place, to which men would bring, not bullocks, but sincerity of spoken words: the incense of lowliness and the gold of obedience; and the offerings laid upon its shrine would be truth in its beauty and love in its tenderness.

Hosea said a single thing about God's view of Israel's *government*: 'They have set up kings, but not by me.'[3] It is likely that he had in mind the royal murderers who followed Jeroboam on the throne of Samaria, and also the misrule that stretched far back

---

[1] W. R. Smith made a famous comment: 'By this judgement Hosea proves the depth of his religious insight; for the whole history of religion shows that no truth is harder to realize than that a worship morally false is in no sense the worship of the true God.' (*Prophets of Israel*, p. 177.)

[2] The writer holds that the great Prophetic protest was unreserved in its condemnation; and pointed not towards desperate efforts to *reform* animal-sacrifices and contemporary cult-forms, but to *transformation*, or sublimation, of Worship in *essentially* new ritual-forms, wherein the natural and the supernatural can interpenetrate in truly spiritual effectiveness—where God can meet men, as well as men seek God. Cp. James, *Origins of Sacrifice*, p. 288 (who cites Quick, *The Christian Sacraments*, pp. 204f.), and Porteous in *Record and Revelation*, p. 237.

[3] Hos. viii. 4; cp. xiii. 11.

through flourishing Jeroboam to bloody Jehu and ruthless Jezebel. But it does not follow (as some have held) from this phrase, or any other references he makes to kings and kingdom, that—doctrinaire dreamer!—he frowned on the very institution of a Monarchy as sin of mistrusting divine guidance.[1] Rather the contrary is true—that he was very conscious of the good which faithful rulers and leaders (kings and priests) might have done, and of the great evil which the great had wrought in Israel. For 'Israel' substitute 'Our World'. Whenever the privileged, the powerful, and the prosperous, to whom much has been entrusted, live in pride and sensuality it is true that, although they are kings in their own eyes, they are the devil's best advocates and are not 'the Anointed of the Lord'.

Hosea was not a sentimentalist in his faith about Divine Love. As rigorously as all the great Prophets he believed God's purpose and the deep meaning of events to be perceptible in the inflexible sequences of moral conduct. 'A corrupt tree cannot bring forth good fruit', and what men sow they reap. The inevitability of harvest (whether of good or of evil) shows that God does not vacillate, but ceaselessly wills that we shall learn from consequences to desire good and not evil. Exactly like Amos, Hosea was sure that Israel's cumulative wickedness had reached a point at which uttermost calamity must ensue, because the eternal purpose is Righteousness. The disaster might take shape in conquest by Assyria (as seemed likely), or it might be the decimation of plague, or the overturning of Nature itself. But whatever the outward form, men ought to see in the event, not some surface cause, but an act of God, the Judgement of God. The point to be stressed is Hosea's full recognition that dire facts had to be faced. The people, menaced by danger or distress, would stage plenty of tearful professions of penitence, but these would be fleeting moods.[2] God—and Hosea—knew such 'repentances'

---

[1] Cp. Welch, op. cit. pp. 117–22, who likewise does not accept the fully sweeping inference. It is true, however, that Organization was not in the foreground of Hosea's thoughts. No Messianic-king figures in his Vision of the life wherein God's purpose has been realized. For Hosea 'the Kingdom of God' is the Realm of loving hearts, and its subjects need no compelling hand to keep them in the right way.

[2] Welch rightly insists that the Prophets were not sensitive political barometers, and their attitude to contemporary affairs is intelligible only as based on fundamental religious-moral conviction. (Op. cit. pp. 105 f.)

only too well—'O Ephraim, what shall I do unto thee? O Judah, what shall I do unto thee? for your goodness is as a morning cloud, and as the dew that goeth early away.'[1] Exactly like Amos, Hosea saw that the nation had sunk to a present baseness incapable of authentic, lasting, reformation. Amos had had to face the sombre truth about the national corruption with no profounder belief than that the merciful God is just, and therefore he could foresee only a Judgement which would be final. Amos (theologically) put an end to Hope. Hosea's genius, confronting the same actualities, put an end to Despair.

Enduring compassion, which reality of pure love had created in his soul, led Hosea through darkness to the door of Hope. Imagine how that could happen within his own home. He looked at unhappy Gomer, and began to see great reason for compassion concerning her, and great need for humility and contrition concerning his own imperfect self. He realized now (too late) how incompatible they had been from the start, and that he had asked of her more than she could give; yet he had felt wronged and righteous when she did not respond to his interests and moods. (There is nothing like intense preoccupation with religious *ideas* for making a man plume himself on being godly, and deem others who are less interested less godly.) Unwittingly but infuriatingly he had made many mistakes in his insistent expectation that she should fully share his thoughts. This suggestion about Hosea's reflection on himself is conjecture, but we may be sure that he became the truer Prophet of God the more humility taught him that he, like Gomer, was in his own way an erring human being standing in the selfsame need of God's all-comprehending patience. Love, said St Paul, is not proud. Compassion taught Hosea to see Gomer in the light of God's concern for her. Compassion pictured what she had been in the innocence and zest of youth—the seeds of good that had not ripened. Hosea's compassionate memory strove to dwell on every glad and hopeful hour. Poor Gomer, who had not seen the beauty there could be in life. Human severity and conceit might

---

[1] Hos. vi. 4. The well-known, preceding *vv.* 1–3 should (almost certainly) not be construed euphemistically, but as tragic irony—contrition of the lips, but not of the heart. The Hebrews are confident Jehovah does not sulk; they have but to profess penitence, and swiftly (one, two, three days) He will be in a good mood and forgive them!

pronounce that the loss had been her own fault. God alone knew how much it had been her misfortune. Hosea knew now that it was not for him to estimate her worth, as if he were omniscient and perfect. If she had married another kind of man, she might have been a happy woman; and there would not have been that tragic figure with the angry, miserable eyes. Ground for compassion, yes. But what vestige of ground for hope that she would ever alter towards life and him? She said he was not 'her husband' and bitterly called him 'her owner' (*Baal*): for had he not *bought* her? Nor did he strive to renew their life upon pretence. Gomer did not love him: therefore he said to her they could not be as once they had been—husband and wife. But he said that to her on this wise: 'Thus shall it be between us many days.' (In Hebrew *many days* is idiom for 'an indefinitely long time'.) God had not said to him 'Be thou this woman's judge', but 'Continue to care for her'. Hosea's hand did not slam the door of Hope to exclude Gomer. If it had, he would have been excluding himself from Love Divine. It was for him to do what, in his imperfection, he still could do— be the servant of God's thought of Gomer, God's ceaseless will that her spirit should be healed.

Hosea had compassion on the multitude in Israel, although he had no illusions about 'the plain man and his wife'. How greatly they had been wronged by those who should have greatly helped. The civil rulers? Example set by those in high responsibility is seen by many eyes. From Samaria it was not health and healing that had been diffused through the community, but deadly, spreading poison. Israel's clergy? It was the function of priests to teach 'the manner of the God'. Israel's priests had been trusted to declare the one God and the one righteousness of brethren. But, in sum, the priests offered to the people the riot and profligacy of the festivals as the worship of Jehovah, and grew fat on the proceeds. What chance had ordinary men and women to understand that their God wanted mercy, and did not delight in the blood of sheep and oxen, or bestow His special favour on pilgrims who were at pains to kiss the flank of the Golden Bull? It was all too true that existing Israel *did not know God*. Yet on Hosea's lips that tragic verdict of fact was not judgement of final condemnation, but compassion throwing wide open the door of opportunity—that those who loved the Lord should continue patiently to teach the uncomprehended knowledge.

Within himself Hosea possessed a deeper reason to hope. In *agony* he had come to know the nature of Divine Love, when the road was blocked against his distracted wish to hate or forget Gomer. He had learnt that Suffering can be a wondrous teacher.[1] Therefore (unlike Amos) he was not shut up to interpreting the coming catastrophe negatively—that is to say, as signifying that, God's forbearance being exhausted, He had no resource left save in justice to give the sinners the thrashing they so richly deserved, and make an End. Hosea could trust that in the furnace of affliction the soul of Israel would be purified. He was right to hope. For, if there be any goodness or greatness latent in men and women, the shock and challenge of common adversity richly evoke it. But let it not be supposed that the man who daily faced the near-impossibility that Gomer would ever be transformed in spirit was facile in expectation concerning Israel. Realistically he pictured alternation of doubt and expectancy, despair and determination, taking place in the mind of God Himself: 'Because of the wickedness of their doings, I will drive them out of my house: I will love them no more'. . . 'How shall I give thee up, Ephraim? . . . mine heart is turned within me, my compassions are kindled together. I will not execute the fierceness of mine anger, I will not return to destroy Ephraim: for I am God, and not man.'[2] Only the last line drawn in that picture explains why for Hosea hope could at last become peace of ultimate assurance. *God is God*—Hosea put final trust in the resources of superhuman love.

The Prophet foresaw the end of Israel's kingdom; the cessation of its ritual worship; horrors of violence so terrible that he longed there might be few children to endure the misery; privation such that it would be like return to the hardship of desert-life.[3] He envisaged the nation driven out of Canaan and scattered in

---

[1] This is the great theme of expiation and deliverance worked out in the dramas of Aeschylus and Sophocles. There is remarkable analogy between the attitude of Hosea and that of Sophocles, 'where the note of sympathy for human weakness makes itself heard throughout his poetry'. (Adam, *Religious Teachers of Greece*, p. 178.) Even more notable is Abbott's remark (*Hellenica*, p. 66—cited by Adam, op. cit. p. 162): 'The undertone of divine vengeance running through the dramas of Aeschylus seems in Sophocles to pass away into an echo of divine compassion, and we move from the gloom of "sin and sorrow" towards the dawning of a brighter day in which strength is made perfect in weakness.'

[2] Hos. xi. 8, 9.   [3] See Hos. ii. 14, 15.

captivity. Nevertheless, he believed that if only the outcome was realization of past wickedness and longing to live rightly, Israel would be restored to dwell again, worthily, in its land. But how could there be restoration from overthrow so utterly shattering? It is clear that the Prophet's conviction rested in belief that 'What God had done once, He could do again'. In the beginning God in His sovran will had called this People out of non-existence. God could renew its life. God, who made all things, can make all things new.

Some have felt Hosea to be the least practical of the great Prophets, on the ground that his hope depended on a miraculous intervention by God in the visible world, and that he looked for a quite literal restoration of historic Israel. The writer (for a reason finally to be suggested) considers that view is unjust to a poetic and tender mind glimpsing transcendent thought upon ultimate meaning in Life, and using the inadequacies of language to express its intuition. Observe what certainly was achieved by Hosea's character as well as by his thoughts. His fidelity, faith and hope influenced Isaiah and Jeremiah after him, and *they* initiated the most practical steps there could be towards making this world a better world. Secondly, in accepting it to be the will of God that he should not cease to *desire* to do all possible for Gomer, whom others accounted worthless, Hosea asserted in relation to this woman the profound principle that there is in human personality indestructible *sacred* value, intrinsic in its very nature. His attitude was indeed assertion of the magnificent claim expressed in the famous words, *Non tantum vile pro quo Christus mortuus est.* Thirdly, Hosea conceived God as the Redeemer: for in the dread realities of moral consequence he saw Divine wisdom and patience enabling men as free beings to discern Good from Evil, and to choose that which is good. This man of sorrows and acquainted with grief kept faith and hope because, beyond the bounds of human affection, he believed that God is Love illimitable. Thus Hosea presents the only reading of the mystery of Good and Evil, and the only conception of Deity, which modern thought should entertain. In himself the Prophet attained the quality of Love. We cannot sensibly suppose that the Creator is inferior to the best in finite beings. Finally, then, consider his ultimate hope. Two ethereal passages, ii. 14–23 and xiv. 1–8, disclose the Prophet's inmost spiritual experience, which may thus be phrased—

'Many days', assuredly, Hosea had to stand at the door of Hope looking towards the Land of Heart's Desire only to find it hidden by mists of perplexity and pain. But there came to him a moment when the clouds vanished, and (whether in the body or out of the body he knew not) he seemed to enter and to see that Holy Land and them that dwelt therein. In his Vision its contours took form as the contours of the beautiful Galilee where he had lived and suffered and longed. It was his homeland of Israel—the same, yet different. For the mountains and valleys were suffused by the light of love, and shadows of sin and grief were absent. Earth and sky were transfigured; and he saw that Nature offered the abundance of its gifts freely, because now there were men to receive and use them lovingly. And as he wondered how this miracle of fertility had come to pass, he heard the voice of Nature's Maker, saying: 'I will be as the dew unto Israel: he shall blossom as the lily, and cast forth his roots as Lebanon. His branches shall spread, and his beauty shall be as the olive tree, and his scent as Lebanon.'[1] [Dreamer of dreams! But to-day, if there were peace and goodwill in the hearts of men, wisdom and skill could make a garden of our world, and the hungry would be fed and the naked clothed.] People were dwelling in this Galilee of Vision—his own People—but they too were different, as if their hearts had been healed; and as if a great menace had passed away, because weapons of war were no longer in all the earth. He saw his People gathered together to offer worship—thankful men and thankful women—grateful because a clean heart had been given to them and a right spirit had been renewed within them. No longer a Land unholy, a People whom God could neither bless nor acknowledge as His own. In his Vision Hosea heard the voice of God proclaiming: JEZREEL! RUHAMAH! AMMI—the very names he had longed that his children could rightly bear—*Holy Land, Beloved, My People.* Then to the Nation God spoke these gentle words: '*I will betroth thee unto me for ever; yea, I will betroth thee unto me in righteousness and justice, in lovingkindness and tender mercy.*' And in response to the Divine promise, Hosea heard Israel's answer—'*My husband!*'

We may believe that, as the Prophet wondered what had made it possible for him to see this Land, and to hear those blessed words, he remembered (as in a dream) that he had suffered; but now knew that God had been with him from the beginning of his

[1] Hos. ii. 21; xiv. 5, 6.

life even unto that hour, because out of the very heart of his
suffering had come his work, and he had been able to open a door
through which others would enter to dwell in the land of the
loving heart. Hosea came back to the life in Time and Space;
wherein men may discern Eternal Verities only imperfectly, as in
a mirror darkly. But as again he faced duty in this world, his
mind was at rest and his patience renewed. It seemed to Hosea
that for a moment he had been allowed to see the *Future*, and
to be certain that God's good purpose would come to pass. He
had seen, not the Future, but the innermost meaning of things
past, present, and to come; the Reality that appearances veil; the
worth (known to God) of our imperfect spirits; the glory of
redeeming and abiding Love; the Eternal in the Temporal.

Some may think as regards all this that a baffled man was
projecting his wishes onto the impenetrable screen of the Inscrutable, and beholding his longings reflected back from the
clouds. But others are free to believe that, where great love is
found in a human soul, the light of Infinite Reality is reflected in
the pool of finite consciousness.

CHAPTER XIV

THE ETERNAL IN THE TEMPORAL

Space and Time—mental conditions of finite consciousness—daunt human imagination. The world is so vast, its inhabitants so numerous. So many passing Ages have passed, so many more seem likely to come. Astronomers chill us by forecasting an eventual frozen finish for Man upon an Earth become too cold to sustain animate life—they alone know how many billion years hence. Even when they add that by a billionth chance collision with a flaming comet might sooner put a flaming end to the whole business, that is still cold comfort. We long to feel assured that there is good *meaning* in life, and great *purpose* to be achieved in the process of history. But is there any solid evidence to sustain such hope? Much Indian philosophy, covering defeat in dust-clouds of Pantheism, would have us throw down our arms and acknowledge—All is Illusion, and all endeavour futile. The ancient Greeks were impressed and depressed because, as they looked anxiously to the past, they saw no sign of continuous progress in civilization, but instead an ebb and flow of tides no human power could control. The poet Hesiod memorably pictured their reluctant conclusion in the notion that Time shows, and will ever show, an inevitable cycle of Epochs—from an Age of *Gold*, to *Silver*, to *Brass*, to *Iron*: when the wheel would come full circle and another 'Age of Gold' recur. Some modern historians in a sophisticated way take much the same sombre, 'circular' view; stressing the fall of civilizations and the inevitability of periods of mental and moral degeneration.[1] To some such, radical, pessimism thinkers are bound to come who do not accept a religious view of human experience, and fail to see eternal values *in* things temporal. In antiquity only the Jews, guided by the wisdom of the great Prophets, held resolutely the 'linear' view of history: that there is ultimate meaning, purpose, progress, in general history and in our brief lives of threescore years and ten

[1] E.g. Spengler, *The Decline of the West*. On the importance of this issue, see Söderblom, *The Living God*; Cairns, *The Riddle of the World*, pp. 242 ff.; Edwyn Bevan, *The Hope of a World to Come*.

(measured by Time). The religious-minded in the Western world are likewise made of sterner stuff in wrestling with the problem. Clough poetically exhorts us: 'Say not the struggle naught availeth, the labour and the wounds are vain.' And not only Western poets and theologians, but many historians and sociologists also, feel that moral values are not illusion, and moral (as well as material) progress a mighty fact, despite the setbacks. Taking the broad view of history, Dodd remarks: 'In that sphere it is not difficult to see a broad rhythm of historic movement which does exhibit something of that inherent justice of things.... The mind of men will not willingly let that discovery drop, however the notion of justice may need to be modified.'[1] But Western stout-heartedness, under the formidable spell of Time, is apt to narrow its hope to expectation of 'some far-off, divine, event to which the whole Creation moves'. And, indeed, confidence that present Imperfection can, and should, be shaped towards Perfection would seem to be a most necessary attitude. But the emancipating thought ('the Eternal *in* the Temporal') is missed, if we allow ourselves to picture Life's meaning and purpose as Humanity striving to reach some far-distant port across the wide ocean of Time. A thousand years may seem to God (as the Psalmist said) like yesterday when it is past; it is distressingly long for distressed humans. Why should remotest Posterity ride blissfully at anchor in the harbour of Utopia, and all previous generations experience only the struggle ''gainst wind and tide to gain the farther shore'? It does not seem fair; and when elemental justice enters protest, it is safe to think that something is amiss or missing in the picture.

The great Prophets of the eighth century, Amos, Hosea, Isaiah (as also later, Jeremiah), believed that God would bring the course of history to an end through 'a sudden and violent upheaval of the physical and social conditions of human life, to be followed by a new order of things in which the divine rule on earth is realized and all nature becomes subservient to the needs of a renewed humanity'. Further they believed the New Creation to be very near in Time: 'the immediate sequel to the political catastrophe which the Prophets saw to be imminent.'[2] In this expectation they were mistaken; but the error affects the *form*, not the *substance* of their

[1] *Authority of the Bible*, pp. 102f.
[2] Skinner, *Isaiah* (*Cambridge Bible Series*, 1915), p. lx.

Faith. The essence of their conviction of the existence and purpose of God, and therefore of the meaning of our life, was a vastly more important matter.

The unthinking care not for all these things: sufficient unto the hour is the occupation thereof. Determined, irreligious men trouble seldom about Final Meaning and Ultimate Values, lest their native resolution should be 'sicklied o'er with the pale cast of thought'. They strive to shape the immediate future, convinced that the battle is to the strong, and they make Efficiency their God. Irresolute men bend before the tempest of their forcefulness. But sometimes they encounter still more resolute men who confront Might by Right. When that happens high significance is revealed in life, and history may be shaped to noble ends. It happened thus in A.D. 1940, when one man steeled the spirit of his nation to attempt the seemingly impossible and fight on. Concerning him an American Journal wrote these words: 'He saved the British people, and through them saved the whole structure of rational and civilized world-society in the hour of its greatest peril';[1] and a British Journal this: 'In 1940 this country had sunk to a lower trough than any nation in modern times has reached without going down. Humanly speaking, we might have gone under had one man, who was there, not been there. One man made all the difference. And the man was Mr Churchill.'[2] History is rightly measured, not by Time, but by the quality of lives. In 740 B.C. one man made all the difference, and turned the future of his race, and the trend of Western civilization, towards belief in Right. The man was Isaiah, a citizen of Jerusalem.[3]

[1] *The New York Herald Tribune* (27 July 1945).

[2] *The Observer*, London (29 July 1945).

[3] Authentic sayings of Isaiah must be sought only in chapters i–xxxiii of the great Book of Isaiah. Even in those chapters there is much not by Isaiah, or doubtfully so—many verses and phrases, and the following longer passages: iv. 2–6 (?); xi. 10–16; xii, xiii–xiv. 23; xv, xvi; xix. 16–25; xxi; xxiii; xxiv–xxvii. But those deductions leave a splendid amount of reliable information concerning the Prophet's 'Call', beliefs, reflections, speech and deeds during the fateful years 740–701 B.C. Chapters xxxvi–xxxix of the Book of Isaiah are in prose—a parallel version of the narrative given in II Kings regarding Isaiah and King Hezekiah at the time of the Assyrian invasion in 701. Chapters xl–lxvi (and probably xxxiv, xxxv) preserve utterances of an anonymous Prophet or Prophets, living at least 150 years after the time of Isaiah. Those chapters are considered in Chapter XVI of this work.

§1. *Things seen and temporal*

Syria and Palestine in the ninth century B.C. suffered at times from
Assyrian armies which came and fought, and slaughtered and
plundered, but then returned home to Mesopotamia. Assyria in
the second half of the eighth century (Isaiah's life-work as a
Prophet covered the years 740–701) was a much more terrible
proposition. Its kings were extending an Empire, and knew how
to do it. Masses of chariots gave their armies bewildering speed.
To that they added invention of siege-engines capable of reducing
fortress-towns their columns had had to by-pass in the swift
advance. They treated the defeated with such brutality that the
hearts of the yet unconquered were appalled. And they carried
away great numbers of the population, replacing them by alien
settlers from distant places. *Blitzkrieg*, Brutality and Captivity—
an efficient trio. Assyrian kings practised the art of propaganda by
bragging about what they had done and what they would do—
'such boasting as the Gentiles use', as Rudyard Kipling termed
the art.[1] Isaiah's words, when the Assyrians were menacing
Jerusalem, preserve an echo of the fanfares of the Nazis of antiquity
in full tide of victory—'As one gathereth eggs that are forsaken,
have I gathered all the earth: and there was none that moved the
wing, or that opened the mouth, or chirped.'...'Hath any of the
gods of the nations delivered his land out of the hand of the king of
Assyria? Where are the gods of Hamath and Arpad? where are
the gods of Sepharvaim? and have they delivered Samaria out of
my hand?'[2] To the men of the little nations in Isaiah's time (but
not to Isaiah) one conclusion seemed inevitable—that Might
makes history. No doubt their own Gods existed, but would even
their combined strength suffice to resist that of *Asshur*, mighty
God of Assyria? Their statesmen found those 40 years a dreadful
time to have to live in: one was so likely ere long to be dead or
deported. Choice between three evils was offered: 'Buy the favour
of Assyria by crippling tribute'—'Stand neutral' (which infuriated neighbouring States resolved on organizing resistance,

---

[1] After the terrific, *drawn* battle at Karkar in 853 B.C., the baffled King of
Assyria (Shalmaneser III), back in his capital at Nineveh, recorded on a
black obelisk—now in the British Museum—such victory as never was over
the Syrians and Palestinians.

[2] See Isa. x. 1–11, 14; xxxvi. 18f.

and left it open to the Assyrians to say that he who had not been for them had been against them)—or 'Unite and fight'. To their credit the minor States were hopeful in facing the menace, and courageous when crisis had to be met. They felt that a coalition of their forces might halt the Assyrian advance, and that, if only Egypt joined in, there was good chance of success. The peril might vanish if a new Assyrian king was a weakling, or if revolt somewhere in the vast Empire put a stop to his plans. The Syrians fought bravely. Israel's capital, Samaria, managed to hold out unaided for over twelve months in 722–721 B.C. Judah and Jerusalem were a step farther south from the peril than Israel, and in difficult country aside from the main track of the Assyrians' march, if their ultimate, precarious, aim was to overthrow Egypt. No wonder Jerusalem's leaders were of doubtful mind.

Appreciate the impact of the growingly awful news as it came to the ears of Jerusalem—place after place conquered: Hamath, Arpad, Sepharvaim; in 734 B.C. Damascus captured, and Galilee ravaged. Then the frightful news in 723–721 that Israel was invaded—Samaria stormed—the sister-kingdom at an end. From then onwards Jerusalem faced Assyrian territory scarce 20 miles distant along an indefensible border. By conquering Samaria the Assyrians had opened the mountain-passes to the Palestinian coast. In 720 Sargon, their king, defeated an Egyptian army at Raphia on the southern border of Palestine. In 711 the coastal towns revolted: the Assyrians came and captured the immensely strong fortress-town of Ashdod. It grew clear that they were preparing for the feat of leaping their army across the 150 miles of desert in order to conquer Egypt. But for that purpose they must hold securely the Palestinian coast as their base of operations. What more likely now than that they would compel the surrender of Jerusalem to protect the flank of their army? Such was the situation in things seen and temporal, when Isaiah was Prophet from 740–701.

The menace of Assyria became dismayingly apparent to the Palestinians about 745 B.C., just when Jeroboam II's forty years of prosperous rule in Samaria drew to its close. During the same forty years the southern kingdom also saw only one king—prosperous Uzziah,[1] who died in 740. In estimating the feelings of the flourishing citizens of Jerusalem when Isaiah began to prophesy

[1] Called *Azariah* in the Book of Kings.

observe that prolonged security had preceded the fear which now beset them. Throughout the ensuing years to 701, during which a mistaken step might entail not only loss of independence but massacre or deportation, Isaiah was never afraid, never hesitant what the nation ought to do.

§2. *Isaiah's Vision of Reality*

Isaiah may have been in the courts of the actual temple in Jerusalem when trance came upon him, but the temple and altar and ministrant, angelic figures mentioned in his description of his Vision are of course not the temple on earth but the 'temple' of heaven—the Holy Place of things eternal. It is not questioned that in Isa. vi. 1–13 we have before us the Prophet's own words concerning his supernormal experience:[1]

In the year that king Uzziah died I saw the Lord sitting upon a throne, high and lifted up, and his train[2] filled the temple. Above him stood the seraphim: each one had six wings; with twain he covered his face, and with twain he covered his feet, and with twain he did fly. And one cried unto another, and said, Holy, holy, holy, is the Lord of hosts: the whole earth is full of his glory. And the foundations of the thresholds were moved at the voice of him that cried, and the house was filled with smoke. Then said I, Woe is me! for I am undone; because I am a man of unclean lips, and I dwell in the midst of a people of unclean lips: for mine eyes have seen the King, the Lord of hosts. Then flew one of the seraphim unto me, having a live coal[3] in his hand, which he had taken with the tongs from off the altar: and he touched my mouth with it, and said, Lo, this hath touched thy lips; and thine iniquity is taken away, and thy sin purged. And I heard the voice of the Lord, saying, Whom shall I send, and who will go for us? Then I said, Here am I; send me.[4] And he said, Go, and tell this people, Hear ye indeed,

[1] Otto, *Das Heilige* (Eng. trans.), pp. 63, 78: 'If a man does not feel what the *numinous* (sense of the Supernatural) is when he reads the sixth chapter of *Isaiah*, then no "preaching, singing, telling" (in Luther's phrase) can avail him.'

[2] I.e. the skirts of His vesture. The impression intended by the phrase is that the Prophet is conscious of the Divine Presence, but does not raise his eyes to look upon the King's person.

[3] Or, *heated stone*.

[4] This is not proud confidence. Cp. W. G. Elmslie, *Memoirs and Sermons*, p. 229: 'If ever Isaiah was not thinking of himself at all, if ever he had utterly forgotten self, and pride, and all things, and was conscious only of God, and goodness, and gratitude, it was then, when his heart was running over with

but understand not; and see ye indeed, but perceive not. Make the heart of this people fat, and make their ears heavy, and shut their eyes; lest they see with their eyes, and hear with their ears, and understand with their heart, and turn again, and be healed.[1] Then said I, Lord, how long? And he answered, Until cities be waste without inhabitant, and houses without man, and the land become utterly waste, and the Lord have removed men far away, and the forsaken places be many in the midst of the land. And if there be yet a tenth in it, it shall again be eaten up: as a terebinth, and as an oak, whose stock remaineth, when they are felled; so the holy seed is the stock thereof.[2]

In the intensity of this trance three convictions were for ever established in Isaiah's mind. First, he knew that the world and all that it contains is as naught beside the reality of GOD, who is its Creator and Controller. Second, nothing that human strength effects could alter God's purpose or avert the end towards which He is directing history. Third, Isaiah felt the splendour of God as measureless moral purity; and yet, in the very instant of his confession of sinfulness, knew himself to be, not only forgiven, but called and accepted by God into the service of the Divine purpose. From these three immutable beliefs his subsequent thought flowed as a river from its source.

§3. *Isaiah's Policy*

Isaiah went to his life-work sure that (however terribly his efforts might prove to be in vain) he must not cease to strive to convince his People of these truths; and he himself became convinced that whosoever among them responded would be accepted by God, and preserved when decimating retribution came upon the nation. It would be God's will through these faithful men to raise up a new

wonder, love, and praise for God's unspeakable mercy to him. It was not presumption; it was a true and beautiful instinct, that made him yearn with resistless longing to do something for God who had shown such grace to him.'

[1] The significance of this verse can readily be misunderstood. As in Hosea i. 2 (see p. 269), it is an instance of the Hebrew idiom which treats the actual outcome of an action as having been its sole intention. Skinner (op. cit. p. 50) well says: 'Isaiah realized the profound truth that the most decisive and searching judgement to which men are subjected lies in the abundance of the revelations of God vouchsafed to them'—and compares St John iii. 19.

[2] The concluding words ('so...thereof') are absent in the LXX text, and in all likelihood are a late, explanatory, addition to the original Hebrew, inserted in view of the development of Isaiah's teaching.

'Israel' in a world renewed.[1] For, further, the Prophet—sure that the good purpose of the omnipotent Deity could not fail—came to believe that after the initial judgement on Israel, a final *universal* act of God would bring to pass a new Age of Righteousness. Stated thus in summary prosaic fashion, these expectations will seem to the reader naïve. Their real depth, and essential value for human issues at any time, will, it is hoped, grow apparent in the course of the Chapter. We cannot date specific utterances of Isaiah as assuredly given in the years immediately following his Vision in 740 B.C., but it is absurd to suppose that he kept silence, or merely attacked ritual and moral evils, saying nothing about these basic convictions. His thought (implicit in the Vision) that God would accept and use those who repented and trusted must have been established in his mind soon afterwards, for we find that in 735 he had a little son called by a name that summed up the belief.[2] We may safely infer that by 735 the citizens of Jerusalem and Ahaz, their king, were well aware of this earnest man and his peculiar message, and that they found him mystifying, frightening and vexatious.

(i) '*Be not afraid.*' In 735 B.C. the kingdoms of Syria and Israel hadresolved that they would fight the Assyrian army, if it came. They needed every man they could muster; and, when Ahaz refused to aid them, the two allied kings marched, or threatened to march, against Jerusalem in order to replace him by one who would be of their mind. Opinion in Jerusalem may have been divided, and Ahaz's position precarious. Isaiah (master of words) says that 'his heart was moved, and the heart of his people, as the trees of the forest are moved by the wind'. Ahaz decided both to defend his city against their threat, and also to invite the Assyrians' good-will by sending tribute. Isaiah saw the situation differently. Inward compulsion came upon him that God called him to make this issue a crucial test for king and people, whether they would calmly trust that God was overruling history; or trust in them-

---

[1] Isaiah called those who would repent by a word, *Shear*, which means *A Remnant*. It is difficult to select a satisfactory English phrase. *The Remnant* sounds too tattered; *The Pious* too smug; *The Loyalists* too vague; *The Survivors* too reminiscent of shipwreck. Best paraphrase perhaps is *The Believing*, or *The Faithful*.

[2] Isa. vii. 3, 4. (*Shear-jashub*; i.e. 'A few will repent' *or* 'return'.) Cp. also viii. 1–4.

selves, striving to shape events to their liking by devices of human policy and power: 'Then said the Lord unto Isaiah, Go forth now to meet Ahaz, thou, and Shear-jashub thy son, at the end of the conduit of the upper pool in the highway of the fuller's field; and say unto him, "Take heed, and be quiet; fear not".'[1]

At this encounter, famous in religious history, Isaiah put his (shall we say?) already well-known alternative in the most solemn possible way. In Jehovah's name he declared that by the time an infant had learnt to say *Father* and *Mother* Syria and Israel would be overthrown by the Assyrians. Jehovah would give the king any token of assurance he liked to name, if only he and his people would take the way of trust and amend their lives.[2] Ahaz knew he was not going to try to become a saint, and that, if he did, his subjects would not follow suit. Politically the Prophet's demand (to do nothing, and keep calm!) seemed to him the least expedient, the most obviously foolish, course to take. Categorically he refused—he replied to the promised assurance that he would not tempt God. Isaiah answered that the rejected assurance ('sign') would come to pass! God's intentions do not change. The only consequence of Ahaz's disbelief was that he, and those who also were not willing to see God's purpose in all events, would be utterly overthrown by calamity when it came.

Some sympathy may be felt for Ahaz, seeking the most expedient way, unconscious that 'God' for him meant naught except his own sagacity. It is arguable that, if Ahaz had allowed the confederates to walk in and Judah at that time been drawn into

---

[1] See the Commentaries on the important passage, Isa. vii. 3–17. The child's name means 'A remnant *shall repent* or *shall be restored*'. Welch rightly stresses that Isaiah's personal experience of divine forgiveness and vocation 'coloured all that he had to say as to God's will for any man. No man who holds this truth as the source of his religious life and his religious work can be a mere prophet of denunciation.' Therefore Isaiah's message to his nation had in it a like offer of reconciliation and renewal. (*The Religion of Israel*, p. 153.)

[2] Isaiah's promise that Syria would be struck down within (say) three or four years came to pass, for its kingdom was overthrown by the Assyrians in 733. But the kingdom of Israel lasted on for twelve years, to 721. The non-fulfilment of the second part of the prediction is excellent evidence that the verse exactly preserves the Prophet's words to Ahaz. A late conjecture about what he had said would have conformed the oracle to the then-known course of events. Regarding vii. 8 (apparently a curious marginal comment brought into the text) see the Commentaries.

overt opposition to Assyria, the Great Power would have gone on to take Jerusalem when Samaria was taken in 721 B.C.; and in that case (humanly speaking) the seeds of profound religion sown by Isaiah could not have had time to ripen and to come to harvest a century later in the time of Jeremiah. Cromwell said (sincerely, however) that he intended both to trust in God, and to keep his powder dry. Ahaz probably felt awed and anxious, because transparently Isaiah was not offering his *opinion*, but conveying the solemn word which Jehovah had inspired him to utter. But there were other prophets who could be relied on ecstatically to say otherwise. Lest the reader should sympathize overmuch with the king, consider this—Ahaz decided (1) to placate Assyria, although acknowledgement of its overlordship would involve paying highest honour to the great God of Assyria in Jerusalem's temple; and (2) to make quite sure of Jehovah's goodwill by offering up his son as a burnt-sacrifice! Jehovah for the mind of Ahaz, and Jehovah for the mind of Isaiah, meant two very different things.

Despairing of Ahaz, Isaiah appealed to the People; and met with no success. He told them that the power of God—the Holy One of Israel—was irresistible. (Pleasant hearing.) He said that the idols of which their land was full, and all the images adored in other lands, were man-made *nothings*,[1] insults to the real God—the One and Only G OD. (Unbelievable! Was Asshur, God of the Assyrians, nothing?) But next he said that all-powerful Jehovah (their own God!) was about to bring disaster upon them for their wickedness—disaster which only those would survive who repented and faced whatever befell as the working of His righteous purpose. Insistently he said: 'In repentance and quietude ye shall be saved; in calm and confidence shall be your strength', and 'If ye will not trust, ye shall not stand.'[2] (What did he mean? It did not seem common sense.) Pungently he rebuked the vice and cruelty that disgraced city and country. (They liked not at all the moral challenge, which they did understand.) So the People waited on events. Down went Syria before the Assyrians in 733! Israel unaided was no menace to Judah, and, best of all, Ahaz had placated the Assyrians. O wise king! O foolish Prophet! The populace had had enough of Isaiah and his incessant sermon: 'Only believe, and thou shalt see that *Yah* is all in all to

---

[1] Cp. Isa. ii. 8, 20; xvii. 8; xxxi. 7.
[2] Isa. xxx. 15 (so translate). Cp. vii. 9.

thee.' The ribald mocked. One day they crowded round him, and someone started the fun, shouting, 'Blah, Blah! Yah, Yah!' Isaiah answered that, if they would not learn truth in plain Hebrew, the day would come when they would be taught the lesson in Assyrian.[1] The Prophet felt at this stage that a last chance had been given both to the rulers and to the citizens in general. What he next did made 'the world of difference' to history; but it is convenient to refer to that later in the Chapter.

(ii) '*God is our refuge and strength.*' About 720 B.C. Ahaz was succeeded by Hezekiah. Hezekiah is credited with specific measures to reform the cult, and it is accepted that religiously and morally he was a sincere man; one therefore who was likely to be impressed by Isaiah. Throughout his twenty and more years on the throne, there was a tug-of-war between those who were for accepting Assyrian dominance, and those who were optimistically in favour of joining schemes of the fortress-towns of the Palestinian coastal plain (formerly the Philistine cities) to concert opposition with the powerful aid of Egypt. In 720 an Assyrian army under Sargon swept down upon them, and showed its might by defeating an Egyptian army on the southern border. Again in 705 Sargon crushed a revolt of the Palestinians led by Ashdod, and captured that powerful fortress. On neither occasion does Judah seem to have been implicated, and that may be due to the influence of Isaiah. At one time a pact with Egypt had been made. Isaiah told the schemers, cock-a-hoop with their success, that instead of ensuring safety they had made a covenant with death.[2] His brilliant word-picture of an invincible Assyrian army tearing south along the highlands to the gates of Jerusalem may belong to this period.[3] He prophesied: 'Woe to them that go down to Egypt for help...and trust in chariots, because they are many, and in horsemen, because they are very strong; but they look not unto the Holy One of Israel, neither seek the Lord!...Now the Egyptians are men, and not God; and their horses flesh, and not spirit.'[4] Because Isaiah in 735 had denounced Ahaz for coming to terms with Assyria, whereas now he opposed those who were for defying Assyria, he has been charged with inconsistency. Isaiah

---

[1] Isa. xxviii. 10–13. Reiterated syllables suggest the mockers' scorn of the Prophet's repeated teaching—ʒav laʒav, qav laqav.

[2] Isa. xxviii. 14, 15, 18.   [3] Isa. x. 28–32.

[4] Isa. xxxi. 1–3.

was not weighing political alternatives, and there is no inconsistency. 'The religious motive in both cases was the same—his antipathy to the spirit of unbelief which he discovered in all attempts to effect political salvation by human wisdom and the help of heathen States.'[1] He told the plotters with Egypt that men who are aware of the only real God do not scurry hither and thither with palpitating hearts.[2]

In 705 B.C. Sargon died, and disturbances were widespread in the great empire. Hopes ran high in Palestine, and this time Hezekiah was completely committed to the revolt. But Sargon's successor, Sennacherib, was no less a grand monarch. In 701 came the climax. He and his great army arrived in the coastal plain, set to work to besiege its fortress-towns, and sent a task-force up to the Judaean hills. Forty-six of its defended places were overrun. High Assyrian officers went to Jerusalem demanding surrender, mocking its citizens for relying on Egypt, 'that broken reed'; jeering at their impotent God, *Jehovah*; offering them choice of 'siege, starvation, defeat, massacre' or 'unconditional surrender—in which case the great king was likely to spare their lives, but perhaps would deport them'. There was an unexpectable sequel. Either plague broke out in the main Assyrian army in the plain, or serious news came from Nineveh that compelled Sennacherib to return. The conquering host suddenly departed, and Jerusalem found itself delivered as by miracle. Had not Jehovah at the last moment saved His city? It was easy for the populace to think so.

Tradition told that in the fateful hour Hezekiah in his desperation had entreated Isaiah to seek Jehovah's guidance,[3] and that the Prophet had answered that Hezekiah was to defy the enemy because Jehovah Himself would now protect the city; protect it in such wise that the Assyrians, blasphemers of the living God, would not so much as be able to shoot an arrow against it.[4] We cannot be sure that tradition correctly remembered. Actually Isaiah may have reiterated his unchanging conviction—that God

[1] Skinner, op. cit. p. xxxvii.   [2] Isa. xxviii. 16.
[3] See the prose account in Isa. xxxvi, xxxvii (cp. II Kings xviii. 13, xix. 37). It may be that Hezekiah answered a first demand by buying pardon at the cost of a heavy tribute, was cheated by the Assyrians who took the payment and then renewed the demand for surrender; and that it was at that stage that the king besought Isaiah's Prophetic guidance. But there are complexities in the narrative, which must be left to the historians to consider.
[4] Isa. xxxvii. 33.

in His own way and *in His own moment* would humble the pride of
Assyria; that neither Hezekiah nor Sennacherib could do anything
against Jehovah's will; that there were those in Zion who trusted
and would certainly be preserved. When the startling sequel of
deliverance occurred, such words might easily be misconstrued
by wishful thinkers. But if the tradition as stated in our texts
is as good as correct, then of this we may be wholly certain—
Isaiah's assurance was given, because at that moment he believed
that king, leaders and people had genuinely repented, and that the
change of heart, to which God could rightly respond, had come to
pass. Never did Isaiah promise immunity to the impenitent. Whatever be fact about his exact words on the occasion, he was
tragically made aware of the city's real state of mind. Certain
verses in chapter xxii tell his heart-broken desolation, and appear
to be the last utterance of his that we possess.[1] Isaiah looked to see
awe and gratitude. What he beheld in the delivered city was
drunken jollification. Jerusalem celebrated the Peace—'What
aileth thee now, that thou art wholly gone up to the housetops?
O thou that art full of shoutings, a tumultuous city, a joyous town;
thy slain are not slain with the sword, neither are they dead in
battle.... Surely this iniquity shall not be expiated till ye die,
saith the Lord.'[2]

§4. *Isaiah's Greatness*

(i) *The Guidance of God.* Once in Hebrew history, when Elijah
fought the influence of Ahab and Jezebel, a Prophet had claimed
final authority over the civil rulers in a momentous issue; and his
disciple, Elisha—although it was told that he sought to uphold the
nation in its struggle against the Syrians—held also to Elijah's
antagonism towards the dynasty of Ahab. Isaiah's intervention in
affairs of State reasserted the high claim on the grand scale, and
was continued through many years. Moreover, 'Isaiah held aloof
from all political combinations, and his influence was simply that

[1] Isa. xxii. 4, 14. In this chapter later additions are most confusingly
blended with Isaiah's words.

[2] *Press extract* (18 August 1945): 'San Francisco's VJ celebrations will go
down as the world's wildest....Dozens of girls danced naked in the streets.
Thousands of girls and boys in their 'teens reeled drunkenly through the
city or lay in the gutters.' San Francisco is not all America; nor is 'Saturday
Night' in (say) Glasgow the whole of Britain. But Jerusalem *was* all that
counted in Judah, and the Prophet had good reason to despair.

of his commanding character, and of the imperial word of Jehovah.'[1] Steadfastly he stood for the principle that in Judah neither *vox populi*, nor *vox regis*, was the Voice of God, but only the wisdom of truth and right which God put into the mind of His Prophet to declare. His hearers chattered and argued about the pros and cons of what he had told the king to do; they discussed the expediency of what he said was right, and, when they decided it was not expedient and found him adamant, called him a dreamer. They told him he had been against conciliating Assyria in 735. Why, now, was he set against seeking help from Egypt? Did he not want to see Judah free and able to defy Assyria? Had he no desire for safety; no dread in face of obvious peril? And (said the priests) by what authority dared he denounce their holy worship?[2] Isaiah had one answer for their questions and agitation. He said to them: 'Mine eyes have seen the King, the Lord of glory.' And one thing reluctantly they knew: this man spake with authority, and not as other prophets.

(ii) *Master and Friends.* After 735, when it was clear that King Ahaz and the people generally would neither comprehend nor accept his reading of things present and to come, Isaiah was inspired to take the simplest but the most practical step there can possibly be towards the making of a better world. Instead of despairingly hugging his belief to his lone and virtuous self, he sought to find a few like-minded men who would study what he meant; men who would meditate on what trust in One God exalted in righteousness implied for worship and for clean living; who would learn to perceive how its strength could give to themselves 'peace in believing' and to the nation a future. A single sentence records his action after Ahaz's refusal: 'I will bind up the testimony. I will seal the teaching, among my disciples. And I will wait for the Lord, that hideth his face from the house of Jacob, and I will hope in him.'[3] Although no other reference is made to Isaiah's *disciples*, the crucial significance is obvious. Few in number the first disciples of Isaiah may have been, but as the years passed they became enough to establish his confidence. These, his friends, who called him *Master*, had understood; and they could transmit the Faith. When the Assyrian 'came down like a wolf on the fold', he could say that 'Jehovah had laid in Zion a

---

[1] W. R. Smith, *Prophets of Israel*, p. 208.
[2] Isa. i. 11 ff.   [3] Isa. viii. 16, 17.

sure foundation-stone', which the engines of the Assyrian could not displace.[1] There were men in Jerusalem ('the Believing'—'the faithful Remnant') ready to endure all things and venture all things in faith that God is righteousness and final power, and that His goodness is to be mirrored in our finite lives. When men of that stamp get together in close association, the persistence of their fellowship is wellnigh unbreakable, and the influence on history astonishingly great. The consequences of Isaiah's act pass far beyond the limits of Hebrew history. He had initiated a bond between men that is not restricted by racial distinctions. As T. W. Manson observes: 'Membership in the nation came by accident of birth; in the *Remnant* it is a matter of deliberate choice by the individual... the vitally important thing is no longer to be a son of Abraham, but to be a disciple of Isaiah with all that that implies.'[2]

(iii) *The City of Righteousness*. There was always danger that the austere Prophetic temperament, shocked by the evils to which luxury tempts, and conscious of the virtues of simplicity, would set its face against the elaborate life of civilization.[3] That would have been fatal. The proverbial garb of the professional prophet was a hairy mantle, and diet of locusts and wild honey supposed to be his taste in food. Townsmen will never be enamoured of such rations, or take kindly to such 'utility' overcoats. There is no turning back the drive of intelligence and ingenuity towards formation of large-scale social organizations, and the problems they create need to be solved, not evaded. None knew better than Isaiah how vile Jerusalem had become. None had clearer eyes to perceive how lust of possessions and seductions of comfort can enfeeble and debase men and women, not least women.[4] When he said that formerly Jerusalem had been 'the faithful city, wherein righteousness lodged', he idealized its past. But when he spoke of its present condition, he was eye-witness. He says Jerusalem had

---

[1] Isa. xxviii. 16. [2] *The Teaching of Jesus*, p. 177.

[3] Contemporary with Isaiah there was in a Judaean village a Prophet called Micah. In Micah's judgement so wicked was Jerusalem that it seemed to him the one thing God could, and should, do with the city was to blast it into a heap of rubble, and plough it as a field. (Mic. iii. 12. Much in the Book of Micah, including perhaps the famous passage vi. 1–8, is of later date. But his acceptedly authentic oracles entitle him to a secure place in 'the goodly fellowship' of true Prophets.)

[4] Isa. iii. 16–24; xxxii. 9–12.

become 'a habitation of murderers', 'red as scarlet its sins': he calls it diseased from head to foot; its great men and its ordinary citizens wicked as the people of Sodom and Gomorrah; their tumultuous worshipping abominable to God, hideous travesty of reverence.[1] In a few early utterances he expects the city's destruction, but he outgrew the phase. Listen to what in maturity he believed the patient grace of God could do, and would do, with Jerusalem: 'Thus saith the Lord, the Lord of hosts, the Mighty One of Israel...I will turn my hand upon thee, and purge away thy dross...afterward thou shalt be called The city of righteousness, the faithful city.'[2] It matters not that actual Jerusalem betrayed his longings. By holding to hope of redeemed *Society*, Isaiah gave Hebrew idealism courage to believe that the complexities of organized life might serve and not defeat the highest ends: in other words, the kingdoms of this earth shall become the Kingdom of our God. That is why Hebrew Prophetic religion has been an immense social incentive, whenever from time to time its implications have been re-seen and faced.

(iv) *The Sword of the Spirit*. The author of the Epistle to the Hebrews wrote: 'The word of God is living, and active, and sharper than any two-edged sword, and piercing even to the dividing of soul and spirit,...and quick to discern the thoughts and intents of the heart.'[3] If this Chapter could be a volume much of its space would be filled with the things Isaiah said concerning good and evil in the daily life of Jerusalem and Judah. For he brought to the task not only the piercing insight of the clean heart, but also extraordinary greatness in diction. He was Scourge of iniquity, Searcher of the thoughts and intents of hearts, and Poet of all that is tender and lovely in the rightful ways of life. Again and again his words fly home like arrows to the mark. 'As a master of style Isaiah is supreme among the Prophets. While others seem conscious of the labour of expression, he wields the resources of the language with the ease and dexterity of a perfect artist in words. There is an astonishing directness and sureness of touch in his phrase, as of one who knows when he has hit the mark and does not need to strike a second time.'[4] How vivid and how forceful, for instance, is the first chapter; and how packed with meaning— if we ponder its many thoughts in their swift sequence.

[1] See Isa. i. 10–23.   [2] Isa. i. 24–26.
[3] Heb. iv. 12.   [4] Skinner, op. cit. p. lxxii.

It brings before our imagination the tragedy of the thankless child—the 'homing' instinct which Man, alone of the creatures, has perverted and lost—terrific exposure of vainglorious Jerusalem that inwardly is like a 'sepulchre full of dead men's bones', like the Church of Laodicea, rich and self-satisfied, but in reality 'naked, poor and blind'[1]—the horrible hypocrisy of worship smugly offered by men whose hearts are stones—and (in a single unforgettable verse) the life of loving-kindness which is precious in God's sight; the purifying redeeming will of God, and its effect. Or, again, note Isaiah's searching Parable of the Vineyard (v. 1–7); his indictments of idolatry, vice and greed (ii. 6–8; iii. 12–15; v. 8–24).

(v) *Faith and the Future.* Isaiah lived in Space and Time. Therefore it was natural that his imagination sought to picture what would come to pass in future time. His reason, resting on the intensity of his Vision of God's Reality, made him sure that God cannot fail, and (*mistakenly*) he believed that the day of Divine achievement was at hand. In that Day of Judgement, and of New Creation, everything that in pride exalted itself against God's holy will would fall: 'The lofty looks of man shall be brought low, and the haughtiness of men shall be bowed down, and the Lord alone shall be exalted in that day.'[2] Therein was the truth concerning mighty *Assyria.* Its awful power was no more than a tool used by God for His own ends, even as a craftsman takes up and discards a saw when it has served his purpose![3] Boastful Sargon and Sennacherib fancy their iron will to be the sole reality; unconscious that they are being used by God to vindicate the reality of the Moral Order, to sift the good from the bad in Israel, and to prepare for God's final, regenerative, purpose with the world. When their work for God, that they intend not, is accomplished, God will lay low their pride, as a woodsman fells a tree in the forest of Lebanon.[4]

[1] Rev. iii. 14–18.
[2] Isa. ii. 11, 17. Only certain verses in this chapter are likely to be by Isaiah. The uncertainty has special interest in regard to the memorable verses 1–4. Most scholars regard these as of later origin. Skinner, however, quotes Wellhausen's remark: 'The prediction is one that would be remarkable in any age; it is perhaps even less surprising from the pen of Isaiah than from that of a later and lesser prophet.'
[3] See Isa. x. 5–34.
[4] Isa. x. 33, 34. Compare *v.* 12: 'I will punish the fruit of the stout heart of the king of Assyria, and the glory of his high looks.'

Isaiah was a lover of his People. Therefore he believed that the truth concerning the future must somehow be the creation of an Israel fully responsive to the Mind of God, which the Israel of the past had failed to be. His expectation rested on conviction that God cannot fail, on his own experience of penitence and restoration, and on confidence in the fellowship of his like-minded friends and disciples. Transfigured Israel was, therefore, central in his imagination of God's realized purpose—not to satisfy Hebrew pride, but for fulfilment of God's universal goodness. For Isaiah conceived the grace of God to be for all. His words about future Israel must not be taken prosaically. Quite certainly he was not trying to say that the realized Ideal would be a tiny island of righteous Hebrews surrounded by nebulous negligible nations, rendered impotent to hurt, but in whom the God of the universe took no other interest. It is true in a sense that Isaiah expected the ideal of the Rule of God to be realized on earth and in the future; but we should do him the justice of recognizing that he did not mean in history as it now is, or in an earth unchanged, or by an Israel unredeemed. He tried to picture that blessed World-to-be. In it there would be harmony: for *The work of righteousness shall be peace; and the effect of righteousness quietness and confidence for ever.*[1] Only the language of poetry could carry him further. Like Hosea, he felt that Nature itself would be transformed—ferocity and poison no longer there: 'The wolf shall dwell with the lamb, and the leopard shall lie down with the kid; and the calf and the young lion and the fatling together; and a little child shall lead them....And the sucking child shall play on the hole of the asp, and the weaned child shall put his hand on the adder's den. They shall not hurt nor destroy in all my holy mountain: for the earth shall be full of the knowledge of God, as the waters cover the sea.'[2]

This Prophet was a citizen of Zion. As Hosea had pictured his lovely Galilee—its people and soil—responding perfectly to the Love Divine, so Isaiah foresaw Jerusalem transformed into the

---

[1] Isa. xxxii. 17.

[2] Isa. xi. 6–9. Scholars are undecided whether the Messianic passages in the Book of Isaiah (viii. 22–ix. 7; xi. 1–9; xxxii. 1) are the work of a later period. There are strong reasons supporting Isaianic origin. Certainly the passages may here be used. Isaiah was a gentle as well as a strong man, and the lovely poetry of these verses could grow from that aspect of his character, as the rose opens from the bud.

City of Righteousness; and on the throne of David in that city of expectation One through whose rule the saving grace of God would bless the life of men. For His royal robes would not be Solomon's golden garments, but righteousness and faithfulness. Wonderful that King would be in wisdom, constant in care of his people; Prince of peace, reigning in blended strength and tenderness, whose kingdom therefore would be an everlasting kingdom. *Magnificatus est Rex pacificus, super omnes reges universae terrae.*

§5. Isaiah's Genius

Soon after the chastisement inflicted on Judah by the Assyrians in 701 B.C., they were back again; and Judah under Hezekiah's successor became a vassal-State, and the Assyrians' Gods were worshipped in Jerusalem. Isaiah was not a false prophet because the surviving humiliated Hebrews did not as one man repent under the discipline, nor yet because the pride of Assyria was not immediately overthrown by God after its victories. Actually Assyria lorded it over the nations for 80 years after 701 B.C., and then succumbed not to a miraculous act of God (as Isaiah expected), but to a combined force of Medes, Babylonians and Scythians.[1] It is neither here nor there that Isaiah was mistaken about the nearness in Time of the Day of Judgement and New Creation. As Jesus said: 'Of that day and hour knoweth no one.' Isaiah's genius is to be perceived not in what he hoped concerning future Time (however high and beautiful those hopes), but in the spiritual meaning he found in *present* Time—in present conditions of life which every generation, every individual, experiences.[2] He found the Eternal in the Temporal, because he saw in evil transient Darkness and Unreality, but in goodness 'Light' and timeless Reality. The same evidence confronts ourselves. God's gift offered to men in this life of Space and Time is opportunity—to learn to do well. In so far as we accept the gift of God, we receive cleansing; and strength and gentleness to continue patient in well-doing; and serenity of the inmost soul which is not overthrown. Thus Isaiah lived, and nobly used both the hopes and sorrows of his experience. It is not known

[1] Isa. xxxi. 8: 'Then shall the Assyrian fall by the sword, not of man....'
[2] Cp. Porteous, in *Record and Revelation*, p. 241: 'Yesterday and to-morrow are less important than the tremendous immediacy of the present moment, in which God's will is either being done or not being done.'

when he died. We may be sure that, when Time ended for Isaiah, he did not die a frightened and disillusioned man. His eyes had 'seen the King, the Lord of glory'; he had stood for truth and right; compassion had filled his heart. Amidst things temporal he had walked in the light of Life Eternal. In all his difficulties he had asked what God would have him say and do, and wisdom and goodness were imparted to him.

Isaiah stands for belief that men who delight in evil lean upon shadows and live in the *Unreal*. Men who are overawed by Time and Space, and look to expediency for guidance, are tossed hither and thither, because they know nothing to consult save their own perplexity. Isaiah sadly watched them missing the spiritual glory that is to be found in present life. He saw that the many evils, to which so easily they surrender as slaves, have the same cause— leaving out God and righteousness. The statesmen of Jerusalem turned now to one quarter, now to another, in order to discover what was expedient, leaving out of their anxious calculations only God and righteousness. The poor were crushed by hardship, and some of them lost freedom of mind and nobility of soul, and then could only laugh in derision when a Prophet talked about God and righteousness. Isaiah watched the rich worshipping wealth, eager to strengthen themselves but not to aid the fallen: God was not in all their thoughts. They heaped up riches to themselves, and behold, their own virtue, and the virtue in their children, consumed away. They clothed their women in purple and fine linen, and gave them perfumes and mirrors and pendants and bracelets and rings; and the women of Jerusalem became proud and greedy and wanton and spiteful. Ah! they walked the streets of Jerusalem ever so daintily; but never deigned to enter the poor dwelling of a sister in distress—forgetting God. In the world of Isaiah's time Hebrews and Assyrians, lords of Nineveh and rulers of Jerusalem, were very busy remembering everything, except the God of righteousness. They were blind to the true values in Life, unaware of the Eternal in the Temporal.

> Far-called our navies melt away;
>   On dune and headland sinks the fire:
> Lo, all our pomp of yesterday
>   Is one with Nineveh and Tyre!
> Judge of the nations, spare us yet,
> Lest we forget, lest we forget!

CHAPTER XV

GOD AND THE INDIVIDUAL

When the life-work of Isaiah had ended, one may say that the Hebrew Prophets had discerned the whole duty of Israel towards God, but by no means the whole Mind of God towards Israelites. Of course each Hebrew felt confident he might seek and expect the favour of Jehovah because he was a Hebrew, but not in virtue of indefeasible right as a human being. Thus far the Prophets had carried over into the higher conception of sole Deity the ancient, unquestioned assumption that Gods are interested in the welfare and continuance of the worshipping tribe or nation as a whole, and in its component individuals only because of their fractional value for its existence. In moments of humility that may seem a sufficient estimate of individual worth in the scheme of the universe, but it involves a deplorably finite measurement of the Mind of Deity. What more, however, could the Prophets think or say, so long as they kept thinking on the *national* scale—*Israel* and God? An impasse had been reached, and the bar to further progress was extremely formidable. An illustration from recent scientific development affords a parallel. When physicists had demonstrated the truth of the atomic theory of matter, it seemed as if analysis could reach no further. But when delicate experiments established that every atom is itself a minute universe of energy, it was seen that a new 'universe' for further investigation had been discovered. A new 'universe' for spiritual discernment was revealed when a Hebrew first learned to say not only 'Our God' but 'My God'. It was not by blows of hammer and chisel that the inner constitution of the atom was discovered. And neither easily nor proudly did Hebrew religion attain belief in a fully personal relation between the individual and God, in which, however, the value in the older collective standpoint was sufficiently conserved. The great transition was effected in the life-experience of a man called *Jeremiah*, between the years 626–586 B.C. Jeremiah was sensitive, and had to learn by the things which he suffered. By a perverse irony he has been styled 'the weeping Prophet'.[1] He did indeed suffer, and he shed tears over Jerusalem as also did Jesus; but, like Jesus, he endured suffering heroically.

Our knowledge of Jeremiah is due to the loyalty of the friend of his later years, Baruch, who preserved what he could of Jeremiah's own words, and himself added much information about him. Unfortunately the present Book of Jeremiah makes quite bewildering reading. It contains much indubitably not by Jeremiah or Baruch. Moreover, the reliable material now stands in no chronological order. Oracular utterances rightly or possibly ascribed to Jeremiah are set together in the first twenty chapters, but without indication of date and circumstance, apart from the quite general heading in i. 1–3. Not until chapter xxi is a specific incident in the Prophet's life mentioned. Chapter xxv refers to the year 586 B.C.; chapter xxvi to events eleven years earlier; and so forth. What happened to Jeremiah, and what he thought, has to be excavated from the Book of Jeremiah by very careful analysis.[2]

---

[1] Authorship of The Book of Lamentations was erroneously attributed to him. The late Apocryphal writing called The Epistle of Jeremy has no historical value in regard to Jeremiah's life.

[2] Peake's edition of *Jeremiah* (*The Century Bible*, 1910) should now be studied in conjunction with the penetrating discussions by A. C. Welch (*Jeremiah*, 1931), by Skinner (*Prophecy and Religion*, 1922) and G. A. Smith (*Jeremiah*, 1923). The German Commentaries by Duhm (1901), and by Cornill and Giesebrecht (who modify Duhm's critical extravagance), were of special importance. But the general comment may here be made that, in dealing with the sublime Prophets, Teutonic scholarship has been gravely marred by certain Teutonic characteristics. The Germans have been apt arrogantly to force a theory through facts, when accumulating evidence ought to have warned them to reconsider. Duhm convinced himself that Jeremiah uttered his oracles in a precise metre. For that reason, and for another (the 'Scythian' theory: see p. 314), he rashly reduced 'authentic Jeremiah' to a pittance of verses—on which, it is to be noted, he commented with keen appreciation of Jeremiah's greatness. Again, the Germans set the fashion of thinking that anything that savours of eschatological or Messianic expectation cannot emanate from a pre-exilic Prophet. Thirdly, the German writers hunt for *political* causes for Prophetic agitation (see further the footnote to p. 314). These tendencies led to a vast amount of rash analysis and dating. Despite its unquestionably great services, not a little German erudition concerning the Prophetic literature recalls the 'bull in a china shop', and needs to be subjected to common sense and artistry. Fortunately, the bull and the shop are literary, not literal; and the scattered crockery remains intact, ready to be gathered up and handled more discreetly.

§ 1. '*Jerusalem the brazen*'

The citizens of Jerusalem learnt nothing theologically from the great deliverance in 701 B.C. Isaiah saw them go up to the roof-tops to jubilate. They came down having fixed in mind precisely what Isaiah had not taught—that Jehovah could be relied on unconditionally to protect His city. Nearly 70 years intervene between that point and 626 B.C., at which date Jeremiah's Prophetic utterances began. In 696 Hezekiah was succeeded by Manasseh, who earned for himself a more villainous reputation than any other Judaean king. Assyria was rising to the zenith of its power (it conquered Egypt in 671), and the new king of Judah must have demonstrated his submissive recognition of its might; for the Assyrians were content to leave Jerusalem intact—like a lone apple on a tree, fruit not worth gathering. Assyrian suzerainty no doubt demanded that reverence be paid to the Assyrian super-Gods in Jerusalem's temple, but Manasseh proved himself worse than a realist in religious matters. It seems certain that he encouraged multiplication of the emblems of the Assyrian astral worship in Jerusalem far beyond the inevitable, and further, in connexion with the cult of Jehovah, revived the sex-ritual and, worst of all, the (Canaanitish) abominable custom of sacrificing first-born children by fire in honour of the national God. This dreadful rite was practised in the valley of Hinnom below Jerusalem.

What was the reaction of his subjects to the king's latitudinarianism? It appears that, to begin with, there was some vehement opposition—presumably from those who had taken to heart Isaiah's real teaching. Manasseh knew a short way with nonconformists: it is written that 'he shed innocent blood till he had filled Jerusalem from end to end'. We hear of no further overt opposition during his long reign of fifty years, and the shocking thing is that for twenty years after his death no sweeping change was made in the religious conditions in the city. What inference can be drawn, except that the bulk of the population—priests, prophets, and laity—were content to have it so? Their kingdom was subject to Assyria. What did that matter, since Jerusalem was unharmed and trade could prosper? They were much obliged to Manasseh's political common sense. And, religiously, why should they cavil because due reverence was offered to the mighty Gods of Assyria? The orgiastic rites in honour of their own Jehovah thrilled and pleased them, even if some old-fashioned 'Puritans' scowled. They would praise Jehovah with all their might. The great festivals at His temple were a riot of excitement. The strong prospered; the weak suffered—Let them suffer!

Jerusalem, the brazen, with milk and honey blest!

§2. The Home of Jeremiah

Jeremiah was born about 645 B.C. in the village of Anathoth some four miles north-east of Jerusalem. In situation Anathoth was a fitting birthplace for one whose sensitive genius was destined to drink deep the significances of nature, history, and the daily life of men. The village was reckoned in the territory of Benjamin, and its people engaged in cultivation of the soil: 'hard thorny soil that needed deep ploughing...the cold northern rains and the tears of a nation's history alike swept across the bare highlands.'[1] Although they lived so close to Jerusalem, the tragedy of vanquished Samaria beset the imagination of the men of Anathoth. To the north were the mountains of Ephraim, and at only a few miles distance the border of the Assyrian province, where a century earlier had been the proud kingdom of Israel. Less than ten miles to the north was the famous altar of Jehovah at Bethel, where alone the Assyrians had permitted sacrifice to the God of Israel to continue; and ten miles beyond that lay the scattered stones of the temple of Shiloh—first temple of Jehovah in the land—which the Philistines had destroyed when Eli (an ancestor of Jeremiah) had been its priest. Eastwards, over rough bare hills, the prospect looked across the depths of the Jordan valley to the mountains of Moab and Gilead. Jeremiah saw the sun rise from behind those distant hills, bringing light to the landscape, but not to benighted minds.[2] All too close to Anathoth was Jerusalem, with its chattering tongues and scheming transactions; its miserable poor; its rich men, royal officials, priests and king; and its golden temple from whose altars rose the smoke of sacrifices that changed not the hearts of men. Not until Jeremiah was 24 years old, and not until five years after he began his work in the name of God, were the flagrant religious abuses fostered by Manasseh brought to an end. Throughout his entire youth he lived only four miles distant from 'Jerusalem the brazen'.

[1] G. A. Smith, *Jeremiah*, p. 70. [2] Jer. viii. 22.

We are told that he was 'the son of Hilkiah, of the priests that were in Anathoth in the land of Benjamin'. From that statement the interesting inference can, almost with certainty, be drawn that his family traced their lineage from Eli through Abiathar, the chief priest, whom Solomon had deposed from the service of his new and splendid temple in favour of Zadok.[1] Presumably the men of his house did not forget their lost ancestral rights when they watched the Zadokites sacrificing at the royal altars in Jerusalem. Presumably they themselves ministered at the High-Place at Anathoth. There is no reason to suppose that the rites in honour of Jehovah at Anathoth were any less gross than at the other local sanctuaries throughout the land; and of this we may be certain— that the young eyes of Jeremiah looked and listened with growing perplexity and with the instinctive repulsion of the pure in heart for such worship. The local cult which Hilkiah served may have been as degraded as elsewhere, yet we may infer that in Jeremiah's home the traditions of Israel's past were proudly cherished, and that in his childhood his impressionable mind heard of Moses and of the desert covenant that had pledged all Israel to be the People of Jehovah and brethren one of another; of Eli his ancestor, and the tragedy of Shiloh; of Samuel's courage and conscience. His own early utterances show that he had pondered deeply the words of Amos and Hosea, and that the ruin which had overtaken the northern kingdom was ever-present in his thoughts. (He compared its desolation to the sobs of a woman lamenting her dead child.[2]) He must have been moved by Isaiah's magnificent witness against the evils in Jerusalem. But what did he make of Isaiah's superb confidence that, when Assyria had humbled the impenitent pride of Judah, Jehovah would then abase Assyria and everything else that exalts itself against the God of righteousness? Nearly a century had passed. That prediction had not been fulfilled!

Jeremiah was probably less than twenty years old when there befell him an experience closely comparable to the 'Call' of Isaiah. He described it thus—

---

[1] Abiathar was the only survivor of the massacre of the family of Eli (I Sam. xiv. 3; xxii. 20). When he was deposed by Solomon he went to live at Anathoth.

[2] 'Rachel, weeping for her children; she refuseth to be comforted' (Jer. xxxi. 15).

Now the word of the Lord came unto me, saying, Before I formed thee in the belly I knew thee, and before thou camest forth out of the womb I sanctified thee; I have appointed thee a prophet unto the nations. Then said I, Ah, Lord God! behold, I cannot speak: for I am a youth.[1] But the Lord said unto me, Say not, I am a youth: for to whomsoever I shall send thee thou shalt go, and whatsoever I command thee thou shalt speak. Be not afraid because of them: for I am with thee to deliver thee, saith the Lord. Then the Lord put forth his hand, and touched my mouth; and the Lord said unto me, Behold, I have put my words in thy mouth: see, I have this day set thee over the nations and over the kingdoms, to pluck up and to break down, and to destroy and to overthrow; to build, and to plant.[2]

Certain features are very notable in this initial trance: (i) The sense of specific relation between his personality and the Divine Being—God had called *him* into existence for a predestined purpose. (ii) The contrast of temperament with Isaiah's un-hesitant response, 'Here am I; send me'. (iii) To his diffident plea the Voice responded only by sterner insistence that he must not shirk the terrific duty, and offered only the promise that he would feel God was 'with him'. (iv) The authority of the truth which he was to speak concerned not merely his People but other nations and kingdoms. The 'Word of the Lord' on the lips of the great Prophets was the Judgement of Righteousness; and Right respects no national boundaries. That truth Amos and Isaiah were led each in his own way to discern. In the consciousness of Jeremiah it was very present from the moment of his 'Call'.

Two further incidents (which may be trance-experiences, but are more probably moments of normally rational insight) are recorded in the first chapter. Together they enabled Jeremiah to conquer youthful dread, and believe that God had indeed summoned him to take up the mantle of Isaiah, and mediate the word of the living God to his own day and generation. One day he found himself gazing at an almond tree, leafless but living. (Now the Hebrew for *Almond-tree* is *Shākēdh*, and for *watching* is *shōkēdh*.) Why had it fixed his attention? Answer flashed into his mind—'God is *watching over* His word to perform it.'[3] That strong

---

[1] The English Versions translate 'a child'; but in reference to Jeremiah *youth* is the right rendering of the Hebrew word.

[2] Jer. i. 4–10.

[3] Jer. i. 11, 12. It has been customary to suppose the tree was showing its early blossom, but there is nothing in the Hebrew to say so. The analogy

clear conviction remained with him through life. On another
occasion he noticed a steaming cauldron of boiling water, the fire
upon which it stood fanned by a wind from the north. He read
this meaning in the sight—The anger of God against men's
iniquity is likewise boiling over, and Judgement is about to be
manifested first against iniquitous Jerusalem. It was for him to do
as Isaiah had done: call men to repent, or else to face imminent
retribution—calamity beyond the power of words to portray.
That mistaken belief in immediate, cataclysmic disaster had to be
shattered so that he might learn in agony of spirit the supreme
truth God predestined him to reach. What was in store for
Jeremiah? He could not foresee that only through the discipline
of disillusionment would he gain assurance of his individual
worth to God. In the innocence of his youth he set forth, taking
up the mistake, as well as the mantle, of Isaiah; for 'the end of all
things' was not at hand. During nearly twenty years (from 626–608
B.C.) he was the impassioned Prophet of that which did not come
to pass. Was not this hesitant youth strange choice for so grim a
duty? Persons of iron determination are not so very scarce. The
real task—which he could not yet comprehend—was so vastly
difficult that it required what Jeremiah *potentially* had it in him to
offer to God—a character made strong as steel in the furnace of
affliction.

§3. *The Signs of the Times*

In 626, when Jeremiah felt the Call of God upon him, the only
storm clouds in the political skies seemed to be looming over
accursed Nineveh, Assyria's capital in the far north. For
Palestine and Jerusalem Spring seemed in the air; the awful Winter
of Assyrian domination was drawing to its end. Men knew that
25 years earlier Egypt had recovered its independence, and felt so
little to fear from Assyria that its interest now lay in giving support
to the tottering empire, lest some other titanic northern power
should take its place. It grew evident that Nineveh was gravely
menaced by the kingdom of the Medes in the eastern mountains;
and (even more so) by its great province of Babylon in southern
Mesopotamia, which indeed revolted in 625 B.C. Moreover about

gains in point if 'the twig was a dry twig, which seemed to promise nothing....
The world was apparently empty of any divine promise.' (Cp. Welch,
Jeremiah, p. 47.)

640 a multitude of barbaric horsemen, Scythians, broke in from the north. But Assyria could absorb them in its wide territories, and indeed after a time found in their hordes a precarious accession to its waning man-power, and could use their help to repulse an attack by the Medes. The Scythians were mobile warriors, who transported their womenfolk and belongings with them in great wheeled carts. They were ready to venture in search of better quarters, and for years their roving bands may have made startling appearances, now here, now there. That general fact is probably the germ of truth in the statement made by the Greek historian, Herodotus, that the Scythians lorded it over all Asia for 25 years, and at one time assailed Ashdod in the Philistine Plain and were a threat to Egypt. It ought to have been plain that Herodotus's remark was not reliable history, and in any event that these barbaric, fleeting, 'allies' of the erstwhile all-powerful Assyrian armies would not strike the hearts of the men of Jerusalem with lasting terror.[1] Jeremiah does not once mention Scythians.[2] The young Prophet enforced his call to repent by invoking not a Scythian bogey-man, but the Lord God Almighty. He took his stand on the logic of righteousness. 'The Prophets', Welch rightly insists, 'did not begin from the Assyrians or Scythians or Babylonians in their threat to Israel's independence . . . They began from Jehovah the God of Israel, from the thought of His character and purpose. A revelation of righteousness in such a world as that in which the Prophets lived meant first a judgement on it. Again, if Jehovah was righteousness, His will involved more than Israel, and His end included all nations.'[3] What precise form, superhuman and human, the act of Divine retribution would take was a secondary matter: it was for the Prophet to awaken men's conscience, and to use all the resources of language to warn the impenitent of the terrors that must ensue. In his early oracles Jeremiah once envisages the coming calamity

[1] Especially if (as is possible) the Scythian assault on Ashdod (if it happened) took place in 640 B.C., some fifteen years before Jeremiah began to predict the near approach of doom.

[2] Observe by contrast that he was quite specific about the Babylonians when, in later years, he was sure that God would use their army to chastise the pride of Jerusalem—exactly as Isaiah became specific about the Assyrians as the axe which Jehovah had taken up in His hand to serve His immediate purpose.

[3] Welch, op. cit. p. 118.

as a scorching wind from the desert, and once (most memorably)
depicts it as a convulsion of Nature itself. Again in xxv. 15–27,
and (?) 30–38, he declares that all nations, 'from Egypt to Elam,
from Babylon to the Mediterranean', must drink the cup of the
wrath of God. But, very vividly in iv. 5–31, the calamity is
depicted as an irresistible invasion coming from the *north*.
Impressive evidence can, however, be gathered from the Old
Testament, and not merely from the Book of Jeremiah, which
goes to show that *the north* had acquired a more than geographical
significance and symbolized the region of terrible possibilities.[1]
For one thing, from its unknown recesses unknown races might
come breaking in on civilization. For another, somewhere in its
many mountains Semitic mythology located 'the mountain of the
Gods'.[2] Add the thought that the north is the quarter whence
comes winter with its icy breath and early darkness. When
Jeremiah (i. 14, 15) predicted that Jehovah will summon 'all the
families of the kingdoms of the north' to come and sit in judgement on Jerusalem, he and his hearers may have interpreted the
threat in the widest, supernatural *and* natural sense—as 'Every
sort (*family*) of awful power (*kingdom*) Deity has at command'.

From 626 to 608 B.C. Jeremiah could specify no northern nation
as bidding fair to overwhelm Palestine and the peoples of the
world. To reply that (though he did not name them) he was
hinting at the Scythians as Jehovah's agents for inflicting doom
will no longer serve.[3] The Prophet spoke vaguely, though
vehemently, of the power and purpose of God, of righteousness
and sin. His fulminations did not in the least ruffle the confidence
of the men of Jerusalem. They saw only excellent reason to hope

[1] See Welch's argument (op. cit. pp. 108–31), which the writer considers
to be generally valid.

[2] Cp. Isa. xiv. 13–15 (on the expectations of the proud king of Babylon).

[3] See Wilke's monograph (*Das Scythenproblem*, in *Studien für Kittel*)
and Welch (op. cit. pp. 100 ff.), who comments drastically on Cornill's
suggestion (*Kommentar*, pp. 86f.) that, when the 'Scythian menace' failed
Jeremiah, he adapted his early oracles to suit the Babylonian danger after
605 B.C. Herodotus' mention of the Scythians was treasure-trove for those
scholars to whom it did not seem possible that Prophets should be roused
to prophesy unless they had shrewdly descried a political peril on the horizon.
Duhm seized on the Scythians with enthusiasm, and, aided by his strict
metrical theory, as good as 'reduced the original elements of Jeremiah's
prophecy to a series of Scythian songs'. Discussion of the Scythians,
or 'the Northern Foe', has occupied undeserved space in the Commentaries.

that the Assyrian Empire was breaking up; so much so that in 621 B.C. (five years after Jeremiah began to prophesy catastrophe) Josiah openly defied Assyria by abolishing the worship of its Gods in Jerusalem and by asserting his royal power in Samaria and perhaps as far north as Hamath in Galilee. The king's temerity was vindicated. In 615 Nineveh was almost overthrown by the Medes; then the Scythians gleefully joined in with its enemies, and in 612 Medes, Babylonians and Scythians captured and destroyed it. For yet another four years Jerusalem seemed secure. But for almost twenty years (from 626–608) Jeremiah had been predicting imminent ruin. O hapless Prophet, refuted by events!

§4. *Twenty Years*

Picture this stripling in the first flush of conviction, setting out from Anathoth to go to Jerusalem; taking his stand near the palace and calling in vain to the king and his great men to give heed to a Prophet's warning; then having to tell his Vision of disaster to a handful who gathered to learn what the fuss might be. Sometimes he would go to speak to the priests and crowds in the temple courts; sometimes to Jerusalem's 'Hyde Park', the open spaces at the city gates where the elders weightily discussed public affairs and their neighbours' disputes. His message fell flat— prophet of blackest woe, when things were going well! If at first there was mild sensation it died down, for familiarity breeds contempt: 'The young fanatic from Anathoth, at it again with the same old story.' He took to walking the narrow streets of Jerusalem, seeking for even one who would listen and be moved.[1] In time he had to recognize that nothing was achieved; he might as well have remained silent at Anathoth. Why was 'the Word of God of none effect'? Surely the fault must be his hearers' obstinacy, obstinacy so great that if, not he, but Moses or Samuel had been pleading the effort would be futile.[2] Did God mean him to desist? His innate diffidence came flooding back: perhaps the failure was due to his own incapacity. But his mind was like a fire, damped down, yet ready to blaze. Facts daunted. Conscience impelled; for the vice and cruelty in men's lives were no illusion. Jeremiah found himself beset by recurrent, and very terrible trances—Visions of slaughter, of wailing women and

[1] Jer. viii. 5, 6.   [2] Jer. xv. 1.

children, corpses rotting in the fields; or of Nature itself in convulsion, the mountains shaking, the earth reeling, the once populous land a silent desolation.[1] Each Vision seemed to him the voice of God driving him back to his duty, entrusting to him alone foreknowledge. If *he* should fail to evoke repentance, these things must be.

In 621 B.C. a Book of religious instruction—perhaps Deuteronomy (in part), or like it—which set forth the right worship of Jehovah, and denounced the abominable customs of the Canaanites, was accidentally found in the temple. King Josiah seized the dramatic moment, and ventured to end the cult of the Assyrian Gods in Jerusalem and the ritual horrors practised during Manasseh's reign. It is obvious that Jeremiah must have welcomed 'the cleansing of the Augean stables'—the cessation of polytheistic and sensual rites. But it is over-against the Reform that the genius of his religious insight begins to appear. Either at once,[2] or very swiftly, he realized that 'the Good' may be the deadly enemy of 'the Best'. Men could use the Reform as a sleeping draught for conscience. Jeremiah saw them flock to the changed ritual, and return unchanged to their sins and selfishness, telling themselves that Jehovah should now be well content. The reform had made only more difficult the Prophet's deeply spiritual task. And when he continued to charge the people with their iniquity and predict ruinous divine retribution, imagine how former indifference towards him would become vexation and fury—not least from those responsible for the Reform. One cannot irritate and threaten one's fellow-men year after year with impunity. Certainly the time came when their indignation developed into resolve to put him to death. If only he could be trapped in an unguarded moment into uttering threats against the State as his own belief, instead of speaking in God's name (and therefore with a prophet's immunity), they could safely kill him. To his horror he found that among the plotters were some of his own kinsfolk at Anathoth.[3]

---

[1] Jer. iv. 23–26.   [2] So Welch, op. cit. pp. 76–96.

[3] An interesting conjecture arises. It is conceivable that one feature in Josiah's Reform restored to Jeremiah's priestly kinsmen at Anathoth their ancestor's right of ministering at the altar in Jerusalem. If so, would they not hail the new measure with delight? But if this odd son of their house now added to his previous pessimistic oddity disinterest and dissatisfaction about the Reform, his attitude may have the more incensed their anger against him. When Josiah suppressed sacrifices at the local sanctuaries, their priests were

In 612 B.C. the complete collapse of the Assyrian empire completed Jeremiah's discomfiture in the eyes of others. Nineveh, the Great, was fallen, was fallen! What a triumphant answer Jeremiah's enemies now had for his predictions of approaching ruin—'False Prophet! False Prophet!' The event might well shake to its foundations his wavering faith in his inspiration.

§5. Agony and Collapse

With such a message down the years Jeremiah was inviting trouble, and received it. The wicked were galled by the sting of his just accusations, and the prosperous by his grim insistence that security was about to end. 'Labour' may at first have relished his onslaught on oppressors; but this man went too far, talking of a disaster that would engulf their little homes as well as rich men's houses. The ribald made him the butt of their mockery. He found himself increasingly isolated, and dislike and loneliness torture a gentle soul that craves for affection and companionship. Pessimists are unpopular. No one invited Jeremiah to a meal, or bade him come to the marriage, or join in rejoicing for the new-born son. Who wanted the death's head at the feast? When he returned dejected from Jerusalem, no smiling faces awaited him in Anathoth, not even in his parents' home. They cannot have relished their neighbours' comments on this peculiar son—accusing everyone of wickedness, threatening disaster, and having these terrifying Visions! Presumably the village mothers said he was inspired by a demon, had the evil eye, and told their children to hide when they saw him. He wanted to have wife and children of his own, and then reflected that for him to marry would be an eloquent way of indicating that he did not really believe in his predictions of doom. God had cut him off from even that solace. It is uncertain if he yet

(so to say) suddenly deprived of their rank and out of a job. That would not promote Josiah's popularity, and he wanted to be no longer 'king of the castle' in Zion, but king of a reunited country. Some action was called for; and it seems possible that wise provision was at once made that the local priests should now be permitted to share with the Zadokite priests in serving the altar at the temple. There is no indication that the Zadokites at that time opposed the generous and sensible arrangement. To think that in a matter of 'Holy Orders' strong-minded men, holding different traditions as to their rights and with practical interests also to consider, should agree the time had come for something new to be done in a changed situation—takes one's breath away. Perhaps it did so happen in 621 B.C.

had won the support of Baruch, loyal friend of his later years. If he had, Baruch did not clearly understand him—much as the disciples of Jesus could not deeply realize their Master's burden. Jeremiah was isolated in mind more than in body. He had to become despised and rejected, mentally separate from men—in order that he might be constrained finally to seek in God alone the strength and wisdom that he needed.

Under the strain his character weakened, for he began to make his personal grievances a central issue. If at that stage he had merely talked *to himself* about himself, that would have put an end to greatness, and perhaps to sanity. But in his perplexity and misery Jeremiah turned to God, willing still to judge his feelings by Absolute Goodness, and striving still to find enlightenment from an understanding greater than his own. Thinking on that wise is *prayer*, and it opens the possibility that a man may yet see what he has not seen, and be able to say 'Thy will, not mine, be done'. Fortunately, the Prophet wrote down a few poignant records of these darkest moments of his soul; and we are thus aware of his reasoning, as he poured out his complaint unto God.[1]

He pleads that he had not refused God's call, but had mastered youthful fears, and persisted—O Lord, how long? How often had he nerved himself to encounter disbelief, ridicule, indifference and then fury? Could God accuse him of being an unwilling servant?—only in the sense that he was by nature a man of peace, hating contention. But for the truth's sake he had endured incessant strife, as if he were the most cantankerous man on earth. The task had cost him every normal human joy for which he longed. All *that* he had surrendered; and truly had sought and found joy in the one thing left—inward gratitude that God entrusted His Word to him, seeming to value and to need him; indeed had brought him into existence for that end. Had he been slack? Nay, he had struggled to find words to stab conscience, enlighten the mind and touch the heart—until there seemed nothing in him left unsaid. Not coldly had he thought and spoken, but in love towards God and his fellows, identifying himself with their need and peril: 'O that my head were waters, and mine eyes a

---

[1] 'It is not too much to say that, if those precious fragments had perished . . . the most vital element in Jeremiah's influence and individuality would have remained unknown.' (Skinner, *Prophecy and Religion*, p. 201.) See Jer. xi. 18–23; xii. 1–6; xv. 10–21; xvii. 9f., 14–18; xviii. 18–23; xx. 7–12.

fountain of tears, that I might weep day and night for my people's slain!'¹ Not arrogance had made him the rebuker of other men. Only what God constrained him to say he had said; but they railed at *him*, venting on *him* their anger because of God's word. Was that just? If God was 'with him' (as the promise had been), his foes, and not he, should have been put to shame. In torment he broke out: 'Let me see thy vengeance upon them...destroy them with double destruction.'² But the uttermost agony that was rending his soul from his body was the seemingly inescapable conclusion that God Himself had failed or deluded him. Again and again the Visions called him to testify that judgement was at hand. Where was vestige of a sign that God would vindicate His righteous purpose? After all these years—Assyria fallen; iniquitous men unscathed and jubilant! God had *not* supported him as He promised, and he was put to shame. That was the horrible, horrible, fact which he felt he could not deny: 'Cursed be the day I was born, the day when my mother bore me, be it unblessed.... Why came I forth from the womb to see trouble and sorrow, to consume my days in shame? O God, Thou hast deceived me, and I was deceived.'³ The suffering Prophet had fallen very low, cursing his lot, reviling his enemies, reproaching God. But when a great soul, spent with fatigue, still wrestles with despair and asks from God the meaning of his perplexity, hope remains. Through the long night Jeremiah kept his face turned toward the east, and the dawn broke.

In the years 626–608 B.C. the greatest event that was taking place was not the decline and fall of Assyria, but the anguished consciousness of Jeremiah learning from his own experience to believe that God cares for an individual human being. Only affliction transformed his youthful confidence into the disciplined humility which is able to believe tenaciously and yet remain

¹ See Jer. ix. 1.

² 'The Prophets were neither vegetables nor machines but men of like passions with ourselves. Jeremiah may have been by temper hasty and raw, with a natural capacity for provoking his fellows....His impatience, honest though it be, needed stern rebuke from the Lord.... When we are tempted to wonder at Jeremiah's passion and cursing, let us try to realize how we should have felt had we, like him, found our *one* service baffled, and the *single* possible fulfilment of our ideals rendered vain. All of which shows the difference that Christ has made.' (G. A. Smith, *Jeremiah*, pp. 332, 335.)

³ Jer. xx. 7, 14, 18.

teachable. Only when he had been humbled to the dust by discovering the weakness in his character did Jeremiah attain that
rare gift, and then discern the truth of God in its perfect simplicity
and unconquerable strength.

§6. *Restoration*

In the second part of Jeremiah's life-work, from 608–586 B.C., we
mark in him an altered and stronger personality. He ceased to
speak in vague terms of an apocalyptic doom, and instead with
cogent force and profoundest insight spoke directly to the
momentous issues of the times—the approaching termination of
the Judaean kingdom and the destruction of the temple. Upon the
existence of city and temple men were resting their faith; and their
hopes, he foreknew, were destined to be shattered. But the event
should be for good; God's meaning and God's purpose could be
found in it. When men could no longer trust in outward things,
then they might discover the fortress within themselves which
cannot be beaten down—*personal religion*, the sense of God's sustaining strength given to those who will govern their life unselfishly and purely. His nation needed the chastening, liberating,
experience through which his own spirit had passed. He began to
try to make that clear, realizing that the task entrusted to him in
the moment of his Call had two aspects: God's Word would be
not merely destructive but constructive also. He knew now that it
would be for the furtherance of the Divine purpose that the actual
Jerusalem should be destroyed; he foresaw now a City of God
which could then be built, such that the future vitality of the
nation would not depend upon vicissitudes of politics, but derive
from the spirituality of its members. The dread which a sensitive
man must always feel in face of bitter antagonism and physical
persecution he did not lose, but now he met it with indomitable
courage. The vehemence of his youth remained, but he had learnt
how to speak commandingly to the authorities, and how to
impress the popular imagination with terrific force. For himself,
he found peace amidst pain; and he gave to his dying nation
amazing newness of life.

What had changed him, and caused his spirit to be born again?
Explanation is found in two facts very briefly recorded. There is
no doubt about the fundamental importance of both allusions, for

in them is foreshadowed the man he actually became. *First,* he says that the Inner Voice answered his despair, not by commiseration with his unhappy lot, but by relentless stimulus—If he would continue to do the work of God, let him realize that what he had hitherto endured at the hands of men was but the lesser part of what he was going to endure.[1] *Second* (in xv. 10–18), Jeremiah, protesting that he had been cruelly wronged by men and unsupported by God, compares himself to a man dying of thirst in the heat of summer who has struggled to a river-bed, where the torrent pours unwanted in winter, only to find no drop of water amidst its pitiless stones—'Why is my grief perpetual? my wound mortal that will not be healed? Wilt Thou be to me as a winter-brook, as waters that fail?' Then, in *vv.* 19–21, follow the words that mark a turning point in pre-Christian religious history: 'Therefore thus saith the Lord—If thou return, I will restore thee; Thou shalt stand before me. If pure thoughts thou utter, unmixed with base, Thou shalt be as my mouth. These men shall come round to thee, But not thou to them. I will make thee to this people a wall strong as brass: They will fight, but shall not overcome thee; For I am with thee to save thee.'[2] Promise—*I am with thee*: and Condition—*If pure thoughts thou utter unmixed with base, thou shalt be as my mouth.* In that sole demand Jeremiah found the one knowledge that is all knowledge, the one truth that is all truth. 'The pure in heart', said Jesus, 'shall see God.'

§7. *The Maturity of Jeremiah*

For four years after the fall of Nineveh in 612 B.C. Josiah reigned in peace. Judaean optimists could see in him a second David on the throne of David, ruler of a free, united, Hebrew State. What Josiah thought himself we know not; but he was personally an upright man—Jeremiah paid him an unhesitant tribute.[3] History was moving apace. The Babylonian (or 'Chaldean') kingdom was bracing itself to be Lord of the Nations in Assyria's stead; and King Necho of Egypt could do no more than send his army in the campaigning seasons north through Palestine and Syria to hold

---

[1] The conviction phrased itself in picturesque metaphor: 'If thou hast run with the footmen, and they have wearied thee, then how canst thou contend with horses?' (Jer. xii. 5.)

[2] Skinner's translation. (Op. cit. p. 204.)　　　[3] Jer. xxii. 15*b*, 16.

the line of the Euphrates at Carchemish against a Babylonian drive when it should come. Very likely Necho had no use for a strong Hebrew kingdom on the flank of his marching army which, if defeated at Carchemish, would have to retreat in disorder over the passes at Megiddo and along the coastal plain. At any rate, in 608 Josiah's life came to a sudden end, and the Jewish historians (puzzled that tragedy should overtake so good a king) cryptically relate that 'Josiah went against him [Necho]; and he slew him at Megiddo, when he had seen him.'[1] It was a shock, not only to Jerusalem's political hopes, but also to its conventional religious ideas.

The dismayed citizens made Jehoahaz, Josiah's *second* son, their king, knowing what manner of man his elder brother, Jehoiakim, was. Three months later Necho, on his return from the northern campaign, carried off Jehoahaz to Egypt, installed Jehoiakim, and imposed a heavy tribute. Jehoiakim was a beast: he had to raise the tribute, but he need not have proceeded further to pour out money and exact forced labour to improve his palace. Possibly the old palace of Solomon was much the better for renovation, but the hovels of the poor were in greater need. Jehoiakim was clear which claim should have priority for building materials. Politically he was an opportunist. In 605 B.C. the Babylonians thrashed the Egyptians in the great battle of Carchemish, and Jehoiakim transferred his allegiance to Babylon. For that he cannot be blamed, but in 598 or 597 he rebelled against Babylon—an utterly rash act. For a while the Babylonians had to deal with the matter by fomenting local attacks, but in 597 their regular army under King Nebuchadrezzar set out for Jerusalem. At that point Jehoiakim died, and his son Jehoiakin was king for two months. When Nebuchadrezzar arrived, he surrendered, and was taken to Babylon together with some thousands of Jerusalem's leading men —a deportation to which we refer as *The First Captivity*. The Babylonians set Zedekiah on the throne, who reigned until 586 and was Judah's last king.

No utterance of Jeremiah can definitely be assigned to the closing years of Josiah's reign. But in the time of Jehoiakim and Zedekiah a series of flaming declarations and bold actions reveal the Prophet and his aim. These we have now to observe:

[1] II Kings xxiii. 29.

IN THE REIGN OF JEHOIAKIM (608–597 B.C.)

(i) '*Speaking against Caesar.*' Jeremiah—voice of eternal Right confronting at all costs the arrogance of temporal Might—denounced despotic Jehoiakim in forthright terms:

Woe unto him that buildeth his house by unrighteousness...that useth his neighbour's service without wages...that saith, I will build me a wide house and spacious chambers, and cutteth out windows; and it is cieled with cedar, and painted with vermilion. Shalt thou reign, because thou strivest to excel in cedar? Did not thy father [Josiah] eat and drink, and do judgement and justice?...He judged the cause of the poor and the needy; then it was well. Was not this to know me? saith the Lord. But thine eyes and thine heart are not but for thy covetousness, and for to shed innocent blood, and for oppression, and for violence, to do it....Therefore thus saith the Lord concerning Jehoiakim...he shall be buried with the burial of an ass, drawn and cast forth beyond the gates of Jerusalem.[1]

(ii) '*Blocks of stone*, and *Scraps of flesh.*' Jeremiah delivered a devastating attack on the externality of the popular trust in the temple and sacrificial rites as automatic guarantee of Jehovah's protection and goodwill. On a festal occasion when crowds from the country as well as the citizens were assembled, he sought to awaken them to the integral relation of morality to worship, essence of the Prophetic-Christian understanding of God and human life. He went to the temple court and there spoke, saying:

Trust ye not in futile words, saying, *The temple of Jehovah, the temple of Jehovah!* ...Behold, ye trust in lying words, that cannot profit. Will ye steal, murder, and commit adultery, and swear falsely, and sacrifice to Baal,...and come and stand before me in this house, which is called by my name, and say, *We are delivered*—that ye may do all these abominations? Is this house, which is called by my name, become a den of robbers in your eyes? Behold, I, even I, have seen it, saith the Lord. But go ye now unto my place which was in Shiloh, where I caused my name to dwell at the first, and see what I did to it for the wickedness of my people Israel.... Therefore will I do unto the house, which is called by my name, wherein ye trust, and unto the place which I gave to you and to your fathers, as I have done to Shiloh. And I will cast you out of my sight, as I have cast out all your brethren, even the whole seed of Ephraim.[2]

[1] Jer. xxii. 13–19.
[2] Jer. vii. 1–15; and xxvi (another record of the event, stressing occasion and sequel).

No less sweeping was his attack on the value ascribed to the two main types of sacrificial offerings—i.e. the 'whole burnt-offerings' (which were entirely consumed on the altar fire), and the 'peace-offerings' (parts of which were devoted to God and the rest of the animal eaten by the worshippers as a meal of sacred meat). Jeremiah said they might with impunity devour the entirety of both kinds: it was just so much ordinary flesh![1] The inference must not be drawn that Jeremiah was a negative iconoclast. But it does mean that the ritual he beheld needed to be broken down, in order that the humble and contrite heart might evolve fitting forms of truly spiritual adoration. Even more clearly than the great Prophets before him, his genius perceived that that truth needed to be declared categorically in the most drastic possible way. As he had said elsewhere: 'Break up your fallow ground, and sow not amongst thorns.'[2] He followed his scathing words on the sacrifices by a very interesting assertion that the solemn command of Moses had concerned, not sacrifices, but simply Israel's fundamental vow to obey Jehovah in the covenantal obligation of His People—therefore as brethren one of another.[3] The feelings of the priests were outraged: they held that his prediction of the destruction of the temple exceeded the limits of liberty of prophesying, and asked the civil authorities to have him put to death. He was saved by the support given by Ahikam and certain of the nobles, and by the protest of men of Judaea who urged that he had said no worse than the Judaean Prophet, Micah, who a century earlier had predicted that Jerusalem would be ploughed up like a field. The State's authority was upheld by a compromise: Jeremiah was forbidden access to the temple precincts.

(iii) '*A Scrap of paper.*' Jeremiah nevertheless found a way to make his voice heard again in the temple courts.[4] He dictated what he wanted to say to Baruch, a scribe, who courageously took the parchment to the temple, and read its contents to the people. Probably this affair took place after Jehoiakim had rebelled against the Babylonians, and the parchment contained a prediction that the Babylonians would take the city. For whereas the priests were not agitated, a group of influential citizens were, and decided Jeremiah's words should be reported to the king. (They must also have been awed and sympathetic, for they warned Baruch to get himself and Jeremiah to safe hiding.) A graphic narrative tells

[1] Jer. vii. 21 ff.   [2] Jer. iv. 3.   [3] Jer. vii. 22, 23.   [4] Jer. xxxvi.

how the parchment was read to the king seated in the winter
palace with a brazier burning beside him. Jehoiakim did not like
what he heard. He seized the pages as they were read, cut them up
with a penknife and cast them into the flames. When the news of
the royal action reached Jeremiah, he dictated the prophecy again,
'adding yet more words'! As Welch comments: 'The divine
purpose stood, whether a king listened or refused. And so a penknife, though Jehoiakim wielded it, could not undo what God was
bringing on Judah.'[1]

(iv) '*A shattered city.*' He impressed the same message—the
coming awful destruction of Jerusalem as the will of God—by
means of a symbolic act. He took representatives of the people
and priests with him down to the valley of Hinnom below
Jerusalem (where in Manasseh's reign children had been sacrificed
by fire), and there dashed to pieces an earthen jar, saying: 'Thus
saith the Lord of hosts: even so will I break this people and this
city, as one breaketh a potter's vessel so that it cannot be made
whole again.'[2] Then, ascending to the temple court,[3] he repeated
the message of Divine Judgement. Pashhur, a high official of the
temple, put Jeremiah in the stocks overnight, very likely
threatening that the utmost possible punishment would be
inflicted on the morrow. Popular concern forced him to release
Jeremiah the next morning, whereupon the Prophet pronounced
that not only would the treasures of Jerusalem be taken to Babylon,
but also Pashhur, himself and his family and friends, and there he
would die.[4]

IN THE REIGN OF ZEDEKIAH (597–586 B.C.)

(i) '*Figs, good and bad.*' After the deportation of King
Jehoiakin (Jehoiakim's two-months successor) in 597 B.C., the
remanent population drew a resilient conclusion from the situation.
They held it had been made clear just whom Jehovah frowned on,
and whom He approved: the exiles removed to Babylonia were
the object of His wrath, whereas they (blest inhabitants of Zion)

---

[1] Op. cit. p. 156.   [2] See Jer. xix–xx. 6.

[3] The interdict against his entering the temple must have been lifted, or
else this event preceded it.

[4] Jeremiah further said that Pashhur's name would be changed in sinister
wise: we may 'English' the point thus—'Sir Aster, thy name shall be called
Dis-aster'. (Hebrews esteemed plays upon words more highly than we do.)

were the objects of His grace—as smug a piece of self-esteem as is known to history. Jeremiah drew an opposite conclusion, and vividly told them so. Baskets of figs were set out for sale in the city, some fine fruit and some the reverse. Jeremiah declared as the word of the Lord to the men of Jerusalem that the exiles were like the good fruit, and they like the bad—'figs so bad that they cannot be eaten'. Let them not deceive themselves; Jehovah purposed to send against them sword, famine and pestilence, till they were consumed.[1]

The Prophet's hope for the exiles was high: theirs was the chance, deprived of State and temple, to discover in righteous life the personal religion of the spirit. But news came that the exiles were bewailing their fate and (encouraged by prophets) pinning their faith on hope of a miraculous intervention soon to restore them and the sacred vessels to Jerusalem. Jeremiah wrote to tell them that what had happened was God's *good* purpose for them; and his letter was so wise and had such momentous historical results (as will be noted at the close of this Chapter) that its words must, in part, be quoted:[2]

Thus saith the Lord of hosts, the God of Israel, to all the captives in Babylon. Build ye houses and dwell in them; and plant gardens, and eat the fruit of them; take ye wives, and beget sons and daughters... and multiply ye there, and be not diminished. And seek the peace of the city whither I have caused you to be carried away captive, and pray unto the Lord for it: for in the peace thereof ye shall have peace.... For I know the thoughts that I think toward you, saith the Lord, thoughts of peace, and not of evil, to give you hope in your latter end. And ye shall call upon me, and ye shall go and pray unto me, and I will hearken unto you. And ye shall seek me, and find me, when ye shall search for me with all your heart.

(ii) *The Test of Inspiration.* In 593 the counsellors of Zedekiah were set on revolt against Babylon: Jehovah (aided by Egypt) would restore the independence of Judah. It was for Jeremiah to urge again the teaching his hearers did not comprehend—God willed no such development, for His purpose was to turn them

---

[1] Jer. xxiv.

[2] See Jer. xxix. 4–7, 11–13; noting that in this chapter and in xxv the text of Jeremiah's letter has been supplemented by additions (especially *vv.* 10, 16–20; cp. similarly xxv. 12), expressing the belief of later times that the captivity lasted only 70 years, and that the Prophet must have said so. See the Commentaries, and Welch, op. cit. pp. 157–79.

from trust in outward things to reliance on the things of the spirit. He appeared in the temple wearing a wooden yoke upon his neck (symbol of the Babylonian dominion), and spoke solemnly to that effect. He was disconcertingly countered by another prophet, Hananiah, who enthusiastically proclaimed, as the word of the Lord given to him, that within two years Jehovah would bring back to Jerusalem the exiled king Jehoiakin, the thousands of captives and the sacred vessels.

When prophet contradicts prophet, both cannot be right. But ought one or the other to have been able to discern that he had been deceiving himself and the truth was not in him, and ought the hearers to have been competent to judge between them?[1] Is there any test of authentic inspiration? Jeremiah had all along had to face the contradiction of optimistic prophets, and in parts of chapter xxiii we possess his earlier reflections on the problem. It is clear that he had felt one test to be assuredly applicable. Many of these prophets were men of vicious life: it must be that their oracles would voice only the promptings of their evil hearts. Their hypocrisy was evident in the glib ease with which they promised 'smooth things', and in their parrot copying of one another's words. But sometimes optimistic prophets seemed sincere. What then? This grave problem drove Jeremiah back on the final significance of moral sensitiveness, and to conviction that men who said God would prosper the nation, but were indifferent to the moral evils in the national life that filled his soul with horror, had not the truth in them. They could not have experienced his own overwhelming sense of God as absolute righteousness.[2] As Skinner admirably says:

The basis of all genuine inspiration is a mind 'in tune with the Infinite', a moral sympathy with the principles on which the universe is governed, and a consciousness, none the less real because incom-

[1] Where Christian Churches have found themselves sincerely divided on deeply important issues, were the reasons quite so impossible to transcend as they appeared, and ought the divisions to have been so intractable and bitter? Did the disputants give sufficient weight to the searching criterion which Jesus stressed? He said concerning true and false prophets: 'By their fruits ye shall know them.'

[2] Cp. Skinner (op. cit. p. 196): 'He who has it knows that he has it, though he who lacks it may be deceived in thinking he has it; just as a man who is awake may be sure he is not dreaming, whereas a man in a dream may readily fancy he is awake.'

municable, of personal fellowship with the God who reigns over all . . . .
Real Prophecy has, as we might say, a cosmic significance. It is not a
series of casual, spasmodic, abnormal, illuminations, having no relation
to ultimate Reality; but a reflexion in human thought of the infinite
Wisdom which reigns throughout the universe and through all the
ages. . . . To Jeremiah the word of Jehovah is the eternal truth of things,
the immutable truth which will shatter the existing order, and
destroy the whole world of lies on which men were building their
confidence.[1]

In Jeremiah's encounter with Hananiah it is obvious that he did
not question Hananiah's sincerity, and the episode reveals
Jeremiah's hard-won ability to unite clear-cut belief with teachable
humility towards the truth. For he answered Hananiah's enthusiasm quietly, 'the Lord perform thy words', adding, however,
that in the past the Prophets of truth had invariably spoken
warnings. When Hananiah proceeded to take the yoke from
Jeremiah's neck and broke it, Jeremiah 'went his way'. Only
after a time was he sure that he, and not Hananiah, had spoken
rightly; then he returned to the temple, and said so in yet more
emphatic terms.[2]

(iii) *The Fall of Jerusalem.* In 598 B.C. Zedekiah rebelled,
relying no doubt on help from Egypt, which did not mature when,
in January 597, Nebuchadrezzar's army began to besiege Jerusalem.
The rebels felt they could not look for mercy. So desperate
was the resistance that not until July 596 did the Babylonians force
an entry. By that time the inhabitants had suffered the last
extremities of starvation.

(a) *God's Word to the besieged.* Jeremiah believed that the ruin
of Jerusalem was needed in order that his People might discover
where their real strength lay. But it is one thing to entertain a
belief; another to hold it fast in frightful circumstances. Not
coldly did this Prophet foretell the end of David's kingdom, and
appalling agonies for men, women and children. Yet from start
to finish of the awful siege Jeremiah could find in his heart no
word of God's relenting; and it was for him to say so honestly. In
the initial stages of the siege he held out one assurance—namely
that the lives of those who would give themselves up to the

[1] Op. cit. pp. 197f., 199f.
[2] Jer. xxviii; also xxvii, where in *v.* 1 Jehoiakim is demonstrably an error
for Zedekiah. Both chapters contain many late interpolations.

Babylonians would be spared![1] In any modern State other than Britain or America he would have been shot. In Jerusalem the authorities were in a fix. They compromised by imprisoning Jeremiah in the court of the guard, so that his words could not weaken the hearts of the people.

(b) *God's Word to His Prophet.* Imprisoned, Jeremiah had a curious premonition that he would be called on to take up a family right concerning a field at Anathoth. It must be explained that the Babylonians had taken the lesser towns of Judah, and were resolved to put an end to the nuisance-value of Jerusalem in high politics, but did not interfere with the cultivation of the land. No doubt they needed all the food supplies they could obtain. It seems they were even willing to permit an individual to pass through their lines into the city on personal business. Hence it happened that Jeremiah's premonition was fulfilled: a kinsman from Anathoth came to his prison concerning this field. The Prophet felt the event as a God-given reassurance that his faith was justified. Therefore, in the presence of witnesses, he signed and sealed a deed of purchase, making the procedure a symbolic affirmation to them of his belief that God had a future in store for His People.[2]

(c) *Scoundrels!* As the siege continued and famine tightened its grip, owners of slaves decided to set them free.—'Surely Jehovah would take favourable note of such brotherly behaviour.' Incidentally, of course, it reduced the mouths to be fed in their houses. The freed slaves must fend for themselves. Shortly thereafter an Egyptian army sallied forth, and the Babylonians had to march off to meet, and to defeat, it. For the moment hopes soared in Jerusalem (would 701 B.C. repeat itself?); and promptly the owners reclaimed their slaves! In flaming anger Jeremiah denounced their hypocritical wickedness. Even as they had brought back their slaves to bondage, so Jehovah would bring back the Babylonians to enslave them and destroy the city.[3]

(d) *Persecution—to the brink of death.* Jeremiah was set free in

---

[1] See xxi. 1–10; xxxvii. 3–10. Duhm's Germanic reaction was inability to credit that Jeremiah had gone to such unpatriotic lengths, and that he would have deserved death, had he done so. Duhm therefore regarded these passages as late additions.

[2] Jer. xxxii (vv. 6–16, 24–27, 42–44—the original narrative).

[3] Jer. xxxiv. 8–22.

the weeks when the Babylonian army broke off the siege, and (perhaps to complete the transaction regarding the field at Anathoth) was leaving the city 'by the gate of Benjamin', when the captain of the ward arrested him and took him to the princes, who accused him of deserting to the foe. Jeremiah denied the charge, but the authorities had found a *secular* pretext for dealing with him. They had him flogged, and put in an underground dungeon 'in the house of Jonathan the scribe', intending to let him die there. The king, however, secretly arranged his release, and asked him now to give a favourable word from the Lord. Jeremiah answered that he had no other word from God than that which he had steadfastly spoken. He entreated not to be sent back to perish in Jonathan's dungeon, and Zedekiah consigned him to custody in the court of the guard.[1] But the royal authority was tottering; and the princes got control of him. This time they lowered him by ropes into an empty water cistern, deep in mud. If, exhausted, he should choke himself to death in the mire, it could not be said they had shed a Prophet's *blood*! Again the scales turned. An Ethiopian at the court told Zedekiah, and Zedekiah contrived to have Jeremiah rescued from the filthy *oubliette*. Even in this extremity the Prophet refused to utter a pretended oracle of hope. Famished, half-dead, and aware it was futile to reiterate what all knew he believed, he made one concession to the king, who at least had respected him, wanted to save his life, and was himself desperate. Now that the end was at hand he promised to keep silent; and Zedekiah was able to preserve him from being put to death.[2]

(*e*) *The Last Refusal.* After the sack of Jerusalem the Babylonians established an administration at Mizpah, five miles north-west of Jerusalem, under a Jewish Governor, Gedaliah.[3] Not long afterwards a fanatical 'Zionist' assassinated Gedaliah. In terror lest the Babylonians should exact indiscriminate vengeance, a large

[1] Jer. xxxvii. 11–21.

[2] Jer. xxxviii. Jeremiah has been criticized for cowardice, on the score that here he was willing to evade duty. To that G. A. Smith makes the reply: 'By now Jeremiah had aged, and was strained by the flogging, the darkness, the filth and the hunger he had suffered. Can we wonder at, or blame him? But with what authenticity does its frankness stamp the whole story!' (Op. cit. p. 284.)

[3] Son of the Ahikam who used his influence on Jeremiah's behalf in the reign of Jehoiakim.

number of Jews besought Jeremiah for guidance whether or not
they should fly for refuge to Egypt, swearing to obey whatever
response he should make in Jehovah's name. For ten days he gave
no reply: only then was he sure; he told them to remain, because
it was now God's will to show them mercy and to build them up.
Whereupon they went back on their promise, and refused his
guidance. Overcome by their fears and the entreaties of their
wives (who tearfully declared that their trials were the result of
ceasing to worship the Queen of Heaven as well as Jehovah), they
fled to Egypt, 'where they would hear no more war'. And they
compelled Jeremiah to go with them.[1] His last utterance in the
land of Judah was that those who fled to Egypt in that frame of
mind would there forget the very name of their fathers' God—
then it would be manifest *whose word stood*.[2] How pardonably
Jeremiah might have written of his life-work: 'Surely I have
laboured in vain and spent my strength for that which is naught.'

§8. *The Gift of God*

Does God demand all things from the loyal heart, and give
nothing in return? Jeremiah did not think so, not even when he
received that last refusal from his fellow-men and was carried down
into Egypt. He had passed through perplexity into the serenity
of settled trust in God. But his friend, Baruch, felt that he had
reached the depths of absolute despair, and came heart-broken to
Jeremiah, saying: 'God does nothing, save add anguish to my
pain.'[3] Jeremiah offered the man he loved the precious, all-
sufficient, gift that God had given him—the same stern and
bracing truth that his own, almost broken, spirit had been taught.
He told him: 'God's purpose extends beyond our individual lives.
Seek not relief, but be prepared for greater strain; God must pull
down more than yet has fallen. One thing alone God gives to thee,
Baruch—thine own life, "in all places whither thou goest".'

[1] 'That was Israel's inveterate habit. They would neither commit themselves absolutely to their prophets, nor would they let them wholly go.'
(Welch, op. cit. p. 243.)

[2] What purport to be oracles of Jeremiah spoken at Tahpanhes in Egypt
(xliii. 8 ff., xliv), and most (if not all) the oracles on foreign nations in the
later chapters of the Book of Jeremiah, are in all likelihood anonymous oracles,
not by him, and of later date.

[3] Jer. xlv. A title-verse dates Baruch's question in the fourth year of
Jehoiakim, but has no great weight. Skinner (op. cit. p. 346; cp. Erbt,

Our life, which we are free to use for righteousness: therein is God's exceeding great reward, preserving us, not from effort and disappointments, but from self-betrayal. For with that gift there comes to whosoever will receive it from the hand of God a sense of the Holy Presence, and a peace no man can take away.

Jeremiah was in no despair about the future of his nation. There had been a day when, disconsolate and baffled, he had noticed a potter in Jerusalem at his work, with skilful hands moulding the clay to the design he had in mind. Then something had gone amiss. But the man did not fling away the errant clay. Jeremiah had watched human patience shaping it again, so that there came forth another vessel perfected to the potter's purpose.[1] He reflected on the ancient covenant with God vowed by all Israel at Sinai, which the forefathers and their descendants had applauded nationally and as individuals had frustrated. But Jeremiah had learnt that it is not for a man to despair concerning the work of God; and he lived to write these words of immortal insight:

Behold, the days are coming, saith the Lord, when I will make a new covenant with the house of Israel, and with the house of Judah. . . . I will put my law in their inward parts, and in their heart will I write it; and I will be their God, and they shall be my people: and they shall teach no more every man his brother, saying, Know the Lord: for they shall all know me, from the least of them unto the greatest of them, saith the Lord: for I will forgive their iniquity, and their sin will I remember no more.[2]

We, restricted to past, present and future tenses, translate *I will make...I will put.* But the Hebrew verbal form equally expresses an action in progress—*I make.* Jeremiah was certain that others would learn what he had been taught, and that there would be an 'Israel', wherever there were Israelites serving God's purpose of righteousness.[3] He had become conscious of the goodness of God

---

Jeremia, p. 86) feels that the contents of the brief poignant passage imply a moment of final, inescapable, parting between the two friends: 'It reads like a farewell oracle, perhaps a death-bed charge'—as if Baruch knew that he must henceforth tread a lonely path.

   [1] Jer. xviii. 1–5.   [2] Jer. xxxi. 31 ff.

   [3] 'Babylon could burn down a temple and carry away its vessels; that was the task which Jehovah Himself had given it. But it was powerless against religion. For the true faith continued wherever Israel offered its prayers and its obedience.' (Welch, op. cit. p. 223.)

eternally at work, in the future as in the past, ever revealing His truth and His Presence to those that seek in spirit and in truth. The Prophet could not know all that God had in store whereby to make known His Presence and His truth; but how near he came to foreknowledge. In a like exaltation of spirit St Paul wrote that, when all else vanishes away, faith, hope and love abide; above all, love—that most excellent gift of God.

§9. *The Influence of Jeremiah*

His courage we can recognize. But was not his labour in vain? The Prophet's treatment at the hands of men was similar to the experience of Christ. At first, it is true, the multitude heard Jesus gladly, but when He taught that His kingdom was not an earthly one they went away, and at the end the mob cried 'Crucify Him'. Like Jeremiah, Christ sadly saw 'the Good' being made the enemy of 'the Best'. Of the Law, which He had come to fulfil, He was forced to say that it could be so misused as even to make men blind to God's truth; and concerning the golden temple Herod had erected, He had to quote Jeremiah's words: 'Ye have made it a den of robbers', and to predict that it would be destroyed. Herod's temple had taken forty years to build, and men trusted in its stability, not knowing that 'three days' suffice to build the temple of God for human souls. When the authorities realized that He might endanger their fixed beliefs and secular interests, from that time forth they sought to put Jesus to death. So also was it with Jeremiah. Him the multitude feared, scorned and hated. The priests, zealous for the reformed worship, asked the Rulers of the State to put him to death: 'These men, who were deeply moved about their religion, would have nothing to do with the most religious man of their time.'[1] In the end the civil Rulers sought to murder him most cruelly.

Christ did not labour in vain: He was able to entrust His significance and His teaching to the disciples who had been with Him three years. Neither did Jeremiah labour in vain. One man had learnt to love and reverence him. For the soul of Baruch had been lifted from the dust; and Baruch wrote down what he could remember about his master and friend, and to his dying day must have spoken much about him. Therefore, it came to pass that Baruch's records of the rejected Prophet were cherished, and

[1] Welch, op. cit. p. 236.

gradually the marvel of Jeremiah's fidelity and wisdom was pondered wherever the manuscripts were copied and studied by Jewish eyes. Moreover, Jeremiah had written to the exiles in Babylon a letter which was a veritable illumination.—They could find God wherever they were, and should pray for the peace of the land where they dwelt. We may be sure that this spiritual conception of life passed from place to place among the Jews in Babylonia; and from Babylonia to other lands, wherever there were groups of thoughtful Jews. All who absorbed its truth found that citizenship of the world was theirs, because (in the New Testament phrase) they could be 'colonists of heaven'. Four hundred years after his death the name of Jeremiah had been inscribed indelibly in the roll of Israel's men of God. The historian of the heroic conflict waged by Judas Maccabaeus in the second century relates that Judas, seeking to nerve his followers for a battle against fearful odds, spoke to them about a dream which had come to Onias, the High Priest. In his dream Onias had seen 'a man appear.... Wonderful and most majestic is the dignity around him. This is the lover of the brethren, he who prayeth much for the people and the holy city, Jeremiah, the Prophet of God.' And in Onias' dream Jeremiah had given to Judas a golden sword, saying: 'Take the holy sword, a gift from God, wherewith thou shalt smite down the adversaries.' [1]

Fortunately, in earlier times far deeper, though not braver, thoughts about Jeremiah had entered many minds. Earnest men realized that his agony had been incurred because he refused to cease to be God's servant; and they saw that his voluntary suffering had enabled him to purify his heart, and had led him to wisdom which became the strength of his People when they were broken and scattered. They saw that his experience had been marvellously transfigured from pain into peace, and from loss into gain; because he had caused the shame and sorrow of outward defeat to become the very means of victory. Above all, after Jeremiah's death one very great man whose name we know not— the last of the supreme Prophets—grasped that profound truth, and discerned in the significance of just such fidelity and innocent suffering as had been Jeremiah's the real vocation of Israel in the providence of God for all peoples.

[1] II Macc. xv. 12–16.

CHAPTER XVI

GOD AND THE NATIONS

Patriotism is an invaluable medicine for self-centred human nature. If the fullest energies and finest qualities of which we are capable are to be evoked, a motive far grander than the interests of the individual self is indispensable. Love of country and of kindred is an incentive of that order, astonishing in its strength, latent in us more deeply than we are aware. In time of national crisis self-sacrifice and endurance are displayed by supposedly unworthy persons in a way that calls to mind the saying: 'There are last that shall be first.' Response to enemy bombs, rather than to appeals for Victory Bonds, tests character in men and women in a way that inhabitants of unblitzed countries will never understand. Patriotism is perhaps the only virtue every respectable person cannot help possessing in some measure, simply because we find ourselves members of a specific land and nation, by which we are ceaselessly affected. If there be in us any graces of affection and gratitude, those qualities are bound to be stimulated by whatsoever is attractive and good in the familiar environment of our daily life. Citizens of the Western States are acutely assertive of their personal rights, but they have been, and remain, violently nationalistic. In this humanitarian Age, and with the assistance of the newspapers, some sympathy may be aroused by a pitiable catastrophe occurring at the other end of the earth; but the emotion is tepid compared with our feelings if inundation is overwhelming our countryside, or epidemic raging in our town. We are not God; and being finite in imagination are sure to care for our fellow-countrymen (with exceptions) far more than for foreigners. Even the most universally-minded idealist cannot love a territory he has never seen, as he may do his own:

> Breathes there the man with soul so dead,
> Who never to himself hath said,
> 'This is my own, my native land'?

Poverty, enterprise, courage have driven many a Briton to distant, and not always unpleasant, parts of the earth. And there some of them have prospered; but 'O hame, hame, hame, to my ain

countree' is the voice of the exiled Scot. R. L. Stevenson, famous
and at ease in his beautiful Pacific Isle of Samoa, was wistful for
Edinburgh:

> I saw rain falling and the rainbow drawn
> On Lammermuir. Hearkening, I heard again
> In my precipitous city beaten bells
> Winnow the keen sea wind. And here afar,
> Intent on my own place and race, I wrote.[1]

Long ago the heart-break of a Hebrew banished to fertile
Babylonia was made audible in these words: 'O Jerusalem, if I
forget thee, let my right hand forget her skill.'[2] Patriotism is a
most permanent and powerful factor in human affairs.

But patriotism throughout history has proved paradoxically to
be a deadly vice as well as a shining virtue. The awkward fact is
that our own beloved People happens not to be the only People
upon the earth; and ardent patriotism too often goes hand in hand
with merciless disregard of the interests of other nations, with
shocking ignorance, prejudice, ill-will, greed, fear, and ferocity
concerning them. Nine-tenths of the space in history books is
occupied by analysis and description of the causes and consequences
of patriotic conflicts. The worst of the record concerns the
relations of highly civilized States. What words are adequate to the
destruction these have inflicted one on another? As for the treatment of uncivilized races by the civilized, sneering comments that
concentrate on injuries done and ignore the good are infuriatingly
unjust; but from the days of the Slave Trade onwards what
arrogance there has been, what cruelties, what exploitation!

In the past, three great efforts were made to eliminate national
conflicts by substituting for local and racial attachments a wider
interest and loyalty. Each failed for diverse reasons. In the fourth
century B.C. Alexander the Great initiated a brilliant effort to unify
Greece and the Near East by kindling enthusiasm for general
Greek (*Hellenic*) culture. Next, between the first and the ninth
centuries A.D., the Roman Empire established a world-domination
intended to secure universal peace and afford all nations willingly
participant an honourable place within its splendid framework.
Neither of those supernational movements was *rooted* in religion;
but both were practical, idealistic, schemes, for a while successful.

---

[1] Dedicatory Sonnet to *Weir of Hermiston*.   [2] Ps. cxxxvii. 5.

In each case, however, as the stimulus of national loyalties loosened, virtues which patriotism had nurtured faded into insipidity, and were replaced by jaded vices that flourished in an atmosphere of cosmopolitan unconcern. The third attempt—the Holy Roman Empire—was built out of the ruins of the second— the political Roman Empire. It was a highly complex blend of the religious concept of the indivisible unity of the Church under Christ, the legacy of imperial Rome's theory of civilization as a single political society, and (later) the philosophical doctrine that 'the One Universal' is the true abiding substance. Nominally the attempt persisted until 1806, and into the intricacies of its history this is no place to enter. In general, the contentions of the Papacy with the kings and feudal lords show the good ship of the religious ingredient in the Holy Roman Empire tossing (and at times disabled) in tumultuous seas of exceedingly irreligious intrigues, ambitions and conflicts of persons, parties and peoples. Neither the Brotherhood of Man, nor the Victory of the Faith, was achieved in Europe between the tenth and the nineteenth centuries.

The fourth attempt to create an overriding World-Organization is now being made. The constraining motives are mixed: *Fear, Food, Finance, Freedom* and *Faith* will serve for catchword summary. When the World-War ended, it seemed that horror and pity would alone suffice to smooth the road to peace. But, in fact, fierce, divisive patriotism survives as untamed and untaught as if nothing significant or moving had taken place, and as if the need were not desperate to prevent the atomic energies in nationalism from finally shattering civilization. Even the parish-pump politics of localities are being recklessly used, and have intensified a thousandfold the terrible major difficulties between the Great Powers. But even if national entities could be eliminated in a cosmopolitan society, history seems to show that would be neither permanent nor wise solution. Love of country is an invaluable stimulus as well as a great virtue. How can the poison be extracted from the plant of patriotism, and its values conserved? It was to the heart of this problem that the final phase of the Hebrew Prophetic Faith was directed.

Thus far the great Prophets had said nothing deep regarding the problem of the passionate patriotism of many nations. The reason for that is obvious. In wrestling to comprehend the mystery of human life, their thoughts had not been wandering to the ends of the earth but concentrated on facts with which they were in immediate contact—the relation of Israel to the God it professed to worship, the ultimate significance of good and evil in the life around them. As soon, however, as their genius had reached the conviction that there is but one God, they were travelling the royal road that must lead to beliefs applicable to mankind. The Prophetic Faith had become implicitly universal, but was not yet explicitly and cogently so. The *ideal* for all nations ('No more war') had been stated; for we may paraphrase Isa. ii. 4 (= Mic. iv. 3) as prediction that 'the nations will turn their tanks into tractors, and their guns into butter'. Hosea and Isaiah had declared, vaguely, that God would bring about that idyllic state of affairs, but only after His miraculous intervention had overthrown the power of the wicked, and put an end to the present, imperfect, World-Order. If, however, history went on (as it has done, and shows no signs of ceasing), the expectation, considered literally, was no more than a woolly wish. It should, however, be noted that at least the Faith was not moving towards hope that Israel would be the Master-Race in the sense that all other nations would have to become its unwilling subordinates! Instead three principles, essential if a right solution of nationalism's dangers is to be reached, had been perceived. First, the Prophets of the eighth century had insisted that Israel's trust in its being the Chosen People of Jehovah had nothing to do with exemption from material hardship or defeat, but everything to do with inescapable spiritual and moral responsibility. Secondly, the resources which belief in One God (morally conceived) could provide to sustain individual courage and social cohesion were being set free from entanglement in national interests (monarchy and independence) and from dependence on local rites (Jerusalem's temple sacrifices)—which had been considered indispensable.[1] Thirdly, and most important of all, in reaching truly personal religion the genius of Jeremiah had been such that 'the Religion of the Old Testament did not become merely

[1] 'The essential task of the prophecy which reached its complete development amid the death-throes of the kingdom of Judah was to separate the vital truths of religion from their embodiment in the institutions of a decadent social organism....That task was finished in the work and life of Jeremiah—in his life even more than in his work; for it was only in a tragic personal experience such as he passed through that the reality of religion could be apprehended and verified.' (Skinner, *Prophecy and Religion*, p. 351.)

individualistic in becoming individual'.[1] No one could consider the unselfish life of Jeremiah, the suffering he chose to endure at the hands of ungrateful men for their welfare, and accuse him of serving individualistic religion! Exactly like the great Prophets before him he had shown that he loved God by caring for his brethren. Hence it was made logically impossible for the Prophetic Faith to develop into a comfortable, self-regarding, piety. In this Religion theory could not be sundered from practice; creed and conduct were made indissolubly one.

§1. *A Literary Problem*

The beliefs which made the Hebrew Prophetic Faith a fully universalist religion are preserved in the extraordinary chapters (xxxiv, xxxv, xl–lxvi)[2] which form the last half of the Book of Isaiah. Nothing in those chapters derives from Isaiah, the Prophet who lived in Jerusalem in the eighth century. They are *at least* 150 years later than his time, and no Prophet is named in them. Since they were attached to the 'Isaianic' collection forming the first half of the Book, scholars found it convenient to refer to their author (or the author of chapters xl–lv) as 'the Second Isaiah'. But that is a drearily academic title for a genius. He will here be called *the Poet-Prophet* or *the Prophet*.

It has long been general opinion that in chapters xl–lxvi the thoughts of more than one unknown Prophet are present. That grandeur pervades the utterances, and that certain passages are sublime, is indisputable and undisputed. 'The exegesis of twenty-four centuries', says S. A. Cook, 'proves that the writers of Is. xl *sqq*. had an insight into spiritual truths which remained unsurpassed in Israel.'[3] But a highly distinctive literary style, and a glorious general theme (like the pattern formed by diverse pieces

---

[1] W. R. Smith and O. C. Whitehouse, in *Ency. Brit.* (11th ed.), vol. XXII, p. 446.

[2] The suggestion that chs. xxxiv, xxxv should be 'reckoned in' is due to Torrey. Ch. xxxv seems convincingly the Poet-Prophet's work. But it is surely probable that the glorious ch. xl ('Comfort ye, my people...') was intentionally the first of the oracles. Where chs. xxxiv, xxxv originally stood is uncertain. Ch. xxxiv (the overthrow and desolation of Edom) might well be the sequel to lxiii. 1–6. The writer, however, is very dubious if either of these 'Edom' passages, or ch. xlvii (on Babylon) derive from the Poet-Prophet: see further, pp. 343, 356.

[3] In *C.A.H.* III, p. 497.

in a rich, multi-coloured mosaic) pervade the twenty-nine chapters. Why should we parcel them out to two or more anonymous prophets? No doubt some phrases, verses, or occasionally a longer passage, should be recognized as late additions ('glosses'), and in all likelihood dislocations in the arrangement of the original order of the utterances have taken place.[1] The text of every Prophetic Book in the Old Testament bids us expect that much. The large problem is whether *major operations* must be performed on the body of 'Second Isaiah'. As to that, the grave symptom which has seemed to necessitate drastic surgical work is that in chapters lvi–lxvi much internal evidence points to conditions in Jerusalem in the *fifth* century B.C.[2] But in xl–lv features occur which (if in the original text) seem to imply that those chapters date from a century earlier—namely from 545–538 B.C., when the Persian king, Cyrus, went from victory to victory and in 538 conquered Babylon. The reasons stressed for dating xl–lv in the *sixth* century are these:

(*a*) Chapter xlvii (xlvi. 1, 2, are detached verses) *expects* the Fall of Babylon, which happened in 538 B.C.

(*b*) Expectation of a joyous return to Jerusalem of Jews from all lands is obviously a leading *motif*; but three verses contain words which narrow the exhortations specifically to the captive Jews in Babylonia.

(*c*) In xlv. 1 it is announced: 'Thus saith the Lord to his anointed, to Cyrus, whose right I have holden, to subdue nations before him...' The chapter proceeds to portray the irresistible march of God's anointed (here stated to be *Cyrus*) to execute the divine intention. This declaration is dumbfounding. Elsewhere in surrounding chapters the executant of God's purpose is exultantly declared to be *Israel*, or 'Israel' as faithful and therefore as achieving its vocation in the high providence of God. *Israel*

---

[1] A special caution, however, is here in place. The repeated, abrupt transitions from 'light' to 'shade' in Isa. xl–lxvi seem, as a rule, to be deliberate; and they are aesthetically effective. They must therefore not readily be assumed to indicate dislocations of order, still less marks of different authorship. It would be a grotesque error to assign the diverse movements (grave and gay, swift and slow) in a sonata to different composers: they play their part in a complex whole.

[2] Between the time when in 518 a makeshift temple was rebuilt at Jerusalem, and the restoration of the ruined walls by Nehemiah most probably *c.* 380 (not 445) B.C.

is His chosen, whom He has called from the beginning, whom He upholds; *Israel* is His servant.[1] Nevertheless the solitary, fantastic identification of the 'chosen and anointed' (*Messiah*) with the Persian king, Cyrus, has been accepted at its face-value, and the then logical conclusion drawn that the Prophet (or Prophets) who gave us chapters xl–lv about the year 545 B.C. obviously cannot be the Prophet (or Prophets) who wrote or spoke chapters lvi–lxvi in the next century.

When, however, Isaiah xl–lxvi has thus been cut in two, the surgeons, considering the sundered halves, see symptoms that prompt further anatomical skill. Some commentators have been guilty of really reckless dissections. 'The paring process', remarks Torrey, 'begun with a penknife, is continued with a hatchet, until the book has been chopped into hopeless chunks.'[2] In particular, one contention, which gave rise to voluminous and intricate discussion, maintains that in four chapters we ought to dissect out certain very wonderful verses concerning the conversion of the Gentiles (which the fidelity of God's suffering servant will achieve), and assign them to one Prophet (call him *the Universalist*); whereas the context which declares the majesty of God, the coming restoration to honour of desolate Israel and Jerusalem, is the work of another (call him *the Monotheist*). This proposal is now generally abandoned. It is like focusing a telescope on the summit of Mont Blanc, and ignoring the fact that its snowy crest is the topmost point of a great mountain, and the mountain part of a magnificent range. The supreme verses cannot justifiably be 'cut out'—they are the culmination of a great argument, announcement of the hitherto hidden truth to which the context leads up. Another and much wider contention, which deserves the closest consideration, concerns the passages that allude to Gentile nations. It is held that, when these are compared, great divergences of attitude towards the Gentiles are evident, such as to indicate more than one Prophet's ideas. But those passages are glorious poetry, on which some who favour this argument have produced some comically prosaic remarks.[3] The writer considers the contention invalid, provided the grand theme is rightly understood. The

---

[1] See xli. 8 ff.; and xlii. 1 (noting the LXX text); cp. also lxi. 1.

[2] *The Second Isaiah*, ch. 1 ('The Eclipse of a great Prophet', p. 13).

[3] Torrey's occasional censures in this connexion are severe, but it is difficult to feel they are undeserved.

'surgeons' are in a quandary regarding the glorious diction that pervades xl–lxvi, and can argue only that the later writers carefully imitated Second Isaiah's style. Lame explanation indeed! Major operations on xl–lxvi are disastrous; to be undertaken only if inevitable.

In 1928 C. C. Torrey in a most refreshing volume urged that the fateful 'Babylonian' features in xl–lv were not part of the original text. If so, the problems are transformed. For nothing then forbids that xl–lv as well as lvi–lxvi may all be dated in the same depressing, fifth, century. If Torrey's case be no more than generally sound, there is cause for thankfulness. In all that shows the grand theme and style ('Gospel for an Age of Doubt') we may see the soul of a single Poet-Prophet, sublime in insight into the problems of suffering and of Nation against Nation.

Students aware of the intricacies of the prolonged, critical, discussion must judge the merits of Torrey's revolutionizing view by reading his book.[1] Torrey gives good reason why 'Babylonian' allusions might be added to manuscripts in the fourth or third centuries B.C.; for the Jews in opposing the Samaritans' claims were anxious to suggest that huge numbers of Jews had actually returned from Babylon in 538 by Cyrus' permission. It may come to be regarded as one of the curiosities in the history of Old Testament criticism that these allusions were not earlier suspected. Torrey is on immensely strong ground in judging them to be glosses. The pivotal point is the equation of Cyrus with God's chosen and anointed servant. It is not credible that the beloved titles of Israel's relation to God, and its achievement of the divine purpose—which in contiguous passages (written in almost identical terms and in the same inimitable style) is asserted to be indeed Israel's privilege and on the eve of fulfilment—should here, and here only, suddenly be flung to an alien king. To invent a parallel enormity, imagine that at the present time there was discovered among German documents a perversion of the famous Christian hymn reading as follows:

> Hail to the Lord's Anointed, TO HITLER,
> Great David's greater son. . . .

That hypothetical document, were it found, we should instantly

[1] *The Second Isaiah* (1928).

recognize as product of an effort to Nazify the German Church!
In xlv. 1 *to Cyrus* was surely no part of the original text.[1]

Torrey is on almost equally strong ground in excising the
references to Babylon and Chaldea in the three verses (xliii. 14;
xlviii. 14 and 20). Delete them (and the cuts come clean),[2] and
the verses are in line with exhortations elsewhere which indubitably
look for a general return of exiled Jews from north, south, east and
west. In xliii. 14 the fugitives *from Babylon* are exhorted to return
in the ships of their rejoicing. That is nonsense; for, as Torrey drily
remarks, exiles in Mesopotamia could not get back to Jerusalem in
ships, the Suez Canal having not yet been cut. Chapter xlvii (the
future fall of Babylon) is in no wise fatal to Torrey's theory.[3]

The writer accepts the validity of Torrey's chief contentions.
Accordingly the view is here taken that in Isa. xxxiv, xxxv, xl–
lxvi, *for the most part* we have to do with a single, profoundly
spiritual, Prophet.[4] He happened also to be a creative literary

---

[1] In the immediately preceding verse (xliv. 28), which is the last verse in
ch. xliv, *Cyrus* is also named. But (before Torrey wrote on the subject) this
verse had been recognized as secondary, a 'tag-on' to the chapter, redundant
after *v.* 26 and inconsistent with the tenor of the context. The sole relevant
question concerns *Cyrus* in xlv. 1.

[2] See Torrey, op. cit. pp. 44–50.

[3] The brilliantly ironic passage, xlvi. 1, 2; xlvii (which contrasts the confidence of Babylon with its coming downfall and humiliation) Torrey
ascribes not to the period of Cyrus, but to a fifth-century date, holding that
Babylon came to be used as a synonym for 'Ungodly Power'—*Edom*,
likewise, as symbol of 'Indelible Infamy'. That may be so (cp. Rev.
xvii, xviii); but another possibility may be preferable. Ought not Isa. xiii,
xiv (on the fallen or falling King of Babylon) to be brought into question?
The three chapters are all-of-a-piece, and their author may well be, not the
Poet-Prophet, but an enthusiast (like-minded with Nahum in reference to
Assyrian Nineveh) who was contemporary with Babylon's collapse. Why
chs. xiii, xiv were inserted in i–xxxix by the compilers of the Book of Isaiah,
one cannot say. But ch. xlvii would readily seem appropriate in chs. xl–lv
because of the Poet-Prophet's scorn of idols and idolaters.

[4] The writer must safeguard his general acceptance by saying that in places
Torrey seems to him to overpress his case, and sometimes unwisely so.
For instance—xlv. 4 is appropriate to Cyrus. Torrey squeezes a meaning out
of the verse consonant with the whole chapter being originally addressed to
Israel. But the verse may be a gloss, either by the author of the fateful 'to
Cyrus' interpolation in xlv. 1, or by someone who, having the words 'to
Cyrus' in his manuscript, wanted to underscore the surprising declaration.
Furthermore, a few passages in chs. lvi–lxvi are not at all convincingly in the
style or of the quality of the great Prophet. Ch. lxvi in especial looks like

genius, who lived in Jerusalem amidst the dismal circumstances of the latter part of the fifth century, preceding the arrival of Nehemiah. Call him *the Poet-Prophet*.

Nothing can be learnt about the Poet-Prophet himself except by inference from his thoughts and the form in which he set them forth. Mastery of language he possessed. The style is noble, impassioned, resourceful, resplendent; poetic in the highest degree. And it is so inimitably individual that, if even a few verses were to be transplanted to some other Prophetic Book, they could scarcely fail to be recognized as a strayed fragment. The Prophet's theme has been entitled *Zion Redeemed*, but is far greater. It is the deliverance of Mankind from ignorance and evil—*God and the Nations*. All that he says concerning Israel's coming honour and joy is spiritually conceived, and in no wise separable from the joy of all the nations. The mode in which he unfolds the sublime conception is, however, disconcerting; so seemingly inconsequential are the abrupt transitions as topic after topic is treated for a few verses, then abandoned, and later resumed or amplified.[1] First reading of these chapters is therefore bewildering, but the impression should deepen that (however strange the method) a great argument is being developed. It is as if one becomes aware that beneath surface-waves that foam and fall and rise again, there flows a mighty current of the ocean. When the Prophet's problem with his hearers is appreciated, his method is most skilful. He was charged to impart an absolutely new conception of Life's meaning and Israel's part therein, and its truth would sound almost unbelievable. The danger was that his supreme disclosure would be made to men with closed minds, offered to the unheeding and uncomprehending. Therefore effort on effort had to be made first to rouse their despondent apathy and compel attention. If he spoke to the citizens of

patchwork, in which fragments only are likely to be the Poet-Prophet. It is hard to suppose these verses were his final utterance: perhaps dislocation of arrangement has occurred in manuscript transmission, and perhaps he recorded a good deal else which chances to have perished.

[1] Comparison has been made with the sequence of parts in an oratorio. True; but the Prophet was not trying to produce an artistic masterpiece: he spoke from the heart as the spirit moved him. R. G. Moulton (*Literary Study of the Bible*, p. 435) suggested as the only suitable classification the term *rhapsodic*—i.e. 'the prophetic form made by the fusion of all literary forms in one'.

Jerusalem in the fifth century, he spoke to men who had good reason to feel done with political and religious hopes. No man can speak powerfully in a time of frustration and disillusionment unless he has felt to the full the facts that have defeated others. The Poet-Prophet must himself have suffered and been near despair, because he could say to Israel as the promise of its God—'When thou passest through the waters, I will be with thee; and through the rivers, they shall not overflow thee: when thou passest through the fire, thou shalt not be burned; neither shall the flame kindle upon thee.' Such words bear the marks of personal experience. So much then we can infer concerning the Poet-Prophet, but 'the rest is silence'. It may seem a grievous loss that we should not know even the name of one whose mind reached out in generosity towards human life everywhere, and who, inspired to discern that there could be purpose of goodness and mercy in the dark mystery of Israel's suffering, spoke to all who suffer and are heavy laden. Yet in this instance our ignorance is not loss but gain. This Prophet gave no place to Self in what he had to say. So far as was humanly possible, he made himself a transparent medium of truth. Hence at this climax of Hebrew Prophecy it is as if not even the screen of a human personality was allowed to interpose between our conscience and the Word of God. In his words God is the speaker—*Attend unto me, O my people; and give ear unto me, O my nation.*

Of course, the great thoughts—their significance deeper than the immediate apprehension of the Prophet could realize—had to pass through the limitations of his mind and were applied by him to the specific circumstances he knew. We are concerned with genius, not omniscience. Two concessions are asked of the reader. *First,* that he will trace the Prophet's expectation in relation to Israel and the world of that period—without concurrently considering 'Has this any lasting significance? Is it in any wise relevant to our problems?' (To those questions we may turn at the close of this Chapter.) *Second,* that the reader should bear in mind that transcribing high poetry into prose, with aid of fragmentary quotations, cannot possibly convey the sense of power and beauty which one feels when the finest expressions of this vision of the world at last redeemed have grown familiar. Then the exaltation of the Prophet's thought, and the strange music of his words, become unforgettable—like the impression one receives of blended strength and serenity indwelling a great cathedral building, or like vivid recollection of some surpassingly lovely scene in Nature.

§2. *God's Power and Purpose*

By the middle of the fifth century B.C. the citizens of Jerusalem had learnt thoroughly a compulsory lesson in geography. They knew now that their city was politically negligible, and 'off-the-map' commercially. Even if Solomon's reign could be renewed, what was that compared to the wealth and magnitude of the Gentile kingdoms? Impoverished, stony, Judah was a speck in the vastness of the inhabited world. *And* they had had enough of religious optimism. When the temple was rebuilt in 518, two Prophets, Haggai and Zechariah, declared that very soon Jehovah would 'shake the heavens and the earth', and earth's welcome resources be at their disposal—which things had by no means come to pass: predicters of miraculous changes were under a cloud. The wicked could scoff, the cynical could invite optimists to use common sense. As for youth, the soil of Judah offered toil and poverty, whereas there were now excellent prospects in Gentile cities for enterprising Hebrews with their wits about them. Could parents say 'No' to the eagerness of Jewish youth to get *out* of the Holy Land? Besides, remittances from loyal children abroad might keep soul and body together for the aged in Judah. But was it in the least likely those migrant children would continue to revere the God of their grandparents in old-fashioned Palestine? In the fifth century voluntary emigration sapped the remanent strength of Jerusalem. The city was like a widow forsaken, her children departed and departing to the ends of the earth. Too long had Jews in Palestine seen the sun rise and the sun set, and nothing new under the sun. For one reason and for another it seemed certain that hope in Jehovah was no longer sensible. Against that despair rang out this Prophet's challenge, declaring God's power and God's purpose.

Let Israel credit its Creed! *ONE GOD, beside Whom there is none other!* What does that truth imply? What folly to imagine (as some did) that God had been unable to protect Israel against mightier Gods. Let Jews ponder their humiliation, poverty and powerlessness on a rational basis—'Who gave Jacob for a spoil, and Israel to the robbers? did not the Lord? he against whom we have sinned, and in whose ways we would not walk?'[1] God, the only God, is inconceivable in greatness—'Who hath measured the waters in the hollow of his hand, and meted out heaven with the span, and comprehended the dust of the earth in a measure, and weighed the mountains in scales?...Behold, the nations are as a drop of a bucket, and are counted as the small dust of the balance.'[2] Timid pietists were afraid that the Maker of heaven and earth would be really interested only in really large nations, and pleased only by the munificence of Gentile worship with which the meagre offerings at Jerusalem's tenth-rate temple could not compete. What incomprehension of reality—'Lebanon is not sufficient to burn, nor the beasts thereof sufficient for a burnt offering. All the nations are as nothing before him; they are counted...less than nothing.' As for the pride of powerful nations, Jews should bethink them of *quality* not *quantity*—the quality of their Faith's unique insistence that God demands mercy not animal-sacrifices—

Is not this the fast that I have chosen? to loose the bonds of wickedness,...and to let the oppressed go free?...Is it not to deal thy bread to the hungry, and that thou bring the poor that are cast out to thy house? when thou seest the naked, that thou cover him; and that thou hide not thyself from thine own flesh? Then shall thy light break forth as the morning, and thy healing shall spring forth speedily: and thy righteousness shall go before thee; the glory of the Lord shall be thy rearward.[3]

Jews can leave ostentatious ritual and childish theology to Gentiles, who think it sense to construct likenesses of the Deity! The Poet-Prophet knew how to use irony. See (he said) how the Rulers of the great nations engage skilful craftsmen, lavish gold and silver on the design, and obtain a resplendent idol. As for the hard-up heathen fellow, carefully he selects a hard-wood tree, himself chops and trims until he has an image that does not wobble; and to it he devoutly addresses his prayers. Of course (poor man) he does not waste the wood left over; with *that* he can make a fire, and warm himself.[4]

If Jews must try to picture God, let it be by imagining

[1] Isa. xlii. 24.

[2] In this section unspecified references to the Prophet's words are taken from Isa. xl.

[3] Isa. lviii. The flaming accusation and demand in the first twelve verses of this chapter should be read in entirety.

[4] Cp. Isa. xl. 18–20; xliv. 9–20; xlv. 20; xlvi. 1 f.

a shepherd, so vigilant that every one of his sheep is known to him, so gentle that he will carry the weakling lamb in his arms. But some replied bitterly that facts made nonsense of the pretty picture, for Israel was cruelly wronged and God did nothing about it, either because He cared not or He would not. Others, again, insisted that the world was so vast its Maker could not be expected to pay attention to the troubles of a minute People— Israel was no bigger than a worm wriggling in the soil.[1] The Prophet called the doubters to look up to the night skies, and consider the might and vigilance of Him who created and controls the ordered galaxies of the stars, wherein not one is missing. He was told to realize that people and city were utterly exhausted. How could this worn-out, tiny nation possibly revive in a world of mighty and vigorous races? He answered that it could, provided it would hear and heed the Word of God—'They that wait upon the Lord shall renew their strength.' But earnest men argued that their forefathers had sinned beyond forgiveness, and that Israel was deservedly rejected by its God. Again and again the Prophet as the voice of God gave healing answer—[2]

Thus saith the Lord that created thee, O Jacob, and he that formed thee, O Israel: Fear not, for I have redeemed thee; I have called thee by thy name, thou art mine.

Remember these things, O Jacob; and Israel, for thou art my servant:...O Israel, thou shalt not be forgotten of me. I have blotted out, as a thick cloud, thy transgressions, and, as a cloud, thy sins.

Comfort ye, comfort ye my people, saith your God. Speak ye comfortingly to Jerusalem, and proclaim unto her, that her distress is ended, that her iniquity is pardoned; that she hath received of the Lord's hand double for all her sins.

Well did the Prophet, however, realize his difficulty. Jerusalem was sunk in a veritable stupor of dejection. He knew that whatever terms he used concerning the thoughts God had imparted to him, men would at first respond by debasing the gold of his real meaning into glitter of material riches and military security—as if the promise were that Solomon's temple should be restored (for Jews' exclusive worship); that strong walls should be built (to keep out foes); that countless exiles (prospering abroad) should come

[1] Isa. xli. 14.
[2] See Isa. xl. 1, 9–11; xliii. 1, 25; xliv. 21; lv. 6, 7.

back (which would cause a worse housing shortage than ever). Jerusalem, half-conscious, would turn uneasily; remember that it had ceased to believe Prophets; and go to sleep again. He had to speak about renewal spiritual and universal; about restoration transcending all hopes that had ever been conceived. Therefore, not once nor twice, the trump of God must sound—'Awake, awake, put on thy strength, O Zion; put on thy beautiful garments, O Jerusalem, the holy city.'[1] The Prophet's voice was vibrant with authority; for he was preparing men to hear what had never been heard, a supreme revelation of the real purpose of God—'Arise, shine, for thy light is come, and the glory of the Lord is risen upon thee.'[2]

Now the unheard-of truth, and astounding promise, which the Prophet had to announce, brought together two conceptions; one seemingly simple, the other subtle and exacting. The first was religious universalism: God's grace is for all—God 'made the earth, and created man upon it'. He gives 'breath unto the people upon it, and spirit to them that walk therein'. He calls men (*not merely Israel*) 'my sons, and the work of my hands'.[3] From the beginning God's real purpose has been that everywhere men shall cease their foolish trust in idols and possess true religious faith; so that they realize God to be 'a just God and a saviour', and reverence Him 'in whom is righteousness and strength'. This shall assuredly come to pass: 'to Him shall men come'—'Unto me every knee shall bow.'[4] Ever and always the only God has been seeking 'to bind up the brokenhearted...to comfort all that mourn'; 'to open the blind eyes, to bring out the prisoners from the dungeon, and them that sit in darkness out of the prison house.'[5] *Now* God commands and invites—*Look unto me, and be ye saved, all ye ends of the earth.* The second intuition of the Prophet concerned a new and wonderful interpretation of the vocation, suffering and destiny, of Israel amidst the nations. In the profoundest way he fused this belief with the universalism, deeming Israel's response necessary for fulfilment of God's worldwide purpose.

God's mercy extends to all. Was that the prodigious revelation? Our reaction is to ask why so obvious a conclusion was not reached

[1] Isa. lii. 1; cp. li. 1.
[2] Isa. lx. 1.
[3] Cp. Isa. xlii. 5; xlv. 6, 11, 12.
[4] Isa. xlv. 21–24.
[5] Isa. lxi. 1; cp. xlii. 7.

earlier; why (in the Prophet's phrase) God had had to keep it 'hidden'. It was not an obvious idea when the Poet-Prophet was the first in this world to assert it. None of the high and mighty nations of antiquity, with their many Gods, would have understood it at all. Nor could the Hebrews have received and credited it, until the great Prophets had talked sense concerning God. Now at last (the Poet-Prophet believed) Israel might comprehend; but only if it would accept God's purpose in its suffering. It was in this discernment that the genius of the Prophet culminated. Modern thought, of course, recognizes that Deity cannot be conceived as showing partiality towards this or that nation or individual! Anyone who to-day takes a religious view of life will readily assent to the theological commonplace: *One God and Father of us all.* But, implicit in the metaphysical assertion, there is a sociological counterpart: *One Brotherhood of Man.* That proposition gives us pause. Avowedly or secretly, individuals and nations tend to keep creed and conduct in watertight compartments. 'Religion for Sundays only' has been only too popular a cult. The Poet-Prophet took both beliefs seriously. Whoever does so is led to the profoundest spiritual principles, and to implications so exacting that the most christian Christian confesses himself a sinful man who does not fulfil his bounden duty.

§3. *God's Providence and Skill*

What provision must God make in order that His Will be done on earth by persons having a measure of freedom? God must endow Man with a glimmer of intelligence and moral discernment. *This* God has done. No sane human being has ever been quite devoid of Reason and Conscience; which faculties, as he makes use of them, produce increasingly wise discrimination between fact and fancy, right and wrong. By and large, men have made use of Reason, with results that, although thrilling, have in the past century become desperately perilous, because they do not make similar good use of Conscience. The nations persist in being as stupid about conduct as they are clever about mechanics. Furthermore, God must provide a stable framework for human life, wherein causes have consequences: an *Order*, not a *Chaos*. *This* God has done. Thorns of cruelty do not produce grapes of gentleness. Mankind ought to have learnt the lesson from the evil consequences of evil. Yet if they had done so, that result would be no better than pale shadow of virtue, the merely negative attitude of not daring to be vicious. If God's purpose is that we should seek truth and love mercy, what can God do about that? Force, even the might of omnipotence, is useless. Not even God can batter affection into our hearts, like a nail into wood. How then can the light of His moral perfection dawn upon our finite consciousness so that we shall desire truth above all things, and long to do right? To accomplish that God needs His servants who do Him service, the followers after truth, the children of light. In their characters and actions contrast of Good against Evil becomes revealingly apparent.

The Poet-Prophet reflected that in Israel this revelation through faithful persons had been happening even from the beginning, and how marvellously—*Abraham*—*Moses*—*David*. To Israel there had indeed been given God's servants the Prophets—*Amos*—*Hosea*—*Isaiah*—*Jeremiah*. Nor had Israel lacked the valour, goodness and faith of unremembered men and women who had not scorned the Prophets, but had sought to receive their teaching into their hearts and minds. Thus Israel had become a Nation that had been told 'There is ONE GOD: Him only shalt thou serve'; taught that God desired mercy; knew that men should treat one another humanely as brethren of one family, because they did not worship the almighty shekel, but God the All-merciful. What then? (Suppose that ancient Israel had learnt some medicinal marvel that would heal the pain-racked bodies of men, would that treasure rightly have been for its exclusive possession? Such knowledge is held in trust for mankind.) To the Poet-Prophet came an inspiration—God has sought to prepare among the Peoples of the earth a People which can witness to Him. In Israel's past God had given a Call to individuals to receive and speak His truth, and faithfully the great Prophets had borne witness. *Now* the Divine Call has come to the whole People, to Israel itself. In the high providence of God His purpose is that Israel should become *Prophet-Nation to the Nations*.

For himself the thought entailed an agony of responsibility: it was laid upon him to make plain the Vision, and persuade. Searing dread assailed him, lest Israel should not hear the Call, or, assenting easily, prove unequal to the burden of its calling. He was no optimist in that matter, and it has been truly said that he might be called *the Prophet of Rebuke* just as much as *the Prophet of*

Comfort. He knew the men of Judah and Jerusalem had eyes they would not use, ears that refused to hear—'Who is blind, but my servant, or deaf, as my messenger that I send?' 'There is an actual Israel which does not call upon its God, is weary of Him, swears falsehood in His name. God (he declared) *will* establish righteousness on earth, although there be no man to help!¹ But in the Prophet courage became master of his fear. He dared to believe that an Israel responsive to the long patience of God had really existed and exists. How could his generous soul think otherwise, who remembered the faithful dead, and knew that the fire of faith was burning in his own heart?² He could regard this ideal-real Israel in various ways—now as an individual ('My chosen', 'My anointed'), now as the nation ('O Israel, thou art my servant').³ He could say that in relation to actual Israel this ideal Israel had a redeeming work to do. Here are the immortal words: 'It is too light a thing that thou shouldest be my servant to raise up the tribes of Jacob, and to restore the preserved of Israel: I will also give thee for a light to the Gentiles, that my salvation may be unto the end of the earth.'⁴ He felt that the power of God would enable this 'faithful Israel' to achieve the Divine purpose; for the true Israel had come into existence through the foreknowledge and providence of God and was no mere dream of human longing— 'He shall not fail nor be discouraged, till he have set justice in the earth; and the isles shall wait for his law.'⁵ In faithful Israel actual

---

¹ Cp. Isa. xlii. 13–17, 19; xliii. 22; xlviii. 1–11; lix. 16; lxiii. 3, 5; lxv 12.

² Isa. xlix. 6: *to restore*—the Hebrew unites two ideas: change of mind as well as change of condition; *conversion* as well as *restoration*.

³ The varying aspects do not point to diversities of authorship. There is perfect parallel in the variations of Christian feeling concerning the Church, ideal and real. (Cp. the famous hymn 'The Church's one foundation....') As Peake (*The Problem of Suffering*, p. 193; cp. also *The Servant of the Lord*, p. 67) remarks: 'The nation is regarded in the light of its purpose in the mind of God. The servant is not an ideal distinct from the nation, but the nation regarded from an ideal point of view.' See further, Skinner (*Isaiah* xl–lxvi, pp. lviii–lxii, 263–81); H. W. Robinson, *The Cross of the Servant*, pp. 32–46; and S. A. Cook in *C.A.H.* vol. III, pp. 488–98.

⁴ Isa. xlix. 6.

⁵ Isa. xlii. 4. *Justice*—so render. The English versions translate *judgement*, which conveys a wrong impression. The meaning is 'right relations between men, rising out of acceptance of right principles'. *Law* is also too rigid a term. The meaning is *instruction* or *guidance*.

Israel and every nation would find unity: God's servant will be the bond of human brotherhood.[1]

It is one thing to offer for service; quite another to prove obedient in the discipline which fits a man to render service. Only the *skill* of God could make His Prophet-Nation, Israel, capable of its work for God. When Bunyan's hero vowed that he would be a pilgrim, he had to travel a long road. When a lad decides that he will be a scientist, he has to toil at his subject and patiently experiment. So it is with every great resolve:

> Let no man think that sudden, in a minute,
> All is accomplished and the work is done;
> Though with thine earliest dawn thou shouldst begin it,
> Scarce were it ended in thy setting sun.[2]

To what discipline had the true Prophets been subjected? They had not lived in honour, hailed as benefactors by their generation. They were given hatred and scorn as their portion, and their efforts seemed to be fruitless. They endured an anguish like the penalty of wrongdoing which the hardhearted and the sinners deserved. And their agony had been incurred voluntarily, inasmuch as they would not selfishly abandon their stern vocation. Jeremiah placed his youth in the hands of God; and the Master-Craftsman hardened and tempered the raw material, until the sword of the Prophet's spirit was wrought and finished. This burden of strain and sorrow they could have escaped by keeping silence, or by saying the 'smooth things' men desired to hear. But because the Prophets bore it for the sake of others, something wonderful happened—the portrait of the faithful servant of God, lover of his brethren, was being drawn in unmistakable lines. After the Prophets were dead, the men of Israel and Judah were contrite; knew that they had slain the innocent, and persecuted those that did them good. Thus the souls of the Prophets reached the one reward they sought. They brought many to righteousness, because they had chosen to be at-one with sinners in their need. That self-sacrifice is demanded from all who say they serve God, and it is a sobering thought whenever we are tempted to speak fluently about *The meaning of Atonement.*

[1] Isa. xlii. 6 and xlix. 8. This is the meaning of the phrase 'I will give thee for *a covenant of the people*, for a light of the Gentiles'.
[2] F. W. H. Myers, *St Paul.*

In these facts of experience the Poet-Prophet found inspiration concerning the affliction of his People. If Israel regarded its suffering resentfully and construed its hardship and strain as showing negligence and injustice on the Deity's part towards a small nation, nothing would be effected. But if Israel were conscious of the need of the whole earth for true belief and goodness, and for that end placed itself in the hands of God, *willing* to endure in order that all nations might be brought to the knowledge of the truth, such contrast of Good with Evil would be manifest that the conscience of mankind might be moved thereby. Light would arise in darkness. For voluntary suffering has an eloquence greater than speech; the gentleness that is born, not of weakness, but of patience is more potent than might: 'Behold my servant, whom I uphold; my chosen, in whom my soul delighteth: I put my spirit upon him; he shall bring forth justice to the Gentiles. He shall not cry, nor lift up his voice, nor cause it to be heard in the street. A bruised reed shall he not break, and a dimly burning wick shall he not quench: he shall bring forth justice in truth.'[1]

Five wonderful, short, passages in Isa. xl–lxvi declare the Prophet's understanding of the inward struggle of faithful Israel— its anguish and despair, its comprehension of God's meaning in the suffering, its acceptance of the burden, its endurance, and its ultimate spiritual victory.[2]

Bring down this Vision to the too, too solid earth. Jews were by this time dispersed abroad in many lands and the influence of

[1] Isa. xlii. 1–3.

[2] See xlii. 1–4; xlix. 1–6; l. 4–9; lii. 13–liii. 12; lxi. 1–3. Presumably these verses are but a fraction of things the Prophet spoke at sundry times concerning Israel as the faithful servant of God; essentials that he deemed sufficient to include in giving permanent record to his message as a whole. Our tidy minds feel that these passages should have been set together to form a unity of presentation. We can but note that, great artist that he was, he went his own way in the matter. The verses present numerous perplexities, above all in lii. 13–liii. 12, where in many places the text is certainly or probably imperfect. In *v.* 8 read *for our transgressions* instead of *transgression of my people* (a minute change in the Hebrew text; cp. LXX). In *v.* 7 the sacrificial allusion is explicitly metaphorical; whilst in *v.* 10 the context of the word *trespass-offering* is unreliable text, and its specific meaning in Hebrew ritual must be clearly understood. Wise comment on those facts may be found in H. W. Robinson, *The Cross of the Servant*, pp. 46–50. As regards lxi. 2 (*the day of vengeance* or *requital*) see §4 of this Chapter.

such of them as worshipped O N E G O D and behaved well was all to the good. But the Prophet's confidence that the mighty kingdoms would be brought to penitent realization of true God and true goodness did not rest on the merits of a handful of relatively good Jews in distant places.[1] His hope depended on two things. First, he believed that a glaring contrast between Good and Evil now existed in the world (or was certainly on the point of existing) as the result of the nations' treatment of faithful Israel compared with *faithful Israel's* treatment of them in its willingness to suffer for their deliverance from error and wickedness. But he did not suppose the mere existence of that moral contrast would *of itself* suffice. Secondly, therefore, he looked to see some action by God which would compel the attention of the nations, making the contrast plain for all to see.

§4. *The Action of God*

The newspapers tantalizingly assure us daily that the masses of mankind want peace. If only 'the plain man' could make his good-will effective, things would be comparatively well: he does not want to impoverish his neighbours, but only not to be poor; he would like a happy life, not to make others miserable; he does not long to enslave, but only not to be enslaved. But throughout history a minority of evilly disposed persons have had the power and the pitilessness to make hell for the rest. Of this fact the Poet-Prophet was sensibly aware; for Hebrews were realistic. There were strong and unalterably wicked persons, he realized, whom no manifestation of sheer goodness would divert from their wrecking purposes. What then? As the Prophet saw the problem—the myriads of ordinary men and women needed to be shocked out of their moral ordinariness, but *they* were convertible, and God at last possessed in the world the means to reach their conscience, and transform their character. Did He not now hold in His hand the sharp sword of His servant's willing self-sacrifice for their sake? Yes, but incorrigibly evil men would not turn a hair! Was it thinkable that in His destined hour the Creator would allow the wicked to thwart His glorious and

[1] As Torrey (op. cit. p. 145) remarks: 'The great nations of the earth had their own religions, to which they were attached. Why should they think that their salvation rested in the faith of this prostrate people, this "root out of a dry ground"?'

gracious purpose for mankind? The Prophet could not believe so, and he thought the omnipotent power of God would then cast down all who obdurately opposed His will—be they wicked Gentiles or (wolves within the fold) wicked Jews. Therefore a 'day' of divine recompense or vengeance (*Dies Irae*) seemed to him necessary for the advent of the Day of Grace.

The Prophet envisaged the Day of Wrath as an irresistible campaign by God Himself, or by Israel His servant whom He upholds—'I will go before thee, and make the rugged places plain: I will break in pieces the doors of brass, and cut in sunder the bars of iron.'[1] A poet is speaking; his words are figurative. This supernatural triumph denotes no conflict between Jews and Gentiles in history; its setting is eschatological, its hour the moment when God creates a world wherein righteousness shall dwell for ever.

There are, however, two lurid passages, highly disconcerting to the prosaic, on which special comment must be made. Edomites, desert-cousins of the Judaeans, had been present at the sack of Jerusalem in 586 B.C., and the way they had incited the Babylonian soldiers to merciless savagery was branded in the memory of the Jews. Edom deserved to be synonymous in their minds with atrocious cruelty—like the *Gestapo* in ours. Now Isaiah xxxiv depicts the awful devastation of Edom after God shall have dealt with it, and in lxiii. 1–6 God is portrayed as returning in red splendour from victory over Edom's capital, Bozrah. The Prophet was neither ferocious nor demented. How could his universalist mind suppose that a destruction of paltry Edom would overawe the entire earth, and confound the wicked everywhere? If these two passages are from the Poet-Prophet they are metaphor: Edom is synonymous with Wickedness.[2] The famous American hymn based on lxiii. 1–6 is not sung bloodthirstily:

> Mine eyes have seen the Glory of the coming of the Lord:
> He is trampling out the vintage where the grapes of wrath are stored;
> He hath loosed the fatal lightning of His terrible swift sword:
> His truth is marching on.

---

[1] xlv. 2; cp. xli. 1–4, 8–16; xlii. 14–17; xlix. 24–26; lix. 15 ff.

[2] Isa. xxxv is in the mood and mode of Second Isaiah. But xxxiv and lxiii. 1–6 may be by a different author (cp. xlvii, and the Book of Nahum), and were deemed by compilers of the Book of Isaiah suitable to include.

To regard what the Prophet says of the Day of Wrath apart from the concomitant beauty of the Day of Grace is foolishness—like gazing at shadow in unconsciousness of light.[1] In the most moving chapter in the Old Testament (Isaiah lii. 13–liii. 12) the Prophet set forth the contrition of the Kings of the Peoples, conscious now that God's faithful servant, whom they had tormented and despised, had for their salvation from evil willingly endured the agony and shame.[2] Awed, penitent and thankful, they confess—'Surely he hath borne our griefs and carried our sorrows: yet we did esteem him stricken, smitten of God, and afflicted. But he was wounded for our transgressions, he was bruised for our iniquities....All we like sheep have gone astray; we have turned every one to his own way; and the Lord hath laid on him the iniquity of us all.' A right spirit had been created in them. Wherefore to the Nations, transformed in mind and heart, God proclaims—'Behold, my servant shall prosper, he shall be exalted and lifted up....He shall see of the travail of his soul, and shall be satisfied...because he poured out his soul unto death, and was numbered with the transgressors: yet he bare the sin of many, and made intercession for the transgressors.' The chapter carries in its heart a significance greater than the Prophet himself could measure.

[1] In the course of all that the Prophet says about the relations of Israel and the Gentiles in the beatific Age, one verse and two words stand in flagrant contradiction of the whole picture of unity and thankfulness. In xlv. 14 delete *in chains*; the rest is conventional Eastern expression of reverence. The whole verse lx. 12 is an abomination. These are additions, bitter and uncomprehending, typical of certain minds in later time. In lx. 11 for 'their kings led' read *leading*. The difference depends on the correct *vocalization* of the original consonants, n–h–g–m. Finally, a curious point arises in regard to lxi. 5, 6 ('And strangers shall stand and feed your flocks, and aliens shall be your ploughmen and vinedressers. But ye shall be named the priests of the Lord: men shall call you the ministers of our God'). Torrey would excise *v.* 5 as a gloss. But are agricultural pursuits dishonourable, or unpleasant occupations in an idyllic Age? After all, if the men of Israel were to discharge priestly functions for the world's religious centre, they would be busy and somebody had to see to their physical wants! The idea may be quaint, but is not necessarily embittered. (A point of grammar favours deletion.)

[2] The text in certain verses is obscure and imperfect.

§5. *The Joy of All Peoples*

God's purpose is eternal. Intuitively the Prophet spoke of the consummation, now as future ('Behold, the Lord God will come as a mighty one'), now as actual ('Arise, shine, for thy light is come'). Remembering that Hebrews expressed ideas in pictures, follow the Prophet's thought of a regenerate world wherein the nations have ceased to be their own worst enemy and enemies of one another.

It is a world of rejoicing: 'Sing unto the Lord a new song, and his praise from the end of the earth; ye that go down to the sea, and all that therein is, the isles and the inhabitants thereof'—'Be ye glad in that which I create: for, behold, I create Jerusalem a rejoicing, and her people a joy.'

It is a world where bombs do not turn cities into rubble, nor stupidity and greed change fertile soil into deserts; because men no longer spend money for that which is not bread, nor labour for that which satisfieth not. Nature can respond to nations who are of one accord to build and to plant: 'They shall build the old wastes, they shall raise up the former desolations'—'Instead of the thorn shall come up the fir-tree.' Even the desert shall blossom like the rose; for there will be pools of water in its irrigated sands, and in its midst a way of holiness for redeemed and thankful men to walk therein.

It is a world where Israel, once desolate, is satisfied, because the travail of its soul had not been in vain. The Israel of God had identified itself with the need of all nations, had been willing that peace should come to it only as they also entered into peace, and that its joy should be fulfilled only when joy was universal. Through faithful Israel's agony the blind have received their sight, the lame walk, the imprisoned are set free in the liberty of the children of God: 'Sing, O heavens, and be joyful, O earth; and break forth into singing, O mountains: for the Lord hath comforted his people....'

In the midst of this transfigured world of unity there is a City of God, a New Jerusalem of heavenly beauty, radiant with light. Its brilliance is the light of God's presence, not the glitter of human pride: 'The sun shall no more be thy light by day; neither for brightness shall the moon give light unto thee; but the Lord shall be unto thee an everlasting light, and thy God thy glory.'

Jerusalem—that had been like Rachel, weeping for her children, because they are not—will lift her sorrowing eyes and (incredulous) see her sons and daughters returning from east and west and north and south. The white-winged ships of the ocean are bringing them home, and the caravans across the deserts. But not all the Jews in all the world could account for a fraction of those that are hastening to the City of God. This is a multitude no man can number: for the children of Jerusalem come not alone. All nations accompany them, led by their rulers and 'singing the praises of the Lord'. All that was Israel's, Israel gave—treasure that gold and silver could not buy. Now all that is theirs shall be hers. Freely and thankfully the Peoples bring the diversities of their treasures to adorn the Holy Place of their unity. Eagerly they build its shattered walls; for New Jerusalem is a city the gates whereof stand open by day and night. 'Are not its walls salvation, and its gates praise'; and its temple 'the house of prayer for all peoples'? [1]

The world of to-day needs to translate the Prophet's Vision into actuality.

§6. Translation

Ought we to look back upon the Prophet's expectation with cynical eyes? Or was he very near to stating the immutable principles by which inestimable possibilities of virtue and welfare could be made actual? He held that human existence is meaningful and intelligible. As he put it: 'Thus saith the Lord that created the heavens (he is God; that formed the earth and made it; he established it, he created it not a waste, he formed it to be inhabited): I am the Lord; and there is none else. I have not spoken in secret, in a place of the land of darkness; I said not unto the seed of Jacob, Seek ye me in vain: I the Lord speak righteousness, I declare the things that are right.' [2] In our words—the Prophet believed that Ultimate Reality is *morally* apprehensible. Was he wrong?

Here is a modern answer from a scientist. 'Nature', writes Crowther, 'is much simpler than might have been expected, and therefore we have a better chance of mastering it and turning it to our uses....Modern *quantum* theory does not suggest that the foundations of Nature are dotty, nor that the Almighty has presented us with a cruel joke.' Crowther then cites a remark of

[1] Isa. lx. [2] Isa. xlv. 18, 19.

Einstein to the same effect: 'Raffiniert ist der Herr Gott, aber Er ist nicht boshaft', adding an American translation thereof: 'God is slick, but He ain't mean.' Was the Prophet wrong in thinking that Ultimate Reality steadfastly makes for construction? From the standpoint of a biochemist, Needham writes: 'Form, or rather Organization, as we might now call it, is present everywhere, at all levels, wherever we look; and the only other fundamental idea we need is that of Energy. We can stop thinking of Form and Matter altogether if we begin thinking of Organization and Energy'; and he draws this conclusion: 'The World co-operative commonwealth is not, as so many people seem to think, a wild, preposterous, optimistic dream; it is a certain resolution of our difficulties, having the full authority of evolution behind it.... Whatever force hinders the coming of the World co-operative commonwealth, where all human races will live in harmony together, and where the old maxim will be true "from each according to his capacities, to each according to his needs"; that force is ultimately doomed. Against the world-process no force can in the end succeed.' And a sociologist, Karl Mannheim, insisting on the values of group-loyalties, remarks that modern sociology tends to follow a trend parallel to one which prevails in modern biology; and says: 'We have now reached the Age of planning, when purposeful reconstruction of society as a whole has to be envisaged.' These comments, drawn from a single volume, are modern assertions of the Poet-Prophet's faith.[1]

Two errors, or inadequacies, in the Prophet's thoughts are patent. *First*, God did not make evil-minded men powerless by an omnipotent intervention, as the Prophet expected Him immediately to do. That indispensable task of imposing restraint on the pitiless is laid upon the servants of truth and goodness in every generation; God gives the light necessary for its accomplishment. *Second*, the Prophet's touching confidence that actual Israel would not fail to be converting manifestation of Goodness was mistaken. Jews have suffered from Gentiles persecutions which disgrace our common humanity, but as a race they have not transparently manifested the Mind of God, nor embodied Love Divine. Every student of Judaism knows the heroism, goodness and faith which multitudes of Jews have shown in the course of history. But everyone knows also how many, Jews by race but

[1] *This Changing World* (ed. Brumwell, 1945), pp. 31, 38, 70, 73, 77.

not by faith, have been anything but shining lights. [That verdict has also to be pronounced upon how many Gentiles?] The Prophet asked more than a nation, being composed generation after generation of saints, sinners, and the 'in-betweens', can accomplish. When his thoughts of faithful Israel were most intense, he individualized his ideal. Is it not true that at the earliest possible moment ineffable Goodness was seen in an incomparable personal life? 'What think ye of Christ?' Light has shined in this dark world of human strife; and many in many lands have come to its brightness—'out of darkness into His marvellous light'. All too often that Light has been tragically obscured, partly by grave intellectual disputes, more so by intellectual niceties which like a dense undergrowth cover up essentials; but chiefly by failure to insist that sincerity of faith is proved by deeds, not words—as Jesus and the Prophets rigorously said.

At the beginning of this Chapter it was remarked that mixed motives—Fear, Food, Finance, Freedom and Faith—are in the present effort to establish a World Order. Terror of atomic warfare, the obvious fact that sustenance and solvency are supranational interests, and the passionate patriotism which is indicated by the demand for freedom, are welcome influences that should work together for good. But unitedly are they adequate to create and maintain peace in this distraught and divided world? And will they pull together, or, fatally, pull at cross purposes? There is a growing weight of apprehension. It seems that nothing can avail to avert catastrophe, unless a radical change of spirit can be brought about, which would heal ancient feuds and present fears through a vitalizing sense of a fresh outlook that made problems soluble on a higher plane. From the Peace Conference of Nations at Paris in August 1946 an experienced commentator wrote these words:

There is needed desperately a voice which will denounce their jealousies and their prevarications, their embittered polemics and their inhuman dialectics. A voice which will remind them that in our human lives there are certain values, certain sins, certain virtues, which are not concerned in any way whatever with the economic and social theories of our time: that cruelty is evil absolutely, that untruthfulness is evil absolutely, that hatred is evil absolutely; and that however harsh and clangorous may seem our present rivalry and suspicion, there is a single strong wish that pulsates in every heart—that never again shall we see fear dart across the eyes of our children, that never again shall we dread lest the word justice may lose its strength and its beauty among men.[1]

In Israel the Prophets were that voice. When their words are not left between the closed pages of a book, they are that voice.

The Poet-Prophet looked not for a Universal State, but for a universal state of mind—assent to the true values in life. Then 'the treasures of the nations', the achievements of their distinctive characteristics, would enrich the common welfare. Second, he thought that the *kings* of the earth would perceive the transfiguring truth: they would comprehend, and would *lead* their Peoples along the Way of Holiness. In the past regenerating movements have sometimes begun in humble circles. The reverse may be the hope in our times. For the irresistible tendency in modern society is that the mind of the masses is increasingly shaped from above by the relatively few. That is true even in the democracies, where variety of information still is provided, and liberty to differ permitted. It is awesomely true of the Soviet Republics, where a few men are able to determine what 200 millions shall know and be caused to think. What those rulers of Russia believe about ultimate truth and goodness, and what the leaders of thought, politics, industry and finance, in the West, China, India, and Africa, believe, is making a 'world' of difference to our world.

In the energetic civilization of to-day, which has seen two devastating wars in half a century and where peace trembles in the balance, there are plenty of reasons to despair of the future, even as there were in the fifth century B.C. Our dread is that, whereas religion can speak redeemingly to the spirit of the individual, it is unable to grapple with the terrible complex of material as well as moral factors involved in *group* interests (economic and national affairs), from which, however, the individual cannot sharply sunder his moral life. The Poet-Prophet saw in such despair blindness to truth which could deliver the nations. We shall never know his name. But he should be remembered as 'The Apostle of Hope', because he called the communities of men to Faith and Love.

[1] Harold Nicolson (*The Listener*, 29 August 1946).

CHAPTER XVII

WISDOM

When men hold definite ideas about Ultimate Right (Ethics) and Ultimate Reality (Metaphysics), what they think about either or both subjects affects their personal lives and their civilizations profoundly. Failure to hold definite ideas does so equally. Consider this observation:

The Germans teach in their schools a certain body of doctrine, which the great mass of them accept, and upon which they are now acting. It has given them unity and a great and fanatical strength; but it has also led them into the crimes that we know of. We, on the other hand, are taught no body of doctrine in our schools, at least none that can be called philosophical, and we are rather proud of the fact.... The Germans have taught their children that they must do everything for the good of Germany....They have been industrious, obedient, and self-sacrificing. They have made their country the tidiest, the most efficient, the most powerful in the world, and an intolerable nuisance to all mankind....Now we see that we cannot remain in this negative state. We must believe either what the Germans believe, or *something positively and splendidly contrary to it.*[1]

That passage might seem comment on the Nazis: it was penned in 1917, and the succeeding twenty years supplied the commentary. Certainly the prevalent disposition of the British and American public is to make do with no very definite opinions about Ultimate Right and Ultimate Reality. Yet in physical problems we appreciate the importance of having sound ideas and paying attention to facts—as, for instance, that men can fly the Atlantic, but not by jumping off the house-top, hopeful they may be upborne on thin air. In Morals few suppose (as Hitler may have done) that, if we tell 'the Lie, the whole Lie, and nothing but the Lie', it will eventually be credited as Truth; or that the habitually treacherous man can build up a reputation that his word is as good as his bond. But we are not positively and splendidly eager about basic ethical convictions, as were the Nazis about their creed of Blood and Soil. Asked whether a religious view of Life is truth

[1] Clutton Brock, *The Ultimate Belief*, pp. 1, 3, 7.

or illusion, we are prone to say 'Another day will serve for that'. We ought to take our stand splendidly and positively on the reading of Life which comes to us through the Prophets and the Christ. There have been, and there are, other interpretations of Existence and Morality. Only summary reference can here be made, but is in point. For light is thrown on a subject by saying, however briefly, *This* is not *That*. The claim is that, by contrast and comparison with these other views, the Prophetic Faith is wise; and is wise because in its essentials it is true.

The cardinal beliefs of the Hebrew Prophets are classified as Ethical Monotheism. In this Chapter let us utilize instead a definition drawn, not from the Greeks, but from the Hebrews' style of speech—ONE GOD, EXALTED IN RIGHTEOUSNESS.[1]

§1. *ONE*

The Prophetic Faith shows psychological wisdom in its demand that we must seek to integrate our personality by holding in thought a single, supreme, standard whereby to measure the validity and value of the manifold interests that excite attention and seek our approval. Few individuals are so fiercely swayed by two radically divergent dispositions that their condition has to be diagnosed as 'Split Personality'. But only the absurdly arrogant man assumes himself to be a perfectly integrated Self. Most of us are often in danger of being 'tossed to and fro and carried about by every wind of doctrine', tempted to toy with the fancy that life is sufficiently devoid of principle to be plastic to our whims and that, if we cannot get what we want by hook, we may get it by crook. 'Unite our hearts to fear Thy name', said a Psalmist, echoing the wisdom of the Prophets. But the Prophets do not invite us to mystical contemplation of undefined, and undefinable, *Oneness*.

---

[1] The Prophets had to pour the wisdom of their convictions through the channel of Semitic speech, but how wonderfully they widened and deepened the channel. 'It is a fascinating sight to see the prophets fighting for a new language, and fighting with it after they have attained it. Although at first Hebrew religion had much in common with the religious languages of the great contemporary civilizations, yet the peculiar element in it, that made it entirely different, ultimately forged its way through, and created a language for humanity. It provided words in which men could pray and express their faith. It made a language suitable for a world-religion.' (Baeck, in *The Religions of the World* (ed. Clemen), p. 270.)

(i) *Primitive Monotheism.* The Prophetic Faith has no relation-ship, in theory or history, to the interesting claim made by a few, gifted, individuals in savage communities that they have an impression of a supreme *Oneness*—a barbaric mysticism unwarran-tably termed 'Primitive Monotheism'. Savages, who thus feel, treat the experience as devoid of any bearing on mundane affairs. 'It is not in the least degree that victory over environment which marks a true monotheism.'[1] Indeed, Polytheism (which is an attempt to understand and grapple with the circumstances of life) is a superior level of thought.[2]

(ii) *Mysticism.* The Prophets at times had supernormal visions, and to the significance of the fact for normal men reference will be made in the closing Chapter. But their Faith stands in contrast to typical *Mysticism.* Usually the mystic can report to others that in the trance he has had an incommunicable sense of oneness with Reality, a consciousness of 'pure light without any object it illuminates, an ecstasy of completely void awareness';[3] and (except for some of the mystics who have been heirs to the Faith of Christ and the Prophets) the experience tempts to consciousness of difference from ordinary men and a longing to renew the blissful rapture, but not to passionate longing to serve the needs of others. The Prophets in their moments of trance felt not 'void awareness', or 'identification with an incommunicable Oneness', but met Reality robed in righteousness, demanding the service of their lives, their all. Instead of being dazed 'by pure light that illumi-nated nothing', they returned to their normal senses resolved to stand for truth, at whatever cost to themselves, for the sake of their fellow-men; and with illuminated minds that perceived the deep

[1] Oman, *The Natural and the Supernatural*, p. 386. He terms it 'the unity of undifferentiated awe of one sacred reality'.

[2] Radin (*Primitive Man as Philosopher*) maintains that savages show as great a range of intellectual and religious capacity as civilized men. There is among them occasionally a man of genius. Such a man may have thoughts far above crude superstition. Some practical-minded savages believe in a Creator Super-God, who intervenes in the world's affairs but not often in a beneficent way. It is only the devout, idealistic savage who experiences the mystical sense of an ultimate Oneness or One. But he does not regard the Oneness or One as approachable by man or interested in the created world.

[3] Oman, *The Natural and the Supernatural*, p. 418. Cp. E. Bevan (in *The Legacy of Israel*, p. 47): 'The mystical experience does not seem, of itself, to have necessarily any spiritual value....The sense of immense awareness which it gives does not mean any extension of real knowledge.'

determining factors in the perils and disorders of their times. 'The mystic', wrote Heiler, 'is one who gives up, renounces and rests; the prophet is a fighter, who perpetually struggles from doubt to assurance, from torturing uncertainty to absolute certainty of life, from weariness to fresh courage, from fear to hope, from the crushing sense of sin to the blessed consciousness of grace and salvation.'[1]

(iii) *A-cosmic Pantheism*. The *One* of the Prophetic Faith is diametrically different from the undifferentiated *Absolute*, which the philosophy of A-cosmic Pantheism regards as Ultimate Reality. According to that philosophy the phenomenal world (including Man's differentiation of Right and Wrong) is Illusion; and our proper aim is therefore not to endeavour to deal positively with the seeming challenges of environment, but to lose the illusion of personality in the blank unity of the Absolute. The moral consequences of that attitude, which has tragically affected Indian civilization, are logically paralysing; for it lays down that 'there is no world in which anything that might be called the divine will could be done'.[2] In contrast, the Prophetic Faith looks upon the universe and human beings as having finite Reality, derived from the infinite, perfect, Reality of God—the O N E, in thought of Whom we should strive to unify our personality.

§2. *One GOD*

For a variety of reasons—some honourable in their sincerity of doubt, some excusable, and some contemptible—we live in a period that is remarkably untheological: which is not the same thing as saying irreligious or immoral. Multitudes fail to believe (to any practical extent) in the existence of God, because in the first place they are at a loss to imagine what is meant. Certainly it is a period

---

[1] *Das Gebet* (Eng. trans.), p. 255. S. A. Cook's pronouncement to the same effect is weighty: 'The Prophets were not mystics—there is for them no *unio mystica*—they were intensely realist and rationalist....Prophecy at its highest was not a psychological phenomenon with psychological criteria: it was the balanced sanity of the Prophets, and not their manticism, that made them such tremendous factors in human history.' (*The Old Testament: A Reinterpretation*, pp. 188, 189.)

[2] Farmer, *The World and God*, p. 69. Cp. MacNicol (*Jerusalem Meeting Report*, vol. I, p. 42): 'The *Vedanta* doctrine presents to us a world-wide view which is serious and profound. But the absolute unity of *Advaita* leaves no room for the spirit to breathe. Its unity reveals itself as a unity of death, not life. Its ultimate end is emptied of all ethical significance.'

in which men generally do not take themselves to task about metaphysics—Ultimate Fact and Right. It follows that morality is neither strongly nor clearly conceived, because all-too-human standards are allowed to occupy in men's minds the place of God (i.e. an absolute standard by which values are to be judged and aims shaped). But, if through disbelief or disinterest men cast the God of the Prophets and of Jesus out of the mansion of the Mind, into its emptiness crowd many jostling demi-gods and devils. Some of these occupants of the house that belongs rightly to God are respectable, some the reverse. In modern times one wing of the mansion is inhabited by well-meaning but quaint 'Fancy Religions'. Many rooms are tenanted by emaciated Ideals to which decent folk try to adhere who suppose that nowadays we have only Mother Earth to appeal to instead of 'Our Father who art in heaven'. The rear quarters are defiled by disreputable, ugly demons known as 'the Lusts of the Flesh'. Administrative quarters in the vast house are staffed by indispensable competent persons, many of whom, however, are financially preoccupied; some cold and calculating, and some showing horns and a cloven hoof. Down in the cobwebby cellars lurk hoary Superstitions that wilt in the light of day. In the upper floors are young, unscientific atheists, cheerful devotees of 'Having-a-good-time', most of whom are not devilish at all, but they are apt to make such a mess of their lives and such a mess of the premises. In the bleak grandeur of the State apartments reside for the most part holders of University degrees who happen either to take a militantly materialistic view of Man and the Universe, or halt agnostically between two opinions, suspending judgement, even when the sirens wail. But among their number are followers of *Humanism*, and those Humanists who are earnest and gentle representatives of its doctrine deserve respectful and honourable mention. One wing is energetically occupied by ardent believers in a revolutionary social theory. These arouse great interest but also acute anxiety, for they are capable of pursuing ideals by most unideal methods. Rumour has it that the rightful owner of the house is in it all the time. Most people laugh at the notion, remarking that, if so, he must be most skilfully disguised. It should be added that the mansion has a chapel, sparsely attended. The worshippers who gather there invoke the presence of their Lord. When they do so in sincerity, there comes an answer: 'Behold, I am among you as he that serves.'

An instructive parallel to our 'GOD-less Age' occurred in the ancient world, when the Greeks from about the fourth century B.C. lost confidence in the early cult of the Olympian Deities, and (unlike the Jews) having no GOD to replace them, made shift with inadequate substitutes. Greek philosophers and physicists, asking of the Universe ' *What* is it?', argued brilliantly that all things are but variant forms of some ultimate material substance; and insistently reported that no Gods can be found at home on Mount Olympus or floating on clouds above the earth, or visiting the homes of mortal men. Moral philosophers joined in, and showed how discreditable was much of the conduct ascribed to the ancient Deities. Interestingly we find that the threatened loss of all religion was felt unbearable, and three devices eased the strain. First, the title *God* was lavishly ascribed by the Greeks to almost anything that exercised influence on human life.[1] Even the well-educated continued to draw pseudo-comfort from speaking of the world as full of Gods. (Thales, the physicist, used the phrase; although he held that the Ultimate Reality, from which all derives and to which all returns, is Water, or Fluidity.) Secondly, conflate systems of belief (*The Mystery Religions*) were evolved around certain divine names. Thirdly (like a rabbit out of a conjuror's hat), the clever Greeks produced that obliging friend, *Allegory*. Zeus and the other Deities (with their benevolences and boastings, their

---

[1] Gilson, *God and Philosophy*, p. 9, instances: 'Earth, Sky, Ocean, Rivers; Sleep, Death; Fear; Strife; Vengeance; Justice; Love; the Muses and the Graces—in short all the immortally living powers that rule the lives of mortal men.' Even Plato, reasoning ontologically that Reality is not anything substantial but is archetypal 'Ideas' and that the Ultimate among the 'Ideas' is the 'Idea' of Goodness, yet speaks freely of the Gods. But by *Gods* he means what has just been said, not the picturesque quarrelsome Deities portrayed by Homer. Plato (*Republic*, 517) could say about Goodness as the Ultimate Reality that 'It is the universal author of all things beautiful and right, parent of light and of the lord of light in the visible world, and the immediate source of reason and truth in the intellectual; and this is the power upon which he who would act rationally either in public or in private life must have his eye fixed.' But Plato was following the Greek inquiry ' *What* is it?', and a chasm divides his philosophy, *intellectually*, from the religion of the Prophets and Christianity. Plato never calls the transcendent Goodness *God*. In his view it exists unconscious of, and indifferent to, any efforts men may make to walk by its light. All that humans can do, and should do, is to practise in earthly relationships what it metaphysically is, but must not look for its interest in their endeavour, nor will receive from it any aid other than of their own making.

rages and peccadillos) could be construed as symbols for this or that force in Nature or some dignified mental or moral quality. As to just what they typified, *quot homines tot sententiae*; for with the aid of Allegory anything can be asserted to mean anything. The Greeks, and the other Gentile Peoples, stood in desperate need of the living God of the Hebrew Prophets and of Christ.

For the Prophetic Faith *God* meant what the word ought to mean—the only Source and Sustainer of absolutely all that exists. That will be evident in what will later be said regarding God as exalted over the universe and concerned with the universe *in righteousness*. The Prophets freely spoke of God as *Jehovah*, because the ancient name denoted in their minds not a national Deity, but the only God there is, whom Israel should revere. If the Prophets had known the term Ultimate Reality, they would surely have used it in their anxiety to emphasize how profoundly their sense of Deity differed from the utmost men had hitherto meant by 'a God'. The Prophets did not conceive the One God in terms of One large *El*, or One big *Baal*; nor yet as a conglomerate of the more pleasing features of all traditional Deities. In their minds God was not (so to say) 'Baal & Co., Amalgamated and Unlimited'. Trust in God as the Prophets conceived God had momentous results.

(i) *Superstition*. For sensible Jews belief in one GOD killed Superstition in its typical ancient form—craven fear of *Demons*. The Prophets rebuked those who foolishly feared demonic malignity, or for nefarious purposes sought to enlist demonic help. Their complete disregard, otherwise, of the subject is significant— so sure were they of the power and goodness of God that they had to look for a deeper explanation than demonic spite to account for the facts of misfortune and suffering. After the sixth century B.C. speculation about superhuman beings (wicked demons, and benevolent angels who were ministers of God, serving His will) developed among the Jews; *but never got out of control*. The truly religious Jew turned to God in his need, and could say: 'Thou wilt keep him in perfect peace, whose mind is stayed on Thee.' Down to a late date in the Christian Era belief in demons was general, and modern psychology is a shade hesitant about dismissing the phenomena called 'demonic possession' as solely morbid imagination. But the various superstitions which are the modern equivalent of ancient fear of demons are kept underground in civilized life, and are no great menace. Mascots are seen on cars, but hope of reaching journey's end is really attached to the driver's skill.

(ii) *Dualism*. Although for two centuries, from 538 B.C., the Jews in Babylonia and Palestine were ruled by the cultured Persians, the Prophetic conception of God safeguarded them from Persian *Dualism*—belief in two supreme Powers, one good, one evil, *Light* and *Darkness*.[1] They held to it—ONE GOD; and refused to regard a Super-Demon ('the Power of Darkness') as final and sufficient explanation of suffering and moral evil. That was great wisdom.

(iii) *Polytheism*. The Prophetic Faith killed ancient *Polytheism*, stone-dead, among sensible Jews, even when they were not devout and exemplary specimens of their race. If men adored as divine actually existent objects such as the sun moon stars, they were foolish; for all such things are but 'the work of God's hands'. Worshipping Baal or Ashtarte, or Isis and Horus, or Zeus and Athene, and so forth, was even more foolish; for all those famous ancient names were but product of human imagination, 'things of naught'! In the Hellenistic Period cultured Greeks, Romans, and Egyptians were endeavouring to buttress up polytheism for various reasons. From lingering awe—'Perhaps after all there might be something substantial in the traditional piety.' For practical purposes—'Ancient customs help to stabilize the State; the priests are a powerful class with a vested interest in the ceremonial of worship, which also pleases the populace.' And for the better reason (as we have said) that men could not bring themselves to feel they exist in a wholly mindless universe that nowhere knows them. But, what between acute philosophers and agile allegorists and unbelieving Jews, Gentile religion was in a quandary. The cultured Greeks, Romans and Egyptians found the scorn of the Jews particularly galling; for the Jews laughed at polytheism, just laughed at it.

The tragedy of the modern world is that, to so great an extent and often so uncomprehendingly, it has dismissed the God of

---

[1] It is questionable whether Zoroastrianism was originally a thoroughgoing Dualism, but popular Persian religion, during the sixth to the fourth centuries when the Jews were subjects of the Persian Empire, was dualistic; and, but for the clarity of the Prophets, the idea might have affected Jewish religion much more deeply than the superficial traces which are all that searching investigation has perceived.

Christ and the Prophets, with the calamitous consequence that disguised polytheism flourishes:

A world which has lost the Christian God cannot but resemble a world which had not yet found Him. Just like the world of Thales or of Plato, our own modern world is 'full of Gods'. There are blind Evolution, clear-sighted Orthogenesis, benevolent Progress, and others which it is advisable not to name. . . .It is important, however, for us to realize that mankind is doomed to live more and more under the spell of a new scientific, social and political mythology, unless we resolutely exorcise these befuddled notions whose influence is becoming appalling. Millions of men are starving or bleeding to death because two or three of these pseudo-scientific, or pseudo-social deified abstractions are now at war. For when Gods fight among themselves men have to die.[1]

§3. One God, EXALTED

Foolish things are said when there is failure to distinguish the crude ideas of early Hebrew religion from the intelligence of the great Prophets, and the subsequent Jewish Faith which was permeated by their influence. The high Faith is then recklessly accused of *Anthropomorphism*, i.e. thinking of the Deity as if He were a man, albeit a very large man and often a very noble man! The charge boomerangs back on its makers; for it is culpable, ignorant rubbish. It was of the essence of the Prophetic Faith that it conceived God transcendentally, as the Creator exalted over His creation. For the first time in history we find men pellucidly aware that the sublimity of God surpasses the range of finite comprehension, and therefore of finite vocabulary. All comparisons are inadequate: 'As far as the heavens are higher than earth, so are my ways than your ways, and my thoughts than your thoughts—saith the Lord.'[2] If there are words or ways in the resources of the Hebrew language that the Prophets did not use to emphasize that belief, what are they? The Prophetic Faith differs fundamentally from every theory that God is a name for the totality of the inscrutable universe; or for anything *within* the universe; or for the Human Race, self-deified in its highest potentialities.

(i) *Cosmic Pantheism*. The Faith is the antithesis of Cosmic Pantheism, the philosophy which regards the universe in its totality as the sole Reality. This system of thought (which like

[1] Gilson, op. cit. pp. 136f.   [2] Isa. xl. 12–18; lv. 9.

A-cosmic Pantheism has been influential in India) is capable of eliciting in those who earnestly entertain it, emotions proper to religion; for the universe is no ignoble subject of contemplation. But its ethical implications are benumbing, since in its view calamitous events and actions normally accounted evil are every whit as much an aspect of 'God' as what we consider beneficial and good. For Cosmic Pantheism moral distinctions have no validity: 'there is no world in which anything that might be called the divine will needs be done.'[1] Indeed it is somewhat misleading that this philosophic system should be called a *theism*.

(ii) *Scientific Materialism.* Modern Physicists, asking of the universe solely the question '*What* is it?', and working by quantitative measurement, have now driven their inquiry so far that the conclusion emerges that what appears to us to be *Matter* (the universe in its immensity; the atom in its minuteness) is in the last analysis not anything that can be called material, but is apparently a mental Reality.[2] At least Physics, following its own line of investigation, now leaves open the door to a religious and ethical valuation. Moreover it is now (belatedly) stressed that to ask merely *What is it?* was an inadequate inquiry, almost sure to lead (although it has not eventually done so) to some non-religious conclusion that the universe—including human life—is no more than a vast machine, however subtle and extraordinary its mechanism. The religious and philosophic questions '*Why* is it?' and 'Is our human sense of *Values* consonant with Reality?' —are equally legitimate questions, not to be ruled out, and indeed are the most important inquiries to be essayed.

But for a long time past Scientific Materialism has been so confidently propounded as final explanation of Existence, and its view so easily assimilated, that in our mechanically-minded Period masses of people were persuaded that religion had conclusively been shown to be superstition, and Christian ideals of Right and Wrong baseless. That was welcome news for the gross; for if religion was moonshine, it was safe to play skittles with the Ten Commandments—God being a name for nothing, and one's fellow-men anybody's prey. It was bleak news for honest folk. The Prophetic Faith summons men to look elsewhere than to the

---

[1] Farmer, op. cit. p. 69.
[2] It looks like a mathematical thought. Cp. Jeans, *The Mysterious Universe* pp. 137–150.

material universe for meaning in their existence and for validity in their valuation of Right.

(iii) *Humanism*. There is, however, one variant of Scientific Materialism—the teachings of *Humanism*—that calls for special comment, both appreciative and critical. Many scientists who reject the validity of any religious metaphysic and contrive still to regard a materialistic philosophy as adequate, or who are practical-minded and unphilosophic, recognize how terrible are the consequences that must ensue if regard for morality cannot be prevented from avalanching down to the abyss along with religion. They seek therefore to salvage Ethics out of the wreck of faith in God and Absolute Goodness; and counsel men to rely on their finest characteristics, and take heart in their latent potentialities for good. They appeal to us to offer the reverence, self-sacrifice and enthusiasm, formerly claimed in the name of religious devotion, henceforth to 'Man at his best', to 'Values which we create', to 'Ideals which imagination presents to us'. To this end they can draw upon the heritage of Greek and Roman virtues and of Christian morality; and they do so to good purpose, but often with curious unconsciousness of the extent of the debt. Moreover, they can utilize the new resources for judging and aiding human conduct which modern research—biological, psychological and sociological—is making available. They do so illuminatingly; yet sometimes with bland unconsciousness that modern theologians are prepared to do likewise. Indeed, the theologians may be on the whole wiser in the matter, because they are historically-minded and are also in no danger of the fallacy of regarding Consciousness as *merely* a mechanism and Behaviour as due *solely* to the glands. The gospel of Humanism at its best offers a splendid conception of Man as he should be, and its sensitive exponents serve an ethical Ideal with a devotion that shames nominal Christians. Of these Jesus surely would say 'Not far from the Kingdom of God', and 'He that is not against us is for us'.

There is, however, place for severe criticism. For by no means all the Humanists show this moral earnestness. Some write with condescension, as if Religion were good riddance, and Ethics an interesting study rather than matter of life and death for humanity. Theirs is an arm-chair detachment from the mortal conflict that makes one glad they are not in fact seated on the throne of God. Some Humanists seem to have little knowledge of theology except in the past tense—as if the argument for Theism still stands where it stood in grandpapa's time. Some obviously relish demolishing the expositions of the Faith current in the verbal-inspiration period. Ridiculing dead theologians is an easier task than coming to grips with contemporary, competent, defenders of the Faith. Most Humanists are more optimistic about human nature than are experts in religious history. They leave themselves scant reason for optimism. For, appealing to Man for the noblest self-sacrificial response, they are bound as Humanists to bid him realize how greatly his behaviour depends on his physical condition, how little on anything for which he need seriously blame himself or feel guilty; and that he exists for a brief while in a mindless physical environment absolutely indifferent to his aspirations or his 'misdeeds' (if the phrase be so much as permissible). This fundamentally pessimistic standpoint the creed of Humanism cannot escape. The more sharply the fact is realized, the more depressing is the effect on moral endeavour.

The Humanists are behind the times metaphysically. Even when things looked darkest for religion, the battle was not lost; and they should have seen so.[1] They 'sold the Pass' of a spiritual interpretation of Life's significance too soon—much as if uninvaded but hard-pressed Britain had surrendered to the Nazis in 1940. It is the dreary country of materialism that is now invaded. Our Faith can stand to it that human life is rightly comprehended as having meaning and value in the exalted Reality of God.

(iv) *Fatalism*. The Prophetic Faith excludes Fatalism as an explanation of the natural calamities, sorrows and evils that are hard to reconcile with an all-wise and all-good Deity. In antiquity the easy way out of the difficulty was to ascribe them to *non-moral Necessity* or *Fate*, to which even God or the Gods must conform. But the easy way was a cul-de-sac; for it reduced God to the pre-prophetic level, to a Power *within* the universe, a well-meaning but insufficiently strong Potentate.

Fatalism—or at any rate a popular cult of *Destiny* or *Luck*—played some part in Semitic (and early Hebrew)[2] religion. We know less about it than we should like. Probably it was never more

---

[1] Analysis and criticism of Humanism may conveniently be found in Cairns, *The Riddle of the World*; K. Walker, *Meaning and Purpose*; Gilson, *God and Philosophy*.

[2] See Skinner's note on Isa. lxv. 11 (*Camb. Bible* (1922), p. 237).

than a minor matter in the system of worship, because the pagan Semites had many Gods and could set down tribulations to the negligence of the worshipper's God, or to a clash of interests between Gods, or to human folly and guilt which had given the Demons a chance to strike.

But the problem whether non-moral necessity is final fact in the scheme of things was taken very seriously by the Greeks, and the theme runs right through ancient Greek literature in intricate and very touching ways. Zeus, although Father of men and of Gods, was obliged to conform to Fate, however unwelcome and unjust the result might seem to him (and to us)![1] The Greek dramatists carried the discussion to profundity. They reasoned that Fate (or The Fates) imposes on men not irrational happenings but the inexorable operation of justice. Aeschylus contends that suffering may in the end actualize good purpose, if willingly endured. Sophocles sustains the hope that the very last word rests not with relentless Fate that takes no account of the wrongdoers' motives and extenuating circumstances, but with the Gods; and is verdict of Mercy and Pardon. When the great Age of Greek philosophizing had run its course and culminated in the Aristotelian metaphysic and ethic, the intellectual atmosphere was too rarified for ordinary men. Hence it happened that, when the Near East was convulsed after Alexander the Great's conquests, and decent citizens were suffering an indecent number of unmerited misfortunes, the strain brought about, not recourse to high philosophical metaphysic, but 'a sudden and enormous spread of the worship of Fortune'.[2] Hope springs eternal in the human breast; but one feels that Semitic or Greek devotees of divine *Fortune* must have feared that their offerings were no better than a gamble on chance.

---

[1] No reproach of injustice was felt to lie against Zeus because all men have to die—that seemed reasonable in the nature of things. But already in the Homeric Ballads (*Iliad* i. 524–7; xvi. 439 ff.) we find the question posed: 'Why should heroic Sarpedon (human child of Zeus, beloved of his divine father) have to die in battle so young?' If Zeus were all-powerful, surely he would have prevented the combat, and so preserved the life of his child? Answer given was that it was *fated* Sarpedon must die there and then. But further the passage implies the important, though muddle-headed, deduction that the supreme God, Zeus, is finally law-abiding, reluctantly defers his inclinations to Necessity, but identifies his innermost will with 'What must be', however cruel the event.

[2] Gilbert Murray, *Five Stages of Greek Religion*, pp. 164f.

But the cult of Fortune was only a popular reaction. Thoughtful Greeks were nobly seeking strength in *Stoicism*—the ancient counterpart to Humanism. Stoic doctrine taught that the universe is indeed wholly indifferent to Man, but that (such is Man's indomitable will) we can steel ourselves to be indifferent to misfortune, and should aim at that. Bloody the Stoic's head might be, but it need not be bowed; in the storm he could remain captain of his soul, and so be master of his fate. Moreover, the Stoics taught that men should not distress themselves about local patriotism, *because* they have learnt to be citizens of the world and by living virtuously can help their fellow-men and promote general social welfare.[1] That was heroic teaching, sure to engender noble sentiment and noble lives. But the metaphysical atheism or agnosticism of Stoic philosophy entailed an undertone of melancholy. It could not provide Virtue with a foundation in Reality, and its morality was marred by moderation. It counselled that 'Friends die and some sorrow is inevitable; but the wise will not break their heart'; that 'Social altruism is praiseworthy; but not to such an extent as to upset one's equanimity'. Modern Humanism would not approve Stoic moderation, but, broadly speaking, ancient Stoicism offers pointed commentary on the defects as well as the virtues in Humanism. What falls to be said about the Prophets' way of facing strain and suffering belongs to the closing Chapter.[2]

---

[1] 'Stoicism comforted Brutus and Cato in the death-agonies of the Roman republic; it fortified the lame slave Epictetus; it inspired the good Emperor, Marcus Aurelius, in his care for a peaceful and well-administered world...it never compromised its lofty spirit and never sank into vulgar superstition or emotionalism' (Gilbert Murray, in *Christianity in the Light of Modern Knowledge*, p. 58). Stoicism stood in splendid contrast to the *Epicurean* philosophy, with its standpoint that 'Gods there may be, but they dwell aloof and aid us not. The cultured may give them a conventional recognition, but the task for wise men is to practise how to extract the maximum happiness in the short span of their years—the quest for pleasure, however, to be practised *as a fine Art*!' It is not unjust to say that Epicureanism resembles the 'polite atheism' of 17th- and 18th-century *Deism*, although the Deists must be credited with a less hedonistic attitude to morals.

[2] Fatalism staged a later appearance in history through the part it plays in Islamic religion, whereof the adherents number about 250,000,000. The Mohammedan doctrine that all events must be faced as 'the will of Allah' breeds stoical endurance of personal tribulations and fanatical courage in battle, but also a temper of resignation that creates shocking indifference to

(v) *Agnosticism.* Since the Prophets realized the exaltation of God over Creation, the Faith had in it the element of *reverential* Agnosticism. The full glory of the Divine Being is incomprehensible by the human mind. But neither the Prophets nor the heirs of their belief were in any danger of jumping from that conclusion into the depths of *defeatist* Agnosticism. On the contrary their teaching 'lived, moved and had its being' in unwavering conviction that knowledge of God wholly adequate for Man's needs and utmost welfare is available. The claim was not that Man by his intelligence could search out God, but that God ceaselessly offers all-sufficient knowledge of His nature and purpose to those who are willing to receive—who seek in the right way by valuing the right things: Truth and Goodness. Limited our power of apprehension may be, but it is entirely competent for that vital purpose, if we will use our Reason and Conscience. Confidence was based on the thought: 'God is not man that He should lie.' Therefore we should be assured that, whatever the unknown and unknowable aspects of God in the exaltation of His eternal Being, they cannot be such as to contradict the known.

§4. *One God, exalted in RIGHTEOUSNESS*

The Prophetic Faith holds that God is Self-revealed through a fact or quality that everywhere characterizes Nature and has its special form in relation to human life. That characteristic they termed *Tsedaqa,* which in our Bible is translated *Righteousness.* Unfortunately, English usage restricts *righteousness* to correct moral behaviour; the Hebrew word had a much wider connotation.

the misfortunes of others. Whatever qualifications may be made as to certain of its theological expressions, Islamic fatalism in its popular manifestations is inimical to moral progress; and the veil of piety that is draped over stark facts is woven out of theological impotence in this problem. If all happenings, good and evil alike, are vaguely accepted as 'the will of Allah', Allah must be a Being often benevolent, but just as often morally callous. There is a world of difference between Islamic pietistic acquiescence and the attitude of Hebrew monotheism. As Oman (op. cit. p. 449) says: 'The Prophets were able to face physical evil as real and terrible, and moral evil as calamitous and perverse, and yet say that, by His own meaning in them and by His good purpose beyond them, the Lord God omnipotent reigneth.' Similarly, the Christian assent *Thy will be done* expresses positive resolve, not negative acquiescence.

Orderliness or *Right Functioning* is the more adequate rendering. If, for instance, a Hebrew had had a motor-car in good running order, he could have said that his car was righteous. Throughout the universe (with the sole exception of human conduct) *Order* or *Righteousness* reigns.[1]

Imagine that *in spirit* Isaiah, Jeremiah and the Unknown Prophet could have met Plato and Aristotle (kindred loyalists to truth) walking in the gardens of the Academy at Athens; and, asking the Greek philosophers upon what subject they were intent, had been told that they were discussing the relation of the Finite to the Infinite and in what sense knowledge of Final Reality is attainable by Man. Isaiah would say: 'The fullness of the whole earth is His glory'; and Jeremiah: 'Am I a God of the near and not also of the far?'; and the Unknown Prophet would solemnly declare: 'God, beside Whom there is none other, hath spoken unto His servant, saying *I, the Lord, have called thee in righteousness.*' Imagine that the Greeks, quick to perceive the point, had answered: 'You urge the metaphysical identity of Virtue and Being. Discourse to us, we pray you, after the manner of your race.'[2]

Hebrew thought observed (as we have said) that, except in human life, Order prevails throughout Creation. With amazing perfection all things fulfil the purpose of their being ('*Why* they

[1] The same assumption underlies all scientific inquiry—that the Universe is orderly and therefore may be intelligible; and so far as the range of our intelligence has penetrated, the facts verify the assumption. A Jewish scholar, C. Roth, stresses the congruity here of Science and Hebrew Monotheism— 'Monotheism, the doctrine of unity of source, implied the inference unity of control, the homogeneity of God's creation. Sporadic or magical interference is at once out of court. Only one supreme God is concerned in the government of things.... Monotheism can have no more dealings with "errant causes", "Chance", or "fortuitousness" in Science, any more than with a host of subordinate controls in Morals.' Noting that Jewish medieval thinkers held that search after truth in the Sciences was a supreme religious duty, Roth continues: 'Not only this idealizing of scientific endeavour, but also the very background of scientific ideology is Hebraic.' (In *The Legacy of Israel*, pp. 436–41.)

[2] Philosophically regarded, the standpoint of the Prophets is in line with those modern thinkers (e.g. Jaspers, Heidegger, and Buber) who insist that knowledge of what is ultimately true has to be won, not simply by the use of speculative reasoning, but also (indeed principally) by the active process of choice and decision in the experiences and personal relationships of life.

are'). Mark how sun, moon and constellations keep 'the Order of their going'. In the night skies the serried ranks of the stars shine out ('Not one of them is missing'). The function of the moon is (poetically and practically!) to give light by night: it does so. The sun gives light by day: unfailingly it rises in the east, exulting like a strong man to run a race, until it sets in the west—its task fulfilled, its *righteousness* accomplished. Thus 'the firmament telleth His handiwork'. All these after their due fashion 'know the Lord', and with all that in them is they praise His holy name. So far as they are able, their unconscious Beings show the Orderliness of Creative Intelligence. As one of our own physicists says concerning the Universe: 'It looks like a mathematical *thought*.' Would that our text-books could be written in Hebraic poetry. How their verses could amplify the marvellous precision and obedience that obtains from the immensities to the infinitesimals. See Nature with the eye of the artist and the farmer. How 'righteous' all things are! The *wild* beasts seek their prey by night: as soon as darkness falls, forth they come.[1] 'The ox knoweth his owner, and the ass his master's crib.'[2] Even the unconstrained birds in the heavens obey their homing instincts.[3] The rain does not fall half-way and then turn skyward leaving its duty unaccomplished, but 'it watereth the earth and maketh it bring forth and bud'. The vegetation responds, and the trees yield their fruits in due season. The Hebrews did not grotesquely suppose that the rest of Creation exists *solely* in order to minister to Man's needs. With gratitude and awe they recognized in the world an environment that richly, yet sternly and challengingly, provides for human life; but also saw that all else exists in its own right, and felt it has value for God which we cannot adequately comprehend.

The Hebrew Bible [Roth remarks], although it gives full measure to the claims of the human heart, is notoriously theocentric. Man is neither the measure nor the centre of things. The cattle of Nineveh, the farmer's ox and ass, the very trees of the forest, are of account to the Maker of all; and 'God in his holy habitation', who is 'father of the fatherless and judge of the widow', gives the raven its food and waters the grass of 'the wilderness wherein there is no man'. In this firm sense of the totality lies the unique character of the Biblical account. Its universality is thoroughgoing. It holds the scales equal between all the

[1] Ps. civ. 20–22.   [2] Isa. i. 3.   [3] Jer. viii. 7.

various parts of creation. Nothing is small, nothing is great. 'They all wait upon Thee.'[1]

On the other hand, firmly and wisely the Faith perceived in Man a unique Being, the crown of Creation, the creature to whom God has given immeasurably most; capacities that truly make him God-like—*Consciousness, Intelligence, Conscience*. Like God, Man can distinguish Order from Disorder; has knowledge of good and of evil, power to create right or wrong. Yet in Man (alone among all created Beings) there is Disorder, Unrighteousness. From the very beginning of truly *human* history, Man has had in this gift of discernment between the better and the worse dawning knowledge of God. In Israel, said the Prophets, men are without excuse: 'He hath shown thee, O man, what is right. And what doth the Lord require of thee save to do justice and to love mercy, and to walk humbly with thy God?'

So it should be. So it is not. The Poet-Prophet wrote to his People: 'Oh that thou hadst hearkened unto my commandments! then had thy peace been as a river, and thy righteousness as the waves of the sea'; and to the proud capital of Judah Isaiah said: 'Oh city of Jerusalem! Behold what tumults and oppressions are in the midst of thee.'

God is not less than the utmost in Creation. In the universe of unconscious things there is regularity and symmetry. And in men there may be found the marvel of intelligence and moral qualities —justice, mercy, love. God excels all that is most wonderful, most noble in Creation. God is perfect Justice, everlasting Mercy, infinite Goodness. When the Prophetic Faith ascribes moral qualities to God, that does not signify that God is conceived as a collection of abstract attributes or as '*A* Person'; but as *not less than personal*—personal, not humanly, but transcendently. 'To find terms that are not in some sense human is like trying to jump out of one's skin.'[2] Moderns have only themselves to blame, if they misconceive such language as naïve. 'Philosophic theism', writes H. W. Robinson, 'has not always recognized its debt to the Hebrew religion for the deepest realization of divine personality.'[3] In the insight of the supreme Prophets we meet with language seeking to body forth exquisite assurance that God is with us,

[1] Op. cit. p. 437. Cp. also Chapter III, pp. 52f.
[2] Matthews, *Studies in Christian Philosophy*, p. 193.
[3] H. W. Robinson, *Religious Ideas of the Old Testament*, p. 65.

revealed alike in the challenge of boundless moral demand and in
the aid of unfailing *personal* relationship: present (if we will) to
lighten our darkness, and to guide our feet into the way of peace.

All the words that men can find to denote union, security, intimacy,
nearness, are in place. To men God is protection and help, refuge and
strength, hope and consolation, light and health, shepherd and keeper,
the merciful and redeemer. Here Hebrew piety has displayed most
clearly its power to invent the language of its needs, and its poetic
genius has sounded the most intimate depths of the human heart. It
calls God the father of men; it speaks of His love for them. The first
personal pronoun is laden with all the meaning it can carry: ' *My* God.' [1]

Western civilization has talked itself into an insanity of confusion on the great spiritual-moral issues, until there is no sure
vision of the loathsomeness of Evil and the beauty of Goodness—
with terrible consequences, social and personal. It has become like
a man lost in the depths of a forest of thick-set pines. Losing his
wits he begins to run aimlessly hither and thither, and flings his
body against the impassive, encompassing, trunks, until he drops
exhausted. That is a macabre picture. But Western civilization has
made a macabre tragedy of its opportunities, especially during the
past fifty years.

The crowning wisdom of the Prophetic Faith is that its cogency
is not addressed merely to the few who can follow a metaphysical
argument. When, however, those few have considered its interpretation of Existence, they find a thought which requires from
them, if they would rationally judge its worth, the same task that
it lays upon their unphilosophic fellow-men. It summons us all to
moral decisions, to a venture of faith—and the strength and validity
of its claim can be tested only by experiment. It points to a way:
'He hath shown thee, O man, what is right.' And it makes a
promise: 'This do, and thou shalt live.'

[1] Baeck, op. cit. p. 276.

CHAPTER XVIII

POWER

Jewish history demonstrated the power which the Faith of the Prophets made available. Politically the small Hebrew Kingdoms were shattered, but the sequel was an immense extension and strengthening of the Hebrew People. This miracle of vitality (repeated in A.D. 70, and again in A.D. 137, and how often since in not dissimilar circumstances) was due, not to the shrewdness of the Jews, but to their virtues; and the virtues demonstrably were created and sustained by the Faith of the great Prophets.

God, revealing in righteousness His changeless purpose; Reason, perceiving what Conscience should command; Mercy, measured by unfailing Love; man's individual worth to God, discovered through self-giving service; the universal acceptance of this way of life—those are the 'Seven Pillars of Wisdom' set up by the Hebrew Prophets. Jesus accepted the essentials of these beliefs, and related them to His own inestimable significance. It is obvious that the Prophetic-Christian Faith offers its resources to mankind. Four things fall to be said concerning its power so regarded. First, the Faith claims that it is not illusion but ultimate truth, truth expressed in dynamic assertions which disclose increasing strength in changing circumstances. As Baeck most rightly says: 'It is an essential characteristic of all that is truly original, of every product of genius, that it means more than it actually says, and implies more than it expresses. It transcends itself by continually forcing the mind and conscience that receive it to wrestle with it. Again and again in different eras men are laid hold of by it, and they cannot let it go until it blesses them. This inward power, this capacity to produce and shape and grow, is peculiar to the Religion of Israel. It is this that makes it a world-religion.'[1]

Secondly, this religion, although individual, is not individualistic. It cannot sincerely be held as a self-regarding piety, but only by incessant effort to advance the welfare of others. No conscientious person can say to himself 'I think this view is

[1] In *The Religions of the World* (ed. Clemen), pp. 267, 271.

right', and then do nothing about it. Recall how the Poet-Prophet expressed the claim of God—'Is not this the *worship* that I have chosen? to loose the bonds of wickedness...and to let the oppressed go free? Is it not to deal thy bread to the hungry, and that thou bring the poor that are cast out into thy house? When thou seest the naked that thou cover him; and that thou hide not thyself from thine own flesh?' One cannot derive from the pages of the Old Testament a ready-made table of 'marks' that should be awarded respectively to Monarchy or Democracy, Capitalism or Communism, to the United States of America, to the British Commonwealth of Nations, or to the Union of the Soviet Republics. 'The Prophets', writes S. A. Cook, 'were detached from all current, social political and religious, presuppositions. They go behind all society and organization and behind the accepted beliefs; they are absolutely fundamental—they go back to the first principles of God and Man.'[1] That is to say, the genius of the Prophets perceived that the prime, social necessity is that every mode of human government shall judge its wisdom and its worth by an absolute standard, alike in respect of its aims and its actual attainments. The standard is that everyone should feel absolute concern for the welfare of each. It is a commandment high as heaven, but it is also 'very nigh unto thee that thou mayest do it'.

Thirdly, the Faith is strong in that it is comprehensive. 'I believe', writes D. S. Cairns, 'that it is still the groundwork of all true Theism, the outline and the way in which we must interpret the great riddle of human existence, before which so much of the graver thought of our age stands bewildered and dumb. Within this interpretation alone can we include and explain the salient features of the riddle, without blunting any of them; the baffling mixture of good and evil in the world, the sacredness of human personality, the glory and tragedy of human life, even the reassuring blend of comedy in it, and finally the astonishing beauty which accompanies it all.'[2]

Fourthly, consider how explicit is its challenge. It deals with issues men perpetually have to face in a way that gives the least learned scant excuse for saying 'I do not understand this doctrine and demand'. On the other hand, the most learned has no excuse

[1] *The 'Truth' of the Bible*, p. 32.
[2] *The Riddle of the World*, pp. 311, 316.

if he does not recognize therein a momentous answer to great questions which it is fatal to seek to evade, and calamitous to answer wrongly. But whoever responds will find himself called upon to make spiritual values his guide in dealing with both the pleasant and the painful aspects of life.

§ 1. *Life's Amenities*

The pleasures felt by those who delight in evil are not the subject of this section. Inasmuch as the Prophets had continually to denounce men who revelled in debauchery and called goodness evil, it is remarkable that they were not morose. On the contrary, they valued intensely all rightful human happiness—they were men who counted the golden hours, and longed that they were not so few. But their wisdom in use of pleasant experience was due to the fact that they possessed a supreme Peace or Joy which transcends happiness, and can meet its loss without defeat. Therefore in regard to Life's amenities they taught two duties with equal emphasis—*Rejoice* and *Beware*. That is counsel which we are apt to receive as a truism, miss the emphasis, ignore the warning, and fail to use its power.

(i) *Rejoice.* Most people derive some degree of pleasure from the diversity and beauty in Nature. But nothing is easier than to take its offered benediction to the spirit with but feeble appreciation. To see Nature with eyes illumined by religious sensitiveness is to find its values incomparably enhanced. The Prophets looked on the hills and valleys, pastures and vineyards, of their land in a way that made them artists, and gave them strength and tenderness. Isaiah presumably had innate aesthetic capacity; the point is that his talent became genius under the touch of his sense of God, the Giver. He saw Nature in relation to the needs of the spirit as well as of the body. Many instances of this intensified appreciation may be found in the records of religious experience. William James cites the following: 'Natural objects were glorified. My spiritual vision was so clarified that I saw beauty in every material object in the universe, the woods were vocal with heavenly music; my soul exulted in the love of God, and I wanted everyone to share my joy.'[1]

For the most part, however, it is in the way we deal with human relationships and bodily sensations that we weave the

[1] *Varieties of Religious Experience,* p. 250.

texture of our life well or ill. The Prophets regarded friendship, marriage, parenthood, and all the natural satisfactions of physical existence as most precious gifts of God, not to be taken as a matter of course, but to be reverenced with intense gratitude. The extremely important consequence has been that both Judaism and Christianity have refused to overvalue asceticism, and repudiate ascetic extravagances; for the positive reason that the pleasures of normal life are to be accounted *sacred*, and will then be rightly used.[1]

(ii) *Beware.* But incessantly the Prophets' teaching had to be warning concerning false pleasures; so environed were they by abominable misuse of things that should have been for men's welfare. The instant we deceive ourselves by supposing that the end to be sought is physical comfort, with most horrible speed we turn material things to the corruption of our own character and to our neighbours' loss. It is solemn fact that conceit, cruelty and covetousness dog the footsteps of prosperity like a shadow. A devil of mercilessness invites himself into every well-appointed house, and seven obsequious devils tender their services to the wealthy. Only the very poor, and the completely callous, can read without heart-searching what the Old Testament says concerning possessions—'Beware lest...when thou hast eaten and art full, and hast built goodly houses, and dwelt therein; and when thy herds and thy flocks multiply, and thy silver and thy gold is multiplied, and all that thou hast is multiplied; then thine heart be lifted up, and thou forget the Lord thy God.'[2] The parable of Dives and Lazarus should suffice those who do not consult the Old Testament.

The shortest way to cynicism and to disbelief in the goodness of God is to count happiness the highest Good. Those who suppose that God's care should be manifested in their immunity from distress have a religion that goes down like a pack of cards at the flick of the lash of suffering. If what the Prophetic Faith meant by the justice of God consisted in His allotting the maximum of prosperity to the most deserving, how account for untimely deaths

---

[1] 'Judaism draws no sharp distinction, in regard to ethics, between body and spirit; it does not regard them as independent, watertight compartments. Both go to make the man, and both deserve care and culture.' (M. Joseph, *Judaism as Creed and Life*, p. 366.)

[2] Deut. viii. 11–14.

and the poverty and hardship endured by countless good men and women, as compared with the security of old 'Mrs Affluent' of 'The Towers', the robust health of 'Miss Katt' with the neatly gloved claws, and the bank balance of 'Mr Shark' so skilful at playing Beggar-my-neighbour? If the object of the Maker of heaven and earth had been to devise an environment in which a sentient, purposive, creature called Man would find suffering absent and merit mechanically receiving material reward, He was singularly inefficient in His planning. But pleasure (in the conventional sense of the word) as the goal of endeavour leaves out of account noble human capacities which have nothing to do with the quest for ease. The Prophets valued normal happiness, but they measured its worth by reference to an incomparably higher understanding of life's meaning. Therefore they knew how to rejoice, because they knew how to encounter sorrow. They were not dazzled by prosperity. Neither was their trust in God defeated by the tragedies that arise from *calamities*, *wickedness*, and *finite limitations*.

§2. *Life's Agonies*

The great Prophets have a right to be heard concerning tragedy. They did not shield themselves from sorrow, nor evade the religious problem fatalistically by thinking that God would like to be more just, but is overruled by a mysterious rigidity in the Scheme of Things which He cannot control. 'Earlier and more vividly than others, the Prophets saw the magnitude of the calamity of the fall of their civilization. They bore their own fullest share, and realized with the deepest sympathy the agony awaiting others. They never sought to shelter their spirits from the horror; they never comforted themselves with the thought that particular evil is universal good; they never took the individual personal sting out of their distress by generalizing it into "All life is misery".'[1]

(i) *Calamity*. Fortuitous circumstances may inflict appalling misery on individuals, and often in ways profoundly detrimental to character. One child is born in surroundings that assist sound thinking and good conduct, another amidst evil influences and crippling poverty. There is no need to detail a catalogue of horrible happenings—such as congenital idiocy or the frightful forms disease may take. What can the Faith say concerning the *chances*

[1] Oman, *The Natural and the Supernatural*, p. 449.

of this fleeting world? One aspect of the daunting facts is here used for consideration—namely, that our physical life is set in perilous places.

Nature's complete unconsciousness of our relative virtues is staggering. But the fact has to be faced. As Jesus said: 'God sends his rain on the just and on the unjust.'[1] The microbe and the midge do not mind our morals. The hungry lion impartially rends the good man or the wicked. The ox knoweth its owner's stall, but not whether he is an honest farmer or unscrupulous. The horse responds to skill and kindness, but does not ascertain whether its rider is a democratic monarch or a despot. The earthquake swallows the innocent and the guilty; the lightning strikes where it listeth; the bomb does not spare the brave; and the motor-car out of control mutilates whoever is in its path, man, woman or child. There is a striking difference between our own and the Hebrews' outlook on physical occurrences, in that they knew so little about the interrelation of physical events and readily regarded any startling occurrence in Nature as an *immediate* act of God. For example—in the time of Amos the kingdom of Israel suffered from earthquake, drought and pestilence. The Prophet called the nation to see in those events God-sent warnings to repent of their sins. Our seismologists would say the earthquake was due to a weakness in the crust of the globe, and the weather experts that the drought was the result of atmospheric conditions. We feel that, if Samaria had had a medical officer of health, he would justifiably have talked about bacteria and the absence of a sewage system. The usual modern reaction is to be struck by ancient ignorance of the sequences of physical phenomena, and *to leave it at that*. What folly on our part! Every calamity that halts complaisant men in the even tenour of their ways is a summons to 'consider our ways'; and in that sense is an act of God indeed. Callous Israelites used the famine to create a 'black market' in wheat. Amos was deeply right that the calamity, and the cruel sufferings it caused, should have shocked the nation into perceiving at last what it

---

[1] When His disciples complacently supposed that the victims crushed by the fall of the Tower of Siloam must themselves, or their fathers, have been notorious sinners, sternly He rebuked them. The question showed no grasp of the nature of the goodness of God. Afterwards the Apostles understood well; but it was St Paul, suffering much in manifold perils, who gave immortal expression to the Faith—Rom. viii. 11, 12.

ought to have seen earlier and prevented—namely, that the poor were left hungry in the midst of plenty and the brotherly spirit almost vanished from the land. What needs to be perceived is that sorrow, pain and humiliation can be met in a way which turns tragedy into a triumph of the human spirit, and may be of immense influence for good. We see it in Jeremiah refusing to let personal anguish quench the light of his witness to truth, and in the Poet-Prophet's inspiration that his People's affliction could be turned to the glory of God and the benefit of mankind.

To sum up, the Faith offers this constructive counsel concerning both pleasure and pain—Exactly, as every event that augments our pleasure is wrongly used unless it turns our thoughts in unselfish thankfulness to the moral significance of life, so also every grievous event is wrongly used if we permit its calamity to increase hardness of heart and bitterness. But if we strive to find in every phase of our experience opportunity the more to do justice and to love mercy, light arises in darkness. For then 'tribulation worketh patience, and patience experience, and experience hope'.

(ii) *Wickedness*. An exponent of Humanism in a jocose and unguarded moment has been guilty of defining the sense of sin and guilt as 'especially in adolescence, a mental disease, something to be avoided if possible, and got over like the measles with the utmost celerity, instead of being paraded as admirable'.[1] As well say that it is childish to be intelligent, and sensible to ignore danger. From the uniquely human capacity to differentiate right from wrong and to obey or defy our conscience, there has ensued, on the one hand, every splendid loyalty to truth and every noble deed the Ages have seen; but also, on the other hand, loathsome depravity.[2] A kindly man who concentrated his attention on humanity's black record could scarce keep his sanity. (And what is reading about deeds of wickedness compared to enduring cruelty, or seeing it inflicted?) Of Belsen Concentration Camp one eyewitness wrote: 'If all the heavens were paper, and all the

---

[1] J. Huxley, *Religion without Revelation*, p. 366.

[2] Scientific research has already thrown invaluable light on human character, revealing how complex are the physical as well as psychical influences that go to the making of behaviour. But that does not imply that we should not make the utmost endeavour to determine what is right, or not feel guilty when we choose to do what our conscience condemns.

water in the world were ink, and all the trees turned into pens, you could not even then record the sufferings and horrors'; and another broadcast these words: 'In Belsen and Buchenwald and other Concentration Camps it seems that men undertook deliberately and with cold calculation to assault the foundation of Western civilization—*Respect for the individual life*, which distinguishes us from the animals.'[1]

Man being what he is (born 'an infant of days', ignorant, passionate, and having to live in community with other passionate persons), less than Divine intelligence suffices to foresee that atrocities of vice and injustice would arise and persist. Indeed a state of static perfection, wherein no effort has to be made to sustain idyllic conditions, cannot exist on this earth, so long as babies continue to be born with diverse temperaments and a lot to learn. Logical recognition that in order to acquire virtue men must necessarily possess liberty to do wrong may content the philosophically-minded; but, so appalling are the deeds of the wicked, that the irrepressible protest, 'A world like this cannot be devised by an intelligent and good God', would be unanswerable, unless God ceaselessly leaves nothing possible undone to deliver us from the love of evil, and unless human personality is more than a momentary and material phenomenon in Time and Space.

Four characteristics of the strength of the Prophets over against the awful realities of wickedness are outstanding. *First*, power is manifest in their adamant conviction that certain qualities are everlastingly right ('the will of God'); in the solemnity with which they held men to it that consequences ensue on moral decisions as inexorably as the sun rises and sets; and in the terrific fearlessness with which they exposed evils and called for active antagonism to the wicked. They did not propound a theory of the origin of Evil:[2] they saw wickedness embodied in wicked persons and entrenched in foul and foolish customs, and they denounced those persons and those customs in flaming words that were a call to action. They did not think that good men would discharge their

---

[1] P. G. Walker in *The Listener* (17 August 1945).

[2] Jewish scholars before and after Christ discussed Man's innate propensities to do good and to do evil, and *death* in relation to the Genesis narrative about Adam and Eve. But Rabbinical exegesis was for the ends of edification, not for the formulation of static doctrines, and St Paul's references are in the same spirit. It was the Greek mentality that elaborated a

full duty by setting good examples and appealing to bad men to be good. With common sense they recognized how tragically improbable it was that (so to say) the Hitlers great and small, the White-Slave Traders and the Dope Merchants, would turn from their intentions. If evil men were not made powerless, they would continue to crush the weak, and spread the poison of their vile influence throughout the community. The Prophets had regard to the interests of the victims. They hated evil with a perfect hatred, and attacked it with all their might. Therefore they called upon all decent men to use every resource in their power to deliver the oppressed from the oppressors. Otherwise, by their supine attitude they have part with the wicked in 'the Slaughter of the Innocents'. Isaiah knew the crowds at Jerusalem's temple were not all murderers and thieves, but because they were inactive in face of flagrant wrongs, he accused them all of having the blood of the wronged dripping from their hands.

Secondly, the Prophets saw why thorns of wickedness grow rampant in human nature, and why their roots are so hard to eradicate. Of necessity men cannot live together except by exercising each a measure of influence or control in relation to his fellows. This inescapable fact operates throughout the entire community in an indescribable variety of obvious and of subtle ways. Statesmen and shopkeepers, financiers and foremen, employers and employed, parents and children, but also friends and neighbours—we influence one another. Every one of us is therefore not merely under control, but to some extent in control, of others. We have to form ideas of what should be done or thought, and when others do not do as we say or think as we think, we are bound to feel they are wrong, to reprimand or to restrain them. But—'Who art thou, O man, that judgest thy brother? Judgement belongeth unto God'. *There* is the insidious and deadly danger, which nevertheless we must incur. Through official position, force of mind, greater age or possessions, one way and another, we are set in positions of comparative strength in relation to others, and exercise power. What is likely to be the

doctrine of Original Sin as prelude to the saving work of God's Grace. Very effectively the Genesis story bids us reflect that, when the time came that there existed on this planet a creature recognizable as *Man*, he had primal instinct to do right, capacity to do wrong, did wrong, and that God did not thereupon abandon him to his tragic weakness and wickedness.

effect on our own character? Lord Acton, the historian, made this
grim reply: 'Power tends to corrupt; absolute power corrupts
absolutely.' Were Lord Acton's declaration absolutely valid, one
might despair; for it would then seem that the Deity would be the
Devil. Retort may, however, be made that the Deity is the
exception that proves the rule. But it is indisputable that possession of power (even the least power) almost irresistibly tempts
men to *pride*, and in the worst instances leads to abominably
ruthless selfishness. Strength and pride are husband and wife, and
their children are cruel. How can the pernicious poison in the
power we severally possess one toward another be checked and
eliminated? On that crucial issue the wisdom of the Prophets'
Faith remains fundamental.

For, *thirdly*, the Prophets saw by what principle alone we can
be saved from self-destruction. Jewish religion states the mind
and example of the great Prophets in the words 'Thou shalt love
the Lord thy God, and thy neighbour as thyself'. This teaching is
not an unpractical, sentimental plea for the feeble man (inefficient
fellow), or for the transgressor (bad fellow) that he should be let
off lightly. Its twofold command is a unity—Every man must
regard himself as under the judgement of God's absolute righteousness (a thought which assuredly humbles), and must not look
upon the interests of any other individual as less inherently
important than his own, still less as negligible.[1] But the principle
transforms our attitude towards whatever power we happen to
possess, and applies from the greatest unto the least, and from the
least unto the greatest. This concept of right relationship between
men, which the Prophets upheld, derives historically from the
social bond accepted as natural and necessary by the tribal
families in the desert, who were eager that all of their brotherhood
(*covenant*) should be strong. The Prophets seized on the one
great virtue in desert-life, and declared its ideal to be the unaltering law of God, obedience to which results in welfare. The
covenant tribes became a nation. The Prophets insisted that the
nation was a *family*, and would not survive unless the law and
love of brotherhood ruled its life. The Poet-Prophet realized that

[1] If Naboth of Jezreel had died a natural death, the State would have
suffered no irreparable loss. But that its Rulers saw fit to use their power to
murder and acquire, was ruinous, and must be answered by denunciation and
effort to dethrone them.

the principle must be given universal range; and Christ declared it to be necessity in His service.[1]

Everything depends on the spirit in which we regard our strength—whether as power to get or to give, to cast down or to lift up. On this infinitely higher level justice will be upheld in a community and mercy will often need to be shown; but only as negative necessities in establishing the nobler purpose. Men who live together as brethren do not want their brother to stand corrected by justice or to be in need of pity. They long that his character should be upright and his affairs prosper; and to that end will use their powers not occasionally but persistently, not reluctantly but rejoicingly. They do not say to themselves 'I am the stronger, therefore I will enrich myself at his expense'; nor do they administer justice proudly, thinking 'Our virtue is superior, therefore we condemn him'. The saints, poets and philosophers—from the Apostles and St Francis to Milton and Niebuhr[2]—have known that *pride* is the tap-root of Evil. Thanks to an extremely diluted dose of Christianity, Western civilization (monarchic and democratic) has paid lip-service to the Prophetic principle, but devastatingly ignored it in practice.[3] Indeed it has never clearly grasped the idea; for Christ and the Prophets have been allowed to seem remote, so far as things political and economic are concerned. In our time a new social theory has arisen, namely, that the interests of the individual are negligible over against those of the State or Race, which are absolute. In Fascist Italy and Nazi Germany we have seen what may ensue along those lines. In Russia the Proletarian Revolution professed the ultimate benefit of all, but the system has concentrated authority in the hands of a very few. Will absolute power corrupt them absolutely into seeking the welfare not of all, nor of

[1] Cp. St Mark x. 42 f.
[2] Cp. *The Nature and Destiny of Man, passim.*
[3] There have been many good monarchs, whose subjects revered their memory—as the Christmas Carol says of Wenceslas, or as Jeremiah said of King Josiah: 'he judged the cause of the poor and the needy; then it was well.' But study the conditions of the poor, and the morals of the aristocrats, of any country in European history—(say) under Louis XIV, the 'Grand Monarch', or prior to the French Revolution in 1789! Democracies are in theory 'the Rule of the People, by the People, for the People'; and have had considerable time and stupendous resources for the purpose. Why have they to so great an extent developed as Plutocracies, where 'Money talks'?

the multitude, but of themselves? Not if the leaders of Russia advance from their present materialistic philosophy to a deeply religious view of Ultimate Reality. The Hebrew Prophets declared that nothing less than the supreme social ideal—*Each for all*, but also *All for each*—is adequate. That attitude is the only means of preventing possession of power from corrupting the powerful, and the only hope that the enormous constructive resources available in the modern world will not be unused or misused to the destruction of civilized life.

Fourthly, inasmuch as the Prophets did not shut their eyes to terrible facts, their courage manifests real strength. (Defeatism wins no victories in this dismaying world.) They propounded no doctrine of original sin, but they were splendidly sure that the Creator does not leave Man's frail and erring nature to its own devices. Therefore the problem is not how to placate an irate Deity, but is in ourselves; in the non-use and abuse of capacities we should develop, the resistance of our wills to the Will of God. Their hope, however, was not built on evasion of the stubborn reality of wickedness; for they knew that so long as men regard one another as objects to exploit, it cannot be well: never will seeds of selfishness yield harvest of peace. But the Prophets looked upon vice as *disease* of the soul, virtue as its *health*; holding that the primal instinct in human nature is to value good. Instincts are not easily eradicated, especially when intelligence can come to their aid. Therefore they dared to believe that normal men and women could change for the better, and amazingly so. History and psychology bear out that when a stimulating idea which has been held in the outskirts of consciousness comes (as it were) into focus, so that there is acute perception and acceptance of its worth, immense power is brought into action. 'Where there's a will, there's a way.' That has happened repeatedly in response to less than noble aims, and for unworthy causes. Why then should not we also remain resolute in hope that the noblest and wisest conception of the necessary relationship between men and men, nation and nation, will inspire the intelligence and conscience of the rulers and the ruled? Strong and gentle, patient and urgent, the Prophets continued in hope. To-day there are almost boundless possibilities for good just out of reach, and out of reach, not because of human incapacity (the sciences have dealt with that), but for lack of right disposition towards one another.

(iii) *Finite Limitations*. 'Life', thought the virtually atheistic author of Ecclesiastes, 'is no better than a sequence of futile efforts to grasp the wind'. The courageous rightly call his dreary opinion pessimism. Nevertheless the agonies inflicted by disappointment, bereavement, loneliness, are dread realities. Human beings strive to achieve their desires in perfection, and to hold secure what they have won; but mortal limitations stand in the way. Our bodies are flesh and blood: therefore there is always struggle to sustain physical health, and in the end it is a losing battle. What aid does the Faith afford whereby to confront 'the *changes* of this fleeting world'?

The more sensitive we become to the best that life can afford, the more poignantly we feel our human imperfection, and the transience of our years. The river of Time carries us on from Youth, to Age, to Death; and we cannot arrest its flow. Hopes tender and true may prove unattainable, and dwell in mind as unforgettable sorrows. And, if we attain, then the great joy is ours to-day. But we know that to-morrow will come, and wonder how long we shall hold fast our heart's desire. The Past lengthens behind us, and may have in it acts we would fain undo; but we cannot re-live past years. Omar Khayyam, holding the Religion of Resignation, could do no more than bid us face the fact—

> The Moving Finger writes; and, having writ,
> Moves on: nor all thy Piety nor Wit
> Shall lure it back to cancel half a line
> Nor all thy Tears wash out a word of it.

The Prophets could speak of the irrevocable Past as though it were not—'Remember ye not the former things, neither consider the things of old... I, even I, am he that blotteth out thy transgressions for mine own sake; and I will not remember thy sins.' Theirs was the strength of the Religion of Renewal.

It is impossible that men so sensitive as the Prophets did not feel the strain inherent in finite limitations. We do not know whether the Prophets felt the validity of their trust in the goodness of God to be challenged by the fact of death. Perhaps they did, and were sore perplexed. (We possess only fragments of their thoughts.) But the problem lay below the horizon of religious questioning in their time. What falls to be emphasized is that, when the challenge came to be taken up, it was the Prophetic conception of God that pointed towards the one profound answer. As for the transience of our years, one feels that the Prophets regarded the successive stages in life—Youth, Maturity, Age— not in resentment that change must take place, but '*in quietness and confidence*' (to quote Isaiah's watchword). Each phase offers its specific gift from God, if we will but deal with it in that spirit. As for the agonies of disappointed hopes, the secret of their courage was that they sought, not for ease and pleasure, but only for strength not to prove unfaithful to truth and goodness. In all things they found God's work given them to do, and felt that God was with them. Hence they are the first, supremely great, example of the way in which men living for an end higher than Self can 'draw from the heart of suffering itself the means of inspiration and survival'.[1]

There is a hard experience in life which many have to endure, namely, *Loneliness*. The Prophets understood loneliness. Moses could not escape the apartness of great leadership. Elijah cried to God, in his solitude in the cave on Horeb, 'I, even I only, am left'. Hosea and Jeremiah were cut off from home-affection for which their spirits craved. Isaiah and Jeremiah in an extreme degree were shunned and dreaded by their fellow-men. All the Prophets were mentally isolated by finding that their contemporaries would not, or could not, share their beliefs. But there is a far deeper solitude which concerns every person, although only a few are acutely sensitive to its pressure. It is the *Aloneness* inherent in the fact that each of us is a conscious individual Self, in a vast, unconscious, physical environment. Are we each, in the last resort, alone in a mindless universe? Our soul protests against the icy thought. The Prophets kept saying that God was with them. How did they gain and retain that sense of a divine, accompanying, Presence? It is all very well to say they had the unusual advantage of setting out filled with confidence in the reality of the living God. As the years passed, it was just as difficult for them as it is for any of us to continue to believe in the living God. Their disturbing message separated them from ordinary men, who told them they were deceived and had dreamt a dream; and when they lifted their tired eyes to the heavens for reassurance, be sure that the stars stared down at them as coldly and remotely as they do now. The

[1] Historic words offered by Mr Winston Churchill to Britain in its darkest and greatest hour.

Prophets had to travel with their own thoughts for company on the path of life's pilgrimage, and found themselves living with ideas of Justice and Mercy, Truth and Goodness. *Abstractions?* In that companionship they felt increasingly they were in touch with unchanging Reality. They did not lose the first rapture of belief that God was strengthening and guiding them; their conviction deepened. Moses understood the promise *I will be with thee* in a wiser way at the end of his journey than at its start. As these Prophets did their duty, the mists of tangible things parted sufficiently. Amos learnt that God had not taken him from his sheep and left him to his own devices, but that He did not fail to reveal the secret of His purpose and the meaning of events. To Jeremiah it seemed once as if he had stood in the very Council of the Most High; and it was in the moment of his deepest dejection that he became sure that God would continue to be with him, an invincible strength. And the last of the supreme Prophets, who could write the words 'I have laboured in vain and spent my strength for that which is naught', must himself have passed through loneliness to assurance, before he could say to his despairing People in the name of God—'O Israel, thou art my servant, I have chosen thee, I have not cast thee away'.

Is the human soul ultimately alone in a mindless universe? The Prophets answer—*Not alone is he with whom keep company on the Pilgrim's Way valiant Truth, and shining Justice, and gentle Mercy: Children of God.*

§3. *The Validity of the Faith*

Persons whose psychic sensitiveness is normal are apt mistakenly to attach sometimes too great, and sometimes too little, importance to the occasional trance-experiences of the Hebrew Prophets in regard to the validity of their belief in God. The Prophets' trances might have been a hundred times more numerous, but they would not have been sure of God and sure there is good meaning in life, if they had not chosen to follow the straight and narrow path of duty. Isaiah would not have become strong in faith and resolute for right, if he had been a man selfishly aloof from the life around him, if he had seen his neighbour's ruin without pity, if he had said of the widow's bereavement 'Is that so?', if hearing talk of orgies in the palace he had shrugged his shoulders, remarking 'Let's hope the next king will be a bit better'. (No one, however psychically normal, is debarred from having a lively conscience.) If Isaiah's Vision had not made him a better man, more concerned for others than he was before the wonderful experience, its impression would have faded until it seemed no more than an empty dream. (Anyone, however psychically normal, may set himself to do his duty, and so join 'the goodly fellowship of the Prophets'.) Very many, however, who strive to live unselfishly, feel that their effort does not afford them any religious experience, or any that they feel convincing. It seems to them that they prefer to do good, and that is all there is to it. But if Ultimate Reality be Absolute Goodness, they walk with God although they know it not. And they should not lightly disregard the testimony of others concerning Divine Reality.

Unquestionably these Hebrew Prophets present a supremely religious interpretation of Existence, which culminated in Jesus Christ. It is understandable that unemotional persons feel it difficult to regard trance-Visions as more than hallucinations. Nevertheless, just as it is a mistake to suppose that the Prophets' faith in God depended on occasional trances, so also on the other hand it is a radical mistake to belittle the significance of their super-normal experiences. Consider how uniquely extraordinary were the Visions of the great Prophets—(i) The Prophets were not dazed 'by pure light that illuminated nothing', but received command to get back to normal life and attack vice and cruelty, defy evil rulers, denounce superstitious 'religion' in the cause of true religion, plead the strength and beauty of goodness, promise that to repentance the door of opportunity stands open, but tell the men of Israel that they lived in a *Moral Order*: God has no favourites.[1] Does that look like hallucination? (ii) It will not do to say that the incentive received in the Visions was only the uprush of the Prophet's own, subconscious, good feelings. 'It is common

---

[1] 'When the Prophets teach God's Righteousness, it is the Law of His Being which they teach....God is Love—but chastening love. God's Righteousness is, so to say, absolutely neutral; of necessity His own people suffer for their sins; of necessity, when they return to Him, He will be reconciled with His own. The Prophets are teaching an absolute theistic law: it would be shattering, if it were not a religious and an ethical one the justice of which man cannot dispute.' (Cook, *The 'Truth' of the Bible*, p. 34.)

decency', remarks Dodd, 'to let the Prophets speak for themselves.' They tell us the experience was as if the rushlight of their
own virtue was made invisible by the blaze of the noonday sun.
They felt themselves apprehended by 'personal' Reality incon-
ceivably great and good—'Holy, holy, holy, is the Lord of hosts:
the whole earth is full of his glory....Woe is me! for I am undone;
because I am a man of unclean lips.' (iii) Although the supreme
Prophets were men of different types living in different centuries,
their Visions did not yield a hotchpotch of conflicting ideas, but
convictions which cohere as a profound ethical Monotheism.
Taken in relation to Jesus Christ, the essential aspects of the
beliefs constitute the *only* religious interpretation of Existence of
which modern thought must take account.   Moreover, the transcendent standard of morality implicit in the transcendent religious
conviction is of such a nature that it has been capable of relating
fresh knowledge to its unchanging ideals.   Does that look like
hallucination? (iv) Consider, above all, the effect of these forma-
tive Visions upon the minds and characters of the Prophets themselves.   Isaiah did not become self-righteous because he had had
a supernatural assurance that his sins were forgiven. The Prophets
did not plume themselves on the score that God deemed them
worthy of spiritual experiences denied to ordinary men.   On the
contrary, all their lives they walked humbly *with God*. But *with
men*, how bold they became in defence of Right! With more
than regal authority they faced kings. The Visions did not lift them
into effortless assurance.   Constantly they were in anguished
perplexity; but how unerring they became in distinguishing truth
from falsehood, because they were subordinating selfishness to
duty.   Men of intense convictions are apt to become intolerant of
others who will not assent to their views. ('This people that
knoweth not the Law is accursed!') The Prophets became very
patient.   Having loved their People, they loved them even unto
the end.   Good men are apt to be hard, although they know they
ought to be forgiving: *they* have found it possible to be upright;
so why not others? The compassion of the Prophets was very
wonderful towards their People, despite the scorn with which
they met. They had learnt not to think about their own rights and
wrongs; so deeply did they care for other men. For their brethren's
sake they drew suffering upon themselves. Of course they longed
as much as any other men for normal happiness, and foresaw its

loss if they tried to be unflinching servants of truth to unwilling
hearers. They counted the cost and accepted it, taking the burden
of the sins and sorrows of others on to their own hearts; until
humanly they shared the anguish they believed to be in the Mind
of God. Yet dare anyone say they would have exchanged that
experience for ease and indifference? We see them attaining
mastery over personal temptation and outward tribulation.
A marvellous quality of life is visible in these men: a higher mode
of existence which can be ours, if we cease to seek satisfaction in
self-centred happiness and avoidance of strain. We speak of the
Prophets as men of genius; the praise is negligible. They were *men
of God*, who answered what they believed to be His Call, and in
singleness of heart lived for a selfless purpose. For themselves
they found steadfastness and inward peace in the midst of storm.
But that strength and quietude they possessed precisely because
their life was not self-regarding, but self-giving. What, in consequence, did they achieve for others? Because of their integrity,
compassion and self-sacrifice, countless deeds of justice and mercy
have been done, and a vision of Infinite Love on the throne of
the Universe has been held before the eyes of men down the Ages.
The Prophets chose for themselves 'The Way of the Cross', and
it was transformed into 'The Way of the Redeemer'. Does that
look like hallucination?

§4. *'The Way of Death' and 'The Way of Life'*

Plato could think it necessary and fitting to let the conclusions of
his metaphysical reasoning take shape and colour in a picture.
A modern writer on religion need not hesitate to use the same
method. An ancient figure of speech—*The Alternative Ways*—
makes vivid the truth that the one thing we cannot do in life
is to stand still morally. Those who protest that they are not
going to be browbeaten into being earnest about anything are, in
fact, making a very definite decision to travel the wrong road.
Physical passions and vigilant self-concern see to it that they travel
fast. A passage in Deuteronomy insists that the necessity to choose
is sharp-set, and the consequences grave: 'See, I have set before
thee this day life and good, and death and evil; in that I command
thee this day to love the Lord thy God, to walk in his ways, and
to keep his commandments....I call heaven and earth to witness

against you this day, that I have set before thee life and death, the blessing and the curse: therefore choose life, that thou mayest live.'[1] One sentence will suffice concerning the broad and tempting Way that leadeth to destruction: along its borders grow trees of corruption, watered by the tears of the wronged.

Think of the other road, which is called *The Way of Life*. Part of its course is amidst green pastures and beside still waters; for in the pleasant phases of life there is Duty to be done, Right to be sought, and Goodness loved. But it could not justly be called *The Way of Life*, if it was not able to carry the feet of men through the waste places of the wilderness. As it traverses the desert of Life's strain and sorrow, it is not an occasional figure of a resolute Prophet that is to be seen following its arid track, but a multitude no man can number of imperfect men and women who, despite hardship, disappointment, pain, try to do right. Among them there are many who have to endure, not hardship, but terrible suffering: 'these are they that are coming out of great tribulation.' Often they stumble in weariness; but they rise and go on. Nor does this host of honest, hard-pressed humanity move dejectedly like a beaten army in retreat. They have a heartening habit of meeting their difficulties by breaking into song. It makes one think that Man cannot be only an ingenious mechanical toy, made for no conceivable purpose. Vast numbers know no other name for the road than *The Path of Duty*, and say they have no notion whither they are bound. But when men who feel they do not know anything about God are faithful to duty, marvellous things happen: at times the glowing sand becomes a pool, and flowers blossom in the wilderness. Even so, they are sorely tempted to doubt if their effort to do right is worth while—wondering whether they will ever arrive and where; perhaps so utterly perplexed that they see nothing in life except a long and thirsty road, stretching ahead. They should lift their eyes from the shimmering heat of the wilderness. Then they would perceive, far off, the strength of the everlasting hills in Galilee and Judah; and would begin to understand that God, who is 'God of the Far', is also 'nigh unto such as remember His commandments to do them'. And they would begin to take thought of One who also knew hunger and thirst in the wilderness, and who steadfastly set His face to go by a very lonely road that brought Him from the

[1] Deut. xxx. 15 ff.

pleasant hills of Galilee to Jerusalem and crucifixion. They would discover that He called ordinary men His friends, and said that He would be with them even unto the end. It is in memory of Him that this Path of Duty was named *The Way of the Cross* and *The Way of the Redeemer*. The Poet-Prophet spoke of it as *The Way of Holiness*. He called those that walk therein *the redeemed of the Lord*, and said that they shall come with singing unto Zion, and that everlasting joy shall be upon their heads. They have a right to the name; because in their faithfulness they are fellow-workers with Him who took The Way of the Cross.

SCRIPTURE REFERENCES INDEX

GENESIS I, 41, 119, 123–4; II, 25, 123; III, 70; IV, 119, 129, 131; IX, 41; XIII, 121; XIV, 65; XVI, 118; XVII, 41; XXII, 45; XXIII, 99; XXIV, 105; XXVII, 125, 214; XXVIII, 143, 148; XXX, 134; XXXV, 118; XLII, 101; XLIII, 200; XLVI, 127; XLIX, 187.

EXODUS II, 201; III, 66, 202–3, 214; VI, 156; XII, 205; XIV, 204; XV, 159; XVI, 120; XIX, 66, 207–9; XX, 216–17; XXI, 67; XXII, 81; XXIII, 105; XXXI, 124; XXXII, 219; XXXIII, 221.

LEVITICUS XXIV, 67, 170.

NUMBERS I, 205; V, 132; VI, 183; XI, 184, 200, 205, 208; XII, 219; XIII, 97; XVI, 220; XX, 220; XXI, 50; XXII–XXIV, 186, 221; XXXIII, 207.

DEUTERONOMY I, 207; V, 216–17; VI, 166; VIII, 385; XI, 95; XIII, 222; XVII, 190; XVIII, 222; XXVI, 105; XXX, 115, 399–400.

JOSHUA VII, 132; XI, 92; XXIII, 105.

JUDGES I, 103, 105; III, 39, 104; V, 47, 50, 102, 105–6, 159, 183; VII, 160; VIII, 160; IX, 118, 149; XI, 160; XIII, 183; XIV, 124; XV, 161; XVI, 48, 127, 146, 161, 183; XVII, 51, 187, 217.

I SAMUEL I, 224; IV, 225; V, 146; VII–VIII, 190, 226; IX, 186, 226, 229; X, 124, 226, 229; XI, 229; XII, 190; XIII, 161, 229; XIV, 229, 230, 232, 310; XV, 230–1; XIX, 217; XXI, 126; XXII, 310; XXV, 117; XXVIII, 143; XXXI, 230.

II SAMUEL I, 39, 53, 162, 230; II, 163; V, 143, 162; VI, 45, 66; IX–XX, 39; XII, 224; XIII, 51; XIV, 167; XV, 167; XVI, 149; XVII, 134; XX, 188; XXI, 190; XXIV, 167.

I KINGS II, 119; V, 171; VIII, 171; IX, 204; XII, 188; XIV, 234; XV, 172; XVI, 149; XVIII, 236 ff.; XIX, 207, 241 ff.; XXI, 159, 236 f.; XXII, 247.

II KINGS I, 144; II, 126, 243–4; III, 119, 150; V, 121, 145; VI, 248; X, 179; XII, 39; XIII, 248; XV, 39; XVIII, 172, 217, 297; XIX, 297; XXIII, 322.

I CHRONICLES VIII, 163; XIV, 163.

JOB XXIX, 134, 181; XXXI, 123; XXXIV, 124.

PSALMS II, 109; VIII, 53; XXIV, 162; XXVI, 73; XXXVII, 136; XXXIX, 124; XLIV, 233; XLV, 46; XLVI, 48; LVIII, 120; LXV, 273; LXVIII, 120; LXXVIII, 15, 223; LXXXV, 136; XCI, 142; XCIX, 152; C, 108; CIII, 56; CIV, 53, 149, 379; CV, 48; CXXXV, 263; CXXXVII, 336.

PROVERBS I, 50; VIII, 50; XXV, 67.

ISAIAH I, 241, 299, 301, 379; II, 295, 302, 338; III, 173, 300, 302; IV, 288; V, 50, 302; VI, 66, 70, 269, 271; VII, 58, 214, 293–5; VIII, 143, 214, 293, 299, 303; IX, 303; X, 289, 296, 302; XI, 124, 288, 303; XII, 288; XIII, 288, 343; XIV, 288, 314, 343; XV–XVI, 288; XVII, 152, 295; XIX, 96, 288; XXI, 288; XXII, 298; XXIII–XXVII, 288; XXVI, 126; XXVII, 50, 297; XXVIII, 296–7, 300; XXX, 295; XXXI, 53, 123, 295 f., 304; XXXII, 300, 303; XXXIV–XXXV, 142, 288, 339, 356, 401; XXXVI–XXXIX, 124, 288–9, 297; XL–LXVI, 288, 339 ff.; XL, 15, 339, 347–8, 371; XLI, 136, 341, 348, 356, 396; XLII, 67, 341, 347, 349, 352–4, 356, 358; XLIII, 343, 345, 348, 352, 394; XLIV, 343, 347–8; XLV, 340, 343, 349, 356–7, 359; XLVI, 340, 347; XLVII, 340, 343, 356; XLVIII, 136, 343, 352, 380; XLIX, 67, 352–4, 356, 396; L, 67, 354; LI, 349; LII–LIII, 67, 348–9, 354, 357;

LV, 126, 348, 358, 371; LVI–LXVI, 340; LVII, 148; LVIII, 347, 383; LIX, 352, 356; LX, 96, 349, 357–9; LXI, 25, 67, 349, 354, 357; LXIII, 352, 356; LXV, 146, 352, 374; LXVI, 343.

JEREMIAH I, 311, 314; IV, 314–16, 324; VII, 199, 323–4; VIII, 309, 315, 379; IX, 319; XI, 318; XII, 318, 321; XV, 95, 127, 315, 318, 321; XVII, 175, 318; XVIII, 78, 184, 318, 332; XIX, 325; XX, 318–19, 325; XXI, 329; XXII, 152, 323; XXIII, 327; XXIV, 326; XXV, 314, 326; XXVI, 323; XXVII, 328; XXVIII, 328; XXIX, 326; XXXI, 310, 332; XXXII, 329; XXXIV, 129, 329; XXXVI, 324; XXXVII, 329–30; XXXVIII, 330; XLIII–XLV, 331; XLIX, 204.

EZEKIEL XVI, 99; XX, 202; XLIV, 188.

DANIEL III, 233.

HOSEA I, 269, 292; II, 165, 272, 276–7, 282–3; III, 269, 274; IV, 241, 277; V, 266; VI, 266, 280; VII, 266; VIII, 277–8; XI, 86, 276–7, 282; XII, 199; XIII, 278; XIV, 284.

AMOS I, 248, 253; II, 65, 183, 248, 251, 257; III, 246, 251, 253, 255–7, 259; IV, 173, 247, 251, 257; V, 214, 247, 259, 260, 262; VI, 251; VII, 192, 251, 254, 258; VIII, 152, 249–51, 254, 258; IX, 103, 247, 254, 258–9.

MICAH III, 300; IV, 338; VI, 241, 300, 380.

ZECHARIAH XII, 152; XIII, 186.

II MACCABEES XV, 334.

ST MATTHEW V, 219, 321, 387; XI, 219; XII, 115, 327; XXIII, 66, 135.

ST MARK X, 392.

ST LUKE II, 246; IV, 67; VII, 270; VIII, 269; XI, 115; XII, 259; XVIII, 109.

ST JOHN I, 84; III, 63, 292; IV, 20; V, 388; VIII, 387.

ROMANS V, 388; VIII, 387.

I CORINTHIANS X, 63; XIII, 264.

HEBREWS IV, 301.

I PETER II, 86, 138.

REVELATION III, 302; XVII, 343; XVIII, 343; XXI, 15.

GENERAL INDEX

Aaron 198, 211 n.
Abbott 282 n.
Abd-el-Krim 213
Abel 129 n.
Abiathar 227 n., 310
Abimelech, 'king' of Shechem 160–1
Aborigines, Australian 34 n.
Aborigines of Palestine 97–8
Abraham 26, 40, 41, 65 n., 127, 128, 211 n., 351
Abrahams, Israel 85 n., 107, 109, 125 n.
Absalom 133 n., 167, 232
Achilles 31
Achor, Valley of 103
Acre 92 n., 96 n.
Acton, Lord 391
Acts of God 56–7, 387
Adad, Canaanite deity 162–3, 165, 172
Adam 277 n.
Addu (Hadad), Canaanite deity 145, 147 n.
Adon, term for deity 144
Adonis 152 n.
Advaita doctrine 366 n.
Aeschylus 277 n., 375
Africa 362
Agag 230, 233
Agamemnon 31, 32
Agape 264 n.
Agar 8 n.
Agnosticism 376, 377
Ahab, king of Israel 120 n., 163 n., 172, 180 n., 182, 184 n., 189 n., 235 n., 298
Ahaz, king of Judah 151, 174, 293 ff., 299
Ahikam 324
Ai 103, 111, 158
Akaba, Gulf of 204 n., 205 n.
Akhetaton, royal city of Amenhotep IV 28
Alamein, El 102
Albright 31 n., 98, 145

Alexander the Great 336, 375
Allah 376–7 n.
Allegory 68 ff., 368
Alphabet, consonantal 99
Amalekites 160, 230, 245
Amarna, Tell-el- 110, 148 n.
Amaziah, priest at Bethel 190 n., 251, 254
Ambrose of Milan 70
Amenhotep IV, king of Egypt (Ikhnaton) 27–9, 31, 100, 202, 208 n.
Ammonites 111, 160, 182, 227, 253
Amnon 133 n.
Amon, Sun-God 28, 145
Amor, land of 92 n., 163
Amorites 33, 91, 92 n., 98–9, 142 n.
Amos, Book of 246, 253
Amos, Prophet 65, 173, 183, 191, 192 n., 199, 231 n., 246 et seq., 275, 278, 279–80, 283, 287, 310, 351, 387, 396
Anath, Canaanite deity 146, 147 n.
Anathoth 146 n., 309, 315, 316 ff., 329, 330
Anatolian plateau 99
Andrew, apostle 61
Andrew of St Victor 76 n.
Animal sacrifices 66, 149–50
Animatism 143 n.
Animism 143 n.
Anselm 76
Anthropomorphism 371
Antioch, theologians of 70 n.
Antiochus IV (Epiphanes) 36 n.
Aphek 225
Apocryphal books of O.T. 36–7, 58 n.
Apollo, Sun-God 139
Apuleius 109
Aquinas, Thomas 70, 76
Arabah, Wadi 93, 204 n., 205 n.
Arabia 31, 129, 208, 213, 235
Arabian desert 92, 93, 112–13
Arabians, Arabs, *see* Bedouin

Aramaeans 92, 99, 200 ff.
Archaeology and the O.T. 26 ff., 41, 42
Aristophanes 186 n.
Aristotle 112, 375, 378
Ark, Noah's 82
Ark of Covenant 66 n., 121 n., 167, 216, 224–6
Arnold, M. 51
Arpad 290
Asa, king of Judah 172
Asceticism 385
Ashdod 146, 290, 296, 313
Asher, land of 168
  tribe of 101, 102 n., 106 n., 111
  Semitic deity 146, 147 n.
Asherah (symbolic pole) 148, 171, 172
Ashtarte, Syrian deity 145, 146, 147 n., 152 n., 173, 370
Asia Minor 26, 96 n., 98 n., 99
Asshur, Assyrian deity 289, 295
Asshurbanipal I 29
Assyria 26, 29 f., 174, 308, 312 ff.
Assyrians 172 n., 247, 248, 257, 267, 289, 293–4 et seq.
Athene, Greek deity 69, 370
Athens 21, 49
Atomic energy 87
Atomic warfare 361
Atonement, meaning of 353
Attis 152 n.
Augustine 58 n., 76
Authorised Version of Bible 46, 47 n.
Authority of Prophecy 298–9

Baal, title of deity 119, 144, 276 f.
Baal in proper names 163
Baalath 144–5
Baal Zebub 144 n.
Baals of Canaan 165 and *passim*, 273
Babylon, city of 29, 312 ff., 340
  return from 340
  a symbol? 343 n.
Babylonia 26, 29 f., 174
Babylonians 304, 322, 324 ff.
Baeck 130, 364 n., 381, 382
Baikie 110

Balaam 186 n., 221 n.
Balak, king of Moab 221 n.
Barak 105, 182
Barnabas, Epistle of 65 n.
Baruch, friend of Jeremiah 307, 318, 324, 331, 333–4
Bashan 93, 104 n., 180
Bates 47 n., 49 n.
Baudissin 155 n.
Bede 76
Bedouin, Arabs 91, 97 n., 112 ff., 131, 137 f.
Beersheba 241–2
Behistun, Plain of (Persia) 29
Benjamin, tribe of 106 n.
Bernard of Clairvaux 76
Bes, Egyptian deity 145
Bethany 61, 245
Bethel 103, 111, 143, 158, 172, 184, 211 n., 217 n., 243, 251, 254, 309
Bethlehem 15, 33, 98 n., 245
Bethshan 146, 162 n.
Bevan, E. 39 n., 286 n., 365 n.
Binyon, L. 49, 54
Blessing of the gods 115 ff.
Blessing of Yahveh 125, 126 f., 132, 135, 190 n.
Blood 123
  abstinence from 40, 41 n.
Body and spirit 123, 385
Boghaz-Keui, Hittite capital 30, 99
Bozrah 356
Brahe, Tycho 77
Breasted 28, 100 n.
British Academy, Proceedings of 65 n.
British Museum 27, 29
Brock, C. 363
Brotherhood of man 350
Brutus 376 n.
Buber, M. 378 n.
Budde 199 n.
Bukkeish 213
Bull-images 172, 211 n., 217 n., 277, 281
Burney 148 n.
Burnt offerings 154
Butler, Bishop 231
Byblos 148 n.

Caesar 61
Caiaphas 7, 61
Cain 129 n., 131 n.
Cairns, D. S. 286 n., 374 n., 383
Calamity 386 ff.
Calvin 77
Cambridge Ancient History 28, 44 n.,
    100 n., 101 n., 102 n., 114, 131,
    180 n., 234 n., 339 n., 352 n.
Cambridge Theological Essays 39 n.
Canaan, land of 99 ff., 221, 273; *see
    also* Palestine
'Canaanism' 177 ff.
Canaanites 55, 85, 98 f., 105–7, 110 f.,
    158 ff., 187 ff.
    deities of 141 ff.
    ideas of 158
Canon of N.T. 57–8, 62
Canonicity, criteria of 37 n.
Cappadocia 103 n.
Carchemish 322
Carlyle, Thomas 107
Carmel, Mount 92, 93, 142 n., 237 ff.
Carthage 150 f.
Cato 376 n.
Celsus 70 n.
Champollion 27
'Charity' 264 n.
Charles, R. H. 216 n.
Chaucer 76
Chemosh, Moabite deity 119
Cherethites 167 n.
Cherubim 171
China 362
Chinese culture 84
'*Christ*' (=Messiah, Anointed One)
    60
Chronicles, Book of 39 n.
Chrysostom 70 n., 76
Churchill, Winston 288, 395
Circumcision 40, 41 n.
City-states, Greek 139
Classical Review 148 n.
Climate of Palestine 94–5
Clough 287
Coastal Plain of Palestine 92 f., 96
Code of Hammurabi 30
Colenso, Bishop 198

Coleridge, S. T. 42
Columbus 77
Communications of Palestine 96
Communism 4
    materialistic 118
    Russian 16, 18
Comparative study of Religion 33 f., 42
Compassion of God 215; *see also*
    Mercy
Comprehensiveness of the Faith 383
Compromise, moral 14
Concentration camps 388 f.
Confessions, Reformed 4, 5
Conquest of Canaan, date of 100–2,
    110 n.
Conscience 14, 67, 224 et seq., 265,
    350, 380
Consciousness, human 373, 380
Cook, S. A. 34 n., 43 f., 44 n., 65, 88,
    101 n., 102, 110, 114, 129 n., 131,
    147 n., 155 n., 156 n., 180 n., 213,
    234 n., 339, 352 n., 366 n., 383,
    397 n.,
Copernicus 77
Cornill 307 n., 314 n.
Court officials 167, 169 f.
Covenant 129, 208 ff., 310, 332
    Book of 198
    obligations 324, 391
Covetousness 237, 385
Cranage 75 n.
Creation 40, 41 n.
Creator, God as 371
Creeds, ancient 4, 5, 16 f., 77
Crete 32, 102
Criticism, meanings of 35, 83 n.
    Higher 37 ff., 74
    Lower (Textual) 35–7, 74
Cromwell 295
Cross, Way of 399, 401; *see also*
    Suffering
Cross of Jesus Christ 61, 75
Crowther, G. 359
Crucifixion 60, 63
Cuneiform script 29, 31, 99
Curse of the gods 115, 133 n.
Curtiss 143 n.
Curzon, Lord 120

Custom 108
Cuthbert, St 75 n.
Cybele 152 n.
Cyclical view of history 57, 286
Cyrus, king of Persia 340, 341

Dagan, Semitic deity 145 f., 147 n.
Dagon, Philistine deity 146
Damascus 92 n., 96 n., 248 f., 267, 290
Damien, Father 270 n.
Dan, tribe of 101, 102 n.
    city of 172, 211 n., 217 n.
Darbyshire, J. R. 65 n.
David, king of the Hebrews 33, 53,
    101 n., 104 n., 120 n., 126, 129,
    133 n., 162, 165 ff., 183, 189,
    190 n., 224 n., 225, 227 n., 230,
    237, 264, 351
    Court History of 39 n.
Davidson, A. B. 6, 212 n.
Davies, J. B. T. 47 n.
Day of Grace 357
Day of the Lord 63, 259
Day of Wrath 355-7
Dead Sea 93, 94, 245
Death, survival of 122 f., 394
Deborah 105, 182
Decalogue 51, 82, 216 f., 222 n., 224
Deism 376 n.
Democracy 4, 8, 49, 118, 139, 189,
    392 n.
Demonic powers 369 f.
Demons and deity 114 f.
Demosthenes 44, 49
Denney, J. 42 n.
Dervishes 182
Desert 112 ff., 139 f.
Destiny, cult of 374-6
Deuteronomy, Book of 56
    Code of 39 n., 40, 189, 222 n.
Diocletian, Emperor of Rome 57
Diodorus 70 n., 151 n.
Dives and Lazarus 385
Diviners 148, 185 f.
Dobschütz 59 n.
Dodd, C. H. 88, 287, 398
Driberg 128 n.
Driver, G. R. 120 n.

Driver, S. R. 30, 38 n., 204 n., 215 n.
Dualism 370
Duhm 307 n., 314 n., 329 n.
Duo-theism 155
Dussaud 156 n.

E (Israelite narrative) 40 f.
Ecclesiastes, Book of 36 n., 37 n., 394
Ecclesiasticus, Book of 36, 58
Ecstasy and prophecy 193 ff.
Edghill, E. A. 63 n.
Edom 92, 167, 343 n.
Edomites 245, 248, 253, 356
Egypt 26 ff., 95 f., 110 f., 196, 198 ff.,
    267, 290, 296, 299, 313 f.
Egypt, language and script 27, 99
    religion of 100, 241 n.
Eichrodt, W. 88
Einstein 79, 360
Eissfeldt 38 n., 225 n.
Ekron 144 n.
El, Elohim 118, 143 f., 155 f.
Elah, king of Israel 234
Elath 167 f., 201, 249
Eli 224 f., 309 f.
Elijah, Prophet 191, 224, 233-44,
    247 f., 257, 283, 298, 395
Elisha, Prophet 191 n., 242 f., 298
Elmslie, W. G. 291 n.
Emigration from Palestine 346
Encyclopaedia Britannica 80 n.
Encyclopaedia of Religion and Ethics
    56 n., 59 n., 65 n., 69 n.
Environment and character 84
Ephraim 106, 111, 266 n.
Epictetus 376 n.
Epicurean philosophy 376 n.
Epistles, Pauline 57, 62, 77
Equality, sense of 164, 182
Erasmus 76
Erbt 331 n.
Eros 264 n.
Esau 125 n., 218
Esdraelon, Plain of 92 f., 96, 104, 106,
    159, 162, 180, 249, 273
Eshcol, Vale of 245
Ethbaal, king of Phoenicia 235
Ethical Monotheism 364 et seq.

Ethics and Religion 51, 262, 373 f.
Euphrates, River 322
Euripides 120 n.
Evans, Sir A. 32
Evil 360, 389 ff.
Evil powers 114 ff.
Evolution 85 n., 371
Excavation 26; see also under Gezer,
    Knossos, Lachish, etc.
Exodus 188, 204 ff., 211 n.
    date of 100–2, 110 n.
Expediency 7, 14
Ezekiel 37 n., 99, 191 n.
Ezra 37 n.

Fall, Genesis story of 389–90 n.
Family, conception of 127
Farmer, H. H. 366, 372
Fascism 392
Fate 374–6
Fatalism 374 ff.
Father of Israel, God as 272 f., 276 f.
Fertility cult 148, 153
Festivals, religious 260; see also
    Practices of religion
First-born, sacrifice of 150 f., 308
Flinders Petrie 32
Flood 29, 30, 41 n.
Fosdick, H. E. 5
Francis, St 392
Frazer, Sir J. G. 33, 34, 107 n., 109 n.
Freedom 136 ff., 389
French Revolution 392 n.
Fullerton 59 n., 71

Gad 106 n., 146, 147 n.
Galilee 92–4, 235, 266, 290, 303
    Sea of 61, 75, 92 f.
Galileo 77, 79
Gama, Vasco da 77
Garstang 91 n., 97 n., 98 n., 101 n.,
    103 n., 110 f., 116 n., 121 n.
    152 n., 156 n., 159 n., 167 n.
Garvie, A. E. 80 n.
Gaster 186 n.
Gath 162
Gaza 92, 96 n., 146
Gedaliah 330

Geffcken 69 n.
Genesis, Book of 40–2, 52, 56, 62 n., 81
Genius, nature of 6, 382
Gentiles, attitude to 341 f.
Gezer 32 f., 97, 148 n., 151 n.
Gibeon 103
Gideon 135, 160, 163, 182, 229
Giesebrecht 307 n.
Gilboa, Mount 53, 162, 230, 232
Gilead 93 f., 104 n., 180, 236, 309
Gilgal 111, 184, 243
Gilson, E. 368 n., 371, 374 n.
Glover, T. R. 68 n.
Gluck, Nelson 93 n.
Gnostics 71
Goliath 55, 126
Gomer 268 ff., 280 ff.
Goshen 200, 202 n., 204
Gospels 57, 62, 77
Grace 209 ff., 265 n.
    Day of 357
Gray, G. B. 120 n., 188 and n.,
    205 n., 261 n.
Greek psychology 122 ff.
Greek versions of O.T. 35 n.
Greeks 6, 17–19, 44, 49, 52, 62, 68 f.,
    84, 286, 336, 368 f., 373
Gressmann 205 n., 216 n.
Gutenberg 76

Habiru 100 ff., 107, 110
Haddon, A. C. 33
Haggai, Prophet 346
Hahn, H. F. 88
Hamath 290, 315
Hammurabi 30, 98 n.
Hananiah 327 f.
Harper 266 n.
Harran 120 n.
Harras, the 207
Hatch, E. 17
Hathor, Egyptian deity 145
Hattin, Horns of 92 n.
Hazor, Canaanite fortress 92 n., 96 n.,
    98 n., 101 n.
Hebert 64 n.
Hebrews, conquest of Canaan 103 ff.
    language of 17 n., 31, 44 ff.

Hebron 96 n., 97, 162, 189, 245
Heidegger 378 n.
Heiler 366
Heine 21
Helvetic Confession of Faith 80 n.
Herder 47 f.
Hermon, Mount 92, 267
Herod 15, 61
Herodotus 91 n., 313, 314 n.
Heroes of Jehovah 160, 182 ff.
Hesiod 286
Hezekiah 193 n., 288 n., 296 ff., 308
High Places 33, 94, 147 f., 174, 277
Hinnom, Valley of 174, 187, 325
Hiram, king of Phoenicia 167 f.
Hiroshima 87 n.
Hissarlik, excavations at 32
Historians, ancient and modern 38–
    9 n., 51 ff.
Historical Books of O.T. 57
Hitler 7, 14, 342
Hittites 27, 30 f., 99, 100, 102, 110
Hivites 98
Holiness, development of thought of
    66, 108 f.
    law of 198 n.
Hölscher 193 n., 234 n.
Holy Roman Empire 337
Homer 21, 31, 68 f., 368 n., 375 n.
Honour, conception of 133 ff., 164
Hooke, S. H. 100 n., 140 n., 152 n.
Horace 72
Horeb, Mount 159, 188, 207 ff., 218 f.,
    225, 242, 395
Horites (Hurrians) 98
Hormah 104 n.
Horus 370
Hosea, Book of 247, 268
Hosea, Prophet 165, 191, 199, 247,
    264 ff., 287, 303, 310, 338, 351,
    395
Hoshea, king of Israel 267
Human nature 255 ff., 283, 390, 393
Humanism 367 ff., 373 f.
Hurrians 98
Husband of Israel, God as 272 f., 276 f.
Huxley, J. 388
Hyksos, see Hittites

Ideas, abstract 396
Ignatius 78
Ikhnaton, see Amenhotep IV
Iliad 21, 31, 68, 375 n.
Immanence of God 107
Immortality 243 f., 394 ff.
Incense trade 96 n.
India 84, 362, 372
Individual and society 10, 13, 306 ff.
Individualism 7, 118 f., 137, 338 f.,
    382 f.
Industrialism 84
Infallibility of Church 80
Infallibility of Scripture 79 ff., 83 n., 86
Inspiration, and authority of Scripture
    71, 79 ff.
Insulin 73
Isaac 40, 41, 70, 105, 125 n.
Isaiah, Book of 288, 339
Isaiah, Prophet 40, 173 f., 191, 193 n.,
    278, 287, 289 ff., 301, 306, 308,
    310, 312, 338 f., 351, 378, 384,
    390, 395 ff.
Ishtar, see Ashtarte
Isis, Egyptian deity 145, 370
Islam 84, 138 n., 376 n.
Issachar, tribe of 101, 102 n., 106 n.
Ithaca 31

J (Judaean narrative) 40 f.
Jabesh-Gilead 162 n., 229
Jack, J. W. 98 n.
Jacob 40, 41, 101, 125 n., 131, 211 n.,
    218
James, E. O. 278 n.
James, M. R. 57 n.
James, W. 194 n., 384
Jarvis, C. S. 205 n.
Jaspers 378 n.
Jeans, Sir J. 372 n.
Jebusites 98 n.
Jehoahaz, king of Judah 322
Jehoiakim, king of Judah 322, 323 f.
Jehoiakin, king of Judah 322, 325, 327
Jehovah 9, 39 n., 56 f., 94, 158 ff.
    163 ff., 369; see also Yahveh
Jehu, king of Israel 29, 179 n., 180 n.
    248 n., 271

Jephthah the Gileadite 160, 182
Jeremiah, Book of 307 ff.
Jeremiah, Prophet 40, 191, 203 n., 278, 287, 306 ff., 351, 353, 378, 388, 392 n., 395, 396
Jeremy, Epistle of 307 n.
Jericho 101 n., 103, 111, 243
Jeroboam I, king of Israel 172, 211 n., 217 n., 234
Jeroboam II, king of Israel 249 f., 254, 258, 267, 278 f., 290
Jerome 57–9
Jerusalem 60, 92, 99, 101 n., 104, 162, 168, 172, 174, 180 n., 234, 245, 250, 293, 298, 300, 305, 308, 312, 315, 322, 325, 328, 330, 340, 356, 358
Jesus Christ 3, 4, 15, 16, 19 f., 21, 22, 33, 42, 43, 58, 60 ff., 66, 67, 70–8 passim, 81, 83–5, 87, 114, 135 n., 264 n., 266, 268, 269–70 n., 321, 333, 337, 361, 364, 369, 371, 382, 387, 392, 397, 398, 400 f.
    as Messiah 60 ff.
Jethro 201
Jewish Quarterly Review 34 n.
Jezebel of Tyre, wife of Ahab 172, 182, 184, 189 n., 235 ff., 271, 298
Jezreel 104, 182, 236 and n., 237, 271, 391 n.
Jinn (demons) 114 f.
Job 44, 47 n., 181 f.
Joel, Book of 191 n.
John, Apostle 62
    Gospel of 20
Jonadab ben Rechab 179
Jonah 55
Jonathan 53, 162, 183, 229 f., 264
Jordan, Valley of 91–3, 94
Joseph 64 and n., 83, 100 n., 127
Joseph, M. 385 n.
Joshua 52, 100 f., 104
Josiah, king of Judah 174, 175, 187 n., 189 n., 315, 316, 321, 392 n.
Journal of Theological Studies 31 n., 155 n.

Judah, Southern kingdom of 92, 94, 290
Judah, tribe of 104 n., 106 n.
Judaism 107, 360 f.
Judas Iscariot 65
Judas Maccabaeus 324
Judges, Book of 39 n., 52, 110
Justice 67, 132 f., 154, 239, 249 f., 265, 352 n.

Kadesh, Canaanite deity 146, 147 n.
    Syrian town 102, 187 n.
Kadesh-Barnea 104 n., 121 n., 212, 216 n.
Kai-Lung 72
Kairwan 120
Karkar, Battle of 247, 289 n.
Kells, Book of 75 n.
Kenites 121 n., 199 n.
Kennedy, A. R. S. 231 n.
Kennett, A. 132 n.
Kennett, R. H. 210 n.
Kepler 77
Keret 167 n.
Khayyam, Omar 394
Khiba (Hipa), Hittite deity 145
Kilpatrick 11
Kings, Book of 39 n., 51
Kingship, oriental 166 ff., 189
Kinnereth 96 n.
Kiriath-Jearim 227 n.
Kish, excavations at 30
Kishon, River 106, 159
Kittel, R. 216 n.
Knossos 32, 102
Kuenen 234 n.
Kurt-Galling 210 n.

Lachish 32, 101 n.
Laish 102 n.
Lamentations, Book of 307 n.
Langdon 116 n., 145 n.
Langton 124 n., 141 n.
Languages and thought 17 n.
Laodicea 302
Law, Hebrew 35 n., 38 n., 56 f., 67, 211 and n.
Law (*Torah*), meaning of 352 n.

Lawrence, T. E. 137
League of Nations 209 n.
Lebanon Mtns 92, 93
Leontes, River 92 n.
Levi, tribe of 101 n., 187 n.
Levirate Law 134 n.
Levites 39 n., 187–8 n.
Libya 102
Lilith, Canaanite deity 142
Lindisfarne Gospels 75 n.
Localization of deity 121 f., 154
Lods, A. 116 n., 120–1 n., 146 n., 153,
    163 n., 179 n., 190 n., 199, 202 n.,
    207 n., 216 n.
Lofthouse, W. F. 51, 216 n.
Louis XIV of France 392 n.
Luck 374–6
Luther 73, 77
Lyall, C. 131
Lycia 103 n.

Maacah, 172
Macalister, R. A. S. 32 f., 91, 95,
    103 n., 144 n., 146 n., 148 n.
Maccabees, Books of 36, 58
McFadyen 216 n.
McNeile 205 n.
MacNicol, N. 366 n.
Magic 34 n., 151 n.
Magnus, L. 76 n.
Malinowski 34 n.
Man and Nature 52 f., 379 f.
Mana 34 n.
Manasseh, king of Judah 151, 174,
    308, 316, 325
Manasseh, tribe of 106 n., 111
Manna 205 n.
Mannheim, K. 360
Manson, T. W. 44 n., 51 n., 91 n., 300
Marcion 58, 71
Marcus Aurelius 376 n.
Marduk, Babylonian deity 172 n.
Margoliouth 121 n.
Marriage, symbolic 152
Mass, the 74
massebah 148, 171
Massoretic Text of O.T. 35 n.
Materialism, scientific 372

Matter, nature of 372
Matthews, W. R. 380
Mecca 207
Medes 304, 312 ff.
Mediterranean Sea 31 f., 91–3, 102
Meekness 219 n.
Megiddo 92 n., 96 n., 103, 168 n., 322
Melek, as title of deity 119, 144, 150 f.
Melkart, Phoenician deity 171, 172,
    235–6 ff.
Menahem, king of Israel 267
Mercy 67, 253 ff., 262 f., 347
Merneptah 111
Mesha, king of Moab 119 n., 216 n.
Mesopotamia 26, 29 f., 96 n., 98,
    145 n., 343
Messiah 60 f., 62
Messianic hope 303 n., 307 n.
Micah, Prophet 191 n., 300 n., 324
Micaiah ben Imlah 184 n., 191 n.
Michelangelo 199
Michmash 230
Micklem, N. 193 n., 195
Midianites 111, 160, 182
Midsummer Feast 149, 152
Milton 109, 392
Minoan-Mycenaean civilization 32, 102
Minotaur 32
Mizpah 226 n., 266 n., 330
Moab 93, 243, 245, 309
Moabites 104 n., 119, 253
Mohammed 12, 114, 213, 217 n.
Monarchy, Hebrew 39 n., 170 f.,
    189 f., 228 ff., 279
Monks 75
Monotheism 85 n., 114–17, 156, 191,
    203, 259, 364 ff., 378 n., 398
Moon-worship 116, 120 f., 145, 201,
    203, 208, 218
Moral consequences of sin 279 f.
Moral order of the world 359 ff.
Morality among Hebrews 51
Moses, Prophet 52, 55, 56, 61, 63, 83,
    84, 101, 107, 141, 145, 166, 184 n.,
    187, 188, 191, 198 et seq., 224,
    240, 255, 310, 324, 351, 396
Moses and Divine Name 119
Moulton, R. G. 44, 51 n., 344 n.

Moulton and Milligan 264 n.
Mountains and Israel's life 94
Mullo-Weir 44 n.
Murray, Sir G. 375, 376 n.
Musa, Mount 207 n.
Musil, A. 114, 207
Mycenae 32
Myers, F. W. H. 353
Myres, J. L. 113
Mystery Religions 368
Mysticism 69 n., 365 ff.

Naaman 121 n.
nabhi 13
Naboth 182, 189 n., 236 f., 271, 391 n.
Nahum 191 n., 343 n.
Naphtali, tribe of 101, 102 n., 106 n.
Napoleon 158
Nathan 191 n., 224 n., 237
Nationalism · 84, 335 ff.
Natural phenomena and faith 116, 387
Nature 52 f., 378 ff., 387 ff.
Nazirites 183
Nazism 8, 13 f., 16, 363 f., 392
Nebo, king of Assyria 29
Nebuchadrezzar, king of Babylon 223, 322, 328
Necho, king of Egypt 321 f.
Needham 360
Nefertiti, wife of Amenhotep IV 28 n.
Negeb 167 n.
Nehemiah 340 n., 344
Neolithic remains 97
nephesh 123 ff.
Nicaea, Council of 5
Nicolson, H. 362
Niebuhr, R. 14, 392
Nile, River 92, 95, 99, 102 f., 200, 201 n., 205
Nineveh, 29, 289 n., 297, 315, 317, 343 n.
Noah 55
Nob 227 n.
Noyes, A. 77 n.

Oakeshott 75 n.
Odysseus 31
Odyssey 21, 31, 68

Oesterley, W. O. E. 38 n.
Oesterley, W. O. E. and Robinson, T. H. 121 n., 141 n., 205 n., 216 n.
Olympus, Mount 68, 388
Oman, J. 138, 209 n., 365, 377 n., 386
Omri, king of Israel 52, 92, 234 f.
Onias 334
Ordeal, trial by 132 n.
Origen of Alexandria 59, 70
Original sin 390 n., 393
Orthodoxy 71 f.
Orthogenesis 371
Osiris, Egyptian deity 145
Otto, R. 66 n., 291 n.
Oxford English Dictionary 63 n.

P (Priestly code) 40 f.
Palace of Solomon 168 f.
Palestine 26, 31, 32 f., 91–6, 289
Palestine Exploration Fund Quarterly 32 n., 33 n., 186 n.
Palmyra 116
Pantheism 286, 366, 371 f.
Paran 205
Parthenon 21
Passhur 325
Patience of God 273 f.
Patience of Prophets 398 f.
Paton, W. 16
Patriarchs 40 f., 52, 188
Patriotism 240, 335 f., 361, 376
Paul, Apostle 62, 195, 387, 389 n.
Peace, conception of 135 ff., 164
Peace-offerings 154
Peake, A. S. 38 n., 307 n., 352 n.
Pedersen 106, 125 n., 126 n., 128, 135 n., 170 f., 182 n.
Pelethites 167 n.
Pentateuch 198
Pentecost 149 n.
Pepy I, king of Egypt 99 n.
Perizzites 98 n.
Persia, dualism of 370
Personal relationship with God 306 ff., 320 ff.
Personality, 15, 122 ff., 128 ff., 380 f.
Peters xi, 143 n., 217 n.

Petra, Edomite city 96 n., 212
Philadelphians, Epistle to 78
Philistines 32, 53, 92, 102 f., 111, 161 f., 182, 184, 225, 229 f.
Philo 69
Phoenicia 31, 92, 103, 240
Phythian-Adams 91 n., 92 n., 198 n., 200, 201 n., 204 n., 207 n., 227 n.
Pilate, Pontius 7, 61
Pindar 44
Planning, social 228, 360
Plato, 12, 44, 69, 74, 368 n., 371, 378, 399
Politics and prophecy 307 n.
Polytheism 28, 30 n., 142 ff., 202, 370
Porteous 195 n., 278 n., 304 n.
Power and corruption 391
Power of God 346 ff.
Practices of religion 240 f., 249 f., 260 f., 277 f. and n., 308, 316, 323 ff., 347
Prediction and prophecy 64 f.
Prefiguration, see Typology
Priam 31
Pride 391 f.
Priestly Code 198 f.
Priests 173, 186 ff.; see also Levites, Zadokites
Primitive ideas, value of 107 f.
Printing 76
Prophet-Nation, conception of 351 ff.
προφήτης 13
Prophetic Books of O.T. 35 n., 38 n., 44, 57
prophets 148 f., 183 ff.
Prophets, the Great 6, 11 f., 45, 64 f., 66 f., 74, 84, 85 n., 91, 191 ff., 196, 351, 353, 364 ff., 371 ff., 382 ff.
Prostitution, sacred 172, 174, 187
Protestantism 58 n., 78 f.
Proverbs, Book of 36 n., 43 f., 47 n., 57
Psalmody 186
Psalms, Books of 43, 47 n., 51, 57
Psalter 21, 40, 131
Psyche in Greek mythology 109

Psychology 122 ff.
Ptah, Egyptian deity 145
Ptolemaic astronomy 77
Puritanism, Hebrew 179 ff.
Pyramids 26

Quails in wilderness 205 n.
Quick, O. C. 278 n.
Quiller-Couch, Sir A. T. 45, 46 n.

Radin 365 n.
Ramah 186, 225 f., 250
Rameses II, king of Egypt 102, 111, 201
Ramman, Rimmon, Canaanite deity 145
Raphia 290
Ras Shamra 31, 156 n., 186 n.
Rawlinson, Sir H. 29
Reality 304 ff., 365 f., 372
Rebecca 70
Rechabites 179
Red Sea 93, 204 f., 249
Redeemer, God as 283 and passim
Redemption of mankind 344 ff.
Redemption of society 301
Reeds, Sea of 204, 208
Reformation, Reformers 58 n., 77 ff.
Rehoboam, king of Judah 170, 233
Relativity, theory of 79
Remnant 292 f., 299 f.
Renaissance 76 ff.
Renan 114
Resheph, Canaanite deity 145, 147 n., 156 n., 165, 172
Resignation 394
Responsibility, personal 84
Restoration, spiritual 349 ff., 352 n.
Restoration of Israel 283
Reuben, tribe of 106 n.
Reuchlin 76 n.
Revelation, Book of 57
Revised Version 47 n.
Rhapsody 44
Riffs, 213
Righteousness 66, 85, 377 ff.
Ritual, see Practices of religion
'Ritual Commandments' 198 n.

Robinson, H. W. 12, 31 n., 38 n., 80 n., 88, 123, 124 n., 128 n., 185, 194 n., 210 n., 352 n., 354 n., 380
Robinson, T. H. 38 n., 148 n., 190, 193 n.; *see also* Oesterley, W. O. E.
Roman Church 78 f.
Roman Empire 76, 84, 336, 373
Rommel 102
Roosevelt, President F. D. 134 n.
Rosenberg, A. 9
Rosetta Stone 27
Roth, L. 45, 378 n., 379
Rowley, H. H. 110
ruach 123 ff.
Russia 84, 362, 392
Ruth, Book of 134

Sabbath observance 40, 41 n., 120 n.
Sacraments in medieval Church 75
Sacred persons (Canaanite) 148
Sacredness of Scripture 56 ff.
Sacrifice 66, 67, 117 f., 150, 153 f., 260 f., 324 f., 347
Sadhu Sundar Singh 194 n.
St Paul's Cathedral 83
Salvation 136 f.; *see also* Redemption, Restoration
Samaria, city of 92, 93, 172, 174, 184, 235, 251, 263, 281, 290
   kingdom of (Israel) 40, 94, 309, 315
   Woman of 20
Samaritans 342
Samson 124, 127, 135, 161, 182
Samuel 111, 161, 182, 183, 186, 191, 195, 224 ff., 237, 240, 250, 257, 283, 310
   Book of 39 n., 51, 110
Sanday, W. 56
Sargon, king of Assyria 290, 296, 297, 302
Sargon of Agade 98 n.
Sarim (nobles) 170 f.
Sarpedon 375 n.
Saul, king of the Hebrews 53, 101 n., 111, 129 n., 161 ff., 182, 190, 195, 225, 226 n., 229 ff., 237
Sayce 145 n.

Schliemann 32
Schofield 91 n., 94 n.
Science and religion 7, 79, 81, 84, 86 n.
Scripture, sacredness of 56 ff.
Scythians 304, 313 ff.
Second Isaiah 130, 191, 339 ff., 378, 380, 383, 388, 391, 396, 401
Seers 148, 185 f.
Sellin 38 n., 41, 199 n.
Semites 6 n., 44, 130 ff.
Sennacherib, king of Assyria 297 f., 302
Sepharvaim 290
Septuagint 35 n., 37 n.
Serbal, Mount 207 n.
Serpent cult 172
Sety I, king of Egypt 102, 111
Sex-ritual 308
Shakespeare 54
Shalmaneser III, king of Assyria 29, 289 n.
Sharon, Plain of 142 n.
Shechem 20, 98 n., 101 n., 266 n.
Shemesh, Canaanite deity 146 n.
Sheol 124 n., 142
Shiloh 161, 187, 224, 225, 309, 310
Shishak, king of Egypt 234 n.
Shubbiluliumma, king of Hittites 100
Sidon 96
Sihon, king of Amorites 104 n.
Siloam, Tower of 387 n.
Simeon, tribe of 101 n., 187 n.
Simon Peter, Apostle 61 f.
Sin, Moon-God 120 n.
Sin, original 390 n., 393
   problem of 262
Sinai, Mount 66 n., 75, 120 n., 207, 261
Sinuhe 99 n.
Sirach, Ben 36
Sirbonian Lake 205 n.
Sisera 102 n., 105, 159, 182
Skinner, J. 37, 41 f., 120 n., 166, 176, 194 n., 233, 234, 269 n., 287, 292 n., 297, 301, 302 n., 307 n., 318 n., 321, 327 f., 331 n., 338 n., 352 n., 374 n.
Slavery 81, 201, 250

Smalley, Miss   75 n., 76 n.
Smith, G.   29
Smith, G. A.   14, 66 n., 91 n., 93, 94,
　95, 112, 114, 116 f., 131, 143 n.,
　159 n., 185, 213, 231, 246, 256,
　266 n., 267, 307 n., 309, 330 n.
Smith, H. P.   231 n.
Smith, W. R.   34 n., 42, 46, 48 n., 53,
　59 n., 71 n., 73, 74, 79 n., 114 f.,
　129 n., 144 n., 147 n., 150 n.,
　213 n., 217 n., 266 and n., 276 n.,
　278, 298 f., 339
Snaith, N. H.   88, 108 n.
Social implications of religion   83 ff.,
　130, 155
Social obligations of Covenant   215 f.,
　219
Socrates   108, 109
Söderblom   85 n., 286 n.
Solomon, king of the Hebrews   37 n.,
　165 ff., 234, 310
　Temple of   39 n.
Song of Songs, Book of   37 n.
Sophocles   282 n., 375
Soul   122 ff.
Speiser, G. A.   98 n.
Spengler   286 n.
Sphinx   26
Spring Festival   149, 152 n.
Stade   234 n.
Star, Evening and Morning (Venus)
　116
Stark, Freya   31 n., 96 n., 113 n.,
　138 n., 163 f.
State and individual   10, 13
Statutes and judgements   222 n.
Stevenson, R. L.   336
Stirling, J.   47 n.
Stoicism   69, 376
Stone, D.   70 n.
Strahan   65 n.
Suez Canal   343
Suffering   282 f., 321, 349 ff., 354 ff.,
　388, 395
Suffering Servant   351 ff.
Sun-worship   116, 145, 170, 201 f.
Supernatural, reality of   304 ff.
Supernatural beings   142 ff.

Superstition and faith   225–7, 369 f.
Sutekh, Egyptian deity   146 n., 163
Syria   26, 31, 92 f., 98, 99, 100, 167,
　289, 294
Syrian cuneiform script   31
Syrians   92, 240 n., 243 n., 247 ff., 253,
　267, 298

Taanach, excavations at   146
Tabor   266 n.
Tadra, Mount   207
Tahpanhes   331 n.
Tamar   133 n.
Tammuz, Babylonian deity   152 n.
Tekoa   245, 246, 250, 253, 256, 263,
　264, 275
Tell-el-Amarna   27 ff., 30, 100
Tell-el-Hesy (? Lachish), excavations
　at   32
Temple of Solomon   39 n.
　building of   168, 171 ff.
　rebuilt   346, 348
Tertullian   64 and n., 151 n.
Teshub, Hittite deity   145, 156 n., 162 f.
Teutonic criticism   307 n.
Thales   368, 371
Thebes   27, 100 n.
Thebez   160
Theocratic government   228
Theocritus   49
Theodore of Mopsuestia   70 n.
Theseus   32
Thomas, L.   138
Thucydides   21
Thutmose III, king of Egypt   92 n.
Time and eternity   286 ff.
Times, The   87, 239 n.
Titles of deity   118 ff.
Torah   211 and n.; see also Law
Torrey, C. C.   339 ff.
Trance   194 f.; see Visionary experi-
　ences
Transcendence of God   107
Transcendental faith   371
Troy   31, 32
Tutankhamen, king of Egypt   29
Tyndale, W.   47 n.
Typology   63 f.

Tyrants, Greek 139
Tyre 92, 96 n.

Universalism 349 ff.
Universe, harmony of 48 f.
Ur 30, 120 n.
Urim and Thummim 132 n.
Uzzah 66 n.
Uzziah, king of Judah 249, 290, 291

Values and reality 372
Vedanta doctrine 366 n.
Venus 145, 152 n.
Virgil 49
Virgin Birth 58–9 n.
Visionary experiences of Amos 258 and n.
Visionary experiences of Isaiah 291 f., 397
Visionary experiences of Jeremiah 310 f.
Visionary experiences of Prophets 396 ff.
Volz 216 n.
Von Rad 88
Vulgate 37 n., 58 f., 74, 76, 80

Walker, K. 374 n.
Walker, P. G. 389
War, effects of 247, 248, 250, 256 f.
Wardle 105 n.
'Way of the East' 96 n.
Weeks, Feast of 149

Welch, A. C. 188, 190 n., 216 n., 222 n., 266 n., 274, 279 n., 294 n., 307 n., 312 n., 313, 314 n., 316 n., 325, 326 n., 331 n., 332 n., 333
Wellhausen 234, 241 n., 302 n.
Whitehouse, O. C. 339
Wilberforce 81
Wilke 314 n.
Willkie, Wendell 229
Winchester Bible 75 n.
Wisdom of Solomon, Book of 36, 58
Witchcraft 81
Woolley, Sir L. 30 n.
Words, power of 125 f.
Wordsworth 195
World organisation, attempts at 336 f
Worms, Diet of 5
Worship. See Practices of religion
Wrath, Day of 355–7
Writings, The Other 35 n., 38 n.

Yahveh 119 f., 152 n., 214 f.
Young 27

Zadok 310
Zadokites 187–8 n., 227 n., 310, 317 n
Zebulun, tribe of 101, 106 n.
Zechariah, Prophet 191 n., 346
Zedekiah, king of Judah 322, 325 ff.
Zephaniah 191 n.
Zeus, Greek deity 69, 368, 370, 375
Zimri, king of Israel 234
Zion 162, 227 n., 303, 344, 401
Zoroastrianism 370 n.